Religion in the Contemporary South

RELIGION
in the CONTEMPORARY
SOUTH

CHANGES,

CONTINUITIES,

AND

CONTEXTS

Edited by

CORRIE E. NORMAN AND DON S. ARMENTROUT

The University of Tennessee Press • Knoxville

Copyright © 2005 by The University of Tennessee Press/Knoxville.
All Rights Reserved. Manufactured in the United States of America.
First Edition.

This book is printed on acid-free paper.

Library of Congress Cataloging-in-Publication Data

Religion in the contemporary South : changes, continuities, and contexts /
edited by Corrie E. Norman and Don S. Armentrout.— 1st ed.
    p. cm.
Includes index.

ISBN 1-57233-361-8 (pbk. : alk. paper)

1. Southern States—Religion.
 I. Norman, Corrie E., 1959–
II. Armentrout, Donald S.

BL2525.R46877 2005

200'.975—dc22   2004014317

CONTENTS

PART I

The Old Story: Common Themes
From Yesterday to Tomorrow

PART 2

The Bible Belt Loosens:
Religious Diversity in the South Today

Behind the Red Door:
The Episcopal Microcosm in the South

Raj and Leon. Colquitt County, Georgia. Photograph courtesy of Corrie Norman.

PREFACE

THE PHOTOGRAPH REPRODUCED ON PAGE viii IS A PICTURE OF MY FATHER, Leon, and one of his neighbors, Raj, standing in front of the shrine that Raj has built on his farm in southwest Georgia. Raj is from Gujarat, India, and is Hindu. He came to Colquitt County to grow vegetables familiar in his homeland for Asian markets on the East Coast. Raj's vegetables fascinated my father, a farmer of soybeans, cotton, and "southern" vegetables all his life. Raj's religion also fascinated my father, a Baptist deacon for most of his life.

I remember when my father became a deacon. I was four and had chicken pox and thus could not attend the mysterious deacon ordination ceremony my family was talking about at supper. When I asked my father what a deacon was, he thought for a minute and gave a reply a child could understand: "Well, deacons take care of things like locking up the church at night." Some of my earliest memories are of accompanying him on his lock-up duties when he would show me things usually off-limits, such as the baptismal pool. One of my last memories of him is of his showing me Raj's shrine and telling me some of the stories Raj had told him about the deities whose images it housed.

Those two memories speak to me not only of my father but also of the scope of religion in the South during his lifetime. Securing the old church and opening the door to new religious forms may seem at opposite ends of the religious spectrum. But as I recall my father entering Raj's shrine in his sock feet, I cannot help but remember that the shrine stands on the same wiregrass-covered ground on which my father played barefoot as a boy. South Georgia (for south Georgians) is "the holy land." To my father, that little piece of it in Colquitt County became more holy, not less, as it supported Raj's faith. What appear to be of the past and of the future, the old-time religion and the new religious pluralism, together locate us in the present. But as we spin about looking to them for a sense of orientation in "southern religion," we can find ourselves dizzied. It is no longer clear what the South is, what "southern religion" is.

What is clear, still, is that religion has lost none of its importance as a cultural factor in the South, even as the South and religion change and resist change. As a scholar of religion in Europe four hundred years ago, I find that this all seems familiar. My period of history is often spoken of as "pivotal." Its present rocked to and fro between reform and resistance, revolution and renaissance. Yet all were part of the same reality of what in historians' hindsight has become "early modern Europe," a term that hides the very point on which it pivoted—religious identity.

But like early modern Europeans, early postmodern southerners find avoiding religion well nigh impossible. Most would not want to anyway. We are also fortunate that today scholarship on the South, past and present, turns more and more to religion as a factor of significant importance. This was not always the case. Before the 1960s little southern religious history existed apart from state denominational histories and "lives" of esteemed white holy men. In that decade a full-scale enterprise began. Especially within the past fifteen to twenty years, work has been extensive and more inclusive.

That development reflects differences in location of the scholars who attempt to place religion in the context of southern history. It also reflects the problem of "locating" the South as a religious place today. Sam Hill's introduction highlights some of the specific difficulties in pinpointing where "southern religion" is that are brought to light in the essays that follow. In a general way, the architecture of this volume is indicative of how religion in the once and future South is taking place in the present. In the first section, the essays observe religious identities in the South today that weave in and out of the past. The first and longest essay in the volume addresses the marginalization of women's religion and the persistence of old myths in the pursuit of positions of power. The shortest essays are on the dominant Baptists and speak in dialogue of persistence and fragmentation. The direction of Pentecostal progress is questioned. Black religious identity is located not just in the churches but in novels and films that bear witness to the sacred myths of Creole identity. The second section reveals new (at least to the South) religious expressions taking place and old "minority" traditions shifting positions in southern society. The final section focuses on the Episcopal Church as a case in point of the difficulties of locating exactly where tradition is in a time of change. Throughout, we meet southerners securing their religious space and southerners seeking what is behind new doors. Take off your shoes as you walk with us through this volume, for everywhere you will find someone claiming southern holy ground.

This volume had its origin at the University of South in the 1999 DuBose Lectures of the School of Theology. We hoped to find the place of southern religion today, sensing that we needed to look back and ahead to do so. We found signs and mileposts. This volume offers further direction and invitation to those who are interested in continuing the search. While we have traveled far and wide into southern religious experience here, we are acutely aware that we have missed some important sites. Most seriously, we regret that we were unable to find a contributor willing to focus on the contemporary experience of black churches in the South. While race is a current that runs through the volume, this is an enormous omission. Attempting to correct it delayed the completion of the manuscript for two years. At present, we can only hope that our experience may serve as a call for more guides into this important territory.

The effort, expertise, and goodwill of so many contributed to this project. Warmest thanks are extended to the University of the South School of Theology, former Dean Guy Fitch Lytle III, and members of the Dubose Lectures committee, as well as the University Lecture Committee and Woods Lecture Endowment. I also thank Don S. Armentrout, my coeditor, and his assistant, Shawn Horton. Charles Lippy's encouragement and advice helped give birth to this book, and Sam Hill's shepherded it along. My research assistant, Heather Barclay, proved so invaluable that she became coauthor of one essay. Jonathan Grieser provided editorial assistance and good sense (as usual). The support and insightful suggestions of the readers for the University of Tennessee Press, especially Paul Harvey and Kendall White, are deeply appreciated. First Joyce Harrison and then Scot Danforth have been enthusiastic and patient editors, and the staff of the University of Tennessee Press congenial professionals. Finally, my warmest thanks to all the contributors to this book, who worked graciously with an editor trespassing from another time, whose only claim to the field of southern religion is that of one who seeks to understand her place in it. Their southern hospitality has made this a truly pleasurable as well as enlightening experience.

Corrie E. Norman
Spartanburg, South Carolina
January 2003

INTRODUCTION

Samuel S. Hill

THIS COLLECTION OF ESSAYS ON RELIGION IN THE AMERICAN SOUTH IS appearing at a time of major change, even dislocation, for that dimension of regional life. Religious diversity is acquiring new significance. It is also contributing to a dominant fact of the contemporary scene, the dismantling of normative religious patterns and conditions. As a consequence of several new forces at work in the region, the new multiplicity of faiths and the challenging of standard forms that have set the pace for all forms are presenting a new picture of religion on the southern landscape.

To be sure, diversity has characterized the religious life of the American South from its beginning in the early seventeenth century. Like the colonies north of them, the southern ones that stretched along the Atlantic seaboard from Maryland to Georgia were "awash in a sea of faith." During the colonial period several Protestant bodies—all of them of quite recent origin and British—intruded upon the pattern of establishment that the English settlers brought with them. Domination by one "denomination" affected the diversity, without ever quite overshadowing it, rendering the "sectaries" legally suspect and socially insignificant. And, of course, the mere presence of Roman Catholicism, Jewish people, and Native American cultural ways, sometimes generating turbulence, further illustrates the complexity of that religious landscape.

However, by the 1830s the old system of domination by the Church of England, long ineffective, was giving way to cultural normativity. A new establishment, this one de facto, proved highly effective, acquiring an unexpected power to take the cultural lead—owing in part to its indigenousness. In its early stages this new arrangement was dynamic, and later it was firm and nearly inviolable. Its season was destined to last a long time.

Evangelical Protestantism owned southern society for 150 years. This study arrives during the waning of that period of "owning," during a time of genuine change. Some of its fourteen chapters give attention to the presence in regional life of hitherto "alien" religious traditions, mostly from cultures that thrive in societies stretching from the eastern Mediterranean to Southeast Asia, thence on to China, Japan, and Korea. Some other essays point to developments in long-present bodies, Jews, Roman Catholics, and several

Protestant groups. Some of these traditions are passing through a period of development involving energetic and painful struggles. By no means do all the changes have to do with denominations and their life, however. The dramatically new roles for women, as well as the exact character of the places women have long been occupying, deserve and receive attention here. Similarly, the heightened and somewhat altered influence of the churches of African-American citizens come in for serious treatment. Both clusterings of the population have been simply elemental in the South's life for centuries, but their influence and significance have shifted and are preserved in clearer light. This collection is particularly astute in capturing the historic roles of women in the region's religious life. The essay "Women and Religion in the South: Myth, Reality, and Meaning" is so thorough and perceptive as to vie for status as a classic.

The weakening and dismantling of normativity is the dominant fact and feature of the past quarter century. The emergence of "foreign" faiths, in greater size and expanded acceptance as well, contribute to that fact and are in position to take advantage of it. Southern society no longer belongs to the Baptists, Methodists, like-minded groups, and the traditional Europe-derived bodies simply for the taking and keeping. The implications of this change are numerous, as suggested, and they include the conflict embroiling the life of the old communities that embodied normativity. Bill Leonard's piece on the Southern Baptists might well have been accompanied by treatment of the rupturing that took many "southern Presbyterians" out of the familiar fold in favor of forming the Presbyterian Church of America. Everybody's foundations are subject to shaking.

When the study of the religious life and history of America's southern region is undertaken, a good many issues and topics arise that are recessive in or absent from "American religious history" broadly considered. That there are many parallels (some of them requiring mutatis mutandis, of course) is to be expected. Similarly, much continuity prevails. These conditions call for little commentary, after all, since this is a single country. Indeed, that profound fact serves to highlight how tragic was the Civil War (that was so important to both, the region and the nation). We rightly ask, How could people and societies with so much in common do that to each other, in reality to themselves?

The essays here offer fresh perspectives on what those distinguishing issues and topics are. They do so indirectly more often than directly, a point of considerable significance. That is, the newly arrived, the newly emergent, and the old bodies that have been displaced from the "catbird seat" from which they ruled the roost and set the pace, even going so far as to claim to be what all religious groups should be, are not animated by the new circum-

Samuel S. Hill

stances; they are simply getting on with what lies at hand to do. The several collections (and many interpretive studies as well) that have been published over the last four decades, when serious inquiry into southern religious history has been underway, have worked to grasp the past without having to consider a present, the present in which we live, that reflects so many shifts and turns. The goal of the contributions here aspires to being up-to-date in an era when "the South" is affected by modern issues that are significantly new there, even though they may have made impact on other parts of the nation at large for most of its history. While the region persists as a distinctive society and culture, it is now experiencing some of the challenges that were overturning the prevailing culture of the Northeast and the West (from Middle to Far) as early as the 1820s in some cases.

What are these challenges, these new conditions? What is this up-to-dateness that occasions the work we authors submit as having promise for contributing to the ongoing inquiry into American religious history? We must take pains to avoid stressing novelty at the expense of continuity, since there is plenty that appears to be the same, more than a little of which really is. Wayne Flynt's article on denominationalism underscores the validity of seeing the religious South through the eyes of Baptists, Presbyterians, Methodists, Episcopalians, and many more. That institutional reality continues to have powerful effect.

It is by now apparent that to the writer of this introduction one condition outranks all the rest: the displacement of the condition of normativity. As noted, the evangelical Protestant tradition has been overwhelming the regional culture ever since the 1830s. As many observers have long been pointing out—and most citizens of the region have simply taken for granted—the Baptist and Methodist forms of church life and kindred movements have set the standard for religious understanding and practice. They remain present, indeed ubiquitous and influential. And some of the "kindred movements"—Pentecostalism and true fundamentalism, for example—have gained much strength since the 1970s, actually attaining to more celebrity than the historic bodies. The hold of the "Baptist-Methodist hegemony" on the society and on the culture is no longer automatic or magical or probably even possible. There are major stories needing to be told concerning this transformation.

One is the particular southern twist on those two historic Protestant denominations. Baptists in the South—white ones for the moment—have differed greatly from people of that persuasion in the rest of the American society. The introduction and coming to dominance of revivalistic evangelicalism has distinguished them from others in that heritage. More importantly, that version of evangelical Protestantism has made an oversized imprint on the region's religious life. It has bequeathed to the Christian religion and to personal Christian faith the stamp of personal salvation as its defining trait. The experience of having one's sins forgiven—consciously, that is, knowing it and being able to talk about it—became the message that was insistently given and that required response. "Getting right with God" has been seen by so many as what life is all about and what the churches must attend to as their consuming passion and urgent mission. Methodists were never so single-minded, the Wesleyan tradition being given to multiple ministries in a large comprehensive framework. But the same outreach agenda, personal conversion, was a driving force there, too. These two rose to be the region's quasi-established churches. Many in other denominations have testified that that message is what they subsumed from cultural transmission, the commonsense view of what religion is, even though they heard both more and less than that single message from pulpits and lecterns in their congregations.

The "kindred movements" just mentioned have inherited much of the same understanding but with some unique turns. Pentecostalism, its regional rootage tracing to the years around 1900, added the gift of speaking in tongues to the gift of personal salvation; the former came to identify the movement to outsiders and, not lightly, to its own adherents, indeed to the point of giving the movement its name. Fundamentalism, a reason-based heritage insisting on correct belief and at war with all teachings judged to be heretical, included this message about conversion on its list of infallible and absolutist doctrines. While it made less of the *experience* of conversion, fundamentalism upheld the indispensability of that action. Even though its identification in the eyes of others and to itself had more to do with sound doctrine than with the moment of entrance into the saved life, personal conversion remained a paramount theme. This movement, too, emerged around 1900, mostly as a northern phenomenon, to check the raging tide of secular, atheistic, liberal thinking in science, philosophy, the social sciences, and, with a vengeance, in theology and the study of the Bible. Its impact on southern church life was minimal and marginal for a long time.

Thus, the span of southern evangelical communities extended over a wide range. In historic terms, center-right to far-right instances of evangelical Protestantism have been popular in the southern setting for a century. Southern religious culture has been in their thrall for a long time. (Leaving aside the kindred movements, recall, the tradition reaches farther back than 1900, to the antebellum period.)

Normativity has been a staple of southern religious culture. Regional religious life was predicated on the definitions provided by revivalist evangelical bodies. But three facts of history require attention as we consider the impact of normativity's decline. The first is the significant presence of black people and the African American heritage in the region. No question about it, evangelical Protestantism has been that people's classification of Christianity. The names give it away: Baptist of this and that sort, three in particular; Methodists in three subcommunities; and, since the early twentieth century, Pentecostalism, in black-only bodies such as the Church of God in Christ and in racially inclusive groups. But caution is in order; titles may mislead as well as suggest. For, especially since freedom expressed itself as distinct black denominations and practical forms, black Baptistism and black Methodism have developed their own variations on those themes. The message of those churches has not forged a heavy line between those who have experienced conversion and those who have not. Praising God and drawing close to him have supplanted the urgent altar call common among slaves and still definitive for many whites. Also, the black church message has been focused as much on social ministries as on issues of personal relation to the Almighty. Moreover, these two themes have been related dynamically, dialectically, not ranked with the implication that the churches should first attend to one, then secondly, even secondarily, to the other. The black churches have seen no need to subordinate one of these ministries; an imperative is an imperative. Also, in the fresh essay here on fiction and black religious-cultural life written by Carolyn M. Jones, we gain new glimpses into the imagination of an imagination-vibrant African American culture.

Forms of religious expression generally described in this way have been widespread, indeed standard, among the region's black Christians since they began to found their own congregations after Emancipation and develop their own style of worship and theological understanding. Patterns existed, in other words, but in forms significantly distinctive. And the large bodies did not define what religious life is about; they embodied the game that was playing in the culture. In certain respects white church and black church patterns have appeared to be first cousins; nevertheless, they differ markedly in manner, emphasis, and impact.

A second historical note requiring attention is that the dominant southern forms of evangelicalism are not the only forms of evangelicalism. In fact, they are not the historic forms either in North America or Europe. They are what they are, and they are intelligible and authentic varieties of this family of Protestant faith. But the point that has to be made in the setting of this book, that addresses the passage from the past to the future through the present in the region, is that in religion as in social arrangements, politics, and cultural heritage, the South has developed and proceeded along its own paths. This phenomenon has meant that collaboration between southern forms of white Baptist life and that of its counterparts elsewhere in the country has been awkward. Even in our own time, as the so-called fundamentalist segment of the Southern Baptist Convention has claimed the title of "evangelical" with vigor not seen before, it has not found it easy to blend with classic evangelicalism in "the North."

The point of greater pertinence, however, is that as many northern evangelical families move to take jobs and create their living in the cities of the South, they look with frustration to find a familiar manifestation of their evangelical faith. Try as it may, southern evangelicalism seems unable to shed its regional historic heritage. Changes have been occurring in the conservative southern churches, but they persist on a regionally distinct axis.

One other historical note needs striking here before we deal more directly with the decline of normativity: namely, timing. Incursions occurred around 1900, as mentioned already, forces that ruffled the equilibrium of the classic southern religious tradition. Pentecostalism appeared and fundamentalism invaded. The former captured the loyalty of many, mostly among the lower classes, who found the established Methodist (most often) churches growing too large, bureaucratic, and high-falutin' for them to feel at home. Pentecostalism offered these people a great deal—a sense of belonging, vigorous faith forms, and an affirmation of their own worth. Startlingly, it opened some doors to racially mixed congregations and afforded women leadership positions, sometimes the right to preach. On their reckoning, when the Spirit is determining church life, institutional forms and traditions take a backseat. These developments bespoke some new currents in the evolution of southern society. Things were changing.

Fundamentalism, modes of faith that challenged the churches to take up arms against a worldliness that is evil, faithless, and perverse, did not meet with a generally warm acceptance in a society in which a happy compatibility linked sacred and secular aspects of living. This movement filtered south, never in great force, from a northern urban society that was infested by immigrants, new industrial-urban ways, and, worst of all, modern modes of thought that fundamentalists derogated as "modernistic." The time had come to hold the line against heresies and radical thinking in social and political arenas.

Glancing at these three historical notations, racial issues, the South's distinctive expressions of evangelical Protestantism, and the introduction of fundamentalism, all of this in the years before and after 1900, tells us about more than that era in religious history in American culture, in the South and broadly. In the couple of decades leading up to 2000, another series of disturbances was occurring; these were assessed not as mere disturbances but as major threats to faithfulness. A century earlier, normativity was, at most, mildly challenged. In the recent fin de siècle, it began to unravel. The title of a historical study de-

Samuel S. Hill

scribing the South from the antebellum period to the late twentieth century, "In the South the Baptists Are the Center of Gravity," now applies inexactly. Perhaps there is no better indicator of this disruptive change than the almost frantic passion of the fundamentalist party in the Southern Baptist Convention, the segment now firmly in power, to dig in, to fight the bitter fight, to resist compromise and negotiation, so as to preserve orthodoxy against the relativistic thinking and compromises in thinking detected in that denomination's ranks and ever more prevalent in the culture at large.

The South's mission to save the world by evangelistic fervor, at home and abroad, has shifted. Still assured that they are "God's last and only hope" (the title of another study), the pure in mind and heart in this one American region now have another urgent mission, preventing alien ideologies from turning absolutist Christian teachings into heresy and granting legitimacy to foreign ideologies, including world religions. It is dazzling to observe how confident these southern religious are of their singular calling to rectify the entire world.

No one enjoys relinquishing the comfort of being dominant, of being taken for granted as the favored group. Individuals and local cultures do not relish it, and institutions, especially those possessed by a spirit of divine destiny, resist such dislocation by a call to battle. Something like these moods make up the new, unprecedented situation in contemporary religious life. This present, through which the past is being funneled to the region's future, is the occasion for the essays in this collection. The essay by Bill Leonard on the fracturing of the Baptist stronghold points to one stratum of the seismic shift. David Roebuck's study of the elevation of the Pentecostal movement to strength in size, social acceptability, and political influence points to another. Two traditions long present in the region, the Roman Catholics and the Jews, can no longer be shunted to the margins or treated with, variously, contempt and curiosity. Pieces by Thomas Tweed, Susan Bales, and Mark Bauman give substance to the necessity of putting those ways of speaking in their place. The old mottoes, "they ought to know better," applied censoriously to Catholic Christians, and "they just can't help it," attached condescendingly to Jews, now have to be seen for what they really are.

Not to mention Buddhists, Hindus, and Muslims—who gain inclusion in this book for far better reasons than so-called political correctness. While adherents to these traditions have made up a tiny percentage of the population for many decades, they are now more visible owing to growth in numbers and, especially, to their prominence as leaders in communities and corporations. They are less and less strangers and more and more active participants. Charles Lippy, in "From Angels to Zen," delineates the vast array of religious groups now present, and accessible, in the region today.

Perhaps there is no better mark of the cultural arrival and internal strength of those in the array that we identify as "Eastern" or "non-Western" or "alien" religions—no defining or describing term is satisfactory—than the challenges that they are facing within their own group life. In his study of Hindu people and temples in the South, Steven Ramey highlights the struggles that that community faces in accommodating to the multiple heritages present within itself. In particular, the new emigrants from India bring their different experiences and ideas to a fairly settled collection of second- and third-generation American Hindus who are comfortable with the forms of religious belief and practice that they have developed. Followers of Islam are relatively new at having to claim a way in the society, tend to be young, and are reeling from association with those who destroyed the World Trade Center in September 2001.

But such confrontations are not unique to the "non-traditional" faiths. Susan Bales makes clear that southern Roman Catholics are confronting comparable challenges. As Latino Catholics become part of the population, often in quite large numbers, they find themselves in long-established Anglo parishes. Settled conditions are forced to give way to mixtures and medleys, as traditions and customs from Mexico, the Caribbean islands, and Central and South America collide with forms long since created and adapted by Irish, German, Italian, Polish, and other European Catholics. Whatever credence we were able to attach to the old melting-pot theory of American life has been upset by the persistence of classical faiths and the variations within them, much of the ferment owed to the same immigration conditions that inspired the use of that metaphor more than a century ago.

The impetus for this book arose from the DuBose Lectures given at the University of the South ("Sewanee") in 1999. Thus the sponsorship of the enterprise belongs, directly and indirectly, to the Episcopal Church, the denomination that owns that university and features this lectureship named for a stalwart priest-theologian long on its seminary faculty. What underlay the conception and effort that resulted in the work that this book embodies? Why should scholars in the Episcopal Church lead in the undertaking of such a study?

Why not? one may respond. The subject is there to be investigated, after all. But we may conjecture that some singular factors were at work. For one thing, the Episcopal Church is the extension of the established church of colonial history, the Church of England, the official religious body of all six colonies of the region. That fact alone surely constitutes a legitimate interest. For another, that Christian denomination may serve as a metaphor for southern religious history. Donald Mathews's essay raises that possibility; he sees it as a "test case." (I confess that I have flirted with the same idea.) In addition, of course, many leaders in the denomination have a concern to assess and perform

Samuel S. Hill

their ministries more faithfully under the present's novel conditions. That is surely enough to provide a powerful incentive for work of this kind.

Surely no branch of the Christian church could have been more at home in regional culture than this one present "at the creation," so markedly English (not even Scottish), and the spiritual home of many who identified themselves as aristocratic families and the better classes. Until pretty recently those who aspired to upward social mobility might evaluate the Episcopal Church as the most appropriate to such status. In the South as elsewhere in American society, belonging to the "right church" has been thought to rank fairly close to living in the right neighborhood, running with the right crowd, and displaying certain manners and tastes as people made their way "up." That ascription, however, no longer applies to a church that has diversified enormously as to membership, worship styles, and connection with its surroundings. But as it has shed that reputation, it has sometimes acquired another, as a kind of alternative option for some for whom evangelicalism is no longer a fit but who do not wish to leave the broad Protestant heritage.

An ingredient part of the South's religious and cultural life the Episcopal Church has always been. However, the essay by Gardiner Shattuck, a lifetime resident of New England and himself a priest, dramatizes the peculiarly southern traits of that very old tradition. Yet wherever churches of that persuasion live, the tradition displays its own distinctive approach to Christian living, worship, and understanding. The Anglican-Episcopal perspective leads to a philosophy of infusion rather than transformation. Its ministry is just there, not characteristically an activity of initiating direct and persuasive appeals to people to convert to Christian faith or affiliate with the church. It always means to bear witness to the faith through offering worship occasions and in the lives of its members in loving service to individuals, families, people with special needs, and social justice. The temperament of the Episcopal Church is patient, acclimated to the long run. Rallying slogans, campaigns, crusades, and a spirit of urgency are simply not part of its modus operandi. Also, while distinguishing between "the church" and "the kingdom," it means to offer its life and ministries toward meeting human and social need irrespective of a person's or group's connection with the Christian movement. Despite the common perception that it is "stodgy" or fastened to old ways, it has offered prophetic leadership fairly often. The essay "Quiet Revolutionaries: Stories of Women Priests in the South," reveals the Episcopal Church's capacity for behavior far removed from the banner displaying the message that "we've always done it this way."

The most prominent, normative patterns in the South, associated with evangelicalism, have practiced intensification, rectification, and evangelization, some or all in different degrees. Those descriptions simply do not capture the pace or theology of the Episcopal Church. In one basic sense, then, the Episcopal Church seems awkwardly out of step with southern culture.

Yet that church, once ineffectual and long viewed with suspicion by much of the population, has fought its way through the South's struggles. It felt the power of the surge of the frontier society, the same surge that contributed so heavily to evangelicalism's acceptance and arrival at quasi-establishment status. It played a role in the Christianizing of the slave population. After emancipation had given way to strident segregation, the Episcopal Church made feints toward alleviating the imprisonment of the region's black citizens. Donald Mathews's essay recounts the Newport, Arkansas, confrontation of 1932 that revealed how short a distance the church was willing to go toward any improvement of the lot of black members of their own communion. Over the past half century the Episcopal Church has provided some of the most courageous and prophetic leadership in the dispelling of discrimination in the interest of social justice. And, as already referred to, the standing of its membership has shifted from an aristocratic (or claimed status) position to being marginalized as one Protestant body among several appealing to a wide variety of people. It is worth noting that the Episcopal Church never really split along regional lines during the mid-nineteenth century when that course of action characterized the behavior of the largest bodies; also, that the structure of the national church ignores Mason-Dixon. (Further, it is sobering to realize that one of its Provinces includes the commonwealth where Gettysburg was fought and the Old Dominion that was home to the government of the Confederate States of America.)

And all that is far from all, as noted. The Episcopal Church has struggled mightily with gender issues. In the general article on women and religion, the three authors paint the picture of women as numerous, active, and forceful members of the churches. That includes the Episcopal Church. The other piece, on "Women Priests," highlights one of the issues prominent in the general article, the limitations imposed on women's specific role-playing. Quite a battle was fought over a long period before women won the right to stand as candidates for the priesthood in the church; they waged that battle themselves.

Accordingly we may say that the Episcopal Church has participated in the life of the southern region in as full and rich a fashion as any other branch of the Christian Church. It has faced a range of issues that includes tradition, race, gender, and class, indeed the dynamics of regional society and culture. The planners of the conference at Sewanee and of this collection of essays, operating under the general auspices of the Episcopal Church, had plenty of incentive to treat the place of the church in a present leading to a future from a lengthy past.

Samuel S. Hill

We commend said planners and promoters for this series of studies meant to cover the hugely complex field of religion in the South. Complexity is hardly something new to this aspect of the region's culture. But the dismantling of the long-in-place pattern of evangelical domination that ascended to normativity makes everything different. We may predict more internal conflict, more puzzlement and uncertainty, and probably enlarged alienation on the part of some in the population. Working through those issues is of great significance to the health of the religious institutions and the people who make up the unique and ever-colorful American South.

PART 1

THE OLD STORY: COMMON THEMES FROM YESTERDAY TO TOMORROW

Corrie E. Norman,
Heather E. Barclay, and
Nancy A. Hardesty

CHAPTER I

WOMEN AND RELIGION IN THE SOUTH: MYTH, REALITY, AND MEANING

PERHAPS THE PHRASE MOST OFTEN USED TO DESCRIBE THE CENTRALITY OF religion to the South was coined by its most respected female author, Flannery O'Connor. The South, she wrote, is "hardly Christ-centered, but certainly *Christ haunted.*"[1] At the center of religion in the South is another figure, the one who keeps the memory of Christ, the haunting of religion, at the center of southern life. Through the years, she has appeared in many manifestations, coming into focus most clearly in the years after the Civil War as a young white woman. Dressed in white and seated in a rocking chair, she cradles the body of a dead Confederate hero across her lap, the scene encircled by her billowing hoopskirt. Motherhood and virginity, purity and sorrow, fragility and strength, passivity and resolve converge in this southern pietà. As one Lost Cause preacher in 1912 put it, "Mary is the soul of the South."[2] How ironic that the primary symbol of Catholic piety should be embraced and refashioned by a predominately Protestant, evangelical culture. Our Lady of the South is the Southern Lady.[3] No more ironic is this, perhaps, than that it took a Roman Catholic woman to come up with the phrase, "Christ haunted" for the Bible Belt.

Of such are the stories of women and their complex relationships to religion in the South—full of the irony and paradox that come when myth and reality meet and find themselves not altogether comfortable with each other. The Confederate pietà seldom appears in the South anymore. There are still a few towns that stage this tableau vivant at public festivals with homecoming queens and football stars in the leading roles. (One Alabama town stages it every Fourth of July!) But she still haunts southern women today.

3

The weight of southern patriarchal culture and religion, so the myth goes, rests in the lap of southern woman. She sustains it by surrounding it with her purity; she upholds it by silently and tenderly nursing it in her arms. An awareness of this paradigmatic model, and their discomfort with it, is present in the stories of real women in the South, historically and today. Few have found its burden light. Some have tried to sit still and bear the weight. Others tell of being pushed back down in place. Very few, even today, find a way to stand on their own feet and walk away completely, for to abandon "*our* Lady" is to leave the South behind. There is much about the southern Mary that many women have not been willing to give up, even if they could. So many women in the South have found themselves somewhere between standing up and sitting back. And many often have not known whether they were sitting or standing because, as it turns out, just sitting there rocking requires a lot of work. All that cooking, cleaning, praying, organizing, teaching, and preaching (usually without calling it that), while confined by hoopskirt and rocker, has not been easy. What they have accomplished in such awkward positions is quite remarkable. They—and she—have kept the South "Christ haunted."

This essay will attempt to bring out some of the stories of real women, diverse in so many ways, who struggle with and against the southern Mary today. It is not the full story or a clear picture. It is based largely on scattered testimony. That is the best we can do, given that their voices, though often strong, have been so muted.

We begin by trying to piece together a history of women and religion in the South. No scholarly survey as such exists. Today, even in the best textbooks on women and religion in America, southern women appear "by the way."[4] The picture that emerges is not far off from the myth. Southern women are religious like other women in many ways and yet "different." The difference is usually described in vague terms of less and more. Southern women are less interested in social justice and more passive in regard to the social consequences of patriarchy. They are less likely to strike out as preachers and more likely to accept their assigned roles in the churches. They had less impact because they went along more often with a more thoroughly entrenched patriarchy.

The South did not invent patriarchy or the notion of separate spheres. The southern Mary has many sisters elsewhere, older and younger. She did not appear suddenly as a response to the Lost Cause; she migrated to the Americas with European culture and religion. In the fertile soil of southern patriarchy, rural isolation, economic hardship, and biblical literalism, there has perhaps been less to inhibit certain aspects of her development in the South than in other parts of the country. Should not that make the story of women's religiosity in the South all the more compelling? The mystique of the south-

Corrie E. Norman, Heather E. Barclay, and Nancy A. Hardesty

ern Mary has haunted well-intentioned (and, in other respects, quite fine) scholarship on women, which has assumed a lot about real southern women's religious motivations and experiences when it has paid attention to them at all. To find the names of southern religious women in the books on women's history is rare. And then it is usually the exceptional women, like the Grimke sisters, who become interesting only once they move to the North.

Thankfully, a few of the most recent works on American women and religion have begun to pay more attention to southern women. In Catherine Brekus's study of women preachers, southern women appear in fuller form alongside their northern sisters than in most women's histories. The number and diversity of southern women who felt the call to "exhort" is well documented, as is the complexity of their situations.[5] Evelyn Brooks Higginbotham's work on African American Baptist women also does justice to women in southern contexts, struggling with northern paternalism and southern patriarchy, with sexism and racism.[6]

In the historical scholarship on women in the South that has emerged and begun to thrive of late, the focus has been elsewhere than on religion.[7] Religion is often the "by the way" factor in these social histories. If southern women are supposed to be so religious, how can this be? In part, it is due to the very importance of religion in women's lives. Economic and political motivations, child-rearing techniques, and notions of community, race, class, and personal identity are so permeated by religion that it has become the silent certainty, taken for granted—sometimes by both scholars and the women they study. Women do not have to worship at the shrine of the southern Mary or write about religion extensively in their diaries or even spend a lot of time in church (although many did and do) for religion and the feminine mythos associated with it to affect them significantly, in often complicated and paradoxical ways that merit closer examination.[8] Here again, we have a happy exception in Drew Gilpin Faust's sensitive study of Confederate women during the Civil War, which devotes an entire chapter to religion.[9]

While social history has not adequately addressed the religion of southern women, historians of southern religion have hardly focused on women. When Norma Taylor Mitchell surveyed women and religion for *The Encyclopedia of Religion in the South* in 1984, she could say more about what needed to be done than what had been done in the field.[10] In some ways, scholars have jumped ahead while lagging behind. Don Mathews set the pace when he considered gender along with race and class in his seminal 1977 work, *Religion in the Old South*.[11] Currently, the best history of religion and women in the South comes in studies like Christine Heyrman's *Southern Cross*. It is not a book of "women's history" per se. It is a work that seriously attends to the gendered nature of the development of southern evangelicalism.[12] Similarly, among social historians, Stephanie McCurry stands out for the analysis of gender and religion in her study of yeomen in antebellum South Carolina.[13] Many works of the past two decades that have given us a rich picture of the religion of slaves in the South have also provided some of the fullest exposures to women's religious lives in southern historiography without focusing specifically on women.[14] Without a focus on women's religious history in the South, however, what we know of them is still a blur, and relying on the myth of southern womanhood to clarify the picture is too much of a temptation.

Studies of contemporary southern women and religion are practically nonexistent at a time when sociologists reaffirm the religiosity of the region. The one sure thing that the reality of women's lives in the South and the myth share is the centrality of religious devotion. Yet the myth-busters, for the most part, have ignored this. To find analysis of recent religious trends among southern women, one might pick through a few of the studies on national trends for southern examples.[15] Or just look around and listen. Our reflections on what we hear and see from the women around us, from the books they read and write and the Web sites they explore, from what religious institutions are asking of and offering to them, are at the heart of this essay.

Perhaps it should not be so surprising that the study of religion in the South has not given adequate attention to the women of the region. The academy in the South and the study of southern religion are still male dominated. It is telling that many women scholars who have contributed to our knowledge of southern women and religion, such as Gilpin Faust, Heyrman, McCurry, and Cynthia Lyerly, are working outside the South, as have many of the southern-born feminist theologians in the last decades (Nell Morton, Carter Heyward, Phyllis Trible, and Carolyn Walker Bynum, to name a few).[16] There is hope that things are changing. Repeated calls for more attention to the study of women and religion in the South have come, along with the promise of forthcoming studies now being prepared within and outside the region by new scholars. "We will find," declares Don Mathews, "that women were more intellectually and spiritually inventive than suspected and that they helped change theology and orientation more than imagined."[17] In the meantime, what follows is an outline of the story of southern women and religion, a story that emerges from the interaction of history and myth.

Out of the Hoop: "Other" Women

Historically, the majority of women in the South never could have lived up to the ideal of the southern Mary. They were marginalized and often brutalized because they deviated from the ideal, while their "difference" helped dominant society define it. Women of color, women too poor or preoccupied with the daily struggle for survival to have much left for the church, and women outside the Protestant chosen were still expected to hold up the standard without enjoying the honor of its status. They could be handmaids to Our Lady, imitating and serving her. At varying times, they were the objects of her charity, maternalism, and scorn. More than occasionally, however, women of different races, classes, and even religions discovered their common "bond" to the southern Mary and worked together for mutual benefit.

Many of the women "out of the hoop" had models more ancient than Mary. When the Europeans arrived in the South bringing the nascent southern Mary with them, they found Native American cultures with more egalitarian social and religious structures. The Creek Indians, for example, had a matrilineal government in which women controlled property and raised children with assistance from the men in the tribe. Tensions surrounding gender-related issues such as divorce (the Creeks permitted it to both women and men) and monogamy (which privileged European patriarchy) existed between the cultures and often led to heated religious debates as Europeans attempted to conquer, Christianize, and civilize the Creeks. Some white women and enslaved black women and men recognized that Creek culture and its vision-centered traditions might offer a less oppressive environment and tried to escape to it.[18]

Many of the African American women who were forced into slavery came from tribal heritages of matrilineal authority and women's religious leadership. While much was lost, the preservation and adaptation of women's religious ways of being and knowing helped African American culture survive as it blended with and profoundly changed Christianity. Afro-Caribbean traditions with female leadership and images of the divine were translated to and fostered in Louisiana by priestesses and healers like Marie Laveau (ca. 1790–1881). A free woman of color, she combined an ardent Roman Catholicism with African traditions, passing her mantle on to her daughter when her work was done.

Southern black women also recaptured some of the charisma they had in traditional African religions as they helped to shape the preaching and worship of American evangelicalism. A few itinerant black women preachers, like the famed Jarena Lee, braved the possibility of violence and enslavement to venture south to preach.[19] A rare example was the slave "Clarinda," who took to street preaching in late-eighteenth-century Georgia. In a remarkable case of paradigmatic inversion, this once "remarkably dissolute and profane" woman made such a dramatic impression on white society that she was held up as a "paragon of piety" by Baptist clergy, supported by "ladies," and eventually emancipated.[20] More black women exhorted in the early evangelical groups that allowed mixed-race worship in the South. But it was within black communities that black women were most likely to exercise spiritual leadership without being seen as anomalies. They continued to attend to the spiritual needs of their people as evangelical churches clamped down on white women's and slaves' religious expression. How many like the "Aunt Silvia" remembered by a former Mississippi slave must have ministered as she did, leading "religious services every week in her quarters"? "She was a good thinker. . . . She was the only preacher we knowed anything about," he recalled.[21]

Although black women, like many Southern white women, met with great resistance within the churches when they felt called to preach, they persevered until a number were granted full ordination in the late nineteenth and early twentieth centuries. The first African American Holiness congregation assembled in 1886 in Charleston, South Carolina, under the leadership of Pastor Jane Williams.[22] Mary Small and Julia Foote were ordained in 1898 and 1900 by the African Methodist Episcopal Zion Church. They were the first women, black or white, to be officially ordained by Methodists in the United States. It took half a century for another Methodist body to grant ordination to women.[23]

But women's leadership was expressed in a number of ways in the African American churches, and its story is made more complicated by the constraints of the models of white southern Mary and her northern Victorian cousins. "Our hope for the race lies in a good Christian education," proclaimed the newspaper of black Baptist women in Alabama.[24] The assumptions about what a "good Christian education" might be for women, particularly for black women, were bound up with idealized images of what white ladies and black handmaidens should be. At first organized with the aid of white philanthropists from the North, schools like Spelman College, named for Laura Spelman Rockefeller, sought to create an elite black society with deportment and values similar to those of Victorian whites that might trickle down to other blacks. Discouraged from "emotional" behavior in church, from spontaneous self-expression, Spelman women were taught to behave "like ladies" and to carry their new manners along with godliness and learning out to black communities as teachers.[25]

Women who came out of the Spelman "Talented Tenth" or similar environments were often to lead the black women's conventions that developed in the late nineteenth century. A watershed was the National Baptist's Woman's Convention in Richmond in 1900, where Nannie Helen Burroughs, reared and educated in Virginia, gave her rousing address "How the Sisters Are Hindered from Helping." Burroughs and other female leaders in the black churches would struggle with racism and sexism within and outside the black community as they tried to establish strategies for women's self-determination. Both their achievements and the constraints of dominant images of ladyhood on black women are seen in the establishment of institutions like the National

Corrie E. Norman, Heather E. Barclay, and Nancy A. Hardesty

Training School for Girls and Women. Burroughs, herself the daughter of a mother who raised her on a domestic's salary, promoted self-help and respect for black women through "Bible, bath, and broom."[26]

Catholic women in the South were beholden to their own Mary, whose differences from her southern counterpart helped keep them apart from the norm as they shared struggles for spiritual expression and leadership not dissimilar to those of Protestant women. While Catholic women religious who came to the New World expected to live a life of service and sacrifice, they often had to fight the imposition of cloistration and control by the male clerical hierarchy. Desperate or unfamiliar contexts in the eighteenth- and nineteenth-century South offered these women the challenges they sought and more. They learned to adapt creatively. Their very survival depended on it, as the Sisters of Loreto so tragically learned in Kentucky when several sisters succumbed to the effects of hard work and hot climate combined with European penitential and dress habits.[27] They often specialized in the care of the most marginalized.

The Ursulines, the first women's order to arrive in the South, had been founded by an Italian laywoman in the sixteenth century for an active ministry of educating girls and women. The French Ursulines who arrived in New Orleans in 1727 intended to perpetuate that charism. After braving a tortuous sea journey and shaky beginning in a city in crisis, they soon found their bearings, setting up a convent and the first school for girls in what is now the United States under the leadership of Marie Tranchepain. The sisters in New Orleans also started the first orphanage, first free school, and first classes for Native Americans and blacks. They held the first religious retreats for Catholic laywomen, whose distinctive history in the South still awaits attention from scholars.

Black women were among the earliest American-born Catholic women to exercise leadership in the church. A native of New Orleans, Henriette DeLille, founded the Sisters of the Holy Family to minister to slaves and free blacks in the first half of the nineteenth century. Currently being considered for canonization, she would be the first African American female saint if her cause succeeds. Women's congregations under "simple" vows, like the Daughters of Charity, even gained the respect and admiration of Protestants by their ministries to the sick and dying during the Civil War.[28]

As in socially conscious Protestant circles, northern Catholic women like the Philadelphia socialite-become-saint Katharine Drexel turned their attention southward. Saint Katherine founded the Sisters of the Blessed Sacrament for Indians and Colored People in 1891. In 1925 Xavier University of Louisiana was founded through her initiative, still the only black Catholic university in the country.[29]

Jewish women have a heritage in the South that goes back to seventeenth-century Charleston, but such grand southern pedigree has not afforded them entrance into the dominant culture without internal and external struggle. Like other southern women, they have been largely responsible for maintaining religious identity by upholding strict gender models and maintaining the home. This was no easy task, particularly in the pork-loving South.[30]

Some recent scholarship argues that Jewish households in the English colonies were more "complementary and interdependent" with regard to gender than Christian households.[31] Among Jews who tried to assimilate, however, women adopted and perpetuated the gender ideals of the dominant Protestant culture. The daughters of immigrant women who had exercised authority in family businesses found themselves occupied in their homes and in women's benevolent societies that were organized along the lines of Protestant women's societies. They also shared the complexities of women's quest to carry on responsibly and actively under the constraints of the model southern lady.[32]

This pattern has been studied in two different parts of the South. Jewish women in nineteenth-century Savannah like Eugenia Levy Phillips and Phoebe Yates Pember were southern women through and through, ardent advocates for the Confederacy. They were the backbone of Jewish life in Savannah as well, establishing and teaching in Jewish Sunday schools and women's societies as well as keeping Judaism alive in their homes. The two went hand in hand for them but not without tensions related to religion and gender. In their active support for the Confederacy, they stepped over the boundaries of Jewish exclusion and women's silence.[33] In central Appalachia, Jewish women who were instrumental in building synagogues had to fight to keep a voice in those institutions that were run by male boards. Like many Christian women, they found autonomy in the Jewish women's groups that were beyond male control.[34]

Other Jewish women have walked a tightrope between southern ladyhood and the impetus to confront injustices. During one of the most heinous episodes in the cult of the southern Mary, Jewish southern women found themselves at odds with the female purity code. In 1915 a Jewish man, Leo Frank, was falsely accused of the murder of a young white woman and lynched by a mob in Cobb County, Georgia. Allying with like-minded black and white churchwomen, southern Jewish women joined the Association of Southern Women to Prevent Lynching and later were active in the civil rights movement.

Ironically, one of the ways in which Jewish women have been responsible for maintaining distinction from Christian women has also turned out to be a bridge between domestic and religious cultures. In her study of southern Jewish foodways, Marcie Cohen Ferris writes that food was a vehicle through which Jewish and African American women could share cultures. Though not a shar-

Corrie E. Norman, Heather E. Barclay, and Nancy A. Hardesty

ing of social equals, many black women working as cooks in Jewish households learned about Judaism through preparing traditional foods for Jewish holidays, while their Jewish employers came to appreciate the soul food and church-dinner favorites that gradually crept into their kitchens through their cooks.[35]

The Southern Lady:
Standing Up While Sitting Down

Our Lady of the South began to bud in the planter-controlled society of the Old South before revivalism began to spread across it. She blossomed as the white "evangelical woman."[36] During the fervor of the earliest Baptist and Methodist successes in the South, evangelicals challenged the gender model against which women in the churches of the South had been measured. Often defying family, traditional religion, and social convention, early evangelical women testified and prayed publicly. They met privately in small groups with men and women, black and white, to share their innermost yearnings. They were the vanguard of a religious revolution that threatened to change families and society. Methodist and Baptist clergy sometimes encouraged evangelical women to lead prayer, to "prophesy," give testimony, and let loose the expressions of spiritual ecstasy in worship. In some congregations, women also had a voice on decision-making bodies and were strategic as well as spiritual advisors to clergy.[37]

The earliest cries against these new sects included warnings about the dangerous behaviors they induced in women. Evangelical worship, according to its detractors, promoted mental illness, promiscuity, and immorality in women.[38] From pre-Revolutionary Anglicans like Charles Woodmason on, traditionalist clergy beseeched southern men to reign in the enthusiasm of their women and slaves lest the church and society fall into disorder. Episcopal churchmen of antebellum North Carolina made a concerted effort to squelch the fervor stirring among elite female communicants and bring them into submission to church, husband, and established social order.[39] Baptist and Methodist churches themselves became progressively more negative about women's expressiveness and leadership as they settled into the culture, eventually denying a voice to women, who had been largely responsible for their dramatic success. Even the Quakers—outside the pale in so many respects, including a long tradition of women's leadership—were silencing women's speech. In place of a voice, women were given a place—the separate sphere—and an image to worship and emulate: the Madonna of the South, the evangelical lady. Women were expected to hear and obey the message given by evangelicals and non-evangelicals alike. As one Disciples preacher put it, "My sisters, be content to stay at home and guide the house . . . a mission a thousand times nobler than any known by those who are continuously croaking about women's rights."[40]

Church was the other place where women were "at home," but their space within it was restricted. The boundaries were literal and visceral for women, as one depiction of a typical Sunday in a postbellum church vividly shows. Women sat on the left side of the church in their layers of stiff, uncomfortable clothing and restrictive shoes. The men who even bothered to enter the church doors sat on the right side, where they spent a good deal of their time sleeping or spitting tobacco into conveniently provided spittoons at the ends of the pews. Other men waited outside until church was over so that they could enjoy the Sunday meal or walk a girlfriend home. Young girls sat silently in church while young boys giggled, shot pistols outside, or let animals loose in the church.[41]

For women, church was still their place, however limited. They burst the boundaries by sheer number. As had been the case elsewhere in America since colonial days, women were much more likely than men to be church members, attend services, and participate in church activities.[42] So many more women were involved in church life in the South that many church officials wondered where the men had gone. Rev. Charles E. Dowman in Quincy, Florida, complained, "There has scarce been a religious young man here in years."[43] Some southern churches did not have a single male member; others were maintained by women while the church waited for enough male committee members to call official church meetings. But women did not wait idly. A woman from Chapel Hill remembered that "as is often the case, the day-by-day business of church work was left to the ladies."[44] During the Civil War, this was even more true. When worship was held, it was often at the insistence of the women left behind. When no clergy were available, women *were* the church, holding their own services in homes, leading worship, and committing their dead to final rest.[45]

And thus the southern Mary stood while sitting, busying herself in her clearly defined spaces. In their homes, white women read the Bible and taught it to their charges (children and slaves) and even admonished their husbands from it. They dutifully cared for the church, embroidered altar linens and vestments, and fed and otherwise cared for ministers and the unfortunate. During the Civil War and its aftermath, the boundaries loosened as southern patriarchy fell into chaos. White women found themselves taking charge, forming organizations such as the Soldiers' Relief Society, the Ladies' Memorial Association, and the Ladies' Christian Association (which kept the Young Men's Christian Association alive).

Other situations necessitated the leadership of women. Male preachers and theology students might visit remote Appalachian communities in the

Corrie E. Norman, Heather E. Barclay, and Nancy A. Hardesty

summers. But during the harsh winters, spiritual leadership was one of the tasks that fell to women, especially women teachers. For communities in Appalachia, educated women were more valuable than male clergy. When Rev. R. P. Smith explained to a congregation that there were not enough Presbyterian ministers for rural churches, one mountain man responded: "We like to hear you fellows preach, and I am not saying anything again ye, but if we can't git both, send us the women teachers. These women teach our children books and good manners during the week and on Sunday they teach all of us a lot of what is in the Bible. Tell your folks to send us the teachers, we can git along mighty well for a good while yet just with them doing the work."[46]

There had always been a few who refused to abide in place, and suffered the consequences. In 1834 a Sister Roberts dared to preach—"mounting the pulpit"—in her Primitive Baptist Church in South Carolina. She was removed from the pulpit and the fellowship.[47] Sometimes a woman was allowed to speak under the cover of patriarchal rhetoric and relationship. Tennessean Nancy Mulkey, daughter of a minister, "exhorted" (as distinguished from "preached") in her church "in a manner neither father nor brother could equal." Other women were known for their fervent and extended praying in church.[48] Few itinerant women preachers from the North came to the South; the prevailing sense was that the resistance of male southerners would make the effort insurmountable for women accustomed to resisting the formidable. When Nancy Towle and Harriet Livermore did come to Charleston, they were put in place, allowed to speak only in "small, private gatherings."[49] "Preaching" was something a southern white woman might fall into within the confines of the gatherings of underlings or peers, where its occurrence was out of earshot of white males or could be dismissed as something else. As one former slave reported, his mistress would lead "prayer meetings" in the slave quarters on Sunday afternoons. "Sometimes she git so happy," he recalled, "she git to shoutin."[50]

Most southern women were themselves ambivalent about the limitations placed on them. Within the restrictions, paradoxically, women had a lot to do, places to go, and even managed to find their voices. They could meet with other women in church and charitable settings. They exercised agency within women's organizations that aimed to affect society at large and eventually, in the case of mission societies, the world. They could be seen, if not always heard, as paragons of Christian virtue. Many believed that the roles ascribed to them were god-sent and that they would be rewarded *because of* the trials of their limitations.

The appeal of evangelical piety for women, even purged of its early gender-egalitarian leanings, cannot be overestimated. The promise of eternity with a loving savior was sweet balm for women who lived in a cruel world of childhood mortality and distant husbands where they had little control. It offered a relationship with a master who was kind, who understood and listened to women. That relationship was often characterized in the language of romance and passion. Jesus was an ardent yet gentle lover. Though rife with potential danger (which no doubt added to the attraction in some cases), the relationship with a pastor as spiritual guide and sympathetic male figure might reinforce devotion. But perhaps more significantly, evangelical piety gave a profound sense of meaning to the roles assigned to women, especially to motherhood. Christian mothers were told that they were the most significant forces for spiritual reform on earth. As a poem (ca. 1820) found among the surviving papers of one woman puts it, "O! rich the mead, that heaven bestows, to bless maternal care: / And large the stream of love that flows, called by a Mother's Prayer."[51]

But it is woman's suffering, especially after the Civil War, that becomes the most powerful force on southern earth—and maybe even heaven itself by some accounts. The famed Georgia evangelist Sam Jones held a number of women's revivals, the last of which drew five thousand women to the Ryman Auditorium in Nashville, built to house his events, in 1895. A sample book of Jones's sermons, designed for home use, re-creates the scene at one of these meetings. Jones begins with a war story. A young Confederate lies wounded in a hospital. Somehow, his mother, described as frail and meek, finds him. At first denied entry by the doctors, she crouches nearby, taking on his pain through her prayers. Eventually, she creeps into her son's room and, with the touch of a hand, saves him from sure death. Jones surmises:

> There are three words in our language that we associate
> perfectly naturally together—mother, home, and heaven.
> These words have always been associated together in my
> mind from my youth up: Mother, the dearest sweetest
> being in all the world; home, with all the memories that
> belong to it; and heaven, the final resting place of bliss for
> the good. God's greatest and best gift to a little child is a
> good mother. . . . If you were this morning to place here to
> my right the Bible, the Church, the preachers, the Sunday
> School, the prayer meeting, put them all here, and stand
> my sweet Christian mother over there and ask me, "Now if
> you would make sure of heaven, which will you take, these
> influences over here or your sweet mother, standing there?"
> I would turn my back on all these, and put my arms around
> my sweet Christian mother's neck and say: "Give me my
> mother; for if there is any chance for me to be saved, my
> mother will take me by the hand and lead me home to

Corrie E. Norman, Heather E. Barclay, and Nancy A. Hardesty

God and heaven." There is nothing, I repeat it, this side
of heaven that can take the place of a good mother. You
can talk about Sunday School (that is good); you may talk
about the Bible (thank God for that precious book); you
may talk about preachers (thank God for every one of
them); but there is nothing in the universe like mother![52]

The image that accompanies the text is a version of the Confederate
Madonna, translated to the domestic realm of Jones's postwar audience. It includes both suffering motherhood and virginal purity: a mother cradles an ail-
ing little boy as a small daughter stands beside the rocker looking on. The
necessity of women overstepping the religious boundaries that war brought
encouraged not only a new independence but also reaffirmed the ideology of
female sacrifice and purity—and their necessity for the salvation of the South.[53]

There were temporal as well as spiritual rewards for women's good behavior. You might avoid being hit or put out of your home or community. Elite
white women, particularly, had a lot to lose when they defied the rules since
they also benefited from the privileges and creature comforts of white patriarchy. Even middling white women came to see that there were advantages to
maintaining their places and the social order.[54] The extent to which white
women stood up depended sometimes on the extent to which they could or
were willing to drop not only the bonds placed on them but also on others,
particularly blacks. For others, especially the elite ladies, asserting their own
independence became strategically linked to preserving white patriarchy—
which meant, paradoxically, affirming their places as "ladies."[55] Most bought
their roles and the social order, if not wholeheartedly. So they stood and sat.
They played "the lady" and did the work. Churches provided the place and
sometimes the rhetoric and rituals for standing. The chief complexities of
myth meeting reality for southern women, and the most compelling aspects of
their stories, are the strategies by which women worked for and against, in and
out, up and down at the same time.

Late-nineteenth-century women were able to use the ideal of women's
innate religious virtue to get out of the house and even travel the world
spreading the gospel. Perhaps the most well-known nineteenth-century southern woman today is Charlotte "Lottie" Moon, who established a mission in
China. Ironically, this never-married, career minister would become the closest thing to a saint that Southern Baptists have, as the icon of Southern Baptist foreign missions. More appropriately, however, Moon would be remembered as the "cookie lady" who starved herself to death out of sacrificial love
for the Chinese. Moon herself masterfully used the rhetoric of femininity to
advance her ministry and Baptist missions. In early reports she did tell how

she gained entrance to Chinese homes by winning the trust of children with her cookies. No doubt she knew that the circulation of that story would endear Baptists to her mission. In a letter calling for more male missionaries to come to China to join the efforts of women, she carefully told a story bound to persuade her audience. She reported that a group of men had asked her to lead a worship service and to preach to them about the Prodigal Son. Demurring at first, Moon did eventually lead the men in worship. Her letter was careful to state, however, that she only prayed and taught, because in "the ancient church" women could not preach to men. Moon clearly was appealing to the "shame" of a woman being pressed to perform an inappropriate role due to lack of male ministers. But she also noted that her first reason for turning the men away was that she was busy with her own ministry: She had been teaching women and girls all day when they approached her. She continued not by calling for male preachers but, rather, for male teachers to serve the miners working in a nearby province.[56] At the same time, softly and directly, she shamed Baptist men into the mission field just as she had shamed Baptist women in 1888 to organize themselves better, in the manner of "the noble Methodist women." She also voiced her feelings about women's roles in church life clearly: "Simple justice demands that women should have equal rights with men in mission meetings and in the conduct of their work."[57]

The rhetoric of women's missionary efforts was often couched in gender-appropriate terms; it was part of their "mothering." The women of the Methodist Episcopal Church, South, were the first to organize a missionary society in 1887. Its founder, Mrs. M. L. Kelly, is known as the "mother of Foreign Missions." Her first "daughters" were Dora and Lochie Rankin, from Milan, Tennessee, who preceded Moon in China.[58] Southern Baptist women followed, founding the Women's Missionary Union in 1888. The experience of the many women who sent others abroad while staying behind eventually helped broaden boundaries at home too. Women in the South as elsewhere took the experience gained in church mission organizations and built on it in civic reform groups.[59]

In a variety of ways in everyday life, southern women worked with and against the boundaries of myth at the same time. In some respects women created and maintained the real influence that religion had in their communities. Through the meals women served at churches, they drew communities together. For many men participation in religion meant primarily (if not exclusively) participating in the meals. As one minister's son remarked, "I was in no hurry to get excited over religion. I would take my time, eat fried chickens and watermelons and think it over."[60] For many southerners meaning-making in the community did not come primarily through preaching and sharing communion. Rather, it was the fried chicken, watermelon, and other

Corrie E. Norman, Heather E. Barclay, and Nancy A. Hardesty

Southern foods prepared and served by women's hands that created *communitas* in Southern religion and the opportunity for religious reflection.

Women used such opportunities to push the boundaries. During these meals young women would often present dramas designed to raise funds for the church while simultaneously teaching moral lessons.[61] More often than preaching and communion, it was the female-led rituals of meal and skit that evoked the sacred for many. Gratitude for a good meal meant the funding of sacred causes undertaken primarily by women.

Perhaps more southern women claimed the rhetoric of Christian patriarchy than Christian egalitarianism to defend their causes. And sometimes they appealed to both simultaneously. In the yeoman society of antebellum South Carolina, women called on the "courts of Jesus Christ" to defend themselves against abusive husbands and fathers. They also called for responsibility within the privileges of male rule. Sometimes they stood up for themselves, claiming their rights as Christians, and at other times they pressured male clergy to take up their causes against husbands and fathers, playing patriarchy against itself.[62]

Perhaps the most radical and yet most gender-appropriate of strategies occurred in the temperance movement. In 1881 the newly elected president of the Woman's Christian Temperance Society, Frances Willard, came south hoping to organize interdenominational temperance societies. Sallie Chapin, a Charlestonian and the daughter of a Methodist minister, organized WCTU chapters first in Charleston and then across the South. Southern women believed drinking to be at the root of many social problems in the South, from the overall violence of the region to the domestic abuse and alcoholism many confronted in their own homes. At once defending the home and challenging patriarchy, Methodist women particularly, white and black, were among the most committed advocates of temperance. This was war and called for extraordinary methods: mothers took to preaching and acts of civil disobedience in order to hold up the Christian home, its values and virtues. They could become fearless crusaders on the streets because they were the embodiment of that most loving and peaceful domain.[63]

The Holiness movement in the late nineteenth century allowed female voices to be raised openly once again, although not uncontested, in southern pulpits. Kentuckian Louisa Woosley began preaching in 1887 and was ordained in 1889 by Holiness Presbyterians, although the ordination was rejected by the General Assembly in 1894. Woosley defended her right in the 1891 book *Shall Woman Preach? Or, The Question Answered.*[64] In Milan, Tennessee, a group of women and men from Methodist and Baptist backgrounds formed the New Testament Church of Christ. The leader of the group was Alabama-born Mary Lee Wasson (1864–1950). When she married "the cowboy preacher,"

Methodist Lee Harris, in 1891, she thought that being a preacher's wife would satisfy her calling. His untimely death in 1894, however, left her with a young Holiness denomination to guide. While preaching across the central South and the Southwest, she met her second husband, evangelist Henry Cagle. Back in Milan, Donie Mitchum became pastor of the home church. When she told her husband, Edwin, a successful businessman, that she was called to preach, he bought her a revival tent. Eventually they settled in Memphis, and from there she conducted meetings in Arkansas and Missouri.[65] In 1905 there were enough such stories across the South that Fannie McDowell Hunter could write the volume *Women Preachers*. While the appeal of their gifts as preachers drew people to these women in the spirit-centered Holiness Movement, the support and "co-ministry" with spouses was a significant legitimizer. The endorsements of both God and man were important if a woman wanted to stand up and be heard.

Rocking Back and Moving On: Women and Religion in the Contemporary South

The mythic southern Mary still haunts women in the South today, but her shape is shifting. The persistent paradoxes of active passivity and unacknowledged leadership in religious settings are met primarily with old strategies and models, revised in light of changing social realities. But women in the South across religious divides are articulating a growing impatience with models that do not fit their lives or spiritual needs. While many stay in place, uncomfortably agitated and agitating, a growing number are acting on their restlessness—sometimes prompted by an inner voice and sometimes prompted by personal or institutional change. More often than not, however, moving on means rocking back in some way. Southern women are confronting and embracing an increasingly multifaceted Mary. Thus the story of women and religion in the South only grows more complex.

Perhaps the most significant challenge to the traditional image of the southern religious female is women's ordination in almost every major denomination. This was long in coming, and the battles for acceptance and equity are far from over. While Methodists recognized women's full ordination in 1956, only forty years later did the Southeast jurisdiction of the United Methodist Church elect its first female bishop, Charlene Kammerer. In those forty years many a small, rural Methodist parish experienced the ministries of women. Fewer large churches have been given that opportunity. Female pastors are far more likely to be assigned to positions that barely offer a living wage with little chance for advancement. A 1998 study of the Virginia Annual Conference revealed that women clergy felt "underutilized" and "insufficiently supported." While the statistics show southern Methodists lagging slightly behind, the experience of Methodist women in the South is not particularly atypical of the rest of the country or of other mainline denominations.[66]

Two things do seem to make the ministries of ordained women in southern churches all the more difficult. The first is the degree to which codes of female "style" conflict with pastoral authority within their churches. (See the article on Episcopal priests later in this volume.) The second is that the "mainline" isn't dominant in the evangelical South; the Southern Baptist Convention is. The general religious climate makes acceptance more difficult for women ministers. The Methodist pastor or Episcopal priest often finds herself the only female minister in a town dominated by the "big men" of the larger, conservative churches who oppose women's ministry. One Episcopal priest related typical experiences. Her own parishioners requested that she "put up" her hair when she celebrates the Eucharist, while her participation in the local clergy association prompted the pastors of the largest Baptist churches to withdraw. This is not the whole story, however. This priest's parish is growing, attracting a number of seekers who no longer fit in the churches of their childhood, including several single and divorced women, single mothers, and even teenage girls seeking new models.

The Presbyterian Church (USA), or PC(USA), recognized women's ordination in 1964, and its statistics on women's ministry bear out comparably to those of other churches nationwide.[67] But Presbyterians in the South are divided over women's roles. The Presbyterian Church in America (PCA) began in Birmingham when 260 churches voted to pull out of the PC(USA) in 1974. It now claims 1,450 member congregations, largely concentrated in the South. It formed in protest to what its members saw as "liberalizing" tendencies in the PC(USA), specifically its stance on women's ministry.[68] The PCA, however, has not been able to avoid tensions over women's roles within its own fold. Over the last two decades, it has undertaken an international mission initiative that has commissioned scores of women as well as men. In 1999 a senior pastor in Knoxville, Tennessee, was rebuked by his presbytery for allowing a female missionary to speak from the pulpit on two Sunday evenings the previous year.[69] Her mission abroad is encouraged, but she is not allowed to "teach" men from the pulpit or elsewhere. Her name generally goes unmentioned in reports. The silencing of this woman has extended to media coverage of her experience.

Women are allowed to teach other women in PC(USA) churches. One popular teacher, Jani Ortlund, is a prime example of how some women claim leadership in fundamentalist churches like the PC(USA). The wife of the senior pastor of the First Presbyterian Church in Augusta, Georgia, she speaks to other women from a position of privilege within the church, all the while emphasizing the "servanthood" of women and pastors' wives particularly. Ortlund not only embraces the boundaries, but she also defends them in the militant tenor permissible to women when they are defending patriarchal privilege and "family values." According to Ortlund, women have a lot to lose by straying from traditional roles. In her book *Fearless Femininity,* she proposes a "model of God's plan for womanhood" for those "who are confused by feminist ideology."[70] Ortlund represents the conservative backlash to secular feminism and women's ministry. Complaining that "the image [of Christian womanhood] has almost faded," she encourages other women to return "fearlessly" to a model that "seek[s] to express itself in appropriate, godly ways as we nurture, affirm, and receive the resources of masculinity surrounding us."[71]

While Ortlund writes and teaches to revive the image, others envision it on television or through the Internet, cloaking their ministries with an often-exaggerated femininity (most vividly illustrated currently by Jan Crouch of Trinity Broadcasting in Nashville) and by being the wives and cohosts of ministers. Conservative Protestant women are not the only ones acting within such boundaries on television. Perhaps the most influential and visible Roman Catholic woman in the South of late is Mother Angelica, founder of the Eternal Word Broadcasting Network in Birmingham and host of the popular primetime show *Mother Angelica Live.* In a devotional posted on her website, Mother Angelica holds up an image of Mary shared by Catholic and southern traditions: "She was humble, hidden, sorrowful and afflicted. . . . She is all things to all men that she might understand their failings, though she failed not. She is compassionate with their falls, though she fell not. She followed in the Master's footsteps in order to experience all the sufferings that poor human nature is subject to."[72]

Mother Angelica, once a formidable presence on screen, tragically has come to embody that image of Mary-Christ. Having suffered a stroke that has affected her speech, she now ministers by "bearing her Cross" in silence in a convent in Hanceville, Alabama. Her Mother Vicar reports with confidence that "her suffering is doing great things for the Church."[73] Viewers of EWTN may still see "the best" episodes of "Mother Angelica Live" as they pray for her recovery and return to the airwaves.

Jani Ortlund, Jan Crouch, and Mother Angelica hardly stand for all or even a majority of women in religious organizations that reject women's equal status with men. Less than an hour's drive from the founding site of the PC(USA) in Birmingham and ten miles from Mother's Angelica's convent in Hanceville is the city of Cullman, home to the Benedictine Sisters of the Monastery of the Sacred Heart. While grounded in the traditions of community and prayer, these Catholic women lead lives of activism reminiscent

Corrie E. Norman, Heather E. Barclay, and Nancy A. Hardesty

in some ways of the earliest nuns who came to the South. Deeply involved in work on behalf of social justice and peace, the sisters include canon and civil lawyers as well as social workers, teachers, and health care professionals. The community is best known for its retreat center, which advances the traditions of hospitality and spiritual practice into new areas, integrating traditional Christian prayer with yoga. One of their most popular workshops is "Woman Spirit Rising," which focused in 2002 not on Mary but on Joan of Arc, the "warrior hero," as a model for women today.[74]

As in so many historical instances, women today step into the breach, exercising "masculine" roles, testing boundaries as they pick up the slack. Catholic women religious and lay professionals are sustaining a church suffering from clergy scandal and a lack of priests. While this "helping" ministry satisfies some, others work with much-tried patience, unable to fulfill their calls to priestly vocation. In Arkansas one woman with whom we spoke left another profession to become a parish assistant. "I have felt a call to the priesthood all my life," she reasons. "This is as close as I can get. And with the limited presence of priests, it does at least feel like I am pastoring the people most of the time."[75]

(Not So) Gracious Submitters, Brides of Christ, and Adulterous Women: The Baptists

Nowhere do we see the range of women's participation, and the challenges and paradoxes that have come with it, more than in Baptist life in the South. Although (a few) Southern Baptist churches had been ordaining women for at least twenty years, the Southern Baptist Convention (SBC) officially condemned women's ordination in 1984 as unbiblical. A number of Baptist churches have ignored the statement and ordained women that they found called, fit, and capable. Despite the fact that the SBC reaffirmed its position in 2000 of prohibiting women from the pastorate, some women still serve in SBC churches as associates in specialized ministry, in educational institutions, or as chaplains.[76] The career path of one of the most stalwart of Baptist women pastors, however, illustrates what is likely to happen today. Nancy Hastings Sehested, the daughter and granddaughter of SBC ministers, was ordained and served as pastor in the 1980s at the socially progressive Oakhurst Baptist Church in Decatur, Georgia. In 1987, after she was called by Prescott Memorial Baptist in Memphis, the Shelby County Baptist Association expelled the church from its membership. Sehested persevered at Prescott until 1995, affiliating with the American Baptist Church. Now living in North Carolina, Sehested is no longer a pastor. She is shaping her own ministry, allying with other progressive Baptists and like-minded Christians in social justice and peace activism and in prison ministry. She is an "itinerant" preacher, retreat leader, and writer, coming out of the Baptist tradition in the South, but certainly not confined to or fully defined by it. As for Prescott Memorial, it left the SBC in 1994. Although affiliated with the American Baptist Church, its current minister, Martha Brahm, comes from the Methodist tradition.[77]

Sehested and Prescott Memorial were not the only ones to part with the SBC. Both the Texas and Virginia Baptist Conventions have repudiated the SBC's teachings on women. In October 2000 former president Jimmy Carter declared that he and his wife, Rosalyn, were severing their own very public ties with the SBC. Declaring that SBC statements concerning women's roles "violate the basic premises of my Christian faith," President Carter said, "I personally feel the Bible says all people are equal in the eyes of God. . . . [W]omen should play an absolutely equal role in service of Christ in the church."[78] Churches across the South left or are leaving the SBC, uniting with one of the new "moderate" Baptist alliances, such as the Cooperative Baptist Fellowship. In 2000 it elected the Reverend Dr. Donna Forrester as its moderator. Forrester, daughter of a Baptist pastor, was ordained in 1976 after a career in nursing. She was chaplain at Southeastern Seminary when fundamentalists took over the institution in the 1980s. Forrester has been able to continue her ministry in a Baptist setting through the CBF. Currently, she is an associate in charge of pastoral counseling at the First Baptist Church in Greenville, South Carolina, a CBF affiliate.[79]

Meanwhile, back at Southeastern Seminary, Dorothy Patterson, wife of Paige Patterson, one of the instigators of the fundamentalist takeover of the SBC, teaches in the "Women's Ministries" program. The SBC hierarchy has strategically placed a number of women like Mrs. Patterson on its boards and in other positions. Like Jani Ortlund, Patterson describes herself first and foremost as a wife and mother who is battling to preserve women's biblically ordained roles. Holding up mothers of the Old Testament as exemplars, Patterson contrasts the "high calling" of submission to men to women's "pleading" to do ministry: "Women [in the Old Testament] were not pining away, pleading with the Almighty to be priests and prophets. They were praying for the blessing of bearing children. . . . [T]he Bible [does not] contain any admonition to place the work of the church ahead of home responsibilities. When a woman has chosen the high calling of being a wife, her submission to her husband is 'as to the Lord' (Eph. 5:22). When she chooses the high calling of motherhood, 'Sons are a heritage from the Lord . . .' (Psalms 127:3); this, too, is itself an offering to the Lord."[80]

Patterson expresses the fear that women's ministry will overshadow traditional roles, the most overt being motherhood. The power-by-association

Corrie E. Norman, Heather E. Barclay, and Nancy A. Hardesty

that women like Patterson have is also threatened by the prospect of legitimizing women's ability to lead outright. In reality, most Baptist women who seek ministry are married and have families. A number happen to be married to other ministers. Nancy Hastings Sehested, for example, is also the wife of a minister and the mother of two children. Family status and the validity of other roles that women play, however, are not the main issues for those advocating a woman's right to live out her call in ordained ministry. But they also know well that these issues are not unrelated.

The vast majority of Baptist women participate in religious life somewhere between the boundaries pushed by ordained women and pulled by women who derive some degree of power through them. Many Baptist women would like to think that the debate over women's ordination does not affect them and would, in fact, assume that women are not supposed to be pastors because that is just the way it has been. But it has become increasingly difficult for laywomen to separate their own roles from that issue, just as it has become increasingly more clear that all women's activities are subject to attempts at increased control by the fundamentalist hierarchy. The ordination of laywomen as deacons is one area where the connection has become very apparent. Even an area where women have historically held autonomous leadership in their "separate sphere" has been under attack. The Women's Missionary Union (WMU), grown from its origins in 1888 to become the largest lay organization in the SBC and of Christian women worldwide, has always functioned as an "auxiliary" of the SBC, with its own budget and a governing body elected by its female membership. During the fundamentalist takeover of the SBC, leaders attempted to "hard wire" the WMU into the SBC by shifting its board appointments and budget to SBC control under the International Board of Missions (IBM). When the women of the WMU fought this, the chairman of the IBM called the WMU an "adulterous woman" and tried to cripple it in a number of ways, perhaps the most cruel being its attempts to trademark and tame Lottie Moon.[81] The IBM, now in direct competition with the WMU, celebrates its Lottie by reproducing her tea cake recipe and a few letters on its Web site, including the one in which Moon tried to persuade men to come to the mission field. All the rhetorical subtlety of her "resistance" to preaching is lost, as are her statements on the equality of men and women in mission efforts.[82]

The WMU still claims a membership of over one million, but it is struggling with identity and position. It had already, before the takeover attempt, made stylistic changes to strengthen its compatibility with contemporary women. Its missions organization for girls went from being the "Girl's Auxiliary," with levels ranging from "lady-in-waiting" to "Queen" and formal coronation ceremonies, to "Girls in Action" for little girls and "Acteens" for teenagers. Blending service with self-fulfillment, the WMU's overarching theme these days is "the joy of missions." While its Web site still describes its "helper" relationship to the SBC, it emphasizes core values that include the "priesthood of all believers" and supporting the "giftedness of women and girls." Lottie's tea cake recipe is there too, but it appears as one strategy of an adventurous and passionate activist for girls and women.[83]

The women with the most popular ministries in Baptist circles today are among those "in between." Perhaps no woman could claim a more privileged beginning in southern evangelical culture than Anne Graham Lotz, daughter of the evangelist Billy Graham. While Reverend Graham himself has called his daughter "the best preacher in the family," he transferred his mantle of authority in Billy Graham Evangelical Association (BGEA) to her brother Franklin.[84] Anne is on the board of BGEA, but she is her own woman, with her own AnGeL Ministries, founded in 1988 and based in Raleigh. Like her brother and father, Anne claims a worldwide following. She spoke before the United Nations General Assembly in 2000 and was among the religious leaders sought out for commentary by the national media soon after the events of September 11, 2001. She has preached on every continent except Antarctica.[85] Unlike her father and brother, however, the "best preacher in the family" is not ordained.

Anne Graham Lotz is within the boundaries of southern womanhood in many respects. As have other women in the past, she had tried making an uncomfortable peace with the boundaries in order to advance her ministry. Or, to use our original analogy, Anne's strategy is rocking back while moving on. She originally found a biblical model she could relate to in Mary Magdalene's proclamation of the risen Christ, as have women preachers at other times in Christian history. But biblical rationale also leads her to the conclusion that ordination for her is out of the question. Ironically, that theology has also provided a rationale that opened up a path to ministry outside the official church. Hurt early on by male rejection and criticism for preaching, Anne made strategic moves.[86] Like many a woman before her, she claims authority given by God over the authority designated by male-dominated institutions: "[T]he power of teaching comes in the Word of God, not in a place, a position or a title." But she also strategically sidesteps conflicting claims of divine and human authority. Instead of claiming to be a preacher, she calls herself a "Bible expositor," just as earlier women "exhorted" or "prayed" at length in public but surely did not preach! By not claiming the right to preach, or the affirmation of that through ordination, she hopes to abate criticism as she pursues her call outside the control of her detractors. She comments, "Preacher. Expositor. There's not much difference. But that's not my problem. I'm not looking for power or authority."[87] In other words, she is no threat to the male-dominated institutional church. Yet she has established her own institution and a following outside its control. Its name reveals the paradox: "AnGeL" is based on her initials, A.G.L. It also implies a more female-appropriate role: she is "an angel," not a preacher. But angels are also messengers sent directly from God, without intervention by men.

AnGeL Ministries and its following are female-centered if not exactly feminist. Its roots go back to the 1970s, when Lotz invited neighbor women for coffee and religious conversation. Soon, she was conducting Bible studies with as many as five hundred in attendance. Her "Just Give Me Jesus" revivals across the nation reach thousands of women today, as do her five books, newsletter, Web site, and public appearances. In 2003 she launched "A Passionate Pursuit" workshops to train scores of other women to teach scripture. Again, securing a place for women by staving off critical interference, Lotz stated, ". . . if a pastor comes in to see what's being taught, if a husband wants to see what his wife is involved in . . . it's fine." It's hardly a hearty invitation; she adds, "I'm not pushing men to come."[88]

Lotz's appeal to evangelical women works similarly. She avoids gender controversy, emphasizing women's internal spiritual needs. For Lotz, it is primarily spiritual empowerment, not social or structural change, that women need. Her ministry is centered on enhancing a personal relationship between women and Christ. The rhetoric she employs comes directly out of the evangelical tradition: passionate, emotive, personal, and "feminine." The relationship she promotes is modeled on an ideal of spousal devotion. She wrote her 2002 book, *My Heart's Cry*, for "those who were desperate for more of Him." In her online newsletter, she describes her own life and derives a spiritual lesson aimed at other women from it. Over the summer she finished a book, continued her traveling ministry, and dealt with a flooded laundry room and gardening dilemmas, hardly having time to see her husband, Danny. Intentionally setting aside time for Danny caused her to reflect, "What about my relationship with my heavenly Husband?" Realizing her "longing for more of Him is insatiable," she encourages other women to nurture their own spirits in the language of being a good wife. This is a nurture that takes precedent over and is modeled on women's submission to men at the same time.[89]

One of the SBC's most popular teachers is Texan Beth Moore, bestselling author of the Bible study *A Woman's Heart* and books such as *Breaking Free: Making Liberty in Christ a Reality in Life*.[90] The titles reflect how Moore negotiates her ministry. She works both within and outside Southern Baptist circles and within and outside traditional gender boundaries at the same time. Petite, stylish, perky, and blonde, she plays up her femininity while playing it down. She uses self-deprecating humor and tears. Her voice is loud and confident. In extensive prayers, she calls on God to "fill her" and overcome her frailty. Then she boldly proclaims (teaching, not preaching) for an hour or more. Her book jackets describe her first as "a dedicated wife and mother of two" and "a member of the pastor's council of the First Baptist Church in Houston." She is a good woman, respected under the auspices of pastor and husband, who speaks from "a woman's heart." But her Web site first introduces her, not her roles: "She loves the Lord, loves to laugh, and loves to be with His people." Beth Moore also reflects the emphasis on the individual believer's spiritual freedom that has historically characterized Baptists. Like Lotz, she has her own organization, Living Proof Ministries, which is not confined to the SBC. While she teaches both men and women in a Sunday School class of three hundred and her writings are used widely in Baptist churches, she also holds interdenominational "ladies" Bible studies in Houston, as well as national and international events that attract thousands. In 2002 she extended her reach with "Believing God," an online Bible study series for subscribers.[91]

A recording of one of her Bible studies, available on her Web site, illustrates part of Moore's strategy. The biblical text is Genesis, chapters 1–3, the story of creation, fall, and male-female relations that is often used to justify female subordination. Moore largely ignores that topic. Eve is never discussed. When she comes to Genesis 3:17, where God punishes Adam "Because you listened to your wife," Moore dismisses it jokingly: "O Lord, I hope this isn't going to be misapplied!" Quickly dispensing with the "curse" of childbearing ("Pain, not childbearing, is the curse"), she focuses on Adam's relationship to God and work. This is not a message about women's subordination under man but one of empowerment under God. Moore tells her students, God "created you with honor. . . . Your desire to matter is God-ordained. . . . You have a place to govern under God." She cautions the "misguided humble" and the "play-it-safes" to find their vocation in God by "seeking training" and "fueling the gift." "We are not powerless" is her concluding message for women.

Breaking Free and *A Woman's Heart* do not simply represent two sides of Beth Moore. Women's liberation and women's boundedness are tied together. *Breaking Free* teaches a message of self-care and fulfillment for women, couched in traditional models of womanhood. Often humorously, sometimes bittersweet, Moore uses the experiences of women she has encountered and her own marriage, motherhood, and even her relationship with her dogs to illustrate the distance between ideals and reality. But she does not let go of the ideals. She works from "what women want," or are taught to want, in childhood: "to be a bride," "to be beautiful," "to be fruitful," and "to be happy everafter."[92] Acknowledging that few find these to their satisfaction, she assures the disillusioned that "Real romance awaits you" and "You will be a beautiful bride."[93] Redirecting but not rejecting the feminine myths, she teaches, "Some of your childhood dreams were meant to come true in Christ."[94] Like Lotz, Moore employs ancient Christian bridal imagery reminiscent of female (and

Corrie E. Norman, Heather E. Barclay, and Nancy A. Hardesty

male) mystics but with a particularly southern cast. Jesus is the perfect southern gentleman who can help a woman find in herself the pure and beautiful belle. All she has to do is look in her own lap where she will see a reflection of her own worthiness in her beloved. Submission, sorrow, and sacrifice, the primary adornments of the southern Mary, are joined and overshadowed in this contemporary image by empowerment, joy, and self-care.

No doubt Lotz's and Moore's appeal to women lies in no small part in the resonance their liberating yet traditional messages have with the conflicts felt by Baptist and other women. In 1998 the SBC modified its doctrinal manifesto, "The Baptist Faith and Message," to include the statement that women should "graciously submit" to their husbands in the home. Dorothy Patterson, who helped write the statement, spelled out its practical and theological implications: "When it comes to submitting to my husband when he is wrong, I just do it. He is accountable to God."[95] The SBC's official position on women was now clear and comprehensive: woman *in essence* is under man, who is under God. That means women's desires, activities, and spiritual lives are subordinated to their husbands or other male superiors. A recent study conducted by sociologists at the University of North Carolina found that the majority of evangelicals "would not endorse the Baptist statement with great conviction." The study found that while evangelicals may use the rhetoric of patriarchy, most believe in and practice "equal partnership" marriages.[96] And the "priesthood of all believers" that the WMU espouses and Beth Moore exemplifies is deeply ingrained in Baptist women. In a society where the individual spiritual search has become a national pastime, Baptist and other evangelical women resonate with the desire for personalized spiritual experience.[97]

The tensions between realities of modern life and the old myths start early for women in Baptist life. While the WMU changed its symbolism for girls from queenly purity to activity, the SBC has revived the image of female purity. In 1993 the SBC launched "True Love Waits" (TLW), now an international campaign designed to persuade teenagers and college students to pledge sexual abstinence until marriage. Campaign leaders estimate that over a million young people have already made a commitment to "purity."[98] Both young men and women are encouraged to sign on, but the symbolic weight of purity is still born by the image of the bride in white. Featured on the TLW home page is the testimony of Kristi, who pledged in 1995. She says of her wedding day: "I was all dressed up in white as my dad escorted me to the front of the church where my groom was waiting for me. Because of my pure heart and body, no guilt was tagging along with me down the aisle. No regrets were hidden under my veil. No past emotional pain accompanied me to my wedding altar. No impurity followed me to my marriage bed."[99]

The TLW Web site celebrates a recent study indicating that youth who pledge abstinence are 34 percent more likely to remain virgins until marriage than others. But the image of female purity that TLW has revived in the South has had an impact beyond those who keep the pledge. Many southern women may buy the rhetoric of purity, but fewer are willing to live it out fully. This, paradoxically, has given the symbol new life. In 2002 the *New York Times* reported the growing phenomenon of "secondary virginity" in the South, fueled by TLW. Couples, having lived together for years in some cases, take vows to remain abstinent for a few months before their weddings. As one Charlotte bride put it, "The closer you get to the wedding . . . a preacher and a church, you start to feel guilty."[100] On her wedding day, another young woman explained, "It's about being prim and proper and perfect . . . it's an ideal we live up to." Southern historian Walter Edgar surmises, "There has been this tradition of putting a white woman on a pedestal. . . . She was supposed to be chaste and pure and worshiped from afar. . . . Now this self-rejuvenating virginity is an open admission that this isn't how the real world operates."[101] But in the mythic world of southern womanhood, it is alive and well, thanks to Baptist enterprise.

"Jan" (a pseudonym for one of various women interviewed for this article) is a poignant example of how real women who want to remain true to themselves and to their churches make sense of their complicated lives with the religious resources available to them. In her late thirties, Jan is a single professional woman who is successful and independent. She says, however, that her personal autonomy developed primarily through caring for her parents before their deaths. Her father's death hit her especially hard. She was "forced" to become independent and to take on "roles in the family that [my] father had fulfilled." Missing "the comfort and security" her dad once gave her, Jan turned to "God her father," finding not only comfort and security but also "a sense of courage."

Jan survives as a single adult in a married world by taking "Christ to be her Lover and Companion." A shy person by nature who has an aversion to public speaking, Jan feels it important that she share her decision to remain a virgin until marriage, made long before TLW existed. Longing to marry and have a family, she remains patient and "content" for now "because God is providing." She shares her testimony by teaching and mentoring young women in her church and through singing. Her "theme song" is entitled, "He's All I Need." Jan explains, "It says to me that when I need someone to talk to, He's there. God is all I need. My identity does not depend on a man or anyone else." Jan hopes that her example will teach younger women that "it's okay to be different, it is okay to stand alone on issues, to stand up for what is right and what you believe; and that being single is okay . . . that a woman's identity does not depend on someone else." Jan has used the traditional female

Corrie E. Norman, Heather E. Barclay, and Nancy A. Hardesty

models of purity and female dependence to develop a sense of personal identity dependent only on herself and God. This mostly works for Jan, although she says that she finds herself "wary of physical and emotional intimacy" with other people, especially men. The message, while mixed, comes through positively to the younger women she mentors. As one of her protégées put it, "I admire her. She's taught me a great deal about self-respect and purity."[102]

"Carol" is an example of the countless women trying to survive when the religious models they have followed can no longer work for them. She spent most of her adult life as the wife of a Southern Baptist minister, with "the responsibility and obligation of living a perfect life." Carol committed herself to her husband and daughters and to multiple, unpaid roles in the church. But one day her husband decided he was through with the church and with marriage. He left the pastorate, their teenage girls, and Carol. Some in the church held her responsible. Her "glass house," as she puts it, shattered.

Almost five years later, Carol is not so much picking up the pieces as trying to leave the mess behind. She does not attend church at the moment, but she does have a lot of questions of God that she would like to have answered. In the meantime, she is, according to one of her daughters, "learning about herself and reaching goals she never thought possible." With a new career and both daughters in college, Carol is finding her own way. What sustains her most is the support of her daughters and women friends: "Women need each other to share their experiences and know that someone else has been there too."

Carol connects her personal situation to the bigger picture of the treatment of women in the church. Knowing that following the model of female perfection and selfless devotion to husband and church can lead to loss of self and disillusion, she thinks, "it is time that women are seen for their leadership potential." She experienced a vision of what that might be like when her own mother, at age seventy, was made the first woman deacon in her church. She hopes her daughters will not have to wait so long to be recognized for their gifts. She is encouraging them to find and develop them first for themselves. Her oldest daughter has found a new admiration for her mother. She has become a role model in new ways: "My mom's greatest wish is that my sister and I will be independent women."[103]

A Time to Dance/A Time to Dust:
Charismatic Women

Pursuing independence is exactly what many women who feel called to lead are doing in African American charismatic communities. Bishop Vera Mae Davis has always been spiritually precocious. As a child she would sing and pray so boisterously that her sisters would tie her up to try to keep her still and quiet until their mother came home from work. Vera Mae Davis was not to be deterred: "The further I went, the further He wanted me to go." She felt the call to preach at age sixteen, preaching her first sermon at seventeen. While marrying and having six children, she continued to preach, holding services in her garage until God told her to build a church. She affiliated with the Church of God in Jesus Christ Apostolic (CGJC), taking degrees in its Bible schools and founding the Nazareth Apostolic Church. Eventually, she became the youngest person elected to its Board of Bishops and second in charge.

Even with her success, Bishop Davis chafed under the male-dominated hierarchy. She accepts gender differences, saying, "Many feel women's ministry to be more powerful and anointed . . . because of women's nourishing abilities. A woman doesn't have to be masculine . . . she just has to let God use her." She is quick to add, however, that gender differences should not dictate ministerial roles, emphasizing, "It's not about us, it's about God." In 1991 she left the CGJC and founded the Apostolic Church in Jesus Christ, Inc., taking with her five male ministers, including the mentor who ordained her. Her organization now includes nine churches, the Elohim Bible School, Elohim "We Care" Outreach Center for at-risk youth and young families, and the Nazareth Day Center. In all her organizations, she posts her motto "We are plundering hell to populate heaven with a can do attitude in a can't do atmosphere." As for herself, she has continued to study toward advanced degrees, but her chief goal is the one she has held since childhood: "I am working to move into the face of God."[104]

Bishop Davis is a very successful example of a trend we discovered among African American women. Many women change their affiliations because of the experience of sexism in a denominational structure, only to find their experiences repeated in new places. The authority of charisma in these traditions can work in their favor, however, because their flocks tend toward loyalty to them rather than to the denomination. Developing organizational experience in a denominational structure, as well as strong roots in their communities and congregations, they eventually hope to branch out on their own, leaving the male hierarchies behind.

Charismatic churches have tended to be open to women's leadership and voices early in their development, becoming more restrictive as they become more mainstream. Among the fastest-growing churches in the South are a number of new, "nondenominational" charismatic organizations that are drawing off members from the SBC and mainline churches and attracting "the unchurched." These "mega-churches" tend to be socially and theologically conservative and uphold traditional roles for women. But they offer much that is attractive to women seeking spiritual fulfillment within the gender boundaries

Corrie E. Norman, Heather E. Barclay, and Nancy A. Hardesty

of southern culture. They tend to be more spiritually and less doctrinally focused than fundamentalist denominations. They offer limited but highly visible roles to women in their elaborately produced worship services. They create small groups in which personal expression is encouraged. Like Lotz and Moore, they focus on women's spiritual empowerment in ways that both affirm and defy gender boundaries. They attend to a diverse range of people who are largely ignored or marginalized by the established churches of the South. These include single mothers, the divorced, interracial couples, and others outside the "typical" family—although there is plenty for it too.

The play of paradox in some of these churches is especially complex in the case of women high school and college students. Some groups have concerted strategies for attracting college students who are unchurched or displaced from religious communities while in school. These sometimes include questionable tactics like stealth infiltration of campus residential life positions. But while teaching young women that their roles are bound by biblically sanctioned limits, they are often the only churches in an area that are even paying attention to them. They offer a place where young women's voices can be heard in devotional settings (though sometimes not in mixed groups). They offer leadership opportunities in mission work, peer groups, and campus outreach. They provide a forum for theological discussion in their young women's Bible studies. They offer an appealing, participatory worship style with emotive music, even opportunities for dance and theatrical performances. They affirm their developing womanhood, offering clear directions for lifestyle and important decisions (as well as opportunities to mingle with eligible young Christian men).

One such group is Redemption World Outreach Center, based in Greenville, South Carolina. Hope Carpenter is co-pastor with her husband. An attractive and youthful blue-eyed blonde, she is the picture of southern womanly perfection (and resembles Beth Moore). She figures prominently, almost equally, with her husband on the organization's Web site. Together, they are the picture-perfect Christians of the New South.

Redemption is an ambitious organization. It already supports multiple ministries, a school of ministry, and missions abroad. Its services were first televised nationally in 2003. Thousands attend them in an area that is home to multiple large independent churches, as well as several large Baptist and mainline congregations. Redemption is growing in part because it caters to "what women want."

An advertisement for a women's convention on Redemption's Web site illustrates its appeal. Hope Carpenter begins by speaking "from my heart to yours," identifying with contemporary women's experience: "I understand the many roles of a woman: mother, pastor's wife, homemaker, business owner; pastor. We always do for others but rarely take time for ourselves." Without questioning women's roles (note their order), she invites women to move beyond them, giving them permission to take care of themselves in "celebration" and "fellowship." She warns, "Don't allow the enemy to employ any device to keep you from this appointment to meet God." Instead, she proclaims, "Dry your eyes, raise your hands; it's time to dance!" And she means it literally. Along with two other youthful, attractive female evangelists who will lead the event, the advertisement features a middle-aged woman in white, head held high and arms extended, dancing in praise.[105] Redemption is offering women permission to pursue self-care among other women, to experience women's spiritual leadership, and to express themselves in body and spirit, and it affirms meaning in the "many roles" women play in daily life.

Will women remain seen and heard if Redemption continues to grow? Will its focus on women's experience outgrow the confines of the models it now subscribes to? Will history repeat itself, or will encouraging women "to dance" have different consequences in the contemporary South?

The most popular male on the charismatic scene today is also encouraging women "to get up." From his base in Houston, Bishop T. D. Jakes runs a national ministry that has reached millions of women through his "Women Thou Art Loosed" events and publications. His book *God's Leading Lady* advises women to "take center stage."[106] Jakes considerably softens but does not disregard the headship of husbands. Speaking to women who already lead "take-charge" lives, he interprets headship as a "covering," providing "a safe place to relax" at home.[107] His main message, however, is one of empowerment for women who do not feel in charge in their lives. Using the language of "ladyhood," he holds up Mary. This Mary is a quite a different one, however, from the southern lady:

> Like Mary, we must . . . believe that through the Lord we
> can achieve so much more than we could ever accomplish on
> our own. Many women get so wrapped up in who they think
> they should be, not who they truly are. They feel pressure
> from their parents . . . from the special man in their life . . .
> from their bosses . . . even from their ministers . . . to be
> someone they may not be. These women wonder why they
> feel empty and detached from life. They have become man-
> nequins dressed up in the showcase windows of other people's
> department stores, not the leading lady on a stage of God's
> greatness. . . . Marrying Joseph and living a quiet life may
> have once offered her [Mary] the vision of security for her
> future, but she is wise enough to know that life is larger
> than her intentions. And only God is larger than life.[108]

Corrie E. Norman, Heather E. Barclay, and Nancy A. Hardesty

The combination of the language of self-fulfillment through God and imagery of traditional feminine submission, translated into a relationship with the divine rather than men, is one that seems to suit many southern (and other) women today better than the "fulfillment-through-submission-to-husband" message of Ortlund, Patterson, and the SBC leadership. Even for churches that embrace feminine submission and sacrifice, however, one thing is clear. Women may embrace the rules, just give lip service to them, or fall somewhere in between. But attention to women's concerns and a sense that, as Beth Moore put it, women "matter" and "are honored" needs to be in the mix to keep women involved. "Sister Pat," who is a member of a charismatic African-American congregation in South Carolina, expresses satisfaction with the gender-defined roles women play in her church. She says, "Women have very important roles to play in my church. . . . Women take care of the tablecloths, get the pastor's water, make sure the place is dusted, pray and fast for the congregation, and teach our children family values which allow them to cope with society and teach them to work hard because life doesn't come easy. Our strength is in the church."[109]

Implied in Sister Pat's statement is much more than a passive acceptance of women's inferiority. Women in her church maintain the rituals of sacred worship. The power of their prayers and fasts protects and sustains the community. They are the vehicles by which community is perpetuated through the generations. They are guardians of the future and models of the kind of perseverance necessary for survival. If their community's strength is "in the church," women are the channels of it. Like women throughout southern history, she may be limited, but Sister Pat does not see it so much that way: She is busy and she matters.

Looking out on a sea of white dresses at a Sunday service, one clearly sees that by sheer numbers women are the strength of Sister Pat's church. A further look reveals how its women find significance, meaning, and sustenance. Special monthly services are dedicated to the women of the church, celebrating their contributions, giving them leadership in worship and making space for their own testimonies of faith. Numerous ministries of social outreach aid women and children and provide leadership and service opportunities for them. Workshops and outreach programs focus on relationships, parenting, and empowerment. The Women's Auxiliary that does all that dusting largely controls church space on a daily basis.[110]

Women's Place: Something Old, Something New

Conservative women do not embrace southern Mary blithely, but more liberal women find much about traditional roles that they cannot reject as well. Joanna Bowen Gillespie's study of laywomen in a southern Episcopal parish reveals the depth of meaning that traditional female duties can have, even for women who no longer accept traditional limitations.[111] "Abigail's" parish is inclusive in terms of gender, race, sexual orientation, and class. Many women who have been disillusioned by the male-centeredness of other churches have been drawn to its inclusive worship style. Women participate in all leadership areas, including the priesthood. While appreciating all these things, Abigail describes her most intense spiritual experiences in a very traditional way: "I love to come and sit in with the women who are preparing the church for Easter. I just love to spend a morning, four hours or so, polishing and burnishing the silver and the brass. I think it's because it is symbolic. . . . I like to think that what we're doing is making the setting new—everything new for rebirth from the grave, the resurrection. We're taking off the tarnish, removing the oxidation, preparing for a brand new life."[112] Like Sister Pat, Abigail finds traditional "women's work" meaningful. But she can choose it over a variety of tasks not limited by gender. Echoing Bishop Vera Mae Davis, another woman in the parish put it this way: "There's no such thing as a woman's place, there are just Christian roles. People ought to be able to 'do' according to their gifts. . . . Women should be able to be on the altar guild or be bishop."[113]

But churches like Abigail's are still few and far between. One woman interviewed by Gillespie acknowledged that even there, tensions still existed over women's roles, with some worrying that so much female visibility and leadership might run off the men.[114] Many southern women are left on their own, longing for a community where they can be seen, heard, and fed. "Melissa" is a twenty-five-year-old single woman who is surviving childhood sexual abuse. Her fundamentalist church and family ignored her pleas for help: "I wasn't allowed to speak up for myself." Having confronted her abuser, still a church member, she no longer attends: "I do not wish to be part of a tradition that teaches its women to be inferior to men." She, like Carol, makes the connection between her own victimization and the denial of women's religious autonomy and leadership. Her truck sports a bumper sticker that reads, "Start Ordaining Women or Stop Baptizing Them." Melissa has found solace in a survivors' group and among women friends. But finding a place to express her faith has been difficult. She still clings to "most of" her church's "beliefs," but feels that feminism has saved her life. She has attended National Organization for Women meetings and shares its social ideals, but she does not feel

Corrie E. Norman, Heather E. Barclay, and Nancy A. Hardesty

that she fits there because she cannot reconcile her religious beliefs with the group's secular tenor. Stuck between feminism and faith, Melissa is trying to make meaning on her own, "finding God in nature" and "solitude." She is considering trying one of the new nondenominational churches. And it may indeed be among their women's ministries that Melissa finds some comfort. Of the leaders spoken of thus far, it is picture-perfect Hope Carpenter who is driven to talk about what she calls her "withered hand." Her own experience of rape as a teenager, a subsequent sense of "unworthiness," and eventual healing is part of the testimony she offers women. Carpenter says that she wants to offer a space for women to "deal with the hidden sins, the bruises and the pain, and leave totally free."[115] But when the service is over and they leave the safe spaces, where will women who suffer violence at home go?

Churches across the board still largely ignore the epidemic of sexual and domestic violence that sweeps the country and, disproportionately, the South. At a well-publicized symposium on domestic violence and religion held in a county with the highest incidence of reported domestic abuse in its state, only three clergy were present in the audience of more than two hundred. One mainline pastor, when asked to support the event, said, "It's just too heavy." Given the prevalence of violence against women in their own homes in the South, any discussion of women and religion ought to be conscious of that context. The following example reveals the implicit dangers of patriarchal theology, even the displacement of patriarchy onto a divine spouse. "Mary" went to the pastor of her church, part of a mainstream evangelical denomination, for advice. Counselors had told her, and she herself sensed, that if she didn't leave her increasingly abusive husband, she might wind up dead. Her pastor sent her home "to try harder," adding, "If he kills you, you'll be in a better place with your heavenly Husband."[116]

While many women may turn to ministries like Hope Carpenter's to find a space that is safe and sacred, a growing number of women in the South are looking outside Christianity for sacred spaces. Looking beyond Mary to a mythic time of female power, worshippers of the Great Goddess in neo-pagan traditions are all over the South. Although such practices are still underground in many places, evidence of their popularity appear openly in Asheville or Atlanta, in stores catering to varieties of New Age spirituality, and in alternative newspapers. When the United States Army finally recognized the pagans in its midst, it was probably surprised to find the most organized communities at Fort Bragg, North Carolina, and Fort Hood in Texas.[117]

One woman who has followed pagan traditions says that she grew up all over the place but mostly in Tennessee. Her family was Protestant but sent her to Catholic school. She says she first felt the "tap of the goddess" in her late teens. She spent her early adulthood studying pagan traditions on her own and in communities, taking "Rowan Anye" as her craft name. When she first moved to South Carolina ten years ago, she practiced primarily alone, occasionally driving the sixty or so miles to worship with the closest neo-pagan community. But when the Christian man she was with pressured her to give up her spiritual practice, she decided it was time to become more public about her spirituality. "I thought I could just be private about it," she reflects, "But when he told me I had to stop being a witch, I told him that was like stopping breathing." Rowan Anye knew she needed a community, so she began one, now called the Nature Spirit Community Church.

She is High Priestess of the group that sometimes has as many as thirty worshippers. It is one of six "out" groups in the Greenville-Spartanburg area. Groups like Rowan Anye's attract a diversity of people. Her church includes a banker, a mechanic, and several people in the helping professions. It has African American members and same-sex couples and has attracted several young people. Some members attend Christian churches with their families as well as practice the craft. Rowan Anye describes herself as "a state worker, a single mother, and a home owner. I'm real people." She emphasizes that the group attempts to find a "balance" between "female and male principles." Some members see the deities as Mary and Jesus. A Jewish member has gotten the group interested in the Kabbala. "We are open to all forms of wisdom," she says. The church is openly active in the community. Members wear their logo-imprinted T-shirts as they participate in causes such as animal welfare, the environment, and domestic violence awareness.[118]

Rowan Anye tells her own story as one of finding her mother roots. Her initial interest in nature worship was spawned by her father, who unlike the rest of the family, totally rejected organized religion. Her mother, however, moved from a nominal Protestantism to fundamentalist Christianity as Rowan Anye was getting into the craft. Convinced Rowan Anye was going to hell, her mother was alienated from her for a number of years. Eventually, she began trying to reconnect with her daughter, even attending some of the pagan rituals. When Rowan Anye's mother revealed to her that women for at least two generations back in their family had practiced practical magic, Rowan Anye felt she had come full circle. "Anye" was her grandmother's name. Now she understands why she took it for herself.

Feeling deep down for roots in the feminine divine is what many women in the South are doing. African Americans tracing their ancestry back to Nigeria, Benin, and Dahomy have established Oyotunji, a Yoruban village near Sheldon, South Carolina. In late June they gather to celebrate Yemoja Moreni, the Mother Goddess of the Yoruba, with rites of passage for women.[119] Arianne King Comer, a native of Detroit, moved nearby in the early 1990s to get closer to her African roots in a tangible way. She is a textile artist whose

Corrie E. Norman, Heather E. Barclay, and Nancy A. Hardesty

medium is the indigo once cultivated by African slaves there. She weaves her "deep spirituality" into the textiles she creates.[120] In part historical irony, in part redemption, African American women seeking connection with the sacred Mother return to a place from which so many of their ancestors were torn from motherly arms in slavery.

Many enslaved Africans were Muslim, and over the past several decades, many southern African Americans have reached back to those roots.[121] Victoria Caldwell was working as a fashion model when she decided to embrace Islam and adopt the modesty of the hijab covering her hair. Growing up in Orangeburg, South Carolina, she attended the Worldwide Church of God, but it is in Islam where she has found peace.[122] Southern Muslim women are taking leadership in the growing communities. The first woman to serve as an imam of a mosque in the Nation of Islam is Minister Ava Muhammad, who ministers in Atlanta.[123]

In the significant Muslim immigrant communities across the South, women like Shagufda Raja, principal of the Charlotte Islamic School, find themselves largely responsible for maintaining and adapting Islam in its new environment through educating children, maintaining dietary laws, and community relations. That women can thrive as both southern and Muslim is brilliantly exemplified by Talia Gangoo, whose parents immigrated to the Carolinas before she was born. A recent graduate of historically Baptist Furman University, with degrees in Religion and Political Science, Talia now pursues graduate work on Islam.

Although Shirin Treadwell is a Caucasian American with southern roots, she feels a bit out of step with southern culture. Having been raised by Baha'i missionary parents in South Africa, Shirin learned to value equality of the races and sexes as part of the nine governing principles of her faith. She is alarmed by the sexism taken for granted by some of her classmates, especially by women her own age. Speaking at a recent forum on women and religion in the Carolinas, Shirin expressed her strong sense of mission, not in South Africa but in the South: "Women need Baha'i here." She is not alone. Baha'is have established a mission center in Hemingway, South Carolina, and have experienced significant growth in the state, largely credited to its inclusive stances on race and gender.

As the South becomes more pluralistic, the exchange between religious cultures is creating some interesting opportunities for women. As immigrant women try to make sense of their lives in a new context, they will encounter both those who are closed to their traditions and those open to rethinking avenues of meaning-making. Shagun Batlaw, a Hindu graduate student and mother, speaks with humor and poignancy of reclaiming her own identity with the traditions of her mothers as she raises her little girl. Her daughter attends day care at a Baptist Church. She feels it important that her daughter know something about Christianity, "because she lives in this culture." But as her daughter learned stories about Jesus at day care, it became important to Shagun that she also learned the traditions that her mother and grandmother taught her in India. So, at home she and her little girl make sand paintings in the yard and light incense before female deities in their domestic shrine. She also devotes significant time to intercultural relations in the community. She wonders what her daughter will make of all this as she grows up and hopes that however she puts it together, she will do so on her own terms.[124]

Spiritual practices of Hinduism and Buddhism have gained popularity in the South as elsewhere in the country. Rev. Teijo Munnich is a dharma heir of the late Dainin Katagiri Roshi and spiritual director of the Zen Center, Magnanimous Mind Temple, in Asheville. She came to North Carolina in 1992 after years of training and teaching at major Zen centers in Japan and the United States. Looking for some personal private time in the mountains, she did not intend to stay long in the South. But southerners interested in meditation sought her out and prevailed upon her to stay. She now ministers not only in the Asheville area but also in Charlotte and conducts retreats across the country.

In the South her ministry has taken on new dimensions in response to the needs of her community. A growing number of families now belong to the Zen Center, and she is developing methods for teaching meditation to children and integrating meditation into family life. But it is here in the South that she especially hopes to realize "more space for women in Zen." What she has missed in all her Zen training were the women role models and community that she experienced growing up in her Catholic girls' school and for a while as an aspiring Catholic nun. She currently is in the process of founding Great Tree Zen Women's Temple, a meditation center for women in the Carolina mountains. She says, "It's important for women to have a place to themselves for meditation."[125]

Seeking Sacred Space and Finding Mary Again

There is no way to tell how many women are seeking sacred spaces and models to replace, reconstruct, or augment what established religious institutions offer. It would be impossible to count all the women who nurture their spirituality privately, but a good indication of the numbers can be gotten by walking through any mall in the Southeast. Everywhere are candles, personal devotional guides, sacred statuary, angels for a variety of tastes, Eastern deities, incense burners, and Feng Shui decorating guides. Another image of Mary is

Corrie E. Norman, Heather E. Barclay, and Nancy A. Hardesty

turning up more frequently: the Virgin of Guadeloupe. With Latino Roman Catholicism now the fastest growing religious tradition in the South, it will be interesting to see her influence expand out of its immigrant context.

At least since the mid-nineteenth century, southern Protestant women, like women elsewhere, were encouraged to make their homes "sacred." While this mainly meant sacralizing domestic life with their industry and other-centered prayers, they have also been responsible for "Scripture" cakes in kitchens, family Bibles on coffee tables, Bible verses embroidered on sofa cushions, pianos adorned with open hymnbooks, and Werner Salmon Jesuses hanging on living room walls. A few, like Clementine Harris, a former slave who sewed "Bible" quilts for her home, are finally being recognized by the art world for the quality of their devotional creations. No doubt such domestic arts were personal creative and religious outlets for many women, but they were legitimized by meeting the family's practical and spiritual needs. Today, religious decor is just as likely to be concentrated in a woman's private sacred space and serve no other purposes than to visibly express what matters most to her and to enhance her own spiritual well-being.

Just two examples illustrate both the diversity and similarity of women's expressions of private yearnings. "Cat" is a cradle Episcopalian who moved to the Charlotte area twenty years ago after following her husband's army career. Coming to the South coincided with a period of profound spiritual growth for Cat. Having struggled early in life with resentment and doubt brought on by physical disabilities and unanswered prayers for healing, she made a spiritual breakthrough. Her "idea of truth" shifted from one of submissive pleading to "accepting [myself] as a woman and loving every part of [myself] as a good thing, created in the image of God." Cat created a personal altar in her home. With its sacred symbols and pictures of people dear to her, it is the center of a rich prayer life and expresses her desire to communicate with God from "her goodness as a woman and not from guilt." Mary figures prominently. She is "a sign of special care for women." As she meditates on her crucifix, Cat is reminded of Christ's love for his mother and all women. She has learned to pray "in her own way," and the confidence she has developed has emboldened her to minister through her prayers to others. She feels her communication with God in private is a powerful vehicle for healing, if not always the type of healing she used to seek. She expresses the power of a woman's private sacred space this way: "Any time a woman reaches for God directly, she is being radical."[126]

"Delores" is an African American pastor, businesswoman, wife, mother, and grandmother. While a successful, take-charge woman with a growing congregation and family (having more than a dozen grandchildren), she struggles under a heavy load of obligations and expectations. She suffers from the sexism of her church hierarchy but cannot quite reconcile her confidence in her leadership and call with "what the Bible teaches about women's place in the home." She sees Mary as a model of strength and perseverance in the face of hardships and suffering. She prays that God will help her to be humbly accepting and to remain faithful, as Mary did, no matter what. But Delores's spirituality moves beyond the model of submissive resignation. She takes time in her "special place" to "dream about things I'd like to do and places I've never been." She even has a "sacrament" during these times: "I eat strawberries and chocolate because they are my favorites and remind me that sweet things are possible." Delores does not call this simply relaxing or indulgence; this is spiritual communion for her, a celebration of the divine presence and possibility within her.[127]

Another place to look for evidence of the blossoming of women's personal spirituality in the South is literary expression. Martha Olds Adams spent her whole life as an active Presbyterian laywoman. Twenty years ago she was introduced to the works of Christian feminist theologians and the idea of the divine feminine. Of her reading back then she says, "I felt like I had been picked up by the back of the neck by a knowing tigress and set down in a wholly new place to grow for a few years." At first trying to integrate what she was experiencing into her life in the church, Martha eventually knew she had to find other outlets: "I learned that to be acceptable, the volcanic eruptions that were going on in my inner life needed to be silenced in these quarters. It wasn't safe."[128] Martha found space for expression through occasional trips to women's retreats and through extensive reading of historical women's spiritual works. But she especially found her space in writing poetry. Here, she could express her anger, sorrow, and "reimagined" faith. Her poetry became an expression of the feminine divine. Martha describes the call of the divine feminine in one of her poems: "She wants us changed/wants us to become weavers/our looms sparking new ideas/high energy networks of creativity/new responses."[129] Martha's poetry has not only woven new responses for herself, but it also ties together women of spirit, past and present. Based on a vision she experienced, Martha has written an "epic" poem that recovers women's longing for connection between the holy and the female throughout history. "She Rises Through the Sickle Moon" is intended to be heard through real female voices. Martha has written stage directions for its performance.[130] At a recent performance in western North Carolina, women of diverse backgrounds and generations packed a college auditorium to witness the incarnation of historical daughters of the divine Mother—almost one hundred of them, from Hypatia, to Joan of Arc, to Teresa of Avila, to Sojourner Truth and a multitude of Marys—in women who looked like them. When "the goddess" herself appeared, the room was charged with energy. Martha's poetry now conjures the goddess in colleges, women's groups, and even some churches throughout the South.

Corrie E. Norman, Heather E. Barclay, and Nancy A. Hardesty

While countless women privately seek the divine, growing numbers of communal spaces for women's spirituality are cropping up in the South. Within an hour of the site where Reverend Munnich is making plans for her women's center, there are multiple neo-pagan communities, an ecumenical Christian retreat house for women, lesbian Christian groups, a convent open to spiritual direction for laywomen, yoga and eclectic meditation centers for women, spiritual therapy groups, and no-one-knows-how-many private groups of spiritually compatible women who gather in each other's homes.

Elaine Lang still recalls fondly the "feel of my first communion dress, the smell of incense, the statue of Mary." But several years ago, she began to realize a spiritual emptiness that could not be filled by her local Catholic parish. She also became disillusioned with her career as a nurse, both because of the sexism in the medical hierarchy and its "narrow" understanding of health. She longs for a day when she can reintegrate the powerful images of her Catholic youth and its sense of community life. But Elaine is not sitting back and waiting. She finds spiritual well-being through yoga, bodywork, and other holistic practices. Becoming a yoga-meditation teacher and therapist, Elaine now nurtures others' well-being in her own holistic practice, Body & Soul of Spartanburg, which offers a variety of classes and programs, as well as a women's reflection group. Many of the women who come to Elaine are active churchwomen. "Church is just another place of responsibility for them," she says. "They turn to yoga and meditation for self-care and an integration of the body and spirit that their churches don't provide." Elaine's women's group provides a space for women to learn to recognize and nurture "the sacred holistically in the everyday." Some are extending that to their church activity. Through the influence of women in her group, Elaine now finds herself invited to teach meditation and yoga in Sunday Schools and women's organizations in local churches.[131]

Is the "sacred" South truly so for women? We have encountered so many paradoxes and ironies related to that question. Yes, in terms of numbers and activities of women in churches. No, in terms of women's full access. Yes, in its honoring of womanhood as the preserve of religious and cultural values. No, in the limitations and liabilities inherent in that model. Yes, to the extent that women have carved out space for themselves in homes, churches, women's institutions, nature, and even shopping malls. No, to the extent that patriarchy violates those spaces.

The assurance that women's sacred space can and does happen in the South comes from surprising places sometimes. Carter Heyward is among the best-known Christian feminists today. A priest and professor of Christian ethics at Episcopal Divinity School in Cambridge, Massachusetts, the Reverend Dr. Heyward has shaken the religious world with several books, including

Saving Jesus From Those Who are Right: Rethinking What It Means to Be a Christian. An activist against racism, sexism, and homophobia, she is a much-sought-after speaker around the country—although not generally in the same circles as Beth Moore or T. D. Jakes. She first attained "notoriety" as one of the "Philadelphia eleven," the women who forced the hand of the Episcopal Church by being ordained "irregularly" in 1974.

But Carter Heyward is a daughter of the South, born and reared in North Carolina and an alumna of one of the South's finest women's colleges, Randolph Macon. How did she become a lesbian-feminist activist? Reverend Heyward says her inspiration was drawn first from her southern upbringing. Her parents "really helped teach us to go for it and not be influenced by the crowd." Two women professors of religion at Randolph Macon encouraged her to develop her theological interests by attending Union Seminary. And she credits the strong women she has known in the South, politically astute and talented "black or white women who would not have had the power they had if they had been men." She still returns regularly to North Carolina to be part of a women's community that shares her commitment to social justice. From her office in Cambridge, she assured us, "There are pockets of women of real strength in the South. . . . I think that the South is a great place for women who are interested in organizing, but I do think we need to reach across race and class."[132]

Within the South another generation of feminist theologians is speaking with increasing strength from positions in its premier schools of theology. These women will help to shape the future of religious institutions primarily through the women and men they teach and through their activist scholarship. But Renita J. Weems, an African American and associate professor of Old Testament at Vanderbilt Divinity School in Nashville, has recently written for all women, presenting another face of Mary for the twenty-first century. Questioning the traditional humble and passive Mary, Professor Weems ask, "What, instead, if God chose Mary because part of her would never belong to any man?"[133] Weems refocuses attention on Mary's passionate testimony for social justice in the Magnificat and challenges other women to stand and follow her. Weems cautions that the road will not be easy: "[I]f after years of living your life one way, you wake up one day, like Mary, and start defining yourself, questioning authority, and taking measures to redirect your life, just know that you are at risk of being accused of disrupting the divine order.[134] She advises women to do what Mary did: look for "Elizabeths" to help and support. Southern women have intuited this all along. Kept isolated from each other, set up to compete for male approval and female perfection, southern women often have been stuck in place, struggle as they might to get up by themselves or by "a hand" from a gentleman. When they join together, however, their strength can propel them forward.

But they need ideals, role models, to keep them going. They need new myths to sanctify the paths they take. For that, we turn back to southern Sapphos, our storytellers who give us characters through which we can see ourselves and the South more clearly. Flannery O'Connor has been followed by a lustrous trail of women writers who imagine southern women and religion into being in their stories. They follow from different paths: Dorothy Allison, Lee Smith, Alice Walker. But we allow a relative newcomer to the trail to have the last word because her tales of fiction and autobiography bring together so many of the themes we have discussed. Sue Monk Kidd spent much of her life "under the archetype of the Gracious Lady," diligently applying the "formulas" for "The Good Christian Woman, the Good Wife, the Good Mother, the Good Daughter." She was already a successful spiritual writer before she figured out that "I needed to find the divine feminine within me." Her journey from her Baptist roots through ancient Christian tradition to the goddess is described in *Dance of the Dissident Daughter*.[135] Feeling deprived, in that her earliest female archetype, the "Southern Baptist Mary," was always described to her as "just a woman," Sue's journey to the goddess was about finding herself through finding images of the Divine Mother that were liberating.[136]

Having told her own story, Kidd turned to fiction, where she has depicted southern womanhood's spiritual quest. Her recent first novel, *The Secret Life of Bees*, centers on a young rural white girl, Lily, who loses her mother and sets out to find herself among the peach orchards of South Carolina. Redemption comes through the aid of a family of black women, who worship a dark image of Mary they keep in their parlor and trace back to slavery. They call her "Our Lady of the Chains," and the reason for that, explains the character August, is "Not because she is chained, but because she breaks chains."[137]

Kidd says that the idea of Our Lady of the Chains "just came to her" in a spiritual vision. She adds that through her own searching, "One thing that became clear to me is that images of a divine mother are surprisingly important in the psychological wholeness of women, especially in the process of women taking up residence in their own authority. . . . [M]y guess is that Mary, fresh with feminist appropriations, has the potential to undergird women's reformations."[138] Through "Our Lady," Lily is able to "take up residence" in herself again, among the black women who guide her into womanhood.

There is something troubling as well as heartening in the story of a little white girl called "Lily" finding solace in surrogate black mothers, given the history of belle and mammy. Of such is the power and paradox of "true" myths.

That Kidd's black Mary must find embodiment for Lily in many mothers of diverse temperaments and talents who worship an ideal liberating to them all may get closer to a truth that can nurture postmodern southern women into the future. The diverse stories of southern women that we have repeated here tell us that Kidd may be right. A new look for the old image is what women in the South desire—a vision shaped by their own experiences. She will still resemble the southern Mary because so much of her continues to shape women in the South today. She will remind us of other Marys, Christian and more, who also belong to the South. She will look older as women draw from history's wisdom but youthful as they draw features from the present. Her coloring cannot be of one shade. And her story? No doubt it will continue to be one of rocking back and moving forward in as many ways as there are women to tell about them, all of them having in common the yearning for sacred myths to transform reality into meaningful existence.

Notes

Several of the interviews on which this essay is based are part of the "Women's Religious Lives" project at Converse College. We thank the many student researchers and women who shared their stories for permission to use their information here. (In many cases, the names of interviewees are withheld by mutual agreement.) Additional thanks are extended to Melissa Walker for her suggestions on the manuscript.

1. Flannery O'Connor, *Mysteries and Manners,* ed. Robert and Sally Fitzgerald (New York: Farrar, Strauss, & Giroux, 1969), 44.

2. J. L. Underwood, "Women of the Confederacy," quoted in Charles Regan Wilson, *Baptized in Blood: The Religion of the Lost Cause, 1865–1920* (Athens: Univ. of Georgia Press, 1980), 46.

3. On the mythology and reality of southern women in two historical periods, see, for example, Catherine Clinton, "Women in the Land of Cotton," in *Myth and Southern History,* vol. 1: *The Old South,* ed. Patrick Gerster and Nicholas Cords (Chicago: Univ. of Illinois Press, 1989), 107–19; and Anne Firor Scott, *The Southern Lady: From Pedestal to Politics, 1830–1930* (Charlottesville: Univ. of Virginia Press, 1970). On the multiple ironies of southern religiosity, see John B. Boles, *The Irony of Southern Religion* (New York: Peter Lang, 1994).

4. For example, see Susan Hill Lindley, *"You Have Stept Out of Your Place": A History of Women and Religion in America* (Louisville, KY: Westminster John Knox Press, 1996).

5. Catherine A. Brekus, *Strangers and Pilgrims: Female Preaching in America, 1740–1845* (Chapel Hill: Univ. of North Carolina Press, 1998).

6. Evelyn Brooks Higginbotham, *Righteous Discontent: The Women's Movement in the Black Baptist Church, 1880–1920* (Cambridge, MA: Harvard Univ. Press, 1993).

Corrie E. Norman, Heather E. Barclay, and Nancy A. Hardesty

7. See, for example, the seminal work of Scott, *The Southern Lady* (1970), and, more recently, Elizabeth Fox-Genovese, *Within the Plantation Household: Black and White Women of the Old South* (Chapel Hill: Univ. of North Carolina Press, 1988).

8. For a recent work that does examine the rich religious life documented in a southern woman's own words, see Joanna Bowen Gillespie, *The Life and Times of Martha Lauren Ramsey, 1759–1811* (Columbia: Univ. of South Carolina Press, 2001).

9. Drew Gilpin Faust, *Mothers of Invention: Women of the Slaveholding South in the American Civil War* (Chapel Hill: Univ. of North Carolina Press, 1996). Two essays in *The Devil's Lane: Sex and Race in the Early South*, ed. Catherine Clinton and Michele Gillespie (New York: Oxford Univ. Press, 1997) focus on southern women's religiosity in specific contexts: Jon F. Sensbach, "Interracial Sects: Religion, Race and Gender among Early North Carolina Moravians," 154–67; and Cynthia Lynn Lyerly, "Passion, Desire, and Ecstasy: The Experiential Religion of Southern Methodist Women, 1770–1810," 168–86.

10. Norma Taylor Mitchell, "Women in Religion," in *Encyclopedia of Religion in the South*, ed. Samuel S. Hill (Macon, GA: Mercer Univ. Press, 1984), 845–51.

11. Donald G. Mathews, *Religion in the Old South* (Chicago: Univ. of Chicago Press, 1977).

12. Christine Leigh Heyrman, *Southern Cross: The Beginnings of the Bible Belt* (North Carolina: Univ. of North Carolina Press, 1998). See also Richard Rankin, *Ambivalent Churchmen and Evangelical Churchwomen: The Religion of the Episcopal Elite in North Carolina, 1800–1860* (Columbia: Univ. of South Carolina Press, 1993). These and other works, notably McCurry and Lyerly (see notes 9, above, and 13, below), are revising aspects of the approach toward evangelical women in the pioneering work of Jean Friedman, *The Enclosed Garden: Women and Community in the Evangelical South, 1830–1900* (Chapel Hill: Univ. of North Carolina Press, 1985).

13. Stephanie McCurry, *Masters of Small Worlds: Yeoman Households, Gender Relations, and the Political Culture of the Antebellum South Carolina Low Country* (New York: Oxford Univ. Press, 1995).

14. Similar sentiments were expressed by Donald G. Mathews, "'We Have Left Undone Those Things Which We Ought to Have Done': Southern Religious History in Retrospect and Prospect," *Church History* 67, no. 2 (1998): 312–13. Two examples of important works that illuminate African American religion are Mechal Sobel, *Trabelin' On: The Slave Journey to an Afro-Baptist Faith* (Westport, CT: Greenwood Press, 1979); and Rhys Isaac, *The Transformation of Virginia, 1740–1790* (Chapel Hill: Univ. of North Carolina Press, 1982).

15. See, for example, R. Marie Griffith, *God's Daughters: Evangelical Women and the Power of Submission* (Berkeley: Univ. of California Press, 1997); and Cynthia Eller, *Living in the Lap of the Goddess: The Feminist Spirituality Movement in America* (New York: Crossroad, 1993). For a recent discussion of

contemporary women and religion in the South, see Nancy A. Hardesty, "From Religion to Spirituality: Southern Women In and Out of the Church," in *The Changing Shape of Protestantism in the South*, ed. Marion D. Aldridge and Kevin Lewis (Macon, GA: Mercer Univ. Press, 1996), 69–78.

16. In *Methodism and the Southern Mind, 1770–1810* (New York: Oxford Univ. Press, 1998), Cynthia Lynn Lyerly also employs gender analysis and gives ample attention to women in this work on the anti-Methodist ideology of male elites.

17. Donald G. Mathews, in "Forum on Southern Religion," *Religion and American Culture* 8, no. 2 (1998): 149; in the same discussion, see also John B. Boles, 174. See also Samuel S. Hill, *Southern Churches in Crisis Revisited* (Tuscaloosa: Univ. of Alabama Press), xx.

18. Joel W. Martin, "Indians, Contact, and Colonialism in the Deep South: Themes for a Postcolonial History of American Religion," in *Retelling U.S. Religious History*, ed. Thomas A. Tweed (California: Univ. of California Press, 1997), 158 and 270n21.

19. Brekus, *Strangers and Pilgrims*, 248.

20. Brekus, *Strangers and Pilgrims*, 130.

21. Brekus, *Strangers and Pilgrims*, 129.

22. Cheryl J. Sanders, *Saints in Exile: The Holiness-Pentecostal Experience in African American Religion and Culture* (New York: Oxford Univ. Press, 1996), 33.

23. Published after this article was written is Elizabeth Elkin Grammer, *Some Wild Vision: Autobiographies by Female Itinerate Evangelists in Nineteenth-Century America* (New York: Oxford Univ. Press, 2003), which discusses the autobiographies of Julia Foote, Jarena Lee, and five other women.

24. *The Baptist Women's Era* (1901), quoted in Higginbotham, *Righteous Discontent*, 61.

25. See Higginbotham, *Righteous Discontent*, 19–80.

26. Higginbotham, *Righteous Discontent*, 211–21. For a recent treatment of women in another African American denomination, see Jualynne E. Dodson, *Engendering Church:Women, Power, and the AME Church* (New York: Rowman and Littlefield, 2002).

27. Lindley, *You Have Stept*, 214–15.

28. On the early history of women's orders in the South, see Francis Jerome Woods, CDP, "Congregations of Religious Women in the Old South," in *Catholics in the Old South: Essays on Church and Culture*, ed. Randall M. Miller and Jon L. Wakelyn (Macon, GA: Mercer Univ. Press, 1983). See also Archdiocese of New Orleans, "History," www.ursulineneworleans.org/.

29. Sisters of the Blessed Sacrament, "Sister Katharine Drexel: A Life Summary," http://www.katharinedrexel.org/.

30. A dissertation in progress by Marcie Cohen Ferris examines women and foodways in Southern Jewish history. See her article, "'From the Recipe File

of Luba Cohen': A Study of Southern Jewish Foodways and Cultural Identity," *Southern Jewish History* 2 (1998), 129–64.

31. Holly Snyder, "Queens of the Household: The Jewish Women of British America, 1700–1800," in *Women and American Judaism: Historical Perspectives,* ed. Pamela S. Nadell and Jonathan D. Sarna (Hanover, NH: Univ. Press of New England, 2001), 15–45. The most recent comprehensive history of American Jewish Women is Hasia Diner and Beryl Lieff Benderly, *Her Work Praise Her: A History of Jewish Women in America from Colonial Times to the Present* (New York: Basic Books, 2002).

32. Deborah Weiner, "Jewish Women in the Central Appalachian Coal Fields, 1890–1960: From Breadwinners to Community Builders" in *American Jewish Archives Journal* 52, no. 1–2 (2000): 10–33.

33. Mark I. Greenberg, "Savannah's Jewish Women and the Shaping of Ethnic and Gender Identity, 1830–1900," in *Georgia Historical Quarterly* 82, no. 4 (1998): 751–74. See also Dianne Ashton, "Shifting Veils: Religion, Politics and Womanhood in the Civil War Writings of American Jewish Women," in *Women and American Judaism,* ed. Nadell and Sarna, 81–106.

34. See Weiner, "Jewish Women." See also Mark K. Bauman, "Southern Jewish Women and Their Social Service Organizations," *Journal of American Ethnic History* (forthcoming).

35. Ferris, "From the Recipe File," 148–52.

36. For use of the terms "the southern lady," and "the evangelical woman," see Taylor Mitchell, "Women in Religion," 849; Firor Scott, *Southern Lady;* and Mathews, *Religion in the Old South.*

37. Cynthia Ann Lyerly, "Enthusiasm, Possession, and Madness: Gender and Opposition to Methodism in the South, 1770–1810," in *Beyond Image and Convention: Explorations in Southern Women's History,* ed. Janet Lee Coryell, Martha H. Swain, Elizabeth Hayes Turner, and Sandra Gioia Treadway (Columbia: Univ. of Missouri Press, 1998), 53–73.

38. Lyerly, "Enthusiasm, Possession, and Madness," 62. Also see Heyrman, *Southern Cross.*

39. On this process among the North Carolina Episcopal elite, see Rankin, *Ambivalent Churchmen.*

40. Rev. Samuel Rogers, quoted in Brekus, *Strangers and Pilgrims,* 130.

41. For a vivid description of gendered divisions in churches, see Ted Ownby, *Subduing Satan: Religion, Recreation, and Manhood in the Rural South, 1865–1920* (Chapel Hill: Univ. of North Carolina Press, 1990), 129–43.

42. Ownby, *Subduing Satan,* 129.

43. Quoted in Ownby, *Subduing Satan,* 129. See also Anne Braude, "Women's History *is* American Religious History" in *Retelling U.S. Religious History,* ed. Tweed, 87–107.

44. Quoted in Ownby, *Subduing Satan*, 129.

45. On women's religious activities during the Civil War, see Gilpin Faust, *Mothers of Invention*, 179–95.

46. Quoted in J. Wayne Flynt, "Feeding the Hungry and Ministering to the Broken Hearted: The Presbyterian Church in the United States and the Social Gospel, 1900–1920," in *Religion in the South*, ed. Charles Reagan Wilson (Jackson: Univ. Press of Mississippi, 1985), 101.

47. McCurry, *Masters of Small Worlds*, 181.

48. Brekus, *Strangers and Pilgrims*, 129, 374 n.21.

49. Brekus, *Strangers and Pilgrims*, 248. It should be underlined, however, that female preaching, especially before the Civil War, was hardly acceptable or common anywhere in the United States.

50. Quoted in Brekus, *Strangers and Pilgrims*, 129.

51. Quoted in Rankin, *Ambivalent Churchmen*, 46–47.

52. Sam P. Jones, *Thunderbolts* (Nashville: Jones and Hayes, 1896), 319–21.

53. See Gilpin Faust, *Mothers of Invention*, 187–95.

54. On women in the yeoman class, see McCurry, *Masters of Small Worlds*.

55. On the role of race in southern women's suffrage strategies, see Gilpin Faust, *Mothers of Invention*, 254. See also Elne C. Green, *Southern Strategies: Southern Women and the Southern Woman Suffrage Question* (Chapel Hill: Univ. of North Carolina Press, 1997).

56. International Mission Board (Southern Baptist Convention), "Lottie's Letters: Who Will Teach the Men," http://ime.imb.org/LottieMoon/letters/letter5.asp.

57. Allen Thompson, "Would Lottie Moon Be Appointed Today?" *Mainstream Messenger* 3, no. 2 (April 2000), http://www.mainstreambaptists.org/mob3/ lottie_today.htm. An edition of Moon's letters was published after this essay was written: Keith Harper, ed., *Send the Light: Lottie Moon's Letters and Other Writings* (Macon, GA: Mercer Univ. Press, 2002).

58. R. Pierce Beaver, *American Protestant Women in World Mission* (Grand Rapids, MI: Eerdmans Publishing, 1968), 100–101.

59. See for example, Elizabeth Hayes Turner, *Women, Culture, and Community: Religion and Reform in Galveston, 1880–1920* (New York: Oxford, 1997).

60. Quoted in Ownby, *Subduing Satan*, 147.

61. Ownby, *Subduing Satan*, 142.

62. McCurry, *Masters of Small Worlds*, 192–93.

63. Hill, *Southern Churches in Crisis*, 113.

64. Robert Stanley Ingersol, "Burden of Dissent: Mary Lee Cagle and the Southern Holiness Movement" (Ph.D. dissertation, Duke Univ., 1989), 130.

65. Ingersol, "Burden of Dissent," 163, 157.

66. Statistics on women in the UMC can be found at http://gcsrw.org/, the Web site of the UMC General Commission on the Status and Role of Women. On national trends, see Paula D. Nesbitt, *Feminization of the Clergy in America: Occupational and Organizational Perspectives* (New York: Oxford, 1997); Barbara Brown Zikmund et al, *Clergy Women: An Uphill Calling* (Louisville: Westminster John Knox, 1998); and Catherine Wessinger, *Religious Institutions and Women's Leadership* (Columbia, SC: Univ. of South Carolina, 1996).

67. In 2000, women made up approximately 18 percent of clergy, compared to 13 percent in the UMC. For more statistics, see Presbyterian Church (USA), "Research Services," http://www.PCUSA.org/rs.

68. Presbyterian Church in America, "A Brief History," http://www.pcanet.org/general/history.htm.

69. "Western Carolina Expresses Deep Concern Over Women Preaching in PCA Pulpits," *Presbyterian International News Service,* Spring 1999, http://presbyteriannews.org/volumes/v5/2/CedarSprings.html.

70. Jani Ortlund, *Fearless Femininity* (Sister, OR: Multnomah Publishers, Inc., 2000).

71. Ortlund, *Fearless Femininity,* 16.

72. Mother M. Angelica, excerpt from *The Promised Woman,* accessible online at *EWTN Global Catholic Network,* http://www.ewtn.com/library/Mother/MA41E.htm.

73. "Two Years After Suffering a Major Stroke Mother Angelica Lives Her Life of Prayer," *EWTN Global Catholic Network,* www.ewtn.com/mother_update.htm.

74. Benedictine Sisters of Cullman, Alabama, Sacred Heart Monastery Web site, http://home.hiwaay.net/~shmon/about/shm.html.

75. Anonymous informant, interviewed by Corrie Norman, Oct. 2001.

76. Sarah Frances Andes and Marilyn Metcalf-Whittaker, "Women as Lay Leaders and Clergy: A Critical Issue," in *Southern Baptists Observed: Multiple Perspectives on a Changing Denomination,* ed. Nancy Tatom Ammerman (Knoxville: Univ. of Tennessee Press, 1993), 201–21.

77. Prescott Church Web site, "The History of Prescott Memorial Baptist Church," www.prescottchurch.org/History/history.html.

78. Kristen Wyatt, "Carter Quits Southern Baptists," *The Greenville News,* 21 Oct. 2000, 1A; Somini Sengupta, "Carter Sadly Turns Back on National Baptist Body," *New York Times,* 23 Oct. 2000, www.nytimes.com/2000/national/21CART.html, accessible for fee.

79. David Wilkinson, "Moderator Profile: Donna Forrester," 1 Nov. 2000, *Cooperative Baptist Fellowship Network,* http://www.cbfonline.org/newsstand/cbfnews.cfm?forumid=1199.

80. Dorothy Patterson, "The High Calling of Wife and Mother in Biblical Perspective," in *Recovering Biblical Manhood and Womanhood: A Response to Evangelical Feminism,* ed. John Piper and Wayne Gruden, (Wheaton, IL:

Crossway Books, 1991), accessible online at http://www.leaderu.com/orgs/cbmw/rbmw/chapter22.html.

81. Bruce Prescott and Rick McClatchy, "Subjugating Women in the SBC," Baptist Freedom and Conscience Pamphlet Series, accessible online at http://www.mainstreambaptists.org/mbn/subjugating_women.htm.

82. International Mission Board (Southern Baptist Convention), "Lottie's Letters: Who Will Teach the Men," http://ime.imb.org/LottieMoon/letters/letter5.asp. Published after this article was completed is David T. Morgan, *Southern Baptists Sisters: In Search of Status, 1845–2000* (Macon, GA: Mercer Univ. Press, 2003).

83. Women's Missionary Union, "WMU Store," *WMU,* http://www.wmustore.com/wmu/whoweare.

84. Cathy Lynn Grossman, "Graham Daughter Spreads the Word," *USA Today Books,* 18 May 2000, http://www.usatoday.com/life/enter/book675.htm (accessed summer 2002). See also Duncan Mansfield, "Like Father, Like Daughter?" Associated Press story, May 4, 2000, accessible online at *Beliefnet,* http://www.beliefnet.com/story/24/story_2406_1.html.

85. "Anne Graham Lotz," *Preach the Word,* http://www.preachtheword.org/lotz.htm.

86. Randy Bishop, "Just Give Me Jesus," *Christianity Today,* Sept.–Oct. 2000, http://www.christianitytoday.com/cr/2000/005/2.18.html.

87. Grossman, "Graham Daughter."

88. Bishop, "Just Give Me Jesus." For information on "A Passionate Pursuit" and Lotz's other activities, refer to Anne Graham Lotz, *AnGeL Ministries,* http://www.angelministries.org/.

89. Anne Graham Lotz, online newsletter, Summer/Fall 2002, *AnGeL Ministries,* http://www.angelministries.org/nl/am_nl0201.html. Adapted from Lotz's introduction to her book *My Heart's Cry* (Nashville: W Publishing Group, 2002).

90. Beth Moore, *Breaking Free: Making Liberty in Christ a Reality in Life* (Nashville: Broadman and Holman), 2000.

91. See Beth Moore, *Living Proof Ministries,* http://www.lproof.org; and Beth Moore, *Believing God: Online Bible Study,* http://www.lifeway.com/BelievingGod/.

92. Moore, *Breaking Free,* 146.

93. Moore, *Breaking Free,* 153–54.

94. Moore, *Breaking Free,* 150.

95. Bruce Prescott, "Why Baptist Families Are Fracturing," *Mainstream Messenger* 2, no. 5 (Dec. 199): http://www.mainstreambaptists.org/mob2/fractured.htm.

96. Christian Smith, *Christian America? What Evangelicals Really Want* (Berkeley: Univ. of California Press, 2000), 191.

97. On spiritual seeking in contemporary society see the work of Wade Clark Roof, especially *A Generation of Seekers: The Spiritual Journey of the Baby Boom*

Generation (San Francisco: Harpers, 1993), and *Spiritual Marketplace: Baby Boomers and the Remaking of American Religion* (Princeton: Princeton Univ. Press, 1999).

98. Terri Lackey, "Internet Becomes Symbol of Purity for 31,000 Teens Who 'Seize the Net'" [Feb. 2001?], Baptist Press story, accessible online by searching at Lifeway Christian Resources Web site, http://www.lifeway.com/.

99. Lifeway Christian Resources, *True Love Waits,* http://www.lifeway.com/tlw.

100. Quoted in Elizabeth Hayt, "It's Never Too Late To Be a Virgin," *New York Times,* 4 Aug. 2002.

101. Walter Edgar, quoted in Hayt, "It's Never Too Late." On the multiple significance of purity in religion in the South, see Hill, *Southern Churches in Crisis,* xxxviii–xlv.

102. Anonymous informant, interviewed by Heather Breitenbach, Spartanburg, SC, Apr. 2000.

103. Anonymous informant, interviewed by Kristin Smith, Apr. 2000.

104. Rev. Vera Mae Davis, interviewed by Mekole Cotton, Apr. 2000.

105. Redemption World Outreach Center, http://www.rwoc.org/. Paula White of Tampa and Janice Sjostrand of Arkansas were two of the evangelists who participated. Both, like Carpenter, minister with their husbands but also participate actively in special women's ministries. See Abe Hardesty, "Carpenter Builds Hope with Outreach Ministry," *Greenville (SC) News,* Sept. 2, 2000, http://greenvilleonline.com/citypeople/news/2003/09/02/2003090213437.htm.

106. T. D. Jakes, *God's Leading Lady* (New York: G. P. Putnam's Sons, 2002). Also in the series are *The Lady, Her Lover, and Her Lord; His Lady: Sacred Promises for God's Woman;* and *Woman, Thou Art Loosed!*

107. Jakes, *God's Leading Lady,* 217–18.

108. Jakes, *God's Leading Lady,* 31.

109. Anonymous informant, interviewed by Heather E. Barclay, 30 June 2002.

110. Convocation Worship Bulletin of Progressive Church of Our Lord Jesus Christ, Inc. "Theme: God's Design for the Family: In the Home, Church, and in Society," 30 June–5 July 2002.

111. Joanna Bowen Gillespie. *Women Speak of God, Congregation, and Change* (Valley Forge, PA: Trinity Press, 1995).

112. Gillespie, *Women Speak of God,* 161.

113. Gillespie, *Women Speak of God,* 183.

114. Gillespie, *Women Speak of God,* 183.

115. Hardesty, "Carpenter Builds Hope."

116. The stories of "Mary" and "Melissa" and other information were reported in four separate interviews in 2000 and 2002. Interviewers, subjects, and locations

remain anonymous due to the sensitive nature of the information and potential danger for some of the subjects.

117. "Wiccan Soldiers Want to Worship on Post," *The Greenville (SC) News,* 9 Aug. 1999; and S. C. Gwynne, "'I Saluted a Witch,'" *Time,* 5 July 1999, 59.

118. Rowan Anye, interviewed by Corrie Norman, Aug. 2002.

119. Oyotunji Afrikan Village Web site, http://www.oyotunjivillage.net/oyo2_004.htm.

120. Ibile Indigo House Web site, www.ibileindigo.com/.

121. Diana Eck, *A New Religious America* (San Francisco: HarperSanFrancisco, 2001), 241–42.

122. Deb Richardson-Moore, "Embracing Islam: A World of Change," *The Greenville News,* 15 Nov. 2001.

123. Eck, *New Religious America,* 255.

124. Shirin, Shagun, and Talia are cited from their talks in the Women of Faith(s) in the Upstate Forum, Converse College, Spring 2001.

125. Rev. Teijo Munnich, interviewed by Heather Barclay and Corrie Norman, 2002–3. The Web site for Great Tree Zen Women's Temple is located at http://www.main.nc.us/greattreetemple/about-greattree.htm.

126. Anonymous informant, interviewed by Katie Strong, Apr. 2000.

127. Anonymous informant, interviewed by Gloria Flemming, Apr. 2000.

128. Martha Olds Adams, *Peeling the Rind* (Hendersonville, NC: House of Mirth, 2000), 4.

129. Adams, "Spiritlinking," in *Peeling the Rind,* 34.

130. Adams, *She Rises Through the Silver Moon* (Hendersonville, NC: House of Mirth, 2000). Packets with staging guidelines and multiple copies of the poem are available from the publisher.

131. Elaine Lang, interviewed by Corrie Norman, July 2002.

132. Carter Heyward, interviewed by Heather Barclay, July 2002; Carter Heyward, *Saving Jesus from Those Who Are Right: Rethinking What It Means to Be a Christian* (Minneapolis; Fortress Press, 1999).

133. Renita J. Weems, *Showing Mary* (New York, Warner Books, 2002), 44. Professor Weems is also a beliefnet.com columnist and founder of www.some-thingwithin.com/, "an e-journal for women seeking balance and wholeness."

134. Weems, *Showing Mary,* 77.

135. Sue Monk Kidd, *The Dance of the Dissident Daughter* (San Francisco: Harper, 1996), 13–14.

136. Kidd, *Dance of the Dissident,* 40.

137. Sue Monk Kidd, *The Secret Life of Bees* (New York: Viking, 2002), 110.

138. Sue Monk Kidd Web site, "Readers' Guide," www.suemonkkidd.com/.

CHAPTER 2

PENTECOSTALISM AT THE END OF THE TWENTIETH CENTURY: FROM POVERTY, PROMISE, AND PASSION TO PROSPERITY, POWER, AND PLACE

AS A PENTECOSTAL I AM OFTEN AMAZED TO SEE MANY OF THE CHANGES IN public discourse regarding Pentecostalism at the beginning of the twenty-first century. That which was once ridiculed for its emotional excesses, or at best defined as a religion of the disinherited, is now often included in discussions about popular religion.[1] Even if Pentecostalism is not fully appreciated or understood, it is, at the least, begrudgingly accepted as a successful and potent segment of the American religious landscape.

For example, in his provocative book *Fire from Heaven: The Rise of Pentecostal Spirituality and the Reshaping of Religion in the Twenty-First Century* (1995), Harvard theologian Harvey Cox noted that the end of the twentieth century had not experienced the "death of God" that many scholars had earlier predicted. Instead, religion was experiencing an upsurge, and Pentecostalism was a significant part of that upsurge. Cox became convinced that if he could "decipher pentecostalism's inner meaning and discern the source of its enormous appeal, this would provide an essential clue to understanding the larger religious upsurge of which it is a part."[2]

The rapid growth of the Pentecostal movement appears to have shifted the level of influence Pentecostalism has in American religious life and the academic study of American religion. In his recent book on pluralism come of age in American religion, Charles H. Lippy noted the "Pentecostal presence" in the worship of many American denominations and independent congregations.[3] This increasing presence of Pentecostalism is noticeably evident in the attention given to the burgeoning movement. Not only have publishers found a growing market among Pentecostals, but scholars are also willing to write, and publishers willing to publish, books that discuss Pentecostalism.[4]

Such voices sound very different from those expressed one hundred years earlier at the beginning of the twentieth century. Following the Pentecostal events in Topeka, Kansas, in 1901, the *Topeka Daily Capital* reported the opinion of one observer:

> I believe the whole of them are crazy. . . . I never saw anything like it. They were racing about the room talking and gesticulating and using this strange and senseless language which they claim is the word from the Most High.[5]

Even less friendly was the front page of the April 18, 1906, issue of the *Los Angeles Times* describing the strange goings-on at Azusa Street. The headlines screeched,

> "Weird Babel of Tongues
> New Sect of Fanatics is Breaking Loose
> Wild Scene Last Night on Azusa Street
> Gurgle of Wordless Talk by a Sister"

The article reported,

> Meetings are held in a tumble-down shack on Azusa Street, near San Pedro Street, and the devotees of the weird doctrine practice the most fanatical rites, preach the wildest theories and work themselves into a state of mad excitement in their peculiar zeal. Colored people and a sprinkling of whites compose the congregation, and night is made hideous in the neighborhood by the howlings of the worshipers, who spend hours swaying forth and back in a nerve-racking attitude of prayer and supplication. They claim to have the "gift of tongues" and to be able to comprehend the babble.[6]

Indeed reactions to the sights and sounds of Pentecostalism changed dramatically over the course of the twentieth century. Yet, in many ways the sights and sounds themselves have also changed as the movement has broadened its reach from barns and storefronts to sprawling suburban worship centers and urban cathedrals.

Telling the story of American Pentecostalism most often begins with the two chapters already noted here: the ministry of Charles Fox Parham and his

Bethel Bible College in Topeka, Kansas (1901), and William J. Seymour at the Azusa Street mission in Los Angeles (1906). In the South, we should also add the Camp Creek community in Cherokee County, North Carolina, where some one hundred persons are reported to have spoken in tongues following a revival in 1896. Even though this did not have national or regional significance at the time, it is an important part of the history of the Church of God (based in Cleveland, Tennessee), which is one of several Pentecostal denominations born in the American South.[7]

Although there is evidence of speaking in tongues at other times and places, Parham formulated and Seymour propagated the connection of tongues speech with the Baptism of the Holy Spirit for the purpose of supernaturally reaching the world for Christ before his imminent return.[8] In addition to tongues speech, others have highlighted the extraordinary role of all the gifts of the Spirit, divine healing, and the presence of love that at least temporarily overcame many racial and gender barriers. The results allowed for extraordinary possibilities, including new worship styles, interracial fellowship, and a radical egalitarianism that emphasized the role of laity and created opportunities for the ministry of women.

In the intervening century Pentecostalism itself has changed, however. In many ways it appears to be the classic case of the institutionalization of a new religious movement. Theologian and historian Walter Hollenweger has suggested that the heart of Pentecostalism can be found in the first ten years following the rise of the Azusa Street revival.[9] If Hollenweger is correct, it seems to me that contemporary Pentecostalism has lost much of that heart.

The subtitle of this chapter applies six evocative words to depict twentieth-century Pentecostalism: "from Poverty, Promise, and Passion to Prosperity, Power, and Place." The purpose of this chapter is not to discuss each of these descriptions at length but simply to suggest a cluster of images that together portray shifts in Pentecostalism over the twentieth century. Certainly, early Pentecostalism expanded primarily among the poor of the lower and working classes. Also characteristic of early Pentecostalism was confidence that their experiences were the fulfillment of the biblical promise "In the last days I will pour out my Spirit." Within this promise resided the assurance of both purity and power, the thrust for revival, the liberty to include all people regardless of race, gender, or age, and the absolute belief that Jesus was coming soon. This belief infused Pentecostals with hope and courage despite the uncertainties of life. Finally, the affections of early Pentecostals were fundamentally driven with an apocalyptic passion. Theologian Steven J. Land calls it "a passion for the Kingdom." It was a passion that transformed people, infused extraordinary missionary zeal, and made Pentecostalism into far more than a "tongues movement."[10]

In many places in North America, twenty-first century Pentecostalism appears strikingly different. To note one prominent example, John Ashcroft, a publicly recognized member of the Assemblies of God, has served as a governor, a U.S. senator, and now attorney general of the United States. If the hosts and preachers of the Trinity Broadcasting Network or the pastors of congregations such as Atlanta's Cathedral of the Holy Spirit are viewed as examples or models, they appear decidedly middle class.[11] Although early Pentecostals spoke of the power of the Holy Spirit, many today are just as at home in the power centers of government, business, and broadcasting. Some, such as Pat Robertson, who built a religious broadcasting empire, ran for president of the United States, and subsequently sold his television network, have at least attempted to prove themselves adept at combining all three. Indeed, Pentecostalism that seemed out of place at the beginning of the twentieth century appears to have found its place in mainstream America by the end of the century—a place at the tables of the National Association of Evangelicals presidential prayer breakfasts.

Shifts in the Role of Women in Ministry

Early Pentecostalism was particularly known for its loud and exuberant expressions. These expressions were found not only in tongues speech but also in preaching, singing, and testifying. While some of this exuberance continues in many places, one of the most deafening changes in the sound of Pentecostalism has been the quieting of women's voices. Here is an obvious case study of the transformation in Pentecostalism in the twentieth century. Women ministers are predominately absent from middle-class Pentecostalism with its complex and intricately developed power structures. The remainder of this chapter will examine this shift in the Church of God as an example of what has occurred in Pentecostalism as a whole.[12]

According to Peter in Acts 2:17, the promise that God would pour out the Spirit included the assurance that daughters would prophesy, and the Pentecostal movement produced many prophesying daughters. In the fluidity of the early movement, there was little institutional control or need for credentials, rarely salaries for Christian service, often only a hair's breadth of difference between a testimony and a sermon, and a great urgency to spread the gospel in the "last days." In such a milieu, women often found ways to speak publicly. The Spirit spoke through women, gifted women with charismata, and empowered them to share the gospel. Many served as missionaries and evangelists. Some found enough of a following to establish and pastor congregations and denominations.

David G. Roebuck

This is not to say that there was complete egalitarianism or that this was a "golden age" for women. Women preached under the authority of the Holy Spirit rather than their own authority. Indeed, most denominations had clear limits on the roles of women. There were clear boundaries in the African American Church of God in Christ, where women could serve as "church mothers" but were ineligible to serve as elders and were excluded from the pulpit. In the Church of God, women could preach in worship services but were forbidden from speaking in business meetings and were denied ordination. Assemblies of God leadership continually resisted the idea of women serving as elders. Both the Church of God and the Assemblies of God discouraged women from serving as pastors, although women sometimes filled the role of pastor out of necessity. Even independent-minded women, such as Aimee Semple McPherson, ministered within certain boundaries. For example, McPherson always had a male minister by her side during water baptisms.[13]

The Church of God is typical in its quieting of women's voices. Women were a prominent part of the ministry of the Church of God in the first half of the twentieth century. The percentage of ministers who were women varied but was generally over 12 percent and as high as 18 percent by 1950. Social and cultural changes quickly followed World War II, however, and the percentage of ministers who were women dropped to less than 8 percent by 1990. Although 8 percent might seem significant, in practice far fewer women served in public ministry—especially as pastors.[14]

Why was there a decline in women ministers in the Church of God in the second half of the twentieth century just as mainline denominations were beginning to open doors for women? To a great extent the Church of God responded negatively to the enlarging of roles for women in American culture. After World War II the intensity of the rhetoric increased, battle lines were clearly delineated, and women were challenged to choose between the church and the world. As Church of God women increasingly saw themselves as part of the middle class, they desired the accouterments of the middle class. For those who came from backgrounds in which women previously had little choice but to work outside the home, a stay-at-home wife and mother was an important symbol—whether grounded in reality or not—that Pentecostals had arrived.[15] Women had found a new place based on economic power rather than spiritual power.

At least part of this phenomenon can be explained by changes that occurred in the structure of the Church of God, particularly in the denomination's approach to ministry. This was especially true in regard to the routinization of ministry in the Women's Ministries Department, which primarily served lay women, and the Evangelism and Home Missions Department, which frequently ignored women ministers. The context for these changes was the Church of God's own understanding of its place in American society.

Rise to Middle Class

The Church of God's self-perception of its new place in society was high-lighted by Mickey Crews in his important study *The Church of God: A Social History*. In his final chapter, "From Back Alleys to Uptown," Crews described the shift of the Church of God from a sect to a mainstream American evangelical church. According to Crews, one of the indications of this shift was the rise of membership into the middle class as a result of the economic boom following World War II. This shift, in turn, resulted in the demand for, as Crews put it, a more "professional clergy and a more sophisticated liturgy."[16]

Crews's chapter title came from two lines in an address by general overseer John C. Jernigan to the Forty-first Assembly in 1946: "There was a time when the Church of God was pushed into the back allies [*sic*] and the outskirts of town. But we have disposed of most of our back-alley property and moved uptown."[17] Jernigan's address was a proud rendering of where the Church of God perceived itself to be. According to Jernigan's telling of the denomination's development, at the beginning of the Pentecostal movement the people were from humble backgrounds and served as common laborers and farmers. They had little education. With thankfulness for whatever opportunities came their way, they preached in "old dilapidated church houses, school houses, empty store buildings, barns, brush arbors, tents and private homes . . ." Their church houses were buildings that no one else wanted. They were talked about, falsely accused, and ridiculed by both ordinary citizens and church people alike.[18]

Everything was different in 1946, however. Some Pentecostal churches and the Church of God in particular now ranked among the most successful churches in Jernigan's estimation. There had been tremendous increase in membership, finances, and property. It was clear to Jernigan that the Church of God was now part of respectable middle-class America. He declared:

> Our ministers today wear good clothes, live in good and
> well-furnished homes, drive fine automobiles, and hold
> the general respect of the public, and their sermons are
> surpassed by no other group of gospel preachers. The radio
> stations are open to them, and they are possibly the best-
> liked group of ministers by the owners of the stations of
> any group that has ever gone on the air. . . . We are not a
> weak, back-alley church. We worship on the front streets
> and the world welcomes us. . . . The Church of God has
> spread over the world to the extent that the sun never
> sets on it. She has taken her place with the other great

David G. Roebuck

religious organizations in the world, and is recognized
in our Nation's Capital, in the courts of the land, and by
business and professional men, and they are made to
realize that we are a fast-growing church and have great
possibilities of becoming the world's leading church.[19]

Despite its grandiose appraisal of the state of the Church of God in 1946,
Jernigan's address was intended to serve as a warning. Its primary purpose was
to warn that the movement was at a dangerous pivot. It was where great
churches of the past had been—churches that had had great opportunities
but had become liberal, backslidden, and compromised. While the Church of
God now had the resources to evangelize the world—"large organizations, big
congregations, fine church houses, plenty of money, and an educated ministry, with the world patting them on the back"[20]—they also had their greatest
temptation to lose their evangelistic zeal, to trust in accumulated wealth and
material possessions, and to be deceived into compromise.[21] Jernigan's address
clearly showed that whatever the actual economic status of most Church of
God members, the church as a whole considered itself as belonging to middle-
class America.

Not surprisingly, as the Church of God developed, the institutional structure of the denomination grew as well in both size and complexity. In his
address to the General Assembly in 1948, Jernigan described a highly organized denomination run by boards and committees. These included the Mission
Board, the Board of Education, the General Editorial and Publications Board,
the National Youth Board, the Orphanage Committee, and the Supreme Council. According to Jernigan, "As the Church has grown it has become necessary
to change our methods, system and policies to fit in with the fast developing
organization."[22] This growth and the resulting changes have had direct implications for women in ministry. Two departments in which this occurred were
the Women's Ministries Department and the Evangelism and Home Missions
Department.

Women's Ministries Department

Despite the inclusion of the words "women" and "ministries" in the name of the
department, the Church of God Women's Ministries Department has never
been specifically related to female clergy. Rather, the department has focused
primarily on laywomen. The organization began with the efforts of Jonnie
Belle Wood. Wife of the overseer of Texas, S. J. Wood, she inspired the women
of the church in Electra to make and sell quilts in order to purchase a piano for

their local church during the difficult financial days of the late 1920s. Quilting and other moneymaking endeavors of the newly formed Ladies Willing Worker Band became crucial aspects of the life of the congregation.

In 1936 the General Assembly approved a motion calling for the organization of a Ladies Willing Worker Band in every local church. Although the primary purpose of these local bands was to raise supplemental funds for local churches, spiritual concerns were also emphasized.[23] The LWWB gained its first national structure in 1950 when the wife of the general overseer was selected as a national president. Then in 1964 a national department was organized under the leadership of an executive secretary and a board of directors, along with a president and vice presidents.[24] Two years later, the department began publishing the periodical *The Willing Worker,* later known as *Unique,* as well as organizing meetings at General Assemblies.[25] Constantly adding to their activities, the name of the department was changed to Ladies Auxiliary in 1970, to Ladies Ministries Department in 1982, and to Women's Ministries Department in 1998.[26]

The department's own telling of the history of women in ministry in the Church of God began with the standard recitation of a golden age of equality. This was followed by a matter-of-fact recounting of the decline of women's participation in pulpit and administrative ministries, along with an accompanying shift to youth and Sunday school ministries. Significant to this recounting of history is a characterization of the department's current activities as "the full development of women's ministries." Without any suggestion that the outcome was in any way negative, the account noted that women's ministries were channeled from pulpit ministries into other ministries. The activities of women changed as the needs of the church changed. Absent from this telling of history was any lamenting of the resulting decline of women in the pulpit or any suggestion that contemporary women ought to aspire to pulpit ministry.[27]

Indeed, the department's publications frequently emphasized the idea that women were not credentialed ministers. The very inaugural issue of *The Willing Worker* focused on ways in which women could respond to the call of Jesus. Opening the response to the question "What can we do?" this issue suggested, "Few women are called to work directly as harvesters, but many are called to sustain those who are on the field."[28] Indeed, the department clearly suggested that women's place was primarily in the home.[29] Recognizing that Jesus treated women as "equals with men" in spiritual matters, one article went on to say that "The sphere of their work is different" because they are different from men.[30]

Regarding women's roles in the church, the department at best sent mixed signals to women. On the one hand, they at times recognized the accomplishments of women ministers. On the other hand, they also taught that women had a different role than men and that this role was primarily to "assist," just as women in the Bible served Jesus and assisted Paul. While the department's position that in the Scriptures only men were ordained and had governmental authority was not a new argument for the Church of God, the language used by the department to describe the work of men was particularly limiting for women: "The disciples were ordained and commanded to take the Gospel to the ends of the world. They were placed in authority and were given instructions to preach repentance, heal the sick, cast out devils, etc. . . . Much credit is to be given to our women today for their dedication and abilities to be helpers and assist in the churches."[31] This language at least implied that women were not commissioned to take the Gospel to the ends of the earth or to "preach repentance, heal the sick, cast out devils, etc." This was clearly more restrictive than the early Church of God position that all Spirit-baptized people should be involved in these activities and that women are called to minister the Word. It implied that these activities demand an authority other than that of Spirit baptism and a personal call.

This is not to say that the department did not recognize women who were credentialed ministers. In 1986 the department published a tribute to women in *Centennial: A Century of Pentecostal Witness,* which included several credentialed ministers.[32] Missionaries such as Ruth Crawford, Dora Myers, Lucille Turner, and Margaret Gaines were regularly featured in department publications.[33] Other ministers were occasionally featured in a series entitled "Getting to Know Them."[34] Additionally, a series of articles on "Pioneer Women," as well as other articles, highlighted a number of credentialed women ministers. These women tended to be older (often retired or deceased), were frequently missionaries, and were typically characterized as doing something outside the ordinary.[35] The implied message was that a woman in pulpit ministry was a relic of the past or an activity of unique women. It certainly was not a likely consideration for the majority of women who knew their contemporary place in the church.

Although it would be unfair to hold the Church of God Women's Ministries Department entirely responsible for the decline in the percentage of women who are ministers, the department's emphasis undoubtedly added to the dilemma that existed for young women considering a call to the ministry. The department emphasized the role of women in the family to the near exclusion of the possibility that a woman might consider the clerical ministry. With the exception of certain exceptional women, the department considered women in the pulpit relics that were out of place in the contemporary prosperous and well-organized Church of God.

Evangelism and Home Missions Department

Although the Women's Ministries Department has never had primary responsibility for the care and promotion of women ministers, the opposite is true for the Evangelism and Home Missions Department. Since women ministers in the Church of God were primarily limited to the role of evangelist, the Evangelism and Home Missions Department—the department specifically organized to serve the evangelism ministries of the church—should have been a place where all evangelists, including women, found support and resources for their ministries. Unfortunately, this was not the case.

Leadership of the Church of God began to recognize a need for more organization in the evangelistic thrust of the denomination in the early 1950s.[36] In 1956 the General Assembly created the National Evangelism Committee to support evangelists and create programs that would assist churches in revival.[37] Then, in March 1963 the Supreme Council created the Evangelism and Home Missions Department to coordinate and direct the numerous evangelism efforts of the church.[38] A survey of the department's various publications such as *Flame* reveals the emphases of the department.[39] Particularly important for this study were the department's publicizing of the efforts of male evangelists, the language used by the department to describe ministries and ministers, and the ways in which the department portrayed women in ministerial activities.

Given the fact that women made up approximately 14 percent of Church of God ministers when the department was established in 1963 and almost 10 percent in the United States as late as 1994 and given the fact that these women were known as "lady evangelists," one might expect that women would be referred to frequently in the publications of the department. But references to women as credentialed evangelists or pastors were very rare.

A concern of the newly created department was the support of evangelists. One of the solutions to the economic needs of evangelists was the appointment of "official" evangelists on state and national levels. In large part this was done to supply financial support to some evangelists so that they would not be dependent on offerings, especially the offerings of small churches.[40] State offices appointed state evangelists for their particular state,[41] and the Church of God's General Executive Committee appointed national and metropolitan evangelists. It was not until 2002 that a woman was appointed as a national evangelist. All of the metropolitan evangelists have been men, and only occasionally have women served as state evangelists.[42] A consequence of this approach was that these officially appointed evangelists were the evangelists most frequently highlighted by the department on both the state and general levels. Since women were not appointed on the national level in the twentieth century, most female evangelists lacked the national exposure that came in the official publications of the department.[43]

Additionally, language the department used to refer to evangelists was largely male language.[44] Although the very first issue of *The Flame* and many later issues used exclusive male language entirely, this went beyond the customary inclusive use of male language.[45] Indeed, these references to male evangelists were frequently accompanied by references to the evangelist's wife. Typical was James B. Reesor who wrote about numerous ways the local church could support "the evangelist and his wife."[46] As an article in the department's *Church Planter* reminded the reader, "The pastor's wife is an integral part of the team. After services, she should always be at the back door with her husband, greeting and loving people."[47] Department director Raymond Crowley, in an article entitled "The Spirit of Sacrifice," included men and women but implied that it was men who took women into difficult places. "Our organization," Crowley wrote, "was begun by men and women who were willing to sacrifice—called men of God who took their families to towns where there was not one Church of God member."[48]

Along with male language, most of the images used in departmental publications were male. This was particularly true in promotional materials designed to convey the image of a minister. This was always true in promotional material for the Ministers' Placement Service, a program administered by the department, and for conferences and publications related to evangelists.[49]

Often, in those few cases where the gender references were mixed, the primacy of the male minister was clear. For example, one article referred to the vision of Evelyn Zingmark, who had served as pastor of a successful church in Waukegan, Michigan. Yet, all other references in that article were clearly to the male planting the church: "The foundation of a New Testament church requires a man called by God, called to a city, and called to plant a church. If a person is going to start a church, he must be confident that God had led him to do so." Again, this was not simply male language used to refer to all people: following the topics of "vision" and "call," the article stressed the importance of having a wife committed to the endeavor. In its final comments the article stated that the church planter should "learn from great men," declaring, "Greatness in the ministry is developed by associating and learning from other men." There was no suggestion that men might learn from women or even that women in ministry might need other women from whom to learn. Here all of the examples of "great men" were males.[50]

In addition to highlighting males in most of the department's publications, the department almost always used males as speakers, leaders, and teachers at the conferences, seminars, and other special meetings the department sponsored. The exceptions to this pattern were the specially designed sessions for ladies, which were most often designed for the wives of male evangelists. For example, the 1980 National Conference for Evangelists included a ladies' program with the theme "Evangelism Breakthrough in the Parsonage."[51] The 1985 "Seminar on Ministry," cosponsored by the department and the Church of God School of Theology, featured six general sessions and twelve workshops. All of the speakers and teachers were male.[52]

Women highlighted in the department's publications were most often seen as ministers to those people with the least place and voice in society; such ministries included lay evangelism, child evangelism, missions, and prison ministry. Soon after its establishment, the department began an emphasis on lay evangelism. This came from recognition that local churches would not grow unless the laity was involved in evangelism. Women were frequently highlighted in photos and occasionally in articles regarding lay evangelism.[53] From this interest in the laity came an additional focus on senior adults. Here, too, the department frequently recognized women—usually as the recipients of ministry, sometimes as ministers to other senior adults, and occasionally as featured speakers at denominational functions.[54]

When the department highlighted the need to evangelize children, women were often recognized for establishing neighborhood "kids klubs" to evangelize children. Sometimes these were laywomen, and at other times they were credentialed ministers.[55] At the department-sponsored national evangelists' conference in 1974, featuring the theme "I Am an Evangelist," the only women listed in the program were the anonymous wife of an evangelist and Kathy Sanders, who was listed under "Innovations" and who spoke on the topic "I Am an Evangelist to Children."[56] Despite the fact that so many women were involved in children's ministry under the direction of the department, a male minister was selected when the department hired a staff person to work in the area of children's ministry at the general level.[57]

Another area of ministry spearheaded by the department was missions to Native Americans. Here, too, women were occasionally featured. The department recognized these women as "missionaries."[58] Terry Goodin was the woman most often featured. Goodin felt a burden for missions as a young girl and later experienced a call to work among Native Americans. When she asked Church of God officials to send her, however, they replied that because of safety concerns the denomination had a policy against sending single women as missionaries. So Goodin saved her own money, attended the Church of God's Indian Bible School in New Mexico at her own expense, and after serving as a student missionary was appointed pastor of the Redrock Church of God.[59] Remarkably, of the twenty-eight churches listed as part of the Southwest Indian Ministries in 1994, nine were served by women pastors.[60]

Along with highlighting women in certain ministries, some programs were initiated by the department specifically for men. An early emphasis of the Evangelism and Home Missions Department was ministry to men through Men's Fellowships.[61] These fellowships primarily were directed toward involving laymen in the life of the local church. In many ways it was the male equivalent of the Women's Ministries Department. Yet, it appears that the separation of the activities into male activities sponsored by the Evangelism Department and female activities sponsored by the Ladies Willing Worker Band further shifted the work of the Evangelism and Home Missions Department away from including women in its activities. To summarize the activities of men and women described in the Evangelism and Home Missions Department publications, official evangelists of the department were most often men, while women were most often reported in ministries to prisoners, laity, children, American Indians, and other women—groups that are generally considered powerless in our society.

But how were the activities of women evangelists noted in the department's publications? In 1985 the department began publication of the *Church of God Evangelist* as part of an initiative to enhance the role of the evangelist. A front-page article in the inaugural issue included recognition that "lady evangelists have played a vital role in the expansion and growth of the Church of God." Nine evangelists were cited in the article. Six of the nine were men, and three were women. Of the six men, five were named contemporary evangelists, and the sixth was a biblical figure. Of the three women listed in the article, none were contemporary ministers, and two went unnamed.[62] In telling the story of "lady evangelists," this article implied that they were more often than not unknown and that their ministries were primarily in the past.

Despite this inauspicious start, this single publication, published from 1985 through 1988, was the place where the Evangelism and Home Missions Department most frequently recognized women. Although there were far more articles about men than women, several issues highlighted "lady evangelists."[63] The second issue included a full-page article on the return of Mrs. J. Frank Culpepper to evangelistic work. Kohatha Culpepper was an exception to the norm, having continued to preach during her husband's career as pastor and denominational official. After his death, she returned to the evangelistic ministry.[64] She personally described her ministry as a "gap filler" commissioned by God to fill gaps where no one else would serve. According to Culpepper, "a gap filler was a man who could do nothing, a man not specialized in any field or trade. He was to do jobs that specialized persons did not do." As the wife of a denominational executive, Culpepper had devoted much of her recent ministry to Church of God women, challenging them "to be all that God wants them to be." One of her emphases was involving them in ministry. "She has helped many churches to grow by inspiring pastor's wives and laity to get their hands into the harvest," the article noted. Significant to the author of the article was Culpepper's position on contemporary women's issues. Kohatha Culpepper led the way in the Church of God's opposition to many women's causes, such as the Equal Rights Amendment. According to the article, Culpepper constantly encouraged women to let their voices be heard on important social issues: "The strengthening of the family has been for a number of years one of Culpepper's deep concerns. She has spoken against the Equal Rights Amendment all over our nation. She has enlisted women to write state senators and representatives to speak out against the dangers of ERA to the family, church and nation. Her research has been thorough and accurate. She has provided women with books and materials to fight in this war."[65]

It was an article by an evangelist in the fourth issue of the *Church of God Evangelist* that most clearly defined the nature of the role of the "lady evangelist" in the Church of God. Betty Shaver began her article, entitled "To Be a Lady Evangelist," by stating that for years she had wanted to "change the outlook of many people on the 'lady minister.'" She was concerned that many women ministers had been put in the background because of the image they portrayed, and she wanted to assure the reader that some women ministers "are ladies and like to be recognized as such without being thrown in a general mold along with those who feel that they must portray masculine authority."[66]

Shaver reminded the female reader that she was a wife, mother, and minister—in that order. As a wife, she was to help people respect her husband for his position. Being a minister did not change the fact that she was the "weaker" vessel who needed her husband's "protection and covering just as the Bible states." The wife can have "authority against the enemy" in the pulpit while still recognizing that her husband is the head of the household. According to Shaver, "We dare not confuse the 'anointing' with 'authority.'" Additionally, it is important that the lady minister present herself as a "real" mother—hosting parties, baking cookies, going on field trips, and all the other things that "real" mothers do. The lady reader is reminded that ministry begins at home—first and foremost with her own children. As a minister, the lady minister is to realize that while there is neither male nor female with God, all vessels must follow the established order in God's word: "A lady minister becomes more of a 'lady' when she gets into her proper position and is led by God's Spirit to do the will of the Father. There is neither male nor female with God. He is ever looking for a vessel to use, and if the vessel is male or female, that person must follow the pattern that is laid out in God's word in order to be a minister."[67]

For Shaver, women could be evangelists, but they must first be wives and mothers. As wives, according to the divine order, they depended on their husband's "protection and covering." As mothers, their first field of ministry was to their children.

The stories of Kohatha Culpepper and Betty Shaver help to give insight into attitudes toward women in ministry in the mid-1980s in the Church of God. They reflect the fact that even in 1988 there was much opposition in the Church of God to women in ministry. In the face of this opposition, it was important for women to know their proper place. Women had to assure others that they were called by God, that they had the approval of their husbands, and that they remained under male authority. Additionally, they had to establish that they could be both ministers and ladies. This was a burden that men did not have to bear. Articles about men focused on their ministries; men did not have to establish that they could be ministers and remain fathers, husbands, and gentlemen.

Despite the lack of attention given to women in publications, the most significant action of the Evangelism and Home Missions Department regarding women ministers has been the occasional Women in the Harvest conferences. Beginning in 1991 these conferences have been conducted approximately every other year and are designed especially for credentialed women ministers. According to the department, this conference was "designed to affirm women in the ministry and to recognize their achievements for the Kingdom and the Church."[68]

Despite these good intentions, there has been little follow-up to facilitate changes in the status or treatment of women ministers. Indeed, the second conference for credentialed women ministers, held in October 1993, was not considered newsworthy for the department's own publication. There was not a single news article in the *Flame* about the conference, either to promote the conference or to report its success. The total press coverage in the official publication of the department was inclusion in the calendar of events and a small, three-by-four-inch advertisement in the issue preceding the conference.[69]

Conclusion

In 1910 A. J. Tomlinson, general overseer of the Church of God, penned this prayer:

> O, God, give us an army of men and women who will
> fear nothing but God. Set them on fire with such holy
> zeal that no cries of fanaticism, delusion of the devil,
> manifestations of the flesh, or anything else will check the
> fervor or impede the progress until this glorious gospel is

heralded to the uttermost parts of the earth and the full
blaze of Pentecostal power, with all its signs, wonders and
divers miracles and gifts of the Holy Ghost are ablaze and
utilized for the glory of God, as at the beginning of this
blessed glorious gospel Age.[70]

By the end of the twentieth century, evangelism and Pentecostalism as a
whole were far more organized and controlled. An almost entirely male army
of clergy marched in step to the ever-growing numbers of officers with frequently changing strategies and orders. With most women now in the home
or increasingly in the workplace in order to sustain a middle-class economic
status, few women were finding their place among the clergy of the Church
of God or other Pentecostal denominations. The sights and sounds of Pentecostalism were less out of place in popular religion in the South and in the
United States as a whole.

The story of the growth and development of the Church of God, with its
increased prosperity, its increased economic power, and its increased sense of
place in Evangelical Christianity and the broader culture, was typical of
Pentecostalism in the last half of the twentieth century. These are certainly not
all of the changes that took place among Pentecostals in the twentieth century,
nor were the changes in the role of women all of the consequences. But this
story is an important part of the fabric of religion in the South over the last
one hundred years. Of course, religious movements and denominations are in
constant flux and change. Evidence already exists that new opportunities will
be available for new voices to be heard in the twenty-first century.[71]

Notes

1. One of the best examples of this characterization is Roberts Mapes Anderson,
   Vision of the Disinherited: The Making of American Pentecostalism (New York:
   Oxford Univ. Press, 1979).

2. Harvey Cox, *Fire from Heaven: The Rise of Pentecostal Spirituality and the
   Reshaping of Religion in the Twenty-First Century* (Reading, Mass.: Addison-
   Wesley Publishing Co., 1995), xvii.

3. Charles H. Lippy, *Pluralism Comes of Age: American Religious Culture in the
   Twentieth Century* (Armonk, N.Y.: M. E. Sharpe, 2000), 3, 16.

4. See, for example, Grant Wacker, *Heaven Below: Early Pentecostals and American
   Culture* (Cambridge, Mass.: Harvard Univ. Press, 2001).

5. Samuel J. Riggins, quoted in Jams R. Goff, *Fields White Unto Harvest: Charles F.
   Parham and the Missionary Origins of Pentecostalism* (Fayetteville: Univ. of
   Arkansas Press, 1988), 79.

6. *Los Angeles Times,* April 18, 1906, 1, quoted in Vinson Synan, *The Holiness-Pentecostal Tradition: Charismatic Movements in the Twentieth Century* (Grand Rapids, MI: William B. Eerdmands, 1997), 84–85.

7. Other denominations that originated in the South include the Church of God in Christ, Church of God (Mountain Assembly), Church of God of Prophecy, Fire-Baptized Holiness Church, Fire-Baptized Holiness Church of the Americas, International Pentecostal Holiness Church, Pentecostal Evangelical Church, Pentecostal Fire-Baptized Holiness Church, and the Pentecostal Free Will Baptist Church. For introductions to each of these, see Stanley M. Burgess, *The New International Dictionary of Pentecostal Charismatic Movements* (Grand Rapids, MI: Zondervan, 2002).

8. For an excellent discussion of tongues speech see Wacker, *Heaven Below,* 35–57.

9. Walter Hollenweger, cited in Steven J. Land, *Pentecostal Spirituality: A Passion for the Kingdom* (Sheffield, England: Sheffield Academic Press, 1993), 26.

10. See Land, *Pentecostal Spirituality,* 58–121.

11. Archbishop Earl Paulk serves as pastor of the Cathedral of the Holy Spirit in Decatur, Georgia, a suburb of Atlanta. With a 212-foot spire and thousands of adherents, the cathedral bears little resemblance to the storefronts, tents, and brush arbors of early Pentecostalism.

12. For a more comprehensive discussion, see David G. Roebuck, "Limiting Liberty: The Church of God and Women Ministers, 1886–1996" (Ph.D. diss., Vanderbilt Univ., 1997).

13. Edith L. Blumhoffer, *Aimee Semple McPherson: Everybody's Sister* (Grand Rapids, MI: William B. Eerdmans, 1993), 362–63.

14. Roebuck, "Limiting Liberty," 57–60.

15. For a more complete discussion, see David G. Roebuck and Karen Carroll Mundy, "Women, Culture, and Post–World War Two Pentecostalism," in *The Spirit and the Mind: Essay in Informed Pentecostalism,* ed. Terry L. Cross and Emerson B. Powery (Lanham, MD: Univ. Press of America, 2000), 191–204.

16. Among the evidences Crews cited to show that the Church of God had gained middle-class respectability—as a part of "mainstream conservative evangelicalism"—were changes in the church's growing educational structure; the tearing away of some ecclesial barriers by joining the National Association of Evangelicals, the Pentecostal Fellowship of North America, and the World Pentecostal Fellowship; the encouragement of members to participate in social and political action; and cooperation with the burgeoning Charismatic movement. Mickey Crews, *The Church of God: A Social History* (Knoxville: Univ. of Tennessee Press, 1990), 138, 139, 146, 151, 156–61.

17. John C. Jernigan, "Annual Address of General Overseer," *Minutes of the 41st Annual Assembly* (Cleveland, TN: Church of God Publishing House, 1946), 17, quoted in Crews, *The Church of God,* 151–52.

18. Jernigan, "Annual Address," 15.

19. Jernigan, "Annual Address," 17.

20. Jernigan, "Annual Address," 17.

21. Jernigan, "Annual Address," 18.

22. Jernigan, "Annual Address," 16.

23. B. L. Hicks, quoted in *Church of God International Ladies Ministries Resource Guide*, rev. ed., ed. Mary L. Fisher and Mary-Margaret Morris (Cleveland, TN: International Ladies Ministries, 1994), 36–37.

24. Fisher and Morris, *Ladies Ministries Resource Guide*, 39.

25. Fisher and Morris, *Ladies Ministries Resource Guide*, 40–41.

26. Fisher and Morris, *Ladies Ministries Resource Guide*, 41–43.

27. Fisher and Morris, *Ladies Ministries Resource Guide*, 31–33.

28. "Wanted: Willing Workers," *The Willing Worker* (Spring 1967), n.p.

29. See Edna Conn, "The Woman's Page: So God Made A Woman," *Church of God Evangel*, Jan. 14, 1963, 16; and Ladies Auxiliary Department, "Introducing Mrs. Cecil B. Knight National Ladies Auxiliary President," *The Willing Worker*, Nov.–Dec. 1976, 3.

30. Mrs. F. W. Goff, "Christ Raised the Status of Women," *The Willing Worker*, July–Aug. 1976, 6.

31. "Family Forum: 20th Century Women Addressing Issues of Our Day," *The Willing Worker*, Jan.–Feb. 1980, 8.

32. Dorothy Jennings, ed., *Centennial: A Century of Pentecostal Witness* (Cleveland, TN: Church of God Department of Ladies Ministries, [1986]).

33. See Lucille Turner, "The Woman's Page: The Story of Hope," *Church of God Evangel*, November 2, 1964, 10; Peggy Humphry, "The Woman's Page: Why Dora Myers Has Been Used of God," *Church of God Evangel*, Nov. 9, 1964, 15; and Ruth Crawford, "Lest We Forget," *Church of God Evangel*, Jan. 25, 1965, 9, 19. (This last article was representative of the publication's revamped "The Woman's Page.") See also "Retired at 81—Far from It," *The Willing Worker*, Jan.–Feb. 1979, 10; Oleda Atkinson, "Dora Myers Was A 'Dorcas,'" *Unique*, Jan.–Feb. 1989, 114–15; and Margaret Gaines, "Lifting About Women," *The Willing Worker*, Nov.–Dec. 1986, 12–13.

34. These included Zoe Brown, Dixie Chambers, and Terry Goodin. See "Getting to Know Them," *The Willing Worker*, Nov.–Dec. 1976, 7; July–Aug. 1977, 6; and Sept.–Oct. 1977, 9.

35. Ruth Morris "preached" to the children in her neighborhood as a child and later assisted her husband as a pastor and as a missionary (Peggy Scarborough, "Ruth [Morris] Cecil: A Woman of Prayer," *The Willing Worker*, Jan.–Feb. 1985, 3-4, 17). Maria Atkinson began her ministry in 1924 and brought the Pentecostal message to Hispanics in Arizona and Mexico (Peggy Scarborough, "Maria Atkinson: A Pioneer Woman," *The Willing Worker*, Mar.–Apr. 1985, 14–15, 17).

Connie McCarley, an abused, abandoned three-time divorcee, ministered to youth in jails (Peggy Scarborough, "Pioneer Women," *The Willing Worker,* May–June 1985, 3–4, 17). Marion Spellman founded a drug rehabilitation program (Peggy Scarborough, "Marion Spellman: Pioneer in Rehabilitation," *The Willing Worker,* July–Aug. 1985, 3-4, 18). Myrtle Tatum, seventy-eight years old at the time of the article, and Terry Goodin were missionaries to the American Indians (Peggy Scarborough, "A Feminine Pioneer in the West," *The Willing Worker,* Nov.–Dec. 1984, 3–4, 16; Peggy Scarborough, "Terry Goodin, Pioneer Woman to the Indians," *The Willing Worker,* Jan.–Feb. 1986, 3–5; and Terry Goodin, "Ministering to Native Americans," *Unique,* July–Aug. 1989, 8). Lettie Cross was deceased at the time of her son's article (Louis H. Cross, "The Ministry of My Mother," *Unique,* May–June 1989, 8–9).

36. Gene D. Rice, "Bridging the Gap . . . How It All Started," *Flame,* Summer 1983, 2–3.

37. "The Directors," Flame, Special Centennial Issue [1986], 2.

38. Conn, *Like A Mighty Army,* 330. According to Rice, these included general, state, district and local efforts ("Bridging the Gap," 2).

39. Volume 1, Number 1 of *The Flame* was published in the winter of 1965. It was variously called *The Flame, Flame,* and *Flame Highlights,* and the publication schedule changed from time to time.

40. Walter E. Pettitt, "Are Evangelists Becoming Extinct?" *The Flame,* Summer 1966, 3.

41. Reports on the development of state evangelists with varying levels of financial and scheduling help from the state office appear in the first issue of *The Flame.* See "What Is the Church Doing?" *The Flame,* Winter 1965, 12–14.

42. According to her résumé, Betty Anita Brown served as state evangelist in Texas from June 1989 to November 1990 (Evangelism and Home Missions Department files, Church of God, Cleveland , TN). Jacqueline E. Smith was appointed as the first female national evangelist in 2001.

43. National and metropolitan evangelists were frequently listed in the masthead of *The Flame,* as well as in other occasional lists of department personnel. Additionally, regular reports were given of their activities. A few examples include "National Evangelists," *The Flame,* Spring 1967, 12; "Metropolitan Evangelists," *The Flame,* Fall 1967, 3; "Evangelists 'Called of God,'" *The Flame* Summer 1968, 3; C. Raymond Spain, "Metropolitan Evangelism: Going Where the People Are," *Flame* [May 1973], 1–2; "Introducing Our National Evangelists," *Flame,* Winter 1979, 10-11; "National Evangelists," *Flame,* Spring 1981, 19; "Keeping A Burden for Souls," *Flame,* Fall/Winter 1988, 6; and "National Evangelists—Praying and Preaching Revival," *Flame,* June 1995, 3.

44. There were occasional references to women ministers but these were rare. Examples include F. Sandford Hopkines, "A Career in Ministry?" *Flame,* Summer 1983, 10; Cecil B. Knight, "Into the Future," *Flame,* Special

Centennial Issue [1986], 4; and Gene D. Rice, "Church Planters: Special People," *The Church Planter,* March–April, 1986, 1.

45. *The Flame,* Winter 1965.

46. James B. Reesor, "An Evangelist Speaks," *The Flame,* Summer 1966: 9.

47. Donald R. Bird, "Starting a New Church," *The Church Planter,* May–June, 1985, 2. This was the first issue of a new publication for those planting churches. The assumption was that church planters would be men.

48. Raymond E. Crowley, "The Spirit of Sacrifice," *Flame,* Spring 1980, 2.

49. For examples, see the Evangelism and Home Missions files in the Dixon Pentecostal Research Center, Cleveland, Tennessee. Exceptions to this pattern primarily involve ministries that women were encouraged to participate in, such as senior adult ministries and child evangelism. The Women in the Harvest conferences were also an exception.

50. Orville Hagan, "Church Planting," *The Church Planter,* Winter 1987, 3–4.

51. *Flame,* Spring 1980, 19. See also "1982 National Conference for Evangelists," *Flame,* Summer 1982, 23, which listed a special afternoon ladies program, "The Royal Wedding."

52. "Seminar On Ministry," *Flame,* Winter/Spring 1985, 15.

53. For examples, see Ray H. Hughes, "Planting Growing Churches," *Flame,* Summer 1979, 10–13; Susan P. Sloan, "'It Works and I Can Do It!'" *Flame,* Spring 1981, 11; Nanette Hardy, "Have You Heard the Good News," *Flame,* Summer 1981, 6.

54. A senior adult luncheon at the General Assembly in 1974 featured Mary E. Graves speaking on the topic "Senior Adults Evangelizing Senior Citizens." The 1990 breakfast featured Lucille Walker. "Senior Adult Fellowship Endeavor," *Flame,* Summer 1974, 10–11; "Breakfast to Honor Senior Adults and Feature Lucille Walker," *Flame,* Summer 1990, 1, 3.

55. "Child Evangelism," *Flame* [ca. 1971], 10; "Jimmy Doesn't Know Jesus," *Flame* [ca. 1972], 12; "Carolina Lady Promotes Klubs," *Flame* [ca. 1972]: 13; "Kids Krusade," *Flame,* Fall 1972, 15; Mrs. Bill Sheeks, "Child Evangelism," *The Flame* [Winter 1972], [3–5]; Helen S. Pilkington, "The Greatest Thing Yet in Reaching Children," *Flame* [May 1973]: 11.

56. "I Am an Evangelist," *Flame,* Summer 1974, 8–9. "A. J. Duncan and Wife" were listed under "Presenting the Evangelists."

57. Doug Anderson, who continued to serve as associate pastor of the Rose Heights church in Tyler, Texas, was appointed to an adjunct position as child evangelism coordinator in 1994. "Department Leadership Named at General Assembly," *Flame,* Feb. 1995, 2.

58. "Missionary Esther Williams" was mentioned in "Indian Flame," *Flame* [ca. 1972]: 14. See also "Bible School for Indian Children," *Flame,* Camp Meeting 1985, 8, which highlights women for raising funds for Bibles.

59. Doyle W. Daugherty, "Angel in the Desert," *Flame*, Spring 1980, 5–8; Billy J. Rayburn, "Bibles for Cross Cultural Ministry," *Flame*, Spring 1983, 10; "After 20 Years, Terry Goodin Is Still an Angel in the Desert," *Flame*, July 1994, 5.

60. "Twenty-eight Churches Make up the Ministry in the Southwest," *Flame*, July 1994, 5.

61. "What Some States Are Doing," *The Flame*, Winter 1966, 4; "Church of God Men's Fellowship," *The Flame*, Spring 1967, 13; Houston R. Morehead, "Evertt, Pennsylvania, Has an Active Men's Fellowship," *The Flame*, Fall 1967, 4; Houston R. Morehead, "Men's Fellowship," *The Flame*, Winter 1968, 6; Houston R. Morehead, "Men's Fellowships," *The Flame*, Summer 1968, 9.

62. Gene D. Rice, "Evangelists are Special People," *Church of God Evangelist* 1, no. 1 (June 1985): 1–2.

63. In addition to those discussed here, Jacqueline Smith was featured in "Why Have a Career When You Can Have a Ministry," *Church of God Evangelist* 1:3 (Nov.–Dec. 1985): 3; Betty Haynie wrote about her ministry in "From the Classroom to the Pulpit," *Church of God Evangelist* 1, no. 4 (Jan.–Feb. 1986): 1; and Phyllis Qualls Freeman reported on the ministry of Faye Whitten and Dorthy Qualls in "Evangelistic Team Ministers in Africa," *Church of God Evangelist* 1, no. 6 (Fall 1986): 4.

64. "Mrs. J. Frank Culpepper—Lady Evangelist," *Church of God Evangelist* 1, no. 2 (Aug. 1985): 2.

65. "Mrs. J. Frank Culpepper—Lady Evangelist," *The Church of God Evangelist* 1, no. 2 (Aug. 1985): 2.

66. Betty Shaver, "To Be A Lady Evangelist," *Church of God Evangelist* 1, no. 4 (Jan.–Feb. 1986): 2.

67. Shaver, "To Be A Lady Evangelist," 2.

68. "First Women Ministers' Conference Meets October 29–31," *Flame*, Summer 1991, 1. See also "Women Attend Historic Conference," *Flame*, Winter 1991, 1, 3.

69. *Flame*, June 1993, 2, 7.

70. A. J. Tomlinson, "Better Obey God Than Listen to Man," *The Evening Light and Church of God Evangel*, May 15, 1910, 1.

71. The 2000 General Assembly of the Church of God changed the title of "licensed minister" to "ordained minister," which effectively ordained women for the first time in the history of the denomination. Additionally, the Assembly created an International Council to allow for more voices from outside of the United States to be heard. Both of these are evidence of sensitivity to cultural issues. Church of God, *Minutes of the 68th General Assembly of the Church of God* (Cleveland, TN: Church of God Publishing House, 2000), 79-81.

CHAPTER 3

A Crumbling Empire: Is There a Baptist Future in the South?

ON THE EVE OF THE AMERICAN REVOLUTION, THE ANGLICAN PARSON Charles Woodmason described the carryings-on among the people called Baptists as observed in the "Carolina backcountry." His assessments were anything but flattering. Woodmason wrote:

> They don't all agree on one Tune. For one sings this
> Doctrine, and the next something different—So that
> Peoples' brains are turn'd and bewildered. And then again
> to see them Divide and Sub divide, split into parties—Rail
> at and excommunicate one another—Turn [members] out
> of one meeting and receive [them back] into another. And
> a Gang of them getting together and gabbling one after
> the other [and sometimes disputing against each other] on
> abstruse Theological Questions . . . such as the greatest
> Metaph[ys]icians and Learned Scholars never yet could
> define, or agree on—To hear Ignorant Wretches, who
> cannot write . . . discussing such Knotty Points for the
> Edification of their Auditors . . . must give High offence
> to all Intelligent and rational Minds.[1]

As far as I can discern, some Anglicans have pretty much felt that way about Baptists from that day to this. Indeed, Anglicans were among the earliest critics of the Baptist communities in England. Their assessments indicate that being Baptist has never been all that respectable. As their earliest critics saw it, Baptists were not simply heretical; they were ignorant peasants who had no class. In 1646 the Reverend Daniel Featley, Anglican priest, wrote a scathing denunciation of a new and unruly sect rampant in England. Entitled, wonderfully, *The Dippers Dipt or, the Anabaptists Duck'd and Plung'd over Head and Ears*, it observed cynically:

> They preach, and print, and practice their Hereticall
> impieties openly; they hold their conventicles weekly in
> our chief cities, and suburbs thereof, and there prophesie
> by turnes. They flock in great multitudes to their Jordans,
> and both sexes enter into the River, and are dipt after their
> manner with a kinde of spell containing . . . their erroneous
> tenets. As they defile our Rivers with their impure washings,
> and our Pulpits with their false prophecies and phanaticall
> enthusiasms, so the presses sweat and groan under the load
> of their blasphemies.[2]

Featley also delineated the so-called "heretical" ideas of the 17th century Baptists. Some sound familiar three and a half centuries later.

> First, that none are rightly baptized but those who
> are dipt.
> Secondly, that no children ought to be baptized.
> Thirdly, that there ought to be no set form of Liturgy
> or prayer by the Book, but onely by the Spirit.
> Fourthly, that there ought to be no distinction by the
> Word of God between the Clergy and the Laity, but that
> all who are gifted may preach the Word, and administer
> the Sacraments.
> Fifthly, that it is not lawful to take an oath at all, no,
> not though it be demanded by the magistrate.
> Sixthly, that no Christian may with good conscience
> execute the office of a civil magistrate.[3]

These "distinctives" remain a part of at least some segments of the Baptist heritage.

Suffice it to say that colonial Baptists generally remained antiestablishment in both Puritan New England and the Anglican South. In the 1630s they invented Rhode Island, the first colony to be founded on the basis of religious liberty, for believer and unbeliever alike. In fact, it attracted such a questionable crowd of dissenters and sectarians that it was sometimes labeled a "Rogues' Harbor."

Bill J. Leonard

Seventeenth-century Baptists also lobbied in various ways for religious freedom. Isaac Backus represented the interests of the Warren Association of New England Baptists at the first Continental Congress. Virginia Baptist John Leland encouraged the Virginia bill on religious liberty and encouraged the likes of Thomas Jefferson and James Madison to support a bill of rights promoting freedom of religion.

On the western frontier during the early nineteenth century, they were a genuine peoples' movement, provoking even the Methodists, themselves a crowd of populists, to severe criticism and ecclesiological apoplexy. Peter Cartwright, the Methodist circuit rider, had little good to say about the frontier Baptists with whom he was in constant competition for converts and church members. He wrote of their activities:

> We [Methodists] preached in new settlements, and the Lord poured out his spirit, and we had many conversions. It was the order of the day, though I am sorry to say it, that we were constantly followed by a certain set of proselytizing Baptist preachers. These new and wicked settlements were seldom visited by these Baptist preachers until the Methodist preachers entered them; then, when a revival was gotten up, or the work of God revived, these Baptist preachers came rushing in, and they generally sung their sermons; and when they struck . . . their sing-song mode of preaching in substance it was water! "Water! You must follow your blessed Lord down to the water!" Indeed, they made so much ado about baptism by immersion, that the uninformed would suppose that heaven was an island and there was no way to get there but by *diving* or *swimming*.[4]

As Cartwright saw it, Baptist beliefs were not only unbiblical; their methods were tricky and manipulative. Being Baptist was disgraceful, and apparently, everybody knew it.

As early as the 1830s, however, Baptists in the South were, with the Methodists, a near majority with churches in the countryside villages and towns. First Baptist in Charleston, the oldest in the South, was served by the erudite Richard Furman, a "Gentleman theologian" if ever there was one. Likewise, Furman's 1822 defense of human slavery gave "biblical and moral" grounds to support the South's peculiar institution. It was slavery (euphemistically referred to as "sectionalism" by generations of Southern Baptist historians) that led to the split between Baptists north and south in 1845. The result of that schism was the Southern Baptist Convention (SBC), a denomination linked irrevocably with the Confederacy. Devastated by defeat, it rose again from the ashes, first as one of the leading ecclesiastical proponents of what Charles Reagan Wilson calls "the religion of the Lost Cause," and then as one of the region's most elaborate ecclesiastical systems.[5] The convention system utilized for the first time by a Baptist denomination in the United States linked local congregations with regional and national organizations and enterprises, creating a framework for cooperation and action among a people who claimed to distrust and resist "hierarchies." A zeal for evangelism helped to create a numerical explosion, and by the late nineteenth century Southern Baptists were establishing a religious hegemony as the "Catholic Church of the South." Indeed, writing in the 1970s, Martin Marty described southern Protestantism in general and the SBC in particular as among the most intact religious subgroups in contemporary America. Intactness meant that the SBC retained a sense of continuity with its past and provided a powerful identity for its members in the present. Such a tradition, Marty believed, revealed "regularities of behavior and consistent norms for evaluation."[6]

The Southern Baptist Convention evolved (some would hate my use of that word) into an elaborate system, creating a powerful identity for its people. That system was grounded in a powerful cultural and religious ethos linking significant elements of Southern culture with a denominational program that carried constituency from the cradle to the grave.

Indeed, by the mid-twentieth century, growing up Southern Baptist seemed relatively easy. You knew where you stood on Sundays and throughout the week. Sundays meant church, all day church. So off you went, armed with the three great symbols of Southern Baptist faith: a King James Version of the Bible (zipper edition); a Sunday School "Quarterly," which contained the weekly lesson studied by all Southern Baptists from Richmond to El Paso; and an offering envelope, in which you placed the weekly tithe and on which you recorded your spirituality through the "Six-point Record System." Check marks detailed such things as studied lesson, attendance, staying for church, offering, visits made, and Bible brought. Convention-wide programs were carried out through Sunday school, "Training Union" (a Sunday evening program in ethics, history, and doctrine), seasonal revivals, and special Sunday observances emphasizing programs for missions, stewardship, youth and children.[7]

The system also provided for the training of future generations. Churches taught children, who were sent to Baptist colleges and universities that kept the Baptist identity alive through chapel services, mission trips, and Baptist Student Union. Those called to ministry then went to one of six national seminaries that networked them into pastoral or staff ministry, missionary service, denominational administration, or teaching. An array of literature provided instruction for bible and doctrinal study, church and Baptist history, specific age groups, and mission education. Suffice it to say that those systems and meth-

Bill J. Leonard

ods inculcated a powerful identity in the Baptist multitudes, whose sheer numbers meant that they developed an undeniable hegemony over religious life in the American South. As one observer noted, "In the South, Baptists are the center of gravity."[8] In 1948 Alabama Baptist leader Levi E. Barton declared, "I am more tremendously convinced than ever that the last hope, the fairest hope, the only hope for evangelizing this world on New Testament principles is the Southern Baptist people represented in that Convention. I mean no unkindness to anybody on earth, but if you call that bigotry then make the most of it."[9] The once-persecuted minority had become an establishment.

Southern Baptist identity and hegemony in the South endured throughout much of the twentieth century. In fact, it endured longer than many might have supposed. At century's end, however, the SBC system was (choose your best phrase) coming apart, being redefined, in dynamic transition, disconnecting, in disarray, reclaimed, and experiencing schisms both implicit and explicit. Reasons are numerous and complex. For the sake of discussion, I survey a short list.

First, Southern culture, never homogenous, witnessed major transitions related to, among other things, race, marriage, and immigration. The civil rights movement, desegregation, and the emerging New South challenged old boundaries and divisions—social, ecclesial, and political. Amid significant exceptions, Southern Baptists as a people generally acquiesced in the South's segregationist, "separate-but-equal" society. Wayne Flynt's history of Alabama Baptists provides a powerful survey of transitions in that region and the work of certain Baptists for and against the civil rights movement.[10] Likewise, as southerners moved outside the region and non-Southerners moved in, the old cultural and religious boundaries were challenged. Southern Baptists doing "pioneer" work in Pennsylvania, for example, in the 1970s wondered out loud why the "natives" failed to appreciate the traditional schedules for worship, Wednesday-night prayer meeting, and other aspects of the SBC system. Intermarriage of Baptist youth to non-Baptists and, God forbid, non-southerners, also brought many persons into Baptist congregations who had little or no experience with the system. (Intermarriage also brought Baptists into the ranks of other traditions, as some in those churches might mourn.)

Second, a twenty-year controversy pitting so-called fundamentalists and moderates against each other for theological and political hegemony inside the denomination ultimately found its way into every corner of SBC life. I, along with others, have written extensively about the controversy, and it has been in all the papers.[11] Suffice it to say that the controversy has impacted the stability and system of the denomination in multiple ways. These include the following:

1. While fundamentalists won control of the national denomination, including mission agencies, publishing houses, and six seminaries, they have watched as many of the old connections to churches and other institutions changed, were redirected, or disappeared.

2. State Baptist conventions, a significant part of the old denominational system, have chosen multiple responses to the fundamentalist control of the national system. Some—South Carolina, Florida, Georgia—have generally supported fundamentalist orientations. Some—especially Texas and Virginia—have identified themselves as moderates, creating actual schisms with fundamentalists in those states. In both Texas and Virginia there are now two state conventions, the old system controlled by moderates and a new organization of fundamentalists. Most states—Kentucky, North Carolina, Alabama, and Mississippi—have sought to steer a course somewhere between the two groups.

3. Many moderates have moved toward new Baptist societies organized out of the controversy. These include the Alliance of Baptists, the Cooperative Baptist Fellowship, and Texas Baptists Committee. Many of the churches linked to these organizations still retain "official" membership in the SBC, though there seems to be an effort to reevaluate that relationship on the part of a growing number of churches.

4. Some moderate congregations long affiliated with the SBC have actually dropped their affiliation. These include First Baptist Churches in Raleigh, North Carolina, and Greenville, South Carolina, both of which antedate the founding of the convention in 1845. Other moderate churches, while retaining membership in the SBC, have essentially disengaged from financial, missionary, or other direct involvement in the denomination.

These and other developments mean that the old convention system described earlier in this essay is collapsing or, in many cases, already has collapsed in its ability to create a common identity in an ever-unruly constituency. Indeed, churches across the theological spectrum are stepping outside the convention system for literature, missionary experience, funding, theological education, and other areas of church life. Many churches of varying theological and liturgical orientation are even dropping the Baptist name, fretting that it

Bill J. Leonard

scares people off as a result of the twenty-year denominational dysfunction, or simply that "brand name" religion no longer attracts.

At century's end, statistics and demography are catching up with the divided denomination. In 1998 the SBC posted its first (acknowledged) membership decline in over thirty years. Most acknowledge, however, that of the thirty-seven thousand churches claiming affiliation with the denomination, some 70 percent are plateaued or declining. While the SBC claims some 17 million members, those figures often include such categories as "non-resident" and "inactive members," numbers that might account for almost half of the 17 million figure.

Which brings me to the third major point. All this suggests that Baptist identity is certainly in major transition at every level of the old SBC system. Younger members—aged forty-five and younger—were not reared in the days of the intact system. Intermarriage has brought many into congregations who have no frame of reference for why Baptists practice immersion, congregational polity, and other historic "distinctives." Generation X young people increasingly reject sectarian divisions in favor of a kind of generic Christianity, highly individualized, often charismatic, and less denominationally oriented.

Fourth, the denominational controversy has in many ways obscured significant theological problems that are only now becoming evident and are generally not addressed. Two examples must suffice. While giving great emphasis to the doctrine of biblical inerrancy, fundamentalists now acknowledge that there are multiple "types" of inerrancy, some of which are more orthodox than others. Thus, underneath the litmus test of inerrancy is another level of assessments as to what kind of inerrancy is acceptable and what kind is not.

Likewise, Southern Baptists have never really dealt with the impact of American revivalism on the nature and methods of their brand of Christian conversion. Issues of child conversion in a denomination that touts a believers' church have not been examined in many congregations. One of the fascinating questions of Southern Baptist evangelicalism is why a communion that claims to be a "believers' church" should baptize children, including a large number of preschoolers. Transactional conversionism in which the sinner prays a "sinner's prayer" and then, when "saved," is "always saved" has received little or no theological reflection in Southern Baptist life. Failure to address these evangelical dilemmas is further evidenced in the ever-increasing number of Southern Baptist church members who have received multiple immersions in what seems an unending quest for a "decisive" conversion experience. All this contributes to a kind of evangelical confusion about the nature of conversion, the nature of baptism, and the meaning of faith itself.

Fifth, changes in Southern Baptist influence and identity are also related to the impact of the so-called mega-church and its tendency to minimize denominational identity and local church ecclesiology. Mega-churches are congregations of several thousand members, led by a CEO charismatic pastor, providing specialized services for target groups, and organized around intentional marketing techniques. Mega-churches are mini-denominations, providing in one congregation many of the services and options previously provided by the denominational structure. These churches, some of which maintain affiliation with the SBC, challenge traditional ways of networking, educating, publishing, and evangelizing. Many reflect a populist, performance-based worship style, combining elements of a production, incorporating praise choruses, skits, sermons oriented toward practical concerns, and liturgical informality. Many Baptists, moderate and fundamentalist, are leaving traditional SBC churches for the mega-churches nearest them. Some Baptists are seeking to apply the mega-church model to traditional congregations, while others eschew it completely. Other churches have developed varying styles of worship with contemporary and traditional services celebrated each Sunday. The full impact of the mega-church movement on Southern Baptist identity remains to be seen.

The result of these transitions, in my view, has been to weaken substantially the Southern Baptist hegemony in the South. Does this mean that the SBC will disappear? Of course it will not. But its constituency is clearly changing, its old system breaking apart, and its identity as a Baptist communion uncertain. Perhaps they are signs, if not of hope, then of possibility.

New Communities—New Localism

During the last years of the twentieth century, moderate Baptists were forced to come to terms with the fact that they had not only lost the Convention but also had no real prospect of retaking it. While many continued to maintain relations with the old denomination, others sought a new connectedness in a variety of loose-knit organizations. In a sense they reaffirmed the old society method that had characterized early Baptist associations and permitted churches and individuals to direct specific funds and energies toward organizations that carried out specific activities such as national or international missions, theological education, publications, or other cooperative endeavors.

Gradually, new moderate-related organizations took shape among moderate churches previously connected to the SBC. The first of these organizations began in 1986 as the Southern Baptist Alliance, an organization of churches formerly connected to the SBC. As those connections waned, the name was changed to the Alliance of Baptists. With offices in Washington, D.C., the Alliance of Baptists receives money from churches and individuals to fund a variety of projects, including direct aid to certain theological schools, support for churches in Cuba, and other international missionary efforts as well as special ministries in the United States. It has also participated in dialogues with American Baptist Churches, USA, the Progressive National Baptist Convention, and the United Churches of Christ. Its churches tend to reflect more liberal perspectives on women's ordination, ecumenical and interfaith dialogues, and the need to respond with hospitality to gays and lesbians.

The Cooperative Baptist Fellowship (CBF) was founded in 1991 by a group of individuals and churches that were increasingly estranged from the Southern Baptist Convention. With offices in Atlanta, Georgia, the CBF identified itself as a "mission-sending" organization for those who did not wish to continue supporting the programs of the SBC. While it did not develop elaborate denominational mechanisms, the CBF expanded its cooperative ministries and connections into publication, mission, theological education, and the promotion of "Baptist principles." By the end of the century, a small but growing number of former SBC churches considered themselves "Cooperative Baptist Fellowship" congregations and accepted the CBF as their primary denominationally related constituency.

The Texas-based group called Mainstream Baptists is another organization founded by individuals formerly related to the SBC. It began in the 1990s as an informal network of Texas churches that successfully resisted conservative/fundamentalist efforts to dominate the Baptist General Convention of Texas. Their success in Texas led to efforts to organize Mainstream groups in other southern states. These Baptists may also relate to the CBF or the Alliance of Baptists, but their intent is to challenge conservative efforts to achieve the same control of state Baptist conventions that they achieved in the national denomination. Its rhetoric tends to be more aggressive and its leaders seem more willing to confront the conservatives on their own turf. Mainstream Baptists generally reflect a more conservative theological agenda amid their militant opposition to fundamentalist tactics.

The decision to distance themselves from the old SBC structures has compelled many Baptist churches to be much more intentional about their identity. Whereas these congregations previously drew much of their identity from the old SBC system, they were forced to ask anew what it means to be Baptist and how they proposed to pass on that identity to a new generation of members. This inevitably led to a reassertion of localism with an emphasis on the congregational autonomy in developing alliances and connections with other Baptists. It also created strife in specific churches as members continued to divide over support for the old denominational system. Many no doubt feared that to leave the SBC was to lose Baptist identity all together. Others suggested that appropriate identity could not be sustained in a re-formed, right-wing Southern Baptist Convention.

New Institutions—Theological Education

Another result of divisions in the SBC has been the proliferation of a new generation of theological schools, many connected to Baptist universities in the South and Southwest. When the controversy first took shape among Southern Baptists in June 1979, there were six Southern Baptist seminaries stretching from North Carolina to California. In those years one out of every five students in schools accredited by the Association of Theological Schools was in an SBC seminary. Since the Southern Baptist Theological Seminary was founded in 1859, Southern Baptists have preferred to fund theological education through a set of six denominationally owned but freestanding graduate schools. They became the primary institutions for providing ministerial training for students connected with the SBC. They were also at the center of numerous debates over theology and ethics in SBC life, with professors at several of the schools accused of heresy or of teaching outside the doctrinal "norm." As conservatives gained control of boards of trustees in the seminaries and throughout the national denomination, they moved to restructure faculty and administrative officers in more rightward directions. Soon, moderate Baptists founded schools that provided opportunities for students in service inside and outside the church. Founded in 1989, Beeson Divinity School at Samford University was the first of these new schools. Its commitments were to both a Baptist and evangelical orientation for its students.

The Baptist Theological Seminary, Richmond, Virginia was established in 1989. It began in facilities near the campus of the Presbyterian Union Theological Seminary, Richmond, where it remains. It was organized with help from the Southern Baptist Alliance (Alliance of Baptists) and later received significant funding from the Cooperative Baptist Fellowship. Today, it is the largest of the moderate Baptist schools, with a student body of more than two hundred students. During the 1990s divinity schools or seminaries were founded at numerous Baptist-related universities. These included George Truett Theological Seminary at Baylor University; Logsdon School of Theology at Hardin Simmons University; McAffee School of Theology at Mercer University; Christopher M. White Divinity School at Gardner-Webb University; Campbell University Divinity School; and Wake Forest University Divinity School. Baptist houses of study were also established at Candler School of Theology at Emory University; Duke University Divinity School; and Brite Divinity School at Texas Christian University.

Baptists and a New Pluralism

One of the most formidable challenges confronting Baptists inside and outside the SBC involves the question of pluralism in the church and the society. Religious pluralism in America is nothing new. Indeed, at their best, the early Baptists in colonial America anticipated religious pluralism with their support of religious liberty, the opposition to ecclesiastical establishments, and their insistence that God alone was judge of conscience.

While Southern Baptists supported religious freedom and what was often known as "the separation of church and state," their close identification with southern culture led many to accept slavery and segregation as divinely sanctioned divisions in their society. Indeed, Southern Baptist leaders such as Richard Furman (1755–1825) were among those who set forth certain "biblical defenses" of slavery. During the civil rights movement, many Southern Baptist churches approved membership policies aimed at keeping people of color, in some cases Africans as well as African-Americans, from membership.

Many Southern Baptists also resisted the presence of Roman Catholics in the South. During the 1920s leaders such as J. Frank Norris offered vehement opposition to the political campaigns of Democrat Al Smith and other Catholic politicians. Many Southern Baptist leaders also opposed John Kennedy's campaign for president in 1960. His election was a symbolic victory for religious pluralism in the United States and in the South.

At the turn of the century, especially following the terrorist attacks on September 11, 2001, the growth of non-Christian religions in the United States became increasingly evident. Many Southern Baptist leaders continued to affirm religious liberty for all religious groups, while resisting the idea that such pluralism implied theological equality of world religions. Amid assertions of the need to evangelize all persons, certain Southern Baptist agencies "targeted" various religious groups—Hindus, Muslims, and Jews—on their respective holy days. Leaders warned that the God addressed by these religions was not the same God as the one whom Jesus called "Father." Representatives of the denomination's North American Mission Board insisted that "interfaith" dialogues would undermine evangelistic activities aimed at the conversion of members of other faiths. All this occurred as many Southern Baptist young people were marrying persons of various faiths, and forcing their families to confront individuals who were once known only as objects of "foreign" missions on the other side of the world.

The pluralism of other world religions in the South presents a major challenge for Southern Baptist theology of evangelism, mission, and religious freedom. Many fret that increased dialogue, intermarriage, and other encounters with persons of other faiths would create an implied "universalism" and the belief that all faiths offer an equally valid way to God.

Facing the Future

All this suggests that Southern Baptist hegemony in the South is on the decline, impacted by forces inside and outside what remains America's largest Protestant denomination. Internal divisions have created realignments at every level of denominational life that will have increasing influence on the convention's organizations and activities. Baptist identity, once passed on through the denominational system, is much less important to the generations under the age of forty. Pluralism and intermarriage will continue to bring persons into families and churches that have little or no sense of the "Southern Baptist way." The Convention remains, but confronts a time of permanent transition in its denominational life and work. In the South, Baptists are no longer "the center of gravity." In the Kingdom of God, they never were. So it goes.

Notes

1. Richard J. Hooker, ed., *The Carolina Backcountry on the Eve of the Revolution: The Journal and Other Writings of Charles Woodmason, Anglican Itinerant* (Chapel Hill: Univ. of North Carolina Press, 1953), 109. See also John G. Crowley, *Primitive Baptists of the Wiregrass South, 1815 to the Present* (Gainesville: Univ. of Florida Press, 1998), 8.

2. Daniel Featley, *The Dippers Dipt, or the Anabaptists Duck'd & Plung'd over Head and Eares, at a Dispute in Southwark* (London: 1646), 36.

3. Ibid., n.p.

4. Peter Cartwright, *The Autobiography of Peter Cartwright* (New York: Phillips & Hunt, 1856), 133.

5. Charles Reagan Wilson, *Baptized in Blood: The Religion of the Lost Cause* (Athens: Univ. of Georgia Press, 1980).

6. Martin E. Marty, "The Protestant Experience and Perspective," in *American Religious Values and the Future of America*, ed. Rodger van Allen (Philadelphia: Fortress, 1978), 40.

7. Bill J. Leonard, *God's Last and Only Hope: The Fragmentation of the Southern Baptist Convention* (Grand Rapids, MI: William B. Eerdmans Publishing Co., 1990), 1–2.

8. Edward L. Queen II, *The Center of Gravity: Southern Baptists, the South, and Social Change, 1930–1980* (Chicago: Univ. of Chicago Press, 1989).

9. Quoted in Queen, *Center of Gravity*, vi.

10. Wayne Flynt, *Alabama Baptists: Southern Baptists in the Heart of Dixie* (Tuscaloosa: Univ. of Alabama Press, 1998).

11. See Leonard, *God's Last and Only Hope*; Nancy Tatom Ammerman, *Baptist Battles: Social Change and Conflict in the Southern Baptist Convention* (New Brunswick, NJ: Rutgers Univ. Press, 1990); and David T. Morgan, *The New Crusades, the New Holy Land: Conflict in the Southern Baptist Convention, 1969–1991* (Tuscaloosa: Univ. of Alabama Press, 1996.)

CHAPTER 4

THE PERSISTENCE OF EVANGELICAL DENOMINATIONALISM IN THE SOUTH AND THE CASE FOR DENOMINATIONAL HISTORY: ALABAMA BAPTISTS

PERHAPS THE CONTINUING RELEVANCE OF DENOMINATIONALISM IN THE South is further evidence of the region's exceptionalism. Whatever direction the nation moves, it sometimes seems that southerners dig in their heels and say, "Never!" Of course, one can make too much of such bullheadedness. The metropolitan South often glances nervously over its urban shoulder to make sure it is dressed fashionably and speaking with a general American accent; it is awash in sushi bars and Starbucks coffee shops, as well as in generic churches sans denominational affiliation. But out there in the boondocks, in the small towns, cities, and rural areas, congregations regularly vote down attempts to delete "Southern" from Southern Baptist Convention or "Methodist" from Calvary Methodist Church. Whether this is an example of religious sectionalism or theological identity is hard to determine. Southern Baptists even in California refuse to eliminate "Southern" from their official title. Perhaps this resistance to change suggests that southern religion is exportable to people in other regions. Or perhaps it means that most Southern Baptists in California are southern migrants and that the most effective evangelism there is conducted near the grits counter at the local Wal-Mart superstore. If this be provincialism, adherents seem to be saying, then make the most of it.

The reason such belligerent cantankerousness seems old-fashioned is that, like our eating habits, our national religion seems to favor the buffet over separate entrées. Begin with a little tradition. Add a touch of modernity. The salad consists of a bit of fundamentalism and even a touch of diversity (liberalism, interracialism, Pentecostalism, contemporary music, almost anything will do!), all mixed thoroughly. Quick, cheap, and modern. Pick your church for the top singles' program in your twenties, the best aerobics dance classes and gymnasium in your thirties, the best youth program in your forties, the finest family counseling staff in your fifties, and the most active "Golden Years" activities for retirement. The last consideration (even the thought of it is embarrassing) would be to die in the denomination into which you were born.

Of course denominations do not die overnight. In fact, despite declining loyalty to them, they continue to represent the ecclesiastical structure through which most Americans seek after God. And in the South particularly, they remain vigorously and self-consciously alive and well.

When Henry F. May wrote about recovering American religious history in 1964, it never occurred to him that a time might soon arrive when historians would need to retrieve denominational history as well as theological ideas and systems. In a seminal essay May noted that religious history restores knowledge of the mode, even the language, in which most Americans did their thinking about human nature and destiny.[1] In no place has May's admonition been more fruitfully pursued than in the South. Better than even he could have imagined, transdenominational books have succeeded in capturing the way in which southerners lived (establishing and maintaining community), believed (theology), and had their being (folkways, gender, and race relations).[2] So satisfying have such broadly based cultural studies of religion become that older, denominationally focused books seem old-fashioned at best and deeply flawed at worst.

Henry Warner Bowden, himself editor of a new series of denominational histories, has observed that early examples of this genre were flawed in a variety of ways: they were apologetic, polemical, triumphalist, defensive, narrow, and often little more than boring, endless lists of pastors, bishops, and other denominational bureaucrats, together with dates of significance to that particular order of Christianity. Beyond preserving essential denominational data and explaining the origins, development, and polity of denominations, they were of little value. A shift after 1930 toward a more scientific history—with emphasis on objectivity, criticism, and cultural context—began to change denominational history. So did the rise and sophistication of intellectual history.[3]

By the end of century, it seemed the tide had turned toward renewed interest in denominational history, albeit in a different species of the original animal. Historian John F. Wilson attributes this renewed interest to a variety of factors. Historians often work out of phase with their times, so that, as denominationalism declines, their interest in it increases. Denominational officials and members refocus on denominational distinctiveness in order to reenergize their denominations. "Lilly largess," the product of Ely Lilly grants made to a new generation of scholars, stimulates research about American denominationalism.[4]

There is irony aplenty here. At the same time that Greenwood Press announces a series entitled "Denominations in America," edited by Henry Bowden, historians of religion confidently announce that America is entering a post-denominational age. Other than the fact that religious historians may be as perverse and unreconstructible as southerners, how can one explain this apparent example of miserable timing?

The answer to this question may not be as obvious as it seems. Perhaps, as in the case of so many epitaphs written for Dixie (the idea of a distinctive southern region of America), we have chosen the pallbearers for denominationalism prematurely. If sociology taught any lessons during the past century, it was not to expect social movements to be linear. Many intellectuals considered traditional, antievolutionary Christianity to be dead in the 1920s and again in the 1960s, only to discover it alive and well and even triumphant in Kansas school laws by the end of the century. We may have made the same mistake with denominationalism. Americans change religious direction as often as they do trendy restaurants. And if denominationalism does, in fact, represent American's most important contribution to world religion, it may be that the forces that nurtured such subcultural Christianity will prove more resilient and resourceful than we imagine. If, as the cliché goes, one generation's heresy is the next generation's orthodoxy, the following generation may rediscover the original heresy. And that is just what denominational pluralism was in the early days of the American nation: a diverse, even radical way by which different ethnic groups and small bodies of dissenters understood God. To those who value religious freedom, tolerance, and separation of church and state, the idea of a transdenominational national religion (be it liberal, fundamentalist, or Pentecostal), rooted in theological "truth" rather than in ethnic or regional identity, sends chills down the spine.

That fact makes a recent book edited by Robert Bruce Mullin and Russell E. Rickey, entitled *Reimaging Denominationalism: Interpretive Essays,* both stimulating and instructive, for it offers a blueprint for a different kind of denominational history for a different kind of denominational world. For members embarrassed by the cultural and political compromises of their churches, this new kind of history reminds one of the way Christianity created new opportunities for women and blacks. Religious spheres were often more open to them than public schools, colleges, or secular society in general. Such histories document that the Civil Rights Movement, like abolitionism before it, owed as much to churches as universities, as much to ordinary believers as to ministerial elites. As Nancy T. Ammerman perceptively observes, a church may be officially connected to a denomination but draws its essence from its community of believers. Her organizational chart is less like a traditional denominational hierarchy and more like a fragile spider web, with complex linkages and hard-to-reconstruct parts, sometimes leading to denominational headquarters but other times to diverse community institutions. Attention paid to doctrine, ritual, belief, discipline, practice, and behavior yields rich insights into complex class and gender relationships. Church members, after all, live both in communities of faith and in secular socioeconomic communities.[5]

The best example of such practical denominationalism may be the Church of Christ, where each congregation is fiercely independent of all central authority. Southern Baptists (SBC) rate a close second, despite attempts by various ideological groups to enforce conformity. Even some national SBC agencies resist control by denominational bureaucrats. A good example is the fully autonomous Woman's Missionary Union, which voluntarily cooperates with the SBC but refuses to allow SBC officials to appoint officers or make decisions for the agency. Individual Baptist churches simply ignore decisions made by their annual state and national conventions unless they concur with the decisions. For instance, hundreds of Southern Baptist churches ordain women deacons and/or ministers despite official rejection of such policy as contrary to scripture. Yet these churches often retain membership in Baptist associations, state conventions, and even the national SBC, which have officially rejected such interpretations. These dissident Baptist churches may be more attuned to other denominational models or even to secular culture when it comes to defining the roles of women in contemporary society than they are to fellow Baptists. And more conservative Baptists often grumble that such "liberal Baptists" (probably one of the most obvious oxymorons in contemporary religious discourse) take their cues more from their culture than from scripture.

In another essay from the same anthology, Jan Shipps emphasizes that the shift away from ecclesiastical and institutional history toward people history energizes denominational history just as it does secular history. Focus on women, minorities, lay people, and examinations of who exercises power and at whose expense should not preclude older ways of understanding but can certainly enrich them.[6]

Shipps could have added also that new kinds of people are now writing denominational history. Once upon a time, virtually all such histories were written by "insiders," members of the group about which they wrote. However objective, even critical, they were, their stories were still fashioned within a faith commitment. Now it is increasingly likely that an "outsider" will be equally fascinated by the story of a group of religious people, how they made sense out of their faith, how they related it to social reality, how they expressed it politically, how it determined their sense of community, and how it differed from other Christian expressions of faith.

Those are essentially the considerations that brought me to a thirty-five year exploration of Alabama Baptists. As an "insider" professional historian with a longtime "lover's quarrel" with my denomination, I was determined to write a different kind of denominational history. I focused on bivocational ministers at the forks of the creeks as well as state convention presidents. Prominent laity who significantly influenced Alabama politics and culture interested me as much as pastors. Women made up more than half the members and were often feisty and discontented with male leadership. But not always, and some females were as hierarchical in their conception of society as the most conservative males. Blacks made up a majority of members of many Alabama Baptist churches for a quarter of the denomination's history. And when they left, they created a separate, often contradictory civil religion. Whereas black Baptists interpreted scripture as a revolutionary document endorsing social justice, white Baptists interpreted the same scripture as a conservative document favoring racial segregation. On neither theology nor politics did Alabama Baptists reach easy consensus. And if we are forced to divide historians into "lumpers," who are inclined to see homogeneity, and "splitters," who focus on heterogeneity, I confess an inclination toward the splitters. (That may, in fact, be a generic Baptist trait!)

From my more than three-decades-long examination of a single denomination (albeit an important one) in a single southern state (although an endlessly fascinating one), I offer the following observations about the new denominational history.[7]

Both internal and external constructions of denominational history contain advantages and disadvantages. Outsiders often perceive meaning that insiders miss. But insiders know and understand certain things by intuition and long experience. They are not as easily misled by rhetoric and official pronouncements that point in one direction while consistent actions point in an opposite one. I understand instinctively and from long personal experience that Alabama Baptists often function like a family when they fight. A nonfamily member observing such squabbles might conclude that the family is dysfunctional and cannot survive. Yet members make up or simply agree to disagree, or somehow muddle along, focusing instead on those beliefs and policies that unite them. Like families, Baptists would probably be happier if they were more unified. But for the sake of past and future generations, they compromise rather than divorce.

Authors, whether they come from inside or outside, have to decide whether they are going to focus on the denomination's external relationship to social and cultural institutions or the internal meaning of the denomination to its adherents, or to some mixture of the two. For instance, black Baptists are related to each other by certain beliefs and traditions such as baptism of believers by immersion. They may also be divided from each other by class, gender, or educational differences. Yet these differences often seem insignificant as members bond in sacred fraternity against the crippling external blows of racism and discrimination. The Christianity that saves them also binds them together and profoundly increases their sense of self-worth and community amidst an exterior world that often demeans and patronizes them. Should the historian, then, focus on their internal disagreements or their remarkable sense of community? Determining how and why people find meaning in identifying with a certain form of Christianity is quite a different matter than examining how that form of Christianity relates to the larger society. Both are important and few denominational histories have successfully retained proper balance between them.

Religion can be viewed from many vantage points: from the perspective of an individual's relationship to God; from the view of a congregation's place within a specific community; as a collective denominational experience that transcends both individual and community; as a mixture of all these. Many historians feel exceedingly uncomfortable describing an inner world of spirituality. Early-nineteenth-century religious journals and newspapers are filled with deathbed affirmations of faith and admonitions to loved ones to repent so that families may be reunited in heaven. Conversion testimonials were a central part of revivalism. Women's diaries contain soul-searching accounts of temptation, sin, repentance, and conversion. Yet many historians avoided such profoundly important evidence either because it was so familiar (insider historians) or so incomprehensible (outsider historians). The result was an American public that, outside the evangelical/Pentecostal communities, had not a clue what Jimmy Carter meant during the 1976 presidential campaign when he proclaimed himself to be a "born-again" Christian. Most historians continue to be much more comfortable examining the threads that bind Christians to society than with those that connect them to God.

Denominations do not exist in a vacuum. They have their being within a specific social and cultural context. They have identities that are shaped by their interaction with this broader culture. Alabama Baptists cannot be understood outside the broader scope of Alabama and southern constructions of race, gender, and class. Does religion conform to or transform the larger culture? Or does it accomplish a little of both? There are many religious subcultures as well. And within denominations these subcultures (fundamentalist, moderate, even liberal) thrive within their separate spheres, sometimes quiescent and other times in stormy conflict. To use a contemporary term, it is possible to be politically correct (to affirm positions because they are considered fashionable or even essential within one's group) nationally, within a state, or even within a denomination. And the political correctness of one group may be quite out of step with the political correctness of a different group, although no less influenced by demands for group identity and groupthink. If one desires to be a good Southern Baptist, for instance, it is useful to accept certain politically correct beliefs about the submissiveness of married women to their godly husbands. In the context, perhaps, of political correctness among faculty of a large, secular research university, such feminine submission might render the same person a source of ridicule.

No denomination does everything equally well. Some are better at evangelism than at social ministries. Others offer compelling worship but do not do so well at evangelism. Each tends to do best what it most highly values. Usually denominations pay lip service to all elements of Christianity but specialize in a few.

Historians have every right to judge a denomination by what it says it values and by how what it says measures up with how it acts. But they have no right to superimpose their own assumptions about what denominations ought to value. This recognition will keep denominational history from being a triumphant narrative on one hand or a sociological satire on the other. No institution is entirely faithful to its highest purposes—not even university faculties. They can be self-serving and engage in petty turf battles just like churches. Denominations should be held to human and not divine standards of judgment. People are complex and flawed; so are the denominations they form.

Denominational history, if done properly, allows us to test macro-historical theories in micro-historical settings. Examples abound from my own work:

1. How were early-nineteenth-century evangelicals able to reconcile Calvinist theology and revivalist practice?

2. Was church discipline a form of punitive, puritanical exclusion or a search for the compassionate standards necessary to maintain sacred community?

3. Was the formal exclusion of women from positions of ministerial leadership matched by their informal disfranchisement within the church? If so, how were women able to feminize church discipline and other aspects of denominational life?

4. How did diverse individual congregations function within more centralized denominational structures?

5. How did an ostensibly democratic denomination fashion hierarchical leadership structures dominated by professional male ministerial elites?

6. Was the prevailing relationship of the denomination to its culture one of Christ against culture, Christ within culture, or Christ outside/beyond culture? Did these relationships change over time? If so, why?

7. How did the denomination decide what political causes were moral, and thus deserving of energetic attention, and which were political, and thus requiring avoidance as potentially divisive, disruptive, and inappropriate for religious comment?

8. How and why did Baptists become the "Catholic church of the South"?

9. Were the roots of fundamentalism among Baptists largely theological, sociological, temperamental, racial, political, or some combination of all these?

10. How did individual Baptists, as opposed to the denomination, relate to the larger political culture?

11. How much internal diversity (theological, political, class, racial, sexual) did the denomination tolerate? Did this level of tolerance change over time? If so, how and why?

Finally, the historian's context must be a consideration, insider or outsider. Can the author find anything bad to say about the groups or theologies with which she agrees and anything good about those she opposes? Another way of phrasing this question is to ask if the historian can transcend personal preferences and ideological assumptions. We all know what the answer to that question ought to be. But we also know how few historians measure up to that ideal. Which is to say that historians are the perfect people to write denominational history because they are as flawed as the subjects about which they write.

Notes

1. Henry F. May, "The Recovery of American Religious History," *American Historical Review* 70, (Oct. 1964): 79.

2. An incomplete list of seminal books that cross denominational lines to recapture an earlier mode and language of grasping "ultimate reality" would certainly include the following: John B. Boles, *The Great Revival, 1787–1805: The Origins of the Southern Evangelical Mind* (Lexington: Univ. Press of Kentucky, 1972); Dickson D. Bruce Jr., *And They All Sang Hallelujah: Plain-Folk Camp-Meeting*

Religion, 1800–1845 (Knoxville: Univ. of Tennessee Press, 1974); Jean E. Friedman, *The Enclosed Garden: Women and Community in the Evangelical South, 1830–1900* (Chapel Hill: Univ. of North Carolina Press, 1985); R. Marie Griffith, *God's Daughters: Evangelical Women and the Power of Submission* (Berkeley: Univ. of California Press, 1997); David Edwin Harrell Jr., *All Things Are Possible: The Healing and Charismatic Revivals in Modern America* (Bloomington: Indiana Univ. Press, 1975); Christine Leigh Heyrman, *Southern Cross: The Beginnings of the Bible Belt* (New York: Alfred A. Knopf, 1997); E. Brooks Hollifield, *The Gentlemen Theologians: American Theology in Southern Culture, 1795–1860* (Durham, NC: Duke Univ. Press, 1978); Donald G. Mathews, *Religion in the Old South* (Chicago: Univ. of Chicago Press, 1977); Ted Ownby, *Subduing Satan: Religion, Recreation, and Manhood in the Rural South, 1865–1920* (Chapel Hill: Univ. of North Carolina Press, 1990); and Charles Reagan Wilson, *Baptized in Blood: The Religion of the Lost Cause, 1865–1920* (Athens: Univ. of Georgia Press, 1980).

3. Henry Warner Bowden, "The Death and Rebirth of Denominational History," in *Reimagining Denominationalism: Interpretive Essays*, ed. Robert Bruce Mullin and Russell E. Rickey (New York: Oxford Univ. Press, 1994), 21–24.

4. John F. Wilson, "A New Denominational Historiography?" *Religion and American Culture: A Journal of Interpretation* 5, (Summer 1995): 249.

5. See Nancy T. Ammerman, "Denominations: Who and What Are We Studying," in *Reimagining Denominationalism*, ed. Mullin and Rickey, 134–61.

6. Jan Shipps, "Remembering, Recovering, and Inventing What Being the People of God Means: Reflections on Method in the Scholarly Writing of Denominational History," in *Reimagining Denominationalism*, ed. Mullin and Rickey, 180–83.

7. Wayne Flynt, *Alabama Baptists: Southern Baptists in the Heart of Dixie* (Tuscaloosa: Univ. of Alabama Press, 1998).

CHAPTER 5

Imagining Race and Religion in Louisiana: Kasi Lemmons's *Eve's Bayou* and Barbara Hambly's Benjamin January Novels

In the film *Live and Let Die*, James Bond faces a master criminal (what else?) who has at his command a voodoo priest. Betrayed by his medium, Solitaire, the villain gives her to the voodoo priest for sacrifice. At the climax of the film, the voodoo priest (played by African American dancer Geoffrey Holder) rises from the grave. He is Baron Cemetery, also called Baron Samedi, he of the white face and glasses. He threatens Solitaire, who is bound between two posts for sacrifice. He dances with a big snake (Damballa) as frenzied black people move in the scene. This scene of the dangerous black man—with a big snake—threatening the helpless white woman repeats images from *The Klansman* and *Birth of a Nation* and is the image of voodoo: black, uncontrollable sexuality, power from the dark side, black people out of control of whites and turning in violence against them.

The reality was and is something different. Gayraud Wilmore in *Black Religion and Black Radicalism* is right in arguing that voodoo—or vodou, as it is most properly called—was bound up with resistance. He argues that the "violent impulses released by such a religion" were bound to be turned against the "real enemy in vindictiveness and revenge" as they were in Haiti. That spiritual force for liberation that is voodoo did liberate Haiti from slaveholders, and it created an exodus of slave masters, with their slaves, into south Louisiana where Haitian voodoo met the Creole, and in that particular and peculiar location, voodoo transformed once again.[1]

There is, in Louisiana, a division between the northern part, which is like the rest of the American South, largely Protestant, and the southern part, which, though a mixture, is Catholic in orientation and which retains, despite its Americanness, a unique culture. A significant element of this culture is the Creole. Creoles, as James D. Hardy Jr. points out, are "a particular," even a peculiar people. They are the descendants of the imperial French, predominantly, but also the imperial Spanish structures that governed pre–Louisiana Purchase Louisiana. Geographically, they are now located in the Gulf South, "from the Cane River valley in northern Louisiana to the New Orleans area and east towards Pensacola."[2] The uniqueness and complexity of this cultural remnant intensified in New Orleans (founded in 1718) as Creoles mixed racially with African slaves, Senegalese brought by the Company of the Indies.[3] Indeed, this mixture created, in New Orleans particularly, but also elsewhere in Louisiana, a second particular class, the *gens libres de couleur,* or free people of color. These free people of color are the subject of the two popular examinations of Louisiana culture and religion I will consider here: Kasi Lemmons's film *Eve's Bayou,* the most successful independent film of 1997, and Barbara Hambly's novels about a free man of color, Benjamin January (or "Janvier" in Creole). In particular, I will discuss *Graveyard Dust,* in which January and Marie Laveau, the queen of New Orleans voodoo, join together to free Ben's sister from prison.

I. Who or What Is a Creole?

Who is a Creole?

This has always been and remains a question. The *Harvard Encyclopedia of American Ethnic Groups* argues that "Louisianans of French and Spanish descent began referring to themselves as Creole following the Louisiana Purchase (1803) in order to distinguish themselves from the Anglo-Americans who started to move into Louisiana at this time. The indigenous whites adopted the term, insisting, most unhistorically, that it be applied exclusively to them." In the twentieth century, the definition continues, "Creole most often refers to the Louisiana Creoles of color."[4] In her classic essay "People of Color in Louisiana" (1917), Alice Moore Dunbar-Nelson, herself a Creole Louisianan, suggests the same conflict:

> It is in the definition of the word Creole that another
> great difficulty arises. The native white Louisianan will tell
> you that a Creole is a white man, whose ancestors contain
> some French or Spanish blood in their veins. But he will
> be disputed by others, who will gravely tell you that

Creoles are to be found only in the lower Delta lands of the state, that there are no Creoles north of New Orleans; and will raise their hands in horror at the idea of being confused with the "Cajuns" . . . The Caucasian will shudder with horror at the idea of including a person of color in the definition, and the person of color will retort with his definition that a Creole is a native of Louisiana, in whose blood runs mixed strains of everything un-American, with the African strain slightly apparent.[5] Creoles, particularly in New Orleans, often became wealthy, owning property. They had their own schools and orchestras, and they, like the white Creoles, maintained connections with France, where they often sent their children to be educated.[6] Many owned slaves—some their own relatives, whom they later freed.[7]

These free people of color from *mariages de la main gauche* ("left-handed marriages") constituted a third class. They were positioned in the in-between, between master and slave, but at home with neither. They became, therefore, a separate caste, according to Joan M. Martin, "bound by ties of language, birth, culture, religion . . . wealth" and power. They were "distinguished poets, artists, musicians, sculptors, novelists, statesmen, valiant soldiers, humanitarians, and excellent family people."[8]

What is creole?

The creole, as a theoretical term, is celebrated in the postmodern. It is the evidence of mixture and of hybridity. Edouard Glissant, in *Caribbean Discourses: Selected Essays,* is one of the theorists who first introduced this term. Glissant suggests that such an identity is not simply a matter of mixture or difference. It is intimately tied to place and is, therefore, a sign of continuity and "concurrence" and rupture, difference. He describes the creole as exploding oneness, as unfixed and involving multiple discourses. The transfer (not transplantation, which implies continuity) of a people involves their being changed into something different, "into a new set of possibilities." What is created in the process of creolization is a combination of traces of the former life and the encountered culture. Such creativity begins, often, as camouflage and diversion. These creations are not inauthentic when they "lead somewhere"—that is, "when the obstacle for which the detour was made tends to develop into concrete 'possibilities.'"[9] The African Traditional Religions that developed in Louisiana are and offer such possibilities for both survival and for self and cultural definition and understanding. The struggle for both, however, is an intense one, as both Benjamin January and Eve show us.

Barbara Hambly's novels—*A Free Man of Color, Graveyard Dust, Fever Season, Sold Down the River*, and *Die Upon a Kiss*—tell the story of Benjamin January, a free man of color. January is a physician, trained in Paris, and a musician. He is the son of Livia Lavesque, a free woman of color who is placed to a Creole sugar broker. January's father, however, was a slave, pure African, whom January barely remembers. January, in the first three novels, does not know his father's name. January moves on the boundaries of several structures. He is dark-skinned and half-African but free (a situation that was not uncommon in Louisiana). He is a physician, one who began his desire to heal on the plantation, learning traditional medicine from Mambo Jeanne, but he cannot practice in New Orleans because of the color of his skin. He earns his living playing piano. Ben is Catholic, but his sister Olympe, daughter of the African father and called Olympia Snakebones, is a voodoo practitioner.

January is haunted by memory. His wife, Ayesha, an Algerian Muslim, died of cholera in their Paris apartment. January, who found her, is still grieving. He remembers the smell of sickness and the first sight of her: "Some part of him, he thought, would never recover from that. Some part of him would always be trapped in that moment, like a ghost returning to repeat endlessly one single action in the same corner of the same house forever: opening the door and finding her. Opening the door and finding her."[10]

Just as January is poised between past and present, so is New Orleans. The novels are set at a significant historical moment: just after the Louisiana Purchase. Polite Louisiana Creole society is being invaded by the "Americans," whom they see as crude and uncultured. Grace King, in "New Orleans, the Place and the People," confirms this. "Americans," she writes, "were despised and ridiculed."[11] Americans who came down river found a diverse city. Dunbar-Nelson tells us: "Writers describing the New Orleans of this period agree in presenting a picture of a continental city, most picturesque, most un-American, and as varied in color as a street of Cairo. There they saw French, Spaniards, English, Bohemians, Negroes, mulattoes; varied clothes, picturesque white dresses of the fairer women, brilliant colors of the darker ones. The streets, banquettes, we should say, were bright with color, the nights filled with song and laughter."[12]

The Americans were horrified by the Creoles, too. Carolyn Morrow Long, in *Spiritual Merchants: Religion, Magic, and Commerce*, writes,

> At the time of the Louisiana Purchase in 1803, the population of New Orleans was French-speaking, Catholic, and a majority had some degree of African blood. The people regardless of color, realized that *les Americains* would eventually destroy their way of life.

The new Anglo-Protestant American citizens viewed
Catholicism as idolatry and looked upon the white Creoles
as indolent, uneducated, and lacking in business sense.
They were horrified by the free-and-easy character and
racial mixture of local society, the permissiveness of
Louisiana slavery, and by the autonomy of free people of
color. Under the Americans, slavery became much more
harsh and the rights of colored Creoles were eroded.[13]

What the Americans do is to begin to challenge the definitions and distinctions that governed Creole society. For example, there was (and, underground, still is) in Creole society a strict hierarchy governing mixture. Hambly describes it this way: ". . . *mulatto* for one white, one black parent; *griffe* or *sambo* for the child of a mulatto and a full black; *quadroon* for the child of a mulatto and a full white; *octoroon* for a quadroon's child by a full white; *musterfino* or *mameloque* for an octoroon's child by a full white."[14] Hambly says that she found that Creoles label each other according to how long families have lived in the city and so on. New Orleans, therefore, was a place that worked on a kind of caste system "fiercely adhered to."[15] Indeed, such mathematically calculated determinations of race continued in Louisiana until 1983.[16] In this configuration, "Americans," Hambly writes, echoing Dunbar-Nelson, "simply did not count."[17]

The Americans, however, do count. Hambly shows us how their presence threatens the delicacies that keep both intimate and public things in place. For example, for the Americans black is black, with no nuance. Under American influence, legal restrictions on black Creoles increased.[18] What the Americans who come down the river bring, therefore, is an intensification of the constant threat of violence and of being kidnapped into slavery under which black people live. January, with his dark skin, feels this pressure. He keeps copies of his papers in a variety of places, and a recurring scene is one in which January is with a white person and another white man assumes he is for sale.

If black Creole culture moved in the space between black and white, women who practiced African traditional religions moved between the in-between. Voodoo queen Marie Laveau was such a figure, creating the "possibilities" that Glissant highlights as important to the Creole. Barbara Rosendale Duggal characterizes her this way:

Laveau is said to have traveled the streets of New
Orleans as though she owned them, counseled the socially
elite of both sexes, won every case she took to court,
influenced city policy, borne fifteen children, grown rich,
and died in bed (though legends hold she was reborn

young again to reign as queen some twenty years more), all as a woman of color in the ante- and postbellum South. In the nineteenth century, a time when women of all races and classes endured legally as well as socially sanctioned sexual oppression, this is remarkable.[19]

January says, "She listened, and she remembered, and she cared."[20] She is a kind of principle of movement in the city, one who constantly crosses boundaries. January describes her this way: "She knew everything, they said. She read your dreams. More to the point, January knew she listened to everything, watched everything." Interacting with everyone from market women and rag pickers to slaves of bankers, and acting as a hairdresser to white and colored, she moves on all levels in the city. "She was queen of secrets," Ben concludes, "And this was not all she was."[21]

Laveau was the recognized leader of New Orleans voodoo from 1846 until her death. Indeed, she was so powerful that she is said to be eternally young. Scholars speculate that this eternal youth is because her daughter became the second Marie Laveau.[22] She was a priestess of Damballa, the snake god. Damballa is symbolic of the umbilical cord and/or the rainbow. According to John Blassingame, "In Africa Damballa was sometimes the god of fertility and the determiner of good and ill fortune."[23] Zora Neale Hurston says that Damballa is the "highest and most powerful of all the gods, the *great source.*"[24] Damballa is also known as Damballa Wedo or Li Grand Zombi.

Laveau, it has been argued, further creolized voodoo—an already creole form, a mixture of African traditional religion and the Catholicism that slaves encountered. That Christianity, Carolyn Morrow Long argues, was full of folk magical beliefs, the use of charms, veneration of saints, and belief in spirits, along with a veneration for the ancestors. The European "vast, interconnected universe" of spirit and natural world met the African one.[25] They were not that different. Laveau was instrumental in making a further development in voodoo—making it more Catholic, maintaining its external form but infusing it with a slightly different meaning in an Americanized New Orleans.

The arrest of Ben's sister puts him in an, at first, undesired union with Marie Laveau. As Ben works to free his sister, we see embodied in him the conflict and eventual reconciliation between the African traditional religion, the voodoo of Marie Laveau, and the Catholic Church. "Graveyard dust," which gives the novel its title, indicates a cursing to the death, the intent to maim and kill, and it is this curse that Ben will undo.[26] Graveyard dust, however, can also be positively powerful: it evokes the power of the dead, so it can connect us to the ancestors.[27]

We are made aware, in the opening of the novel, of the African rhythms that sound underneath the European orchestra music of Creole New Orleans.

Carolyn M. Jones

This rhythm, feared by planters and therefore outlawed, calls to something deep in Ben. As he leaves the ball for which he is playing and enters the darkness, he feels the eyes of the *loa* on him:

> Papa Legba, guardian of all gates and doors,
> warden of the crossroad.
> Beautiful Ezili, in all her many forms.
> Zombi-Damballah, the Serpent King
> Ogu of the sword and the fire . . .
> And the Baron Samedi, the Baron Cemetery,
> boneyard god grinning through the darkness. . . .[28]

Wandering from the party at which he is playing, January finds the veves, drawn with rum and blood, and graveyard dust—in this case, a curse. January has decided that he cannot maintain the balance that many of his fellow African-descended peoples do. He cannot be, he thinks, a child of God and a friend of the *loa*. As he is drawn into the mystery of the disappearance of Isaac Jumon, however, he finds that he is both: that while he loves God, the *loa* also love him.

January begins to find himself under threat of someone trying to "fix" him as he works to free his sister. For example, someone makes a cross at his threshold and leaves a severed chicken foot in the middle of his bed. Though January considers himself intellectually beyond being disturbed by this—he is a Catholic with an Enlightenment education —he goes to Marie Laveau, who identifies the practitioner. Laveau offers January a medicine bag or "luck ball," a tricken bag, to wear: "'Will you wear this?' she asked. 'Give it a name, but don't tell anyone what that name is; wear it next to your skin, under your right armpit, and take it out every now and then and give a drink of whisky. It'll keep you safe.'"[29] Such a charm has a spirit of its own and certain rules the wearer must observe for the charm to work.[30]

For January, such a charm is for those who are afraid. Voodoo is a reminder of the fear and helplessness that is constitutive of slavery. All a slave can do, particularly a child, as January was, "with no strength to meet a capricious world," is to use what power he has to control the world. January believes that such action is a betrayal of God, a mistrust of God's goodness and power. Laveau tries to explain to him that God made the "jack honeysuckle and verbena, with the power to uncross any that's crossed" —in other words, that God is not only transcendent but also immanent. But January cannot accept this.[31]

What Marie Laveau represents is what Karen McCarthy Brown articulates *in Mama Lola: A Vodou Priestess in Brooklyn*. Vodou, Brown writes, is a "this-worldly" religion. The vodou spirits embody contradiction. They represent the "powers at work in and on human life" and are able to contain "conflicting emotions and to model the opposing ways of being in the world." African Traditional Religions are those of people who have not had the luxury of illusions about power.

An open-eyed acceptance of finitude, which is central to the religion, is one reason that the Vodou spirits have emerged as whole, three-dimensional characters. The oppressed are the most practiced analysts of human character and behavior, and Haitian traditional religion is the repository for wisdom accumulated by a people who have lived through slavery, hunger, disease, repression, corruption, and violence—all in excess.[32]

Such a religion operates in the social and natural worlds but has its focus, Brown contends, in the "social arena," the most problematic area in a slave's or ex-slave's life. What African traditional religion does is keep energy flowing, moving as Laveau moves through New Orleans society. When energy moves, things "heat up," and transformation and healing can occur: barriers come down, impediments are cleared, and life moves.[33]

It is using excess to counter excess that disturbs January. He has watched his sister dance and give in to the sexual desire the dancing generates. For January, voodoo generates what the church prohibits: desire, particularly sexual desire. As he watches Laveau dance in Congo Square, however, he must acknowledge her power. Laveau herself makes a distinction between true voodoo and hoodoo and juju, those forms practiced by those practitioners who supply curses for individual clients, for example, and who, if not upright, take advantage of others for money.[34] This power to fight and to harm, as January thinks, is a place for hate to go. He cannot distinguish it from what Laveau is trying to tell him. For him, what she practices represents only an illusion, if a necessary one: "A place to pretend you were free. A place to forget . . . it was a place to hide your mind in, when the pain got too bad."[35]

That, too, the *loa* understand and are, as Laveau tells him: "Sometimes you need to hate, until the hate's all gone. . . . Until you see for yourself what a waste of time it is. The *loa* understand that, the way the saints sometimes don't."[36] What the *loa* really are, Laveau suggests, are those who remain, even in the Hell of slavery, and those who remember. They say, *"We didn't get left behind in Africa. We're here with you on the ships, on the ocean, in this land. We remember your names and what you were about, you and your parents and your children."*[37] As such, they offer another face of God, a spiritual power that is not the master's power and a power other than the Enlightenment self, for whom "God's face [is] like [one's] own in the mirror."[38]

Faces, January finds, are many. As he enters deeper into the mystery of Jumon's disappearance, he enters more deeply the world of the *loa*. For example, at a voodoo ceremony in the cipriere, January encounters Baron Cemetery, who is "riding" one of the participants. Baron Cemetery is like Papa Guede,

Carolyn M. Jones

the boisterous and burlesque, temperamental, and whimsical god of Haitian peasants. He is the lord of the dead, the ruler of the cemetery, but he is also the god of doctors and points out what roots are to be used and how.[39] He may well be January's *loa*.

Baron Cemetery lets January know that he has been watching him and that while January, acting as a doctor, has cheated the Baron of his prey, January the musician, who plays the ivories, the bones, of the piano, pleases him: "But you know, I just kind of like a man what got a way with bones." Hambly continues, "And he mimed playing the piano again, this time down his own chest, as if his fingers danced down the empty ribs of the animate skeleton that was the Baron's true form."[40] The Baron tells January that Jumon is not dead—that he does not have him. Later, January encounters the man, now spent from his encounter with the god. He asks what the man meant, but those around the man say that he does not remember anything, that the *loa* had him.

The climax of the novel is one in which human and spiritual agents bring about an end. January and Marie Laveau enter the bayou to find a house where Jumon is being held. Laveau, who handles the serpent Damballah, tells the snakes not to strike, though she will later have them strike Dr. Yellowjacket, the hoodoo man who is part of the plot and who has kidnapped Olympe's son. Yellowjacket throws a powder into the fire in the house, and January is overcome by the smoke. He either hallucinates or begins to see the *loa*.

As January rescues Jumon, he encounters again Baron Cemetery, who demands payment. A young man, Pedro, has been shot by someone who is trying to kill January, and January must pay for his death. January promises to pay the Baron. At that promise, his own *loa* comes to help him. Papa Legba tells January where Yellowjacket is: "'He'll head north across Bayou Metarie,' said Papa Legba, leaning against the corner of the house with his keys in his belt and his pipe in his hand. He jerked with the pipe to show the direction."[41]

Later, when January feels that he will not make it to save his nephew, the voice of Papa Legba assures him that he will make it. January looks up and realizes that Legba is with him: "January thought he glimpsed the old man in the mists again, though now he looked more like the battered old statue of St. Peter at the back of St. Anthony's Chapel. Heaven's keys dangling from his belt. His face was black rather than white."[42] As January rushes to save his nephew, he prays both to "Papa Legba, lord of bridges" and the Virgin Mary. Then, something happens. As Yellowjacket tries to escape, Baron Cemetery appears to Yellowjacket: "Just for an instant, January thought he saw clearly the silhouette in the darkness and the fog: thought he saw the outline of a top hat, the gleam of spectacles, the white glimmer of bones."[43] Yellowjacket, in fear, throws himself in the water. As January runs to help him, the shape comes from the mists. It is Marie Laveau, who strikes the final blow. The snakes, to whom she sends a message, strike him. Laveau does not let him die; she draws out the poison, but January's nephew Gabriel is the voice that confirms her power:

> "The Grand Zombi's her friend," said the boy . . . Without
> a trace of surprise . . . "Course all the snakes in the bayou
> would go after Yellowjacket, once she told them to. He
> was really stupid to try and swim."[44]

Was it Laveau or was it the *loa*? Was January feeling the effects of the poison in the smoke or did he experience the power of the *loa*? Those questions, January has to resolve for himself.

January, at the end of *Graveyard Dust*, finds that he can be a child of God and a friend of the *loa*. The bayou in the night, the dancing and ecstatic power of the *loa*, finally, are not January's mode. Indeed, those become, in the later part of the nineteenth century mere tourist attractions. Like organized voodoo, which goes underground, January reaches a private understanding. He returns to church. He contemplates, as he moves into the church, words from the Gospel of Luke: "In my father's house, there are many mansions." He goes to the rear of the church, to the statue of Saint Peter:

> An old man in a robe, with a beard and a bunch of keys.
> As January knelt at the rear bench, self-conscious and a
> little embarrassed, he noticed two or three pralines, a slice
> of pound cake, and a couple of cigars had been left on the
> base of the statue; another slice of pound cake and a dozen
> or more silver half-reale bits were tucked into the corners
> behind the railing. *To let those still in fear know that prayers
> do get heard.*[45]

January thinks that in the many mansions of the Father's house, there may be many manifestations of god, even the top hat and spectacles of Baron Cemetery. "Why wouldn't," he thinks, "God like the smell of rum and cigars as well as that of incense?" With that he prays his rosary, but he also leaves a piece of pound cake at the feet of St. Peter, who is also Lebga. He says simply, "Thank you."[46]

II. Eve's Bayou

What January's experience confirms is that we are not alone. Who is acting—the human being or the god? What he finds is that both are, and in many different spaces and in every aspect of human life. The question of who is acting is central to *Eve's Bayou* as well. Kasi Lemmons's gorgeous film is set south of New Orleans, perhaps in Plaquemines Parish, in the late 1950s or early 1960s. There, the Gulf of Mexico and the Mississippi River mingle, making brackish water. This mixed water is a place of mixed people. The film has been compared to other coming-of-age stories, including *To Kill A Mockingbird*. It has been called southern gothic and has been both praised and criticized for its stylized presentation of the lives of the Batiste women. It is about a family poised for change. Their lives seem static and enclosed—we are surprised to see buses and trains in the story—in an almost nineteenth-century mode, in an America poised for the civil rights movement and change.

In their genres, Barbara Hambly and Kasi Lemmons are as good as Toni Morrison, for example, is in hers at showing us the casual violence that slavery and racism mean—particularly against women. Sexuality is the tool of exploitation. What Hambly is so good at showing us is that this exploitation was part of the ordinary, the everyday. Our modern outrage would have surprised an eighteenth- or nineteenth-century man who ordered a woman on the block • to strip down and show herself, or a planter sending for a woman from the slave quarters or sending his son there, or an overseer keeping a slave tied to a bed for his pleasure.

Hambly juxtaposes the violence against enslaved black women to the violence in the *placée* system. At quadroon balls (which took place near and at the same time as Creole balls), Creole girls' mothers (usually *placée* themselves) barter and contract to "place" their daughters with a wealthy Creole for security and property for their children and grandchildren.[47] Hambly writes,

> The ladies of Rue des Ramparts implicitly understood the price they would have to pay.
> To have a wealthy lover, but not a husband.
> To love, maybe, and have love, but never to be secure in that love.
> To bequeath to her children the property and education that they might not otherwise have. And with that property and education, to bequeath the fairer skin that altered the way people looked at you, white and black and colored alike.[48]

These relationships, therefore, were important but also precarious for the women. Since these were not legal marriages, Joan M. Martin confirms, the woman "lived with the fact that she lacked the social and legal protection inherent in marriage." Indeed, the man could leave the relationship at any time, particularly once he married. Ben January's sister Minou faces this in the novels. Also, though the man was legally obligated to take care of his children, he was not obligated to be a true father, and his families would not interact. Many women and children, according to Martin, "were denied the familial closeness of the paternal relations."[49] These "left-handed marriages" were advantageous, however. Violet Harrington Bryan tells us of Eugene Macarty, of one of the most powerful of South Louisiana families, who left his *placee*, referred to as "Mrs. Macarty," property worth $12,000. He had lived with her forty-nine years (1796–1845). She herself was a descendent of another powerful family, the Mandevilles. When she died in 1848, her estate was worth $155,000.[50]

A few critics of the film *Eve's Bayou* wondered how these African American people had so much money. The answer is that they are Creole, educated, and property-owning, like Mrs. Macarty. The town, Eve tells us in the film's opening voice-over, is named after a slave; later, we see the words "Eve's Bayou" on a bus marker. A slave woman, Eve saved General Jean-Paul Batiste from cholera. He freed her and gave her land. They had sixteen children. The *loa* that governs this family, I think, is Erzulie Freda. She is, Zora Neale Hurston says, "the pagan goddess of love," and "the ideal of the love bed."[51] She is a beautiful mulatto woman, like Roz Batiste. She is a goddess who is loving to men but "implacable" to women: "No girl will gain a husband if an altar to Erzulie is in the house."[52] Erzulie has no children—like Mozelle Batiste—only husbands. She is a jealous spirit. In her love song is mentioned "General Jean Baptiste," echoing the ancestor of the Batiste family in the film.[53] Through the women in the line Eve's power is passed most strongly, but like Benjamin January and his sister Olympe, Louis Batiste and his sister Mozelle are both healers.

Louis is a physician, and Mozelle is a psychic counselor, healer, and, sometimes, voodoo practitioner. They are, Mozelle tells us, just alike. Louis can be understood as having accepted Western modalities of power in contrast to his sister, who mixes the indigenous and the West. Louis, I think, mimics his male ancestor. In his white suit and carrying his bag, Louis moves through the town like General Batiste must have moved in earlier times, in ownership and without any check: all women are his. Mozelle, in contrast, is contained, in a sense. She has lost three husbands; one is shot by a lover just as Mozelle realizes she loves him. Louis is sleeping with many of his female patients. His infidelity is the open secret of the family, and it warps his relationships, particularly with his daughters. Cecily, the eldest child, ultimately accuses her father of an attempted incest, and that accusation makes Eve turn from him and "fix" him, she believes, to death. The film begins, "The summer I killed my father I was ten years old."

The Batistes are a death-haunted family. Mozelle's threat to all, including Eve, is "I will kill you" or "I will do you harm." When Eve teases her sister about starting her period, Cecily responds by trying to choke Eve and has to be pulled off her. Later, when Cecily leaves the family, Eve feels that she will die. Mozelle, who cannot have children, believes that she is cursed. Though she marries Julian Gray Raven at the end of the film, she believes that he will die, like her other husbands, and only hopes that she may go with him. Sex and death, so connected in human psychology and in religious understanding, are linked intimately here. Eve's "fall" from innocence is witnessing her father's infidelity, an infidelity that will lead to his death. The need for love—desire, *eros*—drives the Batistes, particularly the love of the father and the desire to possess him utterly. That need must go back, as the film's emphasis on memory suggests, to the "original" father, the French general who, with the first Eve, fathers the line. Mozelle is not sure what the drive is towards, besides meaningless death. As Cecily leaves the family, Mozelle muses: "There must be a point to it all. It's just over my head. . . . Sometimes I think there is no point at all and that's the point. . . . No one leaves this earth without feeling terrible pain, and if there is no divine point to it all, that's sad." This thought comes as Eve, feeling pain over her sister, has decided to use voodoo to kill her father. "How do you kill someone with voodoo?" Eve asks. Mozelle demands Eve's hands—touching hands is the way she reads—and what she sees makes her draw back in horror. She tells Eve that you cannot kill people with voodoo, that that is "ridiculous."

Mozelle, though she uses herbal and other remedies, sees herself as a psychic counselor. Like Marie Laveau, she works both from a Christian orientation—praying with her clients before she begins a session—and with voodoo, making charms and spells. For example, she gives one client a chamois tricken bag with lodestone and St. John the Conqueror root to wear.[54] When Eve questions her, Mozelle responds somewhat cynically:

> Eve: You told Daddy you don't practice no voodoo.
> Mozelle: She was desperate.
> Eve: Does it work?
> Mozelle: We'll see . . . I don't think she'll sue me.

Indeed, we find that both Louis, with his pills, and Mozelle are treating the same patients.

Mozelle's gift is also her curse. Mozelle, as much as she can see for others, cannot see her own life. In a magnificent scene, which is echoed in Louis's death later, as we will see, Mozelle tells Eve about the death of her husband Menard. She steps back in time, through a mirror, to show Eve how, when her lover, Hosea, came to the house to take her away, she found that she loved Menard. The moment that she realizes that she loves Menard, Hosea shoots him. Mozelle has lost three husbands and cannot understand why. The desire to know her own future brings Mozelle into contact with Elzora who tells fortunes and sells spells at the farmer's market.

Elzora paints her face white, echoing the figure of Baron Cemetery in *Graveyard Dust,* and uses cat bones to cast fortunes, for which she charges a dollar. When Mozelle and Roz approach her, she tells them what turn out to be related fortunes. She tells Roz that there is an unexpected solution to her problems with Louis, one that she does not imagine. "Sometimes," she says, "a soldier falls on his own sword." She warns Roz to "look to her children." Roz is disappointed in this fortune and wants to leave. Mozelle, however, sees something in Elzora and demands that Elzora tell her fortune. Elzora echoes what Eve sees in a dream just as Harry, Mozelle's third husband, dies in a car that Mozelle is driving. She tells Mozelle that she is a black widow and that she brings death: "Always be true." We are seeing professional jealousy of the same kind between Dr. Yellowjacket and Marie Laveau in *Graveyard Dust.* Later, when Eve approaches Elzora to kill someone, Elzora asks if she is not sure that she wants it to be Mozelle. When Eve says no, Elzora says, "Too bad."

Mozelle recognizes either Elzora's power or her own fear. She runs from her past and passes into a vision of the future. She sees a man walking on tracks. She sees something bearing down on someone and a child scream and fall. Roz, Eve's mother, believes that Mozelle has seen the death of one of her children. Louis says that Mozelle is unstable, that she has been in and out of mental hospitals. But what we come to see, as images of the vision are echoed in Louis's death at the end of the film, is that vision may be clear but human understanding is imperfect. Elements of the vision are present in Louis's death. It is Mr. Mereaux, the husband of Louis's lover, Mattie, who walks down the tracks. A train comes through just as Louis dies, and he pushes Eve out of the way of the gunshot. Eve screams and falls. Mozelle sees, but human understanding is limited. We can know and not know what, know and not be able to tell. Truth, as Eve says at the end of the film, "changes color, depending on the light."

Eve's Bayou raises the same questions as *Graveyard Dust:* who is acting, human beings or the *loa* and God? Eve, in her rage, goes to Elzora to have her father fixed. Elzora tells Eve that "people have a way of dying at their own speed" but says that she will see what she can do. She casts the death spell. She buries Louis's hair in a snake's mouth in a wax coffin in the Batiste plot. Eve is distraught. She wanted, she tells Elzora, a voodoo doll. For her, voodoo, is as Benjamin January realized, a place to put her hurt and anger. Eve wants something that she can control herself. Indeed, we see her practicing sticking pins into a doll, practicing for what she will do. She wants the choice to kill her father, but Elzora tells her that, in bringing his hair, she has already chosen. Her choice to seek out Elzora, to take his hair, to demand his death: these are actions.

We see Eve acting in other ways as well. At the farmer's market, she plants the seed in Mr. Mereaux's mind about his wife and her father. When Eve finds out that the spell is cast, she tries to stop it. She goes to a bar where Louis and Mattie are drinking and begs him to come home with her. Mr. Mereaux comes in drunk and tells Louis, who has been his friend and has betrayed him, that he must not speak to Mattie again. As they leave the bar, Louis, cocky and careless, calls goodnight to Mattie. Mereaux draws a gun, and in a scene that mirrors the death of Mozelle's husband, kills him, as Louis pushes Eve out of the way and as Eve realizes that she loves her father. The death that Mozelle saw in her distress, as she felt cursed, happens here. It is Louis's and Eve's: he loses his life, and Eve loses her innocence. There seems to be a curse on the house.

Does Eve kill Louis, or does he die "at his own speed"? Death does not end his influence. At his funeral, Eve seems to see Elzora in the cemetery, just as January sees Baron Cemetery. This seems to confirm that she is to blame, and she prays the line of the Lord's Prayer that asks for forgiveness of our trespasses. Blame, however, is hard to place. In this Creole family, truth is always mixed.

After Louis's death, Louis seems to understand and to beg for understanding. He communicates to Mozelle in a dream that she should not look back, that she should let the old Mozelle die, and she decides to marry Julian. Louis also sends a message to Eve: "Tell Eve I still owe her that dance," the dance he promises her after the party that begins the film. Eve, touching his things, finds a letter to Mozelle. Louis tells Mozelle, who has confronted him about Cecily, that Cecily kissed him, "like a woman," and that he knocked her to the floor. "Mozelle," he writes, "I would give my life to have that moment back." Perhaps he does give his life, and perhaps he does get the moment back. When he pushes Eve out of the way, it is a redemptive repetition of his pushing, whether in anger or surprise, of Cecily. In this family, moments are lived again and again.

Eve, reading the letter, confronts Cecily, who confesses that she does not know what happened—only that her father hurt her so badly that she wanted to die. Mirroring Mozelle, Eve demands her hands and enters Cecily's memory. All the events are there, but Eve, reliving the moment with her sister and father, cannot see what really happened, what the motivations were, who kissed whom and why. What we do know is that Eve is taking her place as a Batiste woman with sight and power. Recognizing the ambiguity, she sends her father's letter into the bayou, forgiving him, as she embraces her sister, forgiving her.

Our final image is of Eve and Cecily. They stand on a narrow strip of land between two parts of the bayou. They stand between two trees. They are the future, taking their place in the past. Eve concludes not with "When I killed my father" but with "When my father said goodnight," suggesting, as Alice Walker's poem "Goodnight Willie Lee, I'll See You in the Morning" does, that they will be together in the resurrection, in the "great getting up morning." There is, the ending suggests, some meaning beyond the repetition of sex and death that is the Batiste legacy. Telling the story places his actions and hers in the context of the Batiste family and its story, where they are together. She concludes: "We are the daughters of Eve and Jean-Paul Batiste. I was named for her. Like others before me, I have the gift of sight, but the truth changes color, depending on the light, and tomorrow can be clearer than yesterday. Memory is a selection of images, some elusive, others printed indelibly on the brain. Each image is like a thread, each thread woven together to make a tapestry of intricate texture. The tapestry tells a story, and the story is our past."

Conclusions

I want to end with two quotations. The first is from Vincent Harding's *There Is A River: The Black Struggle for Freedom in America*. Harding says that "Bambara, Malinka, Fon, Dinka, Ewe, Bakongo, Ibo, Yoruba, and hundreds more" were loaded onto slave ships. Among them were miners, weavers, potters, metalworkers, tradesmen, herders, farmers, priests, and musicians. Harding continues:

> Now all these histories were jammed into one frightening present, and it was evident that we were being rushed forward into a new history, one which had no real precedent in the countless centuries of our past.[55]

Charles H. Long, in "Perspectives for a Study of Afro-American Religion in the United States" (from his book *Significations*), writes:

> The slaves had to come to terms with the opaqueness of their condition and at the same time oppose it. They had to experience the truth of their negativity and at the same time transform and create an-other reality. Given the limitations imposed upon them, they created on the level of the religious consciousness. Not only did this transformation produce new cultural forms but its significance must be understood from the point of view of the creativity of the transforming process itself.[56]

The two important phrases in these passages—the problem of the "frightening present" and the reality of living in the "transforming process" that combines a double reality—point to W. E. B. DuBois's double consciousness as a reality of African American life. Such "twoness" suggests a unique orientation of the "religious consciousness." Long argues, for example, that to see slaves as becoming Christian in any sense that their white owners understood the meaning of that word is a mistake. Africans in America used and adapted what was "at hand," including the religious forms they found. Such a process, he argues, is neither simple nor wholesale. In identity and new community formation, the people who came reinvested what they brought into new forms, whether those were chosen or forced upon them.[57] They creolized.

There is, therefore, in the creole several levels of activity. The creole is mixture, as Edouard Glissant suggests, a bringing together in a surprising new form traces of the past—what is left when collective memory is lost—with the encountered reality—the radical immediate with which we must cope.[58] Creole identity is living this rupture, strangeness, mixture, daily. "We abandon," Glissant writes, "the idea of fixed being."[59]

Glissant suggests that the rupture with our "matrix" is the "mother beyond our reach."[60] In Eve Batiste's and Benjamin January's stories, Africa, the motherland, is far behind. The father is the one beyond reach. The father provides a particular part of structure: the father is order, continuity (in the sense of a "house"), and name, legitimacy. For Benjamin January, his father is only memory, as Africa is for slaves, and Benjamin loses his connection to his Africanness. The Batiste women, particularly, feel this absence. They are powerful, but frustrated; loving, but unloved. For Eve, Louis is beloved and absent, and she has to come to terms with that absence before and after his death.

Both Benjamin and Eve are at a point of arrival. Eve is ten, verging on her teens, coming to know what it means to be a Batiste woman, standing between the Batiste past and her own future. Benjamin January is about forty. Barbara Hambly describes him this way: "A very intelligent man who is of an age where intelligence and experience are transforming into wisdom; a man who has a clear idea of what goodness is, and is willing to pursue it; a man whose heart is rooted in the love of his family, and his love for music."[61] He is grieving for his wife, living at home and coping with the "custom of the country," as he calls racism, and feeling the pain of the exile. Both Benjamin and Eve must come to be at home in a place that is both familiar and alien. Voodoo works towards this integration. *Vodu* means "spiritual forces" in the Fon language.[62] Those forces are at work in both stories, and they work, as power does, in unexpected ways. The *loa*, as Yoruba priest Gerald Joseph describes them, are aspects of reality, god-given aspects of life. They are real, and they are part of the poetic imagination. Both Ben and Eve, therefore, face what they must integrate—in their worlds and in themselves. Such a process leads to spiritual balance, proper connection to the ancestors, and respect for the power in the world, which constitute the good life and which are the goals of African-based religions. In a beautiful statement, Glissant says that "the poetic imagination struggles against the marauding shadows within us." The inner and the outer are linked. The desire for the "other," original country is always unfulfilled, but, as Glissant notes, "When one discovers one's landscape, desire for the other country ceases to be a form of alienation."[63]

Papa Legba, open the gate. Saint Peter, hand me the key.

South Louisiana—particularly New Orleans—is a weird place—weird, in the old sense of that word: uncanny. It is a place of meeting and of mixture. Barbara Hambly, in an interview, calls it a funnel. It is, to me, the limen in Victor Turner's sense of the word, an in-between place and a place of convergence of cultures—European, American, Caribbean, and African—and of religious practice—Catholic, African, Native American, and Protestant. It is bounded by structure. In many ways South Louisiana is typically American. Commercial American activity, for example, has turned Marie Laveau into an industry and Bourbon Street into a commercial strip. But that structure bounds something older—older modes of relation and some deeper memory, both still operating under the surface. Off Bourbon, on Royal or Rampart, say, while walking at night and smelling coffee, alcohol, and the stench of the old city, one can believe that Benjamin January could still step from a side street and nod good evening. One can hear the drums of Congo Square under the yelling of drunks and feel the misery rise from the streets on which slaves once walked to the Cabildo, prison and slave pen, to be held and sold. And one can believe that Marie Laveau, in her elaborate tignon, could still enter a house on Rampart Street and, first, make a roux.

In New Orleans, it is all present in the moment, and it is all always changing.

Notes

1. Gayraud S. Wilmore, *Black Religion and Black Radicalism: An Interpretation of the Religious History of African Americans* (Maryknoll, NY: Orbis Press, 1983), 45.

2. James D. Hardy Jr., "Freedom in the Interstices: Ambiguity and Paradox in the American South" (paper presented at Southern Humanities Council meeting, New Orleans, Feb. 2000), 9.

3. Fehintola Mosadomi, "The Origin of Louisiana Creole," in *Creole: The History and Legacy of Louisiana's Free People of Color*, ed. Sybil Kein (Baton Rouge: Louisiana State Univ. Press, 2000), 229.

4. Kein, *Creole*, xii-iii.

5. Alice Moore Dunbar-Nelson, "People of Color in Louisiana," in *Creole*, ed. Kein, 8.

6. Dunbar-Nelson, "People of Color," 29.

Carolyn M. Jones

7. Joan M. Martin, "*Placage* and the Louisiana *Gens de Couleur Libre:* How Race and Sex Defined the Lifestyles of Free Women of Color," in *Creole,* ed. Kein, 69–70.

8. Martin, "*Placage,*" 68–69.

9. Edouard Glissant, *Caribbean Discourses: Selected Essays* (Charlottesville, VA: Univ. Press of Virginia, CARAF Books, 1989), 4, 14–15, 19–22, 34.

10. Barbara Hambly, *Graveyard Dust* (New York: Bantam Books, 1999), 339.

11. Grace King, "New Orleans, the Place and the People," quoted in Dunbar-Nelson, "People of Color," 19.

12. Dunbar-Nelson, "People of Color," 21.

13. Carolyn Morrow Long, *Spiritual Merchants: Religion, Magic, and Commerce* (Knoxville: Univ. of Tennessee Press, 2001), 41.

14. Barbara Hambly, *Free Man of Color* (New York: Bantam, 1997), 2. See also Anthony G. Barthelemy, "Light, Bright, and Damn *Near* White: Race, the Politics of Genealogy, and the Strange Case of Susie Guillory," in *Creole,* ed. Kein, 255.

15. Hambly, *Free Man,* 17; Dunbar-Nelson, "People of Color," 26.

16. Barthelemy, "Light, Bright," 253.

17. Hambly, *Free Man,* 2.

18. See Violet Harrington Bryan, "Marcus Christian's Treatment of *Les Gens de Couleur Libres,*" in *Creole,* ed. Kein, 53.

19. Barbara Rosendale Duggal, "Marie Laveau: The Voodoo Queen Repossessed," in *Creole,* ed. Kein, 163.

20. Hambly, *Graveyard Dust,* 321.

21. Hambly, *Graveyard Dust,* 26–27.

22. Long, *Spiritual Merchants,* 47–48.

23. John W. Blassingame, *The Slave Community: Plantation Life in the Antebellum South* (New York: Oxford Univ. Press, 1972), 41. See also Albert J. Raboteau, *Slave Religion: The "Invisible Institution" in the Antebellum South* (New York: Oxford Univ. Press, 1980), 76–77.

24. Zora Neale Hurston, *Tell My Horse: Voodoo and Life in Haiti and Jamaica* (New York: Harper & Row, 1990), 118–19.

25. Long, *Spiritual Merchants,* 8–13.

26. Hambly, *Graveyard Dust,* 10; Hurston, *Tell My Horse,* 237; Raboteau, *Slave Religion,* 82.

27. Long, *Spiritual Merchants,* 6.

28. Hambly, *Graveyard Dust,* 12.

29. Hambly, *Graveyard Dust,* 78.

30. On charms such as the "luck ball," see Raboteau, *Slave Religion,* 82.

31. Hambly, *Graveyard Dust,* 78–79.

32. Karen McCarthy Brown, *Mama Lola: A Vodou Priestess in Brooklyn* (Berkeley: Univ. of California Press, 1999), 98.

33. Brown, *Mama Lola,* 98, 124, 134–35.

34. On the distinctions in forms, see Long, *Spiritual Merchants,* 52.

35. Hambly, *Graveyard Dust,* 243.

36. Hambly, *Graveyard Dust,* 322.

37. Hambly, *Graveyard Dust,* 323.

38. Hambly, *Graveyard Dust,* 323.

39. On Baron Cemetery, see Hurston, *Tell My Horse,* 219-20.

40. Hambly, *Graveyard Dust,* 298.

41. Hambly, *Graveyard Dust,* 368.

42. Hambly, *Graveyard Dust,* 368–69.

43. Hambly, *Graveyard Dust,* 371–72.

44. Hambly, *Graveyard Dust,* 371.

45. Hambly, *Graveyard Dust,* 399.

46. Hambly, *Graveyard Dust,* 399–400.

47. Bryan, "Marcus Christian's Treatment," 50–51.

48. Barbara Hambly, *Die Upon A Kiss* (New York: Bantam, 2001), 77–78.

49. Martin, "*Placage,*" 69.

50. Bryan, "Marcus Christian's Treatment," 18–19.

51. Hurston, *Tell My Horse,* 121.

52. Hurston, *Tell My Horse,* 122.

53. Hurston, *Tell My Horse,* 127. The change in spelling from "Baptiste" to "Batiste" is common in relations between Creole black and Creole white Louisiana families. "Baptiste" is still the white Creole, and "Batiste" the black. Other names include Dominique, pronounced in the French way in the white Creole family, but in the black Creole family pronounced "Domain." A particularly interesting example of differences in spelling and pronunciation concerns the names "McNell" and "McNair." In the white family, "McNell" is pronounced as it is spelled; in the Creole black family, however, "McNair" is pronounced "McNell." Non-Creole blacks, meanwhile, pronounce the name "McNair" as it is spelled.

54. On such preparations, see Long, *Spiritual Merchants,* 221–46.

55. Vincent Harding, *There is a River: The Black Struggle For Freedom in America* (New York: Harcourt Brace, 1981), 4-5.

56. Charles H. Long, *Significations: Signs, Symbols, and Images in the Interpretation of Religion* (Philadelphia: Fortress Press, 1986), 177.

57. Long, *Significations,* 179.

58. Glissant, *Caribbean Discourses,* 231.

59. Glissant, *Caribbean Discourses,* 14.

60. Glissant, *Caribbean Discourses,* 231.

61. Barbara Hambly, interviewed by Joe Hartlaub for *Bookreporter.com,* Dec. 10, 1999, http://www.bookreporter.com/authors/au-hambly-barbara.asp.

62. Long, *Spiritual Merchants,* 37.

63. Glissant, *Caribbean Discourses,* 134.

CHAPTER 6

FROM ANGELS TO ZEN: RELIGION AND CULTURE IN THE CONTEMPORARY SOUTH

"THE MOST STRIKING FEATURE OF RELIGION IN THE SOUTH," WROTE SOCI-ologist John Shelton Reed in his 1972 book *The Enduring South,* "is that the region is, and has been since antebellum times, monolithically Protestant."[1] Reed cited polls conducted between 1954 and 1966 that found some 90 percent of southerners identifying themselves as Protestants, compared with 60 percent of non-southerners. At that time, Reed also insisted that these southern Protestants, regardless of denominational label, had some distinguishing features. Most striking was a consistent orthodox consensus in belief and practice. A decade later, Reed echoed those conclusions in a subsequent study. Despite the significant urbanization and industrialization that had steadily swept through much of the South in the decades after World War II and a population growth resulting more from in-migration than natural propagation, the region, as Reed saw it, continued to retain a singular identity based on the cultural and religious patterns long intact. In Reed's words, "Data on trends often show *change,* in the South and elsewhere, but the *differences* between South and non-South are no smaller now than a generation ago, despite the dramatic changes in Southern society since then . . . the data strongly suggest that the religion of the New South will be as vigorous and as distinctive as that of the Old."[2]

In other words, regardless of change, the perception of the South is the Bible Belt endures. Much in the arena of common culture provides ample evidence to sustain that claim. It is unlikely that in any other region of the country as many collegiate football games each fall include public prayer as part of the regular opening ceremonies. Such a public presence of religion, often a least-common-denominator Protestant Christianity, too thinly disguised for critics, still permeates the culture. In Alabama a state judge received national attention in the late 1990s when he insisted on posting the Ten Commandments in his courtroom, despite legal orders to the contrary. Public opinion was so overwhelmingly supportive that despite the court orders prohibiting such a seemingly overt endorsement of a particular religious heritage, the judge in question received popular vindication when Alabama voters in 2000 elected him chief justice of the state supreme court.[3]

But other forces may lurk beneath the surface. At about the same time that Reed argued for a continuing distinctive religious presence in southern culture, Wade Clark Roof, a South Carolina native who teaches sociology of religion at the University of California at Santa Barbara, seemed to echo Reed's position. Roof concurred that "religion in Dixie is still characterized by high visibility, strong conservatism and moral traditionalism," observing, "[W]hat is truly remarkable about the South, and the Sunbelt generally, is that, though it welcomes new technologies and new migrants, regional ideologies and loyalties are not seriously undermined." But then Roof called attention to another dimension of the total picture when he went on to contend that "no longer can an intact Southern religious culture be simply assumed." Why not? Roof added another reason to the mix, besides demographic change, urbanization, and industrialization, when he pointed out that more than 40 percent of southerners, despite their response to pollsters, claimed no affiliation with any religious organization. While that figure is the lowest for any region of the country—the national average hovers around 50 percent, according to Roof—it does make popular images of the South as being permeated by a religious culture somewhat paradoxical.[4]

In this essay, I shall explore how this southern religious culture, though still dominated in the popular mind by an evangelical Protestant ethos, beneath the surface reflects some of the same trends that mark American religious life as a whole. I shall look first at the erosion of the mainline denominations—particularly the Southern Baptist Convention, which has long had a firm grip on white Protestant life in the South. Then I shall examine how a new pluralism is beginning to enrich southern religion. Finally, I shall note how popular religiosity, much of it associated with the current fascination with spirituality and disdain for religion, has found a home in the South.

First, some observations about the white evangelical presence in the South, particularly the Southern Baptist Convention (SBC): In the past four decades, the Southern Baptist Convention surged ahead of its competitors to become the largest Protestant body in the nation, not just the region. Now numbering almost 16 million, the domination of the SBC would seem secure. Yet inner

Charles H. Lippy

turmoil has wrenched the SBC for more than two decades, bringing what is now dubbed the "fundamentalist takeover" of the denomination and the emergence of a "moderate" counter-church, the Cooperative Baptist Fellowship.[5] The moderates have strength, if not power, within the denomination, especially in Texas, where the state convention in the fall of 2000 cut back financial support for denominational agencies because they were under fundamentalist control. Moderates have been opening theological schools across the South to train clergy sympathetic to their views; they fund more missionaries than the formal SBC agencies; and they have established Smyth and Helwys, a publishing arm associated with Mercer University Press, to produce materials for churches as well as more academic works. In other words, there is already in place all the apparatus for the formation of a separate denomination. Throughout the South, individual congregations are severing ties with the SBC, although in some cases maintaining affiliation with state conventions.

At the same time, it is often forgotten that the SBC was growing faster outside the South than within Dixie for more than two decades before the internal difficulties came to the surface. If fundamentalists decried the decline of the denomination's influence while the moderates were in control, they should look at the statistics that show a decline in the total number of baptisms—the mode of entry for membership in a Southern Baptist congregation—almost every year since the fundamentalists came to power, yielding a growth rate that, while impressive, nevertheless lags behind the growth of rate of the nation's population as a whole. Indeed, the growth rate between 2000 and 2001, as reported by the National Council of Churches, was just 0.7 percent.[6]

Figures for one southern state, Tennessee, will bring the erosion of loyalty to the SBC and other mainline groups into sharper focus.[7] According to the Bureau of the Census, between 1970 and 1990 Tennessee's population grew 24.2 percent. During that time, the state's largest religious body, the Southern Baptist Convention, grew as well, but by 22.6 percent, failing to keep pace with overall population growth. The second-largest group, the United Methodist Church, fared worse, posting a growth of just 2.4 percent over the two decades and between 1980 and 1990 actually showing a loss. The Episcopal Church dropped by 13.1 percent between 1970 and 1990, meaning that Episcopalians accounted for less than 1 percent of the state's population in 1990.

At the same time, some groups were growing at rates outstripping that of the population at large, even if their total numbers were dwarfed by the Baptist and Methodist giants. The Roman Catholic Church posted a 48.2 percent growth between 1970 and 1990 to become the fifth largest single religious body in Tennessee. Within the Protestant fold, the Pentecostally oriented Assemblies of God, not even reported in the 1970 accounting, showed a 32.5 percent increase between 1980 and 1990. Another Pentecostal body, the

Church of God, with its international headquarters in Cleveland, Tennessee, experienced an even more impressive harvest; that denomination boasted an increase of 66.9 percent between 1970 and 1990. The Church of Jesus Christ of Latter-day Saints, better known as the Mormons, did even better; over the twenty-year period, the Saints more than doubled—showing growth of 113.4 percent. In addition, the 1990 figures for the first time included a category labeled "independent charismatic churches." In neighboring South Carolina, Baha'i ranks among the fastest-growing religious communities, although the total number of adherents remains small. The Louis G. Gregory Baha'i Institute in Hemingway, South Carolina, established by the group's National Spiritual Assembly to serve much of the southern region, and the Baha'i-owned radio station WLGI, which operates in the larger Myrtle Beach area, signal that the northern coastal area of South Carolina is home to one of the nation's largest enclaves of Baha'is.[8] Baha'i also maintains a literature distribution facility in Tennessee that ships materials throughout the nation.

There are clear trends here that are unlikely to change, even if the numerical percentages shift. The evangelical bodies whose names are almost synonymous with the religious life of Tennessee and the South as a whole are simply not doing very well. A reconfiguration is under way, although it is one unlikely to challenge Southern Baptist hegemony, especially in the near future. After all, even if the SBC growth rate lags behind the state's, the Convention can still claim more than one-quarter of the entire population of Tennessee (27.5 percent) as adherents.

Accounting for this erosion of membership in the old-line bodies is more complex.[9] A major factor is the growing number of persons moving into the South from other parts of the country and the mobility of the population living in the region, along with the movement to suburbia, another phenomenon most striking in the South since the close of World War II. If persons once sought out a congregation identified with the religious tradition in which they were raised when they moved to a different community or suburban development, the tendency became to pick a congregation that had the most auxiliary programs to suit personal and family needs.[10] Sociologists more than historians have also documented the rapid increase over the last half-century of marriage across denominational lines and now even across religious traditions. In many cases, the couple affiliated with a third religious group, rather than either of those with which each had been identified before, or dropped out of organized religion altogether—at least for a time.[11] Then, too, religious presentations on the media tended to homogenize differences and made Protestant denominations seem almost like carbon copies of each other. These patterns are not unique to the South, but they do undercut the image of the South as a place where a monolith of orthodox Protestantism prevails. In ret-

Charles H. Lippy

rospect, the first signs of this erosion appeared in the 1950s, a decade often trumpeted as a time of religious revival in the United States but a time when mobility, higher education levels, the mushrooming of suburbs, and a host of other factors began to nudge American Protestants, regardless of region, to think in new ways about denominational labels and affiliation.

Then, too, recall Wade Clark Roof's urging us to remember the flip side of the figures that show that for about half a century the proportion of Americans (across the nation, not just in the South) affiliated with a religious institution has remained constant, hovering around or just over 50 percent. That means, however, that more than 40 percent—in the West, more than 50 percent—are unaffiliated with a religious group in any way. Roof suggested that in the South the figure is around 41 percent and although the lowest for any region in the nation, the figure is rising. The 1990 figures from the Glenmary Research Center, by counting "adherents" rather than "members," make Tennessee seem a tad more religious, with just 38.8 percent not aligned with any group; Texas is even more religious in this accounting, with only 35.9 percent not claiming any religious identification whatsoever. Unaffiliated persons are not necessarily hostile to religion or even irreligious. Yet, as the proportion of unaffiliated persons grows, it will be increasingly difficult to assume that there is a religious base, such as Reed's orthodox Protestant consensus, supporting southern culture.

At the same time, there are signs that a vital new pluralism is coming to southern religious life. At one time, students of American religious life used the word pluralism to accent the sheer variety of religious institutions that had found a home in the United States, most of them Protestant groups of one stripe or another. Historically, the term emerged in contrast to the European cultures where a single state church, a religious establishment, prevailed to the exclusion of others. So we talked about the United States as a "denominational society."[12] In the South that pluralism usually zeroed in on the Baptists and Methodists—often hard to tell apart in some areas—but recognized the enormous number of so-called "sects" that had southern roots or established enclaves in the South. One thinks, for example, of groups ranging from the Macedonian Churches of Virginia to the Christadelphians, the serpent-handling congregations, the Two-Seed in the Spirit Baptists, the independent Holiness and Pentecostal congregations in more rural areas with names so long one cannot remember them. Nor should we forget more widely known clusters such as the enclave of Seventh-Day Adventists gathered around Southern Adventist University in Collegedale, Tennessee; the Adventists in Tennessee grew by 84.4 percent between 1970 and 1990.

Pluralism in recent decades has taken many additional faces. In the wake of the civil rights movement, scholars began to look again at the African

American religious experience, ever so slowly recognizing that the African American Protestant denominations are not just mirror images of white groups that bear the same name, perhaps with a dash more enthusiasm in their worship services. Since the introduction of slavery in 1619, the African American presence in the South has meant that the region is the most thoroughly multicultural section of the country. Too often, discussion of groups that are primarily African American is omitted from studies, especially when talking about which groups are the largest and which the smallest. Precious few lists of the nation's (not just the South's) largest Protestant denominations give the overwhelmingly African American National Baptist Convention its due; when one checks statistics, it is the seventh-largest Protestant denomination in the nation by membership.

Nearly four decades ago, Samuel S. Hill issued his indictment of the region's religious culture, *Southern Churches in Crisis*. Hill castigated southern Protestantism because of its racism, arguing that the way racist presuppositions from the larger culture had penetrated the churches rendered southern Protestant Christianity little more than a cultural religion and definitely not a prophetic religion. Appearing at the peak of the civil rights movement, Hill's book was a call to arms, for integration was the watchword of the day. Southern religion is still racist, although perhaps not in the same way it was when the first edition of *Southern Churches in Crisis* appeared. Dismantling the legal apparatus of segregation has not proved the antidote to racism. The common cliché that Sunday morning at 11:00 A.M. remains the most segregated hour of the week in the South, as elsewhere in the nation, holds true. Perhaps because historically the African American denominations—even those such as the African Methodist Episcopal Zion Church, with national headquarters in Charlotte, North Carolina, or the Christian Methodist Episcopal Church, founded and headquartered in Nashville, Tennessee—have never had the same political influence as their white counterparts, it has been easy to skip over them. We do that at our own peril if we want to understand the pluralism that is central to the story of religion in the South today.

The late John Fenton of Emory University led the way in calling attention to the dramatic increase in the number of Asian Americans and Asian immigrants moving into the South, at first primarily in and around major urban areas such as Atlanta.[13] In many cases, these immigrants and in-migrants established traditional Asian religious institutions, often so quietly and inconspicuously that communities were unaware of their presence. That they eschew active proselytizing also contributes to their almost hidden presence. One example is the establishment of a Hindu temple in Chattanooga, Tennessee, that opened in the summer of 1996, housed in a facility that was formerly home to a Southern Baptist congregation. Its only identifying features are small signs on the doors; there is no large marquee or other sign. This Hindu temple joined at least three others in the Volunteer State; the one in Nashville is especially striking since it was built as a temple, not converted to Hindu use from another purpose.

Islam is growing rapidly throughout the South, though numbers of adherents are still difficult to come by. Islam's growth in the South, as elsewhere in the nation, has resulted from a surge in immigrants from the Arab world in the last four decades, thanks to changes in immigration laws in the mid-1960s. Estimates hold that at least three-quarters of Muslims in the United States, excluding African Americans affiliated with the Nation of Islam, are foreign-born.[14] Friday Muslim prayer services have been incorporated into the religious life of most urban areas across the South. Most of the newer facilities are not affiliated with the Nation of Islam or Black Muslims but serve the Muslim immigrant community and a small number of American converts to Islam. As with other newer religious communities in the South, Islam has made its way by adapting other religious structures to its own use. The merger of two dwindling United Methodist congregations in Chattanooga in the late 1990s, for example, left the building that had housed one of them vacant; local Muslims purchased the structure to transform it into a mosque. The Muslim presence, however, is easy to overlook. Prior to the September 11 tragedy, analysts reported that many Muslim immigrants believe most other Americans harbor such a fear and suspicion of Islam, based on perceived connections of Muslims with terrorism and memories of the Iran hostage crisis of the late 1970s, that becoming more visible in the larger religious culture would produce a backlash of resentment and prejudice.[15]

Buddhism has perhaps an even deeper presence in the South, ranging from a lone American convert and monk residing on Lookout Mountain, just across the Alabama border outside Chattanooga, Tennessee, who ministers to the Tibetan Buddhist Bodhi Center that opened in Chattanooga in August 2000, to the sprawling Southern Dharma Retreat Center near Asheville, North Carolina. The Web site for that center reveals a full schedule of programs, ranging from short, weekend retreats that introduce those interested to the basic tenets of Buddhism to ones that last for a week or longer for more serious practitioners. Directories identify Zen centers, Tibetan Buddhist centers, and a host of other Buddhist-related organizations throughout the South. There may not as yet be as many Buddhists as there are Baptists in the South, but it seems likely that Buddhism in its various expressions is growing at a more rapid rate than the Southern Baptist Convention. In the South as elsewhere, those drawn to Buddhism include not only Asian immigrants who desire to practice their religion of origin but also many American converts. But even Vietnamese, Thai, and other Asian immigrants have had to adapt practice to the mores of the evangelical culture that cascades across the southern religious landscape. Thomas Tweed reports that a small Vietnamese congregation in Raleigh, North Carolina, gathers every Sunday morning to read Buddhist scriptures and meditate together, whereas in Vietnam they would come together twice a month and on festival occasions.[16] But in the southern setting, Vietnamese Buddhists now go to temple on Sundays when their Christian neighbors and co-workers go to church. The community thus blends in with the surrounding religious culture and becomes both Americanized and religiously acceptable.

A cursory look at many areas of the South requires taking account of another dimension of ethnic pluralism. The Hispanic presence in southern life is no longer restricted to areas of Texas and those parts of Florida that have for decades been home to a Cuban immigrant community. Virtually every southern city has Roman Catholic churches that offer a schedule of Masses in Spanish; in many of those cities, Protestant churches, often of a Pentecostal inclination, also provide worship opportunities in Spanish. As workers gathered figures for the 2000 census, speculation was wide that Whitfield County in northwest Georgia, home to the many carpet factories in and around Dalton, would have a majority Hispanic population. Although preliminary figures suggested that this estimate was too high, newspaper reports indicated that the Hispanic population of the county would exceed 40 percent. Rather than seeing this Hispanic infusion as an aberration, we should take it very seriously. If present global trends continue, within two generations more than half the world's Roman Catholics will be found in Central and South America. The Hispanic style fuses traditional Roman elements with features rooted in colonial Spanish culture and especially the native religious expression of the indigenous peoples of Latin America. Already found in parts of the South today, it may be the norm a century from now. Southern religious life beats with the pulse of a new pluralism.

Finally, a fresh fascination with spirituality has found a home in the southern religious landscape. Spirituality, what Quaker mystic Rufus Jones once called "immediate awareness of relation to God, or direct and intimate consciousness of the divine presence,"[17] is somewhat elusive. Sociologists would no doubt talk about the privatization of religion that is touted as a hallmark of industrialized cultures; such has surely been one stratum of southern religious life long before industrialization invaded the region in the postbellum period. In the past decade, numerous analysts have looked at the religious life of the baby boom generation, concluding that boomers and probably the so-called "Generation X" make a sharp distinction between religion and spirituality.[18] The former is tied to doctrine and dogma, creed and clergy, institutions and irrelevance; the latter shines with vitality, invigorating individuals as they pursue personal religious quests. Robert Wuthnow, looking at trends in spirituality in the United States—not just the South—claims that since the 1950s the Americans of the baby boom generation have jettisoned the idea of a spiritual dwelling, an abode or tradition in which one finds clues to meaning and purpose in life, instead regarding the spiritual life as a journey, a quest, that traverses many paths.[19] In its July–August 1998 issue, the *Utne Reader* carried a piece on how to "Design Your Own God" that talked about a "cafeteria" spirituality in which individuals picked and chose elements from this tradition and that to create a personal diet that nourished the soul.[20] Wade Clark Roof's latest book on the baby boomers captures the mood well in its two-word title: *Spiritual Marketplace.*[21]

The religious environment of the South has provided particularly fertile ground for this surge of interest in spirituality. Tucked away in the very nature of the evangelical style that fed the Baptists and Methodists generations ago is some direct inner experience of the divine that no one could undergo for you. In evangelical Protestantism, one might speak of a direct encounter with Jesus Christ or of accepting Jesus Christ as one's personal savior. Although there are countless accounts of dramatic personal conversions at public events such as camp meetings or revivals, conversion is essentially private. It is a personal experience that is self-authenticating because of its private nature. At best, one gains confirmation of the authenticity of this personal, private experience through conversation with others of like inclination or through testimonies of others who have had similar experiences.

Spirituality often moves in directions dichotomous with the style of evangelical Protestantism, particularly when it incorporates elements from outside the Christian orbit. But like the experience of conversion in the evangelical context, it is personal and private. Women, including southern women, have been probing resources that take them well beyond the standard denominations to forge a spirituality that speaks to female experience.[22] Some of the explorations for women's spirituality have delved into nature religions long suppressed (or co-opted) by Christianity; many have links to Native American forms of spirituality that once flourished across much of the South. Some invoke the goddess and therefore send shivers up the spines of men who shriek "heresy." Yet others have looked to Wicca and blended features of neo-pagan practice with more traditional forms of religious expression. Once consigned to urban areas and popularly linked with anything vaguely identified as New Age, Wicca has also penetrated the South, even the rural South. Newspaper wire services in January 1999, for example, carried a feature about a young woman raising her son in a Wiccan community in rural Alabama.[23] The result is an eclectic spirituality that blends together features of orthodox Christianity with much that is not specifically Christian.

Another component of this spirituality that turns from orthodox religion inward is the growing interest in labyrinths, rich in association with mandalas and other near-universal symbols of the religious quest. Vicki Brown, an Associated Press writer, focused on an Episcopal parish in Nashville, Tennessee, in a wire-service feature in December 1998:

> Cary Stephenson was so impressed with the way he felt while walking circles in a labyrinth he had to share it. He outlined a pattern in paint on a field outside his church.
>
> Then he started walking.
>
> That was two years ago. The labyrinth at St. Mark's Episcopal Church in Nashville now attracts a group of regular walkers and is being made permanent with brick and concrete.
>
> "It helps you have your mind in the present instead of thinking about what you are going to have for dinner or problems you're having with someone at work," said Stephenson, a 39-year-old sheet-metal layout mechanic.
>
> A labyrinth is made of circles, each one inside the other. A walker can start at the outside and meditate while walking in circles until reaching the center. Unlike a maze, there are no dead ends or tricks, just a single path that leads to the center and out again.[24]

Even though several people may walk a labyrinth at any one time, their journeys are solitary endeavors, as one by one each seeks peace within. While the labyrinth mentioned here is at an Episcopal parish in Nashville, most who walk its circles are not parishioners. They come quite literally from many religious walks of life.

The intensely personal nature of spirituality helps explain why Buddhism can attract former Christians as converts or even as practitioners who combine Buddhist meditation with more traditional Christian practice. Whatever works to bring some sense of wholeness and centeredness to life becomes part of one's personal spiritual life. One may worship in a Christian church on Sunday but practice Buddhist meditation in the privacy of one's home at other times. The increasing privatization of spirituality may also account in part for the way in which religious television, whether through local Christian programming or through the onetime televangelists such as Jimmy Swaggart and Jim and Tammy Faye Bakker, has found its audience concentrated in the South. An older but carefully documented study of the televangelism phenomenon revealed that the typical viewer of religious broadcasting is a southern female over fifty years of age.[25] Televangelism represents one of the most significant ways religion and spirituality become privatized, if not almost invisible. The casual viewer absorbs whatever doctrine is proclaimed, combines it with long-held opinions and prejudices, and fashions them all together into a private religious perspective. Pluralism in idiosyncratic spirituality here takes yet another form.

Southern worship life, reflecting moves that are national in scope, reveals other facets of diversity and eclecticism. A recent cartoon is to the point. A man and a woman entering a church ask the usher greeting them, "Which way to the service?" The usher replies, "The contemporary or classic? Participatory or non-participatory? Southern traditional or 'baby boomer'?" What has been dubbed "contemporary Christian worship" or a "seeker service" by that first of the mega-churches, Willow Creek Community Church in the Chicago suburb of South Barrington, Illinois, has come to the South.[26] Churches from many Protestant denominations have sent clergy and other staff members to Willow Creek seminars so that they might institute such styles of multimedia worship in their own congregations. Tapes and electronic keyboards replace pipe organs. Rock groups and singers with handheld mikes belt out rather different anthems than robed choirs. In blue jeans or shorts and sometimes shoeless, worshipers catch words of upbeat gospel choruses flashed on screens without having to rifle through the pages of hymnals and prayer books. Not wanting to offend anyone, pastors offer short, very practical discourses rather than theologically based sermons. There is no mystery of the Mass here, not even an altar call while the choir croons, "Just As I Am." What one feels becomes the barometer to measure the effectiveness of worship, just as what one feels determines personal spirituality. And the people are there. One such congregation just outside Atlanta attracts in the range of twelve thousand people to its schedule of weekend services. Preliminary studies indicate that Christian congregations offering some form of contemporary worship with social outreach are those that are witnessing numerical growth, not just in the South but throughout the United States.[27]

Add to all of this the increasing fascination with angels, only part of which can be attributed to the popularity of Della Reese's *Touched by an Angel* television series. Again Chattanooga, Tennessee, provides examples. A shop on Market Street, in the heart of downtown, called "Christian Concepts" and one called "Holy Moses," on a trendy street lined with small art galleries and coffee shops, both carry a line of angel-related items, some more traditional than others.[28] At a nearby shopping mall, the Christian Lifestyle Center, formerly known as the Baptist Book Store, reports it has difficulty keeping in stock anything pertaining to angels, from coffee mugs to earrings, because of the high demand. Why angels? Why angels now? With the collapse of trust in a scientific, rationalist worldview, more and more southerners, like other Americans, are willing to explore belief in a realm of supernatural power more fundamental and more pervasive than a divine being trapped in a religious institution. Angels provide direct, immediate access to that realm of power; one does not need imam, priest, or rabbi to point the way. Angels, as beneficent beings, may have come to the fore in part because, throughout the decade of the 1990s, economic times were good, giving Americans a more positive spin on life and its possibilities. A generation ago, in the mid-1970s when the nation confronted recession, a fuel crisis, the last gasp of the Vietnam War, Watergate, and more, there was also a lively belief in the supernatural, but then in those bleaker days it was *Rosemary's Baby* and people looked to *The Exorcist* to remove the demons from their midst.

Existing alongside the churches and other religious institutions, these manifestations of spirituality have given southern religious life a new face as it moves into the twenty-first century. The challenge it presents, however, is precisely its dissociation from traditional religious institutions. Whatever their ties to prevailing mores, as in the racism that penetrated southern Protestant culture, institutions offer structures that facilitate transmission of a religious worldview and its attendant practices from one generation to the next. The highly individualized nature of spirituality and the personal quest that it embodies cannot be readily transmitted. Hence, as succeeding generations, now dubbed Generation X and then the Millennial Generation, come to maturity, southern religious life may be pushed in yet other directions.

The public face of southern religion remains dominated by white evangelical Protestantism. Many Baptists, not as many Methodists, and even fewer Episcopalians are still in southern church pews, but more and more of their neighbors are not Baptist, Methodist, or Episcopalian. Some may be nurturing the religious heritage of their culture of origins as Muslims, Buddhists, or Hindus, much the way European Christians brought a variety of brands of Christianity to the South in the seventeenth and eighteenth centuries. Others may be in a church pew on Sunday morning but walk a labyrinth during the week to gain spiritual energy or attend a croning ceremony for a woman in a forest grove. Southern religious life in the twenty-first century spans the gamut from angels to Zen.

Charles H. Lippy

Notes

1. John Shelton Reed, *The Enduring South: Subcultural Persistence in Mass Society* (Chapel Hill: Univ. of North Carolina Press, 1972), 57.

2. John Shelton Reed, *One South: An Ethnic Approach to Regional Culture* (Baton Rouge: Louisiana State Univ. Press, 1982), 135.

3. The state university where the author of this essay teaches continues to have invocations and benedictions at graduation ceremonies and prayers at university-sponsored banquets and other official occasions, tokens of the public presence of religion in the surrounding culture. Ironically, the chapel on the campus, a reminder that the school was once a private, church-related institution, has been stripped of all explicit religious symbols (apart from those in windows and wood or stone carvings), and policy prohibits holding religious services in the chapel itself, other than weddings and memorial services, on the grounds that such are inappropriate for a secular, state-supported university.

4. Wade Clark Roof, "Religious Change in the American South: The Case of the Unchurched," in *Varieties of Southern Religious Experience,* ed. Samuel S. Hill (Baton Rouge: Louisiana State Univ. Press, 1980), 192–210; quotations from pp. 192, 197, 208.

5. On the internal conflict within the SBC, see Nancy Tatom Ammerman, *Baptist Battles: Social Change and Conflict in the Southern Baptist Convention* (New Brunswick, NJ: Rutgers Univ. Press, 1990); Bill J. Leonard, *"God's Last and Only Hope": The Fragmentation of the Southern Baptist Convention* (Grand Rapids, MI: William B. Eerdmans, 1990); and David T. Morgan, *The New Crusades, the New Holy Land: Conflict in the Southern Baptist Convention, 1969–1991* (Tuscaloosa: Univ. of Alabama Press, 1996).

6. The figure was reported in "Doing the Numbers," *Christian Century* 118, no. 8 (7 March 2001): 7, and was derived from the *2001 Yearbook of American and Canadian Churches,* published by the National Council of Churches in February 2001.

7. I am not claiming that Tennessee is representative of every southern state, only that it is illustrative of trends that prevail across the South. The figures for religious groups come from material provided by the Glenmary Research Center in Nashville; they are updated every ten years after new census figures are available.

8. See Preston L. McKever-Floyd, "Masks of the Sacred: Religious Pluralism in South Carolina," in *Religion in South Carolina,* ed. Charles H. Lippy (Columbia: Univ. of South Carolina Press, 1993), 159–61.

9. A fuller discussion is found in Charles H. Lippy, *Pluralism Comes of Age: American Religious Culture in the Twentieth Century* (Armonk, NY: M. E. Sharpe, 2000), chap. 2.

10. A Presbyterian pastor in South Carolina commented to me more than a decade ago that he could no longer assume that members of his congregation understood anything about the Presbyterian heritage or its history because, with the exception of those children who grew up in that particular church and had just been confirmed, not one single person who had joined the congregation in the previous year had ever been a Presbyterian.

11. Helpful here, although not restricted to the South, is Larry Bumpass, "The Trend of Interfaith Marriage in the United States," *Social Biology* 17 (1970): 253–59.

12. See, for example, Andrew M. Greeley, *The Denominational Society: A Sociological Approach to Religion in America* (Glenview, IL: Scott, Foresman, 1972).

13. See John Y. Fenton, *South Asian Religions in the Americas: An Annotated Bibliography of Religious Traditions* (Westport, CT: Greenwood, 1995). The periodical *Hinduism Today* from time to time publishes a listing of all Hindu centers in the United States, including the South. Now outdated but helpful for locating many of the Buddhist centers is Don Morreale, *Buddhist America: Centers, Retreats, Practices* (Santa Fe, NM: John Muir, 1988). The best overview of developments nationally is Thomas A. Tweed, "Asian Religions in the United States: Reflections on an Emerging Subfield," in *Religious Diversity and American Religious History: Studies in Traditions and Cultures,* ed. Walter H. Conser Jr. and Sumner B. Twiss (Athens: Univ. of Georgia Press, 1997), 189–217. For historical developments, see Thomas A. Tweed and Stephen Prothero, eds., *Asian Religions in America: A Documentary History* (New York: Oxford Univ. Press, 1999).

14. See Yvonne Yazbeck Haddad, "Make Room for the Muslims?" in *Religious Diversity,* ed. Conser and Twiss, 226.

15. Ibid., 228–30.

16. Tweed and Prothero, *Asian Religions,* 194.

17. Rufus Jones, *Studies in Mystical Religion* (London: Macmillan, 1909), xv.

18. An early study still of value is Robert N. Bellah, William M. Sullivan, Ann Swidler, and Steven M. Tipton, *Habits of the Heart: Individualism and Commitment in American Life* (Berkeley: Univ. of California Press, 1985). More directly, see Wade Clark Roof, *A Generation of Seekers: The Spiritual Journeys of the Baby Boom Generation* (San Francisco: HarperSanFrancisco, 1994). Looking specifically at boomers raised as Presbyterians is Benton Johnson, Donald A. Luidens, and Dean M. Hoge, *Vanishing Boundaries: The Religion of Mainline Protestant Baby Boomers* (Louisville, KY: Westminster–John Knox, 1994).

19. Robert Wuthnow, *After Heaven: Spirituality in America since the 1950s* (Berkeley: Univ. of California Press, 1998).

20. Jeremiah Creedon, "God with a Million Faces," *Utne Reader* (July–August 1998): 42–48.

21. Wade Clark Roof, *Spiritual Marketplace* (Princeton, NJ: Princeton Univ. Press, 1999).

22. See, for example, Nancy A. Hardesty, "Seeking the Great Mother: The Goddess for Today" (paper presented at the annual meeting of the South Carolina Academy of Religion, Feb. 1993), and Hardesty, "Seeking the Great Mother Among the Magnolias: Southern Women and the Search for Spiritual Wholeness" (paper presented at the annual meeting of the American Society of Church History, Vanderbilt Univ., Apr. 1997).

23. Jeremy Martin, "Ala. Pagans Following Little-Known Religious Practices," *Chattanooga Free Press*, 3 January 1999.

24. Vicki Brown, "Labyrinths Now Popular," *Chattanooga Free Press*, 27 December 1998.

25. Jeffrey K. Hadden and Charles E. Swann, *Prime-Time Preachers: The Rising Power of Televangelism* (Reading, MA: Addison-Wesley, 1981).

26. A breezy but perceptive overview of this phenomenon more generally is Charles Truehart, "Welcome to the Next Church," *Atlantic Monthly*, Aug. 1996, 37–58. The most sustained analysis is Kimon Howland Sargeant, *Seeker Churches: Promoting Traditional Religion in a Nontraditional Way* (New Brunswick, NJ: Rutgers Univ. Press, 2000).

27. David Roozen and Carl Dudley at the Hartford Seminary Foundation have been conducting a study of congregations across the nation entitled "Faith Communities Today: A Report on Religion in the United States." While the final report was not available at the time of this writing, preliminary news releases touted the numerical success of congregations combining contemporary worship and social outreach, especially in California (a state long popularly regarded as among the least religious in the nation by standard measurement). See Hartford Seminary Foundation Web site, "Faith Communities Today," http://www.fact.hartsem.edu/.

28. Randall Higgins, "Christianity Finds an Unusual Niche," *Chattanooga Times–Chattanooga Free Press*, 16 January 1999.

CHAPTER 7

OUR LADY OF GUADELOUPE VISITS THE CONFEDERATE MEMORIAL: LATINO AND ASIAN RELIGIONS IN THE SOUTH

TRUISMS ARE SOMETIMES TRUE. AND IF ANYTHING HAS SEEMED SELF-evident to interpreters of the South, it is the religious homogeneity of the Bible Belt. With the exception of the Mormon cultural area in Utah and adjoining states, no U.S. region seems less diverse. Fervent revivalism, civil war, and minimal immigration allowed a southern evangelical Protestant establishment—mostly Baptist and Methodist—to form by the nineteenth century, and, free of challenges by immigrants, that evangelical alliance shaped the religious landscape. Observers have offered divergent assessments of that landscape. Some evangelicals have trumpeted the South as the last stronghold of faithful Christian witness; while others, like the Baltimore-born iconoclast H. L. Mencken, have dismissed it as "the bunghole of the United States, a cesspool of Baptists, a miasma of Methodism, snake-charmers, phony real-estate operators, and syphilitic evangelists." However the assessments diverge—and they still do—almost all interpreters have agreed: the South looks more homogenous than the rest of the nation. Charles Lippy has already quoted John Shelton Reed's pronouncement of the South's "monolithically Protestant" character. And historian Samuel Hill spoke for many interpreters when he noted that more than any other feature "the absence of pluralism and diversity from popular denominations" has characterized the South's religious life.[1]

There is much truth to the still standard interpretation: the South seems more uniformly Protestant and more institutionally pious. Surveys indicate that southerners join churches and attend services more than Americans do in other regions. Even the unchurched in the South admit to a lingering piety: in one 1978 poll nearly three-fourths of those surveyed said that they believed that Jesus was the son of God and rose from the dead, and another survey a decade later found that almost two-thirds of the unaffiliated believed in life after death. Recent surveys reveal the same patterns of attendance, membership, and belief. For example, the spring 1998 Southern Focus Poll found that almost two out of ten southerners attend services more than once a week, more than double the rate for non-southerners, and significantly more southerners (41.6 percent, as opposed to 33.2 percent for non-southerners) say that religion is "extremely important" in their lives. More southerners believe in God (87.5 percent), and more than six out of ten say they prefer the biblical creation account to Darwinian evolutionary theory to explain the universe's origins. And some geographers and sociologists have argued that this regional pattern of piety shows few signs of changing.[2]

Furthermore, the South is not just more pious, it is also still predominantly Protestant. As religious historian Grant Wacker argued when considering the national trend toward personal autonomy and away from congregational involvement, the South still diverges in important ways. Wacker was talking about North Carolina, but his point holds for most southern states: the evangelical Protestant establishment in the late twentieth century "remains extraordinarily strong."[3]

Two sociologists who have conducted the most comprehensive telephone survey of the last decade agree. Barry A. Kosmin and Seymour P. Lachman have suggested in a chapter entitled "Geography Is Destiny" (from their book *One Nation Under God*) that there are "homogenous religious subcultures" in the nation: Lutherans in the upper-Midwest farm belt, Roman Catholics in the Northeast, Mormons in Utah and the Rocky Mountain states, and Baptists in the South. They note that Baptists, both black and white, concentrate south of the Mason-Dixon Line. They are the largest religious group in fourteen states (nearly all of those are in the South), and Baptists constitute more than half the residents of Mississippi, Alabama, and Georgia. Further, Kosmin and Lachman suggest, a "relatively stable" southern Protestantism, evangelical and Pentecostal, persisted into the 1990s.[4]

Truisms, however, require nuances. We need to qualify the claims about the continuing evangelical Protestant dominance in several ways. First, diversity has a long history in the South. Scholars have emphasized the mixing of African and European peoples and practices in the South, but, as historians of southeastern Indians remind us, the territory has also been the home of Indian peoples for more than ten thousand years. Those tribes spoke multiple languages and cultivated divergent religions long before Europeans or Africans arrived. Spanish Catholics first traveled through the South in the sixteenth century, and Protestants first visited only three centuries ago. As historian Joel Martin points out, "Non-natives became the majority population only 180 years ago, or after ninety-eight percent of the region's history had passed." The South was multiethnic, multicultural, and multireligious before anyone crossed the Atlantic.[5]

And, as southern religious historians know, there had been religious and ethnic diversity among the European and African settlers. West African religious practices mixed with Christian piety to produce new creole spiritual forms, and even the Christian faiths Europeans transplanted bore varied fruits. Roman Catholics built the first permanent settlement in the South (and North America) at St. Augustine in 1565. They have a long history in Texas and Louisiana, and Catholics built churches in small towns and larger cities. Jews also found a place in some southern cities—Charleston, Wilmington, Savannah, and Miami Beach. Furthermore, Presbyterians, Episcopalians, Quakers, Lutherans, Adventists, Disciples, Unitarians, Universalists, and other Protestants competed with Baptists and Methodists for the allegiance of the region's faithful.

Second, some recent surveys suggest that while Protestantism continues to be the majority faith, the longstanding southern evangelical alliance might not be as "stable" as Kosmin and Lachman and others, have suggested. By some measures, the South does not appear much more religiously conservative. For instance, the 1998 Southern Focus Poll asked respondents who identified themselves as Protestant how they would describe their own faith. Slightly more southerners said they were "Pentecostal" (12.1 percent, as opposed to 10 percent for non-southerners), but fewer below the Mason-Dixon line identified themselves as "evangelical," only 8.4 percent. The South even had slightly more self-described "theological liberals." As with all surveys, there is much that this intriguing finding does not tell us. It does not tell us whether old patterns of belief and practice endure, but southerners now are less inclined to use the traditional labels. We do not know whether the South has become less evangelical or the rest of the country has become more so, although other evidence suggests that the latter is the case. And even if there are fewer southern evangelicals and even if they will confront increased cultural pluralism, that does not doom evangelicalism in the region. If sociologist Christian Smith's "subcultural identity theory" of religious strength is right, U.S. evangelicalism "thrives on distinction, engagement, tension, conflict, and threat." Cultural pluralism, Smith argues, "provides an environment within which well-adapted religious traditions—like evangelicalism—can flourish." Whether or not southern evangelicalism flourishes in the decades ahead, at the start of the twenty-first century the South looks somewhat less distinct. Seven out of ten southerners still affiliate with Protestantism, and the old Baptist dominance persists (46.5 percent), but there is evidence that the region is less disproportionately "fundamentalist" and "evangelical" in its theological vision.[6]

Third, some places in the South have been more religiously diverse than others. It still makes sense to talk about the South as a distinct religious and cultural region, but we should not minimize the intra-regional variation. That was true before Europeans arrived and long afterwards. The U.S. census in 1906 documented this variation, for example. Methodists and Baptists dominated in Alabama, Arkansas, Florida, Georgia, Mississippi, Tennessee, Virginia, and the Carolinas. Yet Catholics formed a majority in Louisiana, and showed significant strength in Kentucky. When we add Texas to the mix, the religious demography becomes less homogenous. And even within states with a legacy of Baptist-Methodist predominance, religious outsiders congregated here and there: for example, in the early twentieth century Greek Orthodox Christians gathered in Atlanta, Jews built a synagogue in central Savannah, and Italian Catholics worshiped in St. Helena, North Carolina.[7]

Fourth—and this brings me to my main point—diversity has been intensifying in the South since the 1970s. In 1999, 15.3 percent of southerners claimed Catholic identity, and altogether more than one in five (21.1 percent) affiliated with some non-Protestant faith—Catholicism, Judaism, Hinduism, Islam, Buddhism, or another religious tradition. The Bible Belt has loosened a bit, I suggest, even if its hold on the region still can be felt on Sunday mornings in white-wood and red-brick Protestant churches all across the South. Transregional and transnational migration has been changing the religious and ethnic character of the South. Economic realignments—and a variety of social and technological changes, including the introduction of air conditioning—have lured migrants from the North and Midwest to the Sunbelt, including areas of the South. That has meant, for example, more Catholics from the Northeast and Lutherans from the Midwest. Just as importantly, temporary, circular, and permanent transnational migrants from Asia, the Caribbean, and Latin America have been changing the southern religious landscape. The national immigrant population almost doubled between 1970 and 1990. By 1994, 22.6 million Americans—nearly one in eleven U.S. residents—were foreign born. Of course, Atlanta is not Los Angeles and Richmond is not New York, but transnational migrants have found their way to the South, too. Even if some states, including Mississippi and Kentucky, show less demographic change, Latinos and Asians taken together now make up almost 14 percent of southerners, and the 2000 census counted 8.1 million southern immigrants, or 8.8 percent of the regional population. The South's foreign-born population more than quadrupled between 1960 and 2000. In Texas, 2.9 million foreign-born residents formed 14 percent of the state's population, and almost 17 percent of Floridians were born outside the United States.[8]

These new migrants have come for varied reasons. Political crises have pushed refugees from their homelands, and some of those have settled in southern cities. The obvious example is Miami, which was a southern Protestant town when Fidel Castro's revolutionary army marched into Havana in January 1959. Fleeing the new socialist state, hundreds of thousands of Cuban exiles boarded planes, boats, and rafts to cross the warm waters of the Straits of Florida. Other refugees from Central America and the Caribbean joined them. By the 1990s, Latinos formed the majority, and Roman Catholicism had become the city's predominant faith. Those new Latino Catholics have transformed Miami: for example, at the Shrine of Our Lady of Charity, where hundreds of thousands of exiles pray to Cuba's national patroness. Other refugees have made their homes in other cities and towns all across the South, including the Hmong in Selma and the Vietnamese in New Orleans, and they have done their part to reconfigure the region's religious landscape, too.[9]

Political changes in the United States also have played a role: the 1965 Immigration Act altered the old national quota system and allowed larger numbers of voluntary migrants from Asia and Latin America to legally cross U.S. borders. Those migrants have brought with them multiple religions, including Hinduism, Catholicism, Islam, Sikhism, Jainism, Vodou, Santeria, and Buddhism. By 2000, when a new federal law allowed even more immigration visas, approximately 24,358 Vietnamese—Buddhist, Catholic, and Confucian—claimed residence in Louisiana. Approximately 46,132 Asian Indians, many of the them Hindu or Sikh, found their way to Georgia, and 47,609 Filipinos, the overwhelming majority of them Catholic, had settled in Virginia. Atlanta boasted approximately 10,000 Buddhists, 12,000 Hindus, and 30,000 Muslims; and followers had built temples and mosques in and around the city. Even in southern states with smaller Asian immigrant populations—such as Arkansas, Alabama, and Tennessee—observers could notice signs of the new religious diversity: for example, at Wat Buddhasamakeedham, a Theravada Buddhist temple in Fort Smith, Arkansas, and at the Sri Ganesha Temple, an Indian-style Hindu building in the capital of country music, Nashville. And the new (and not so new) Latino presence is even harder to miss. It is obvious in Texas, where a quarter of the residents claim Hispanic heritage. But elsewhere in the South—defined as the Gallup Poll does, as the eleven former Confederate states plus Kentucky and Oklahoma—more recent Latino migrants have transformed some states, especially Florida with its 2000 Hispanic population of more than 2.7 million. And all across the region, Latinos, both circulatory migrants who leave when the growing season ends as well as those who have made the South their home, have filled the pews of Catholic, and some Protestant, churches. Even unchurched Latinos, like the Mexican migrant laborer who chalked an image of Our Lady of Guadeloupe on a railroad overpass in Raleigh, have left their mark on the landscape.[10]

Asians and Latinos in Contemporary North Carolina: A Case Study

We might expect to find ethnic and religious diversity in Texas, with its unbroken Hispanic heritage, and in Florida, with its influx of migrants since the 1960s, but this new diversity is evident throughout the South. Consider North Carolina, which traditionally has been one of the region's Protestant strongholds and, as recently as 1990, had foreign-born Hispanic and Asian populations of less than 2 percent. Even though the older patterns of Protestant ascendancy persist, Latinos and Asians have had an impact in North Carolina. According to the 2000 census, which did not count illegal migrants, 113,689 Asians and 378,963 Hispanics lived in the state. Between 1990 and 2000, every county saw an increase in Asians and Hispanics. The Asian population of Mecklenberg County rose 197 percent (to 25,186), Guilford County increased 226 percent (to 12,168), and Wake County swelled 201 percent (to 24,622). The Hispanic increases between 1990 and 2000 were even more dramatic, as the number of Latinos grew from 77,000 in 1990 to more than 377,000 ten years later. Six counties boasted increases of more than 1,000 percent, and many others found themselves transformed by migration. Durham County's Hispanic population rose 729 percent in the decade, and the city of Durham became an "all-minority" municipality where no racial or ethnic group could claim a majority. In 2000 Durham was 48 percent white, 39 percent African American, 8 percent Hispanic, and 3 percent Asian.[11]

Those demographic changes were evident, for example, in public schools throughout the state. By 1993 school officials in Charlotte began to sense the changes as children from sixty-seven nations, who spoke forty-four languages, showed up for school on the first day. The majority of those new students were the children of Southeast Asian immigrants, especially Vietnamese. And in 1999 hundreds of parents attended a school board meeting in Siler City, a small town in central North Carolina, to express their worries about the ethnic and linguistic shifts that their traditional southern town had witnessed in recent years. When schools opened in Siler City in fall 1994, 15 percent of the students were Latinos; five years later that proportion had grown to 41 percent. Hispanics had become the largest ethnic group.[12]

And North Carolina's new migrants, young and old, have not always received a warm welcome. In June 1998 Durham's community leaders felt the need to organize the "Operation TRUCE Campaign," which was aimed at reducing the rising violence against Latinos. And consider events in McAdenville, which locals dubbed "Christmastown, USA" because it draws a million visitors every December to view the dazzling display of 425,000 Christmas lights. In the summer of 2001, the 616 residents of that small mill

Thomas A. Tweed

town did what so many other communities across the region and the nation have done: they used zoning codes to prevent Asian American Buddhists from transforming an existing building into a new temple. Officials and residents pointed to legitimate concerns—about traffic and parking—and they suggested that "it wouldn't have been any different if they'd been Baptist or Methodist." But not far beneath the surface were other worries about the Lao and Thai migrants and their unfamiliar religion, as with a forty-nine-year-old neighbor who worried about "what it might bring into the neighborhood." Those same worries surfaced even more clearly in Siler City, the largest town in rural Chatham County, which witnessed a 741 percent increase in the Hispanic population during the 1990s. On February 19, 2000, four hundred residents gathered at the steps of city hall to hear David Duke, the former Louisiana state legislator and current director of the National Organization for European American Rights. A service station owner, whose license plate reads "ARYAN," had invited Duke to condemn Siler City's new ethnic diversity at a public rally. And the former Ku Klux Klan grand wizard did not disappoint the crowd. "Siler City is at a crossroads," said Duke. "Either you get your public officials to get the INS in here and get these illegal immigrants out or you'll lose your homes, you'll lose your schools, you'll lose your way of life." As some Latino migrants and their supporters stood by with signs that signaled their dissent, Duke ended by linking local and national developments: "Siler City is symbolic of what's happening in America. Your battle here is America's battle."[13]

And those on both sides of the battle lines could not fail to notice that the increase in the Asian and Latino populations also has affected religious life in North Carolina. Most of the state's 12,600 Koreans are Protestants, as are some of the 19,000 Chinese. Some Latinos converted to Pentecostal and evangelical Protestantism after they arrived, in response to vigorous missionary efforts by some congregations. But most of the newcomers have added to the spiritual heterogeneity of North Carolina. For example, they have increased dramatically the state's Catholic population. Across the nation Latinos are a growing presence in the Catholic Church, where they now constitute about one-quarter of all U.S. Catholics. And, according to a 2000 report by the National Conference of Catholic Bishops, North Carolina included two of the four U.S. dioceses with the highest percentage of growth among Hispanic Catholics: Charlotte, which topped the list, and Raleigh, which was fourth. The Latino Catholics in North Carolina have continued their traditions of domestic devotion to Mary and the saints that they learned in their homelands, but many also attend the local parish, when they can find Spanish-language masses. As recently as 1990, that was much more difficult than it might seem. The Diocese of Raleigh was caught off guard by the rising migrant population, and it scrambled to find Spanish-speaking priests. Sometimes that caused tensions, as when most of the Latinos left Holy Cross Church in Durham in 1996, after the new pastor discontinued the bilingual mass. On October 13 of that year, the Latino parishioners walked out, with one middle-aged Mexican migrant carrying the statue of Our Lady of Guadeloupe down the church's front steps. Those exiled Latinos found a spiritual home across town at Immaculate Conception Parish, where the priest established a Spanish mass for the 284 Latinos, and more than two hundred other unregistered Hispanic households. As at Immaculate Conception, the state's Catholic leaders slowly began to respond to the new Latino presence. By 2000 fifty-four parishes in the Diocese of Raleigh had at least one Spanish-language mass, including Saint Julia's in Siler City, where parallel congregations of Anglos and Latinos meet on Sunday mornings in the small white church for the English mass at 9:00 A.M. and the Spanish celebration at 11:15. This would not be news in Florida or Texas, of course, but in the home of Billy Graham, a state with the traditionally southern Baptist-Methodist dominance, it is noteworthy.[14]

It is noteworthy, too, that several dozen Buddhist, Muslim, Jain, and Hindu congregations now meet across the state in converted homes and renovated churches and even in new structures built according to traditional Asian architectural models. Approximately twenty thousand Asian Indian immigrants made their homes in North Carolina in 2000, and the Hindus and Jains among them meet for worship in centers across the state, including a Swaminaryan Temple in Charlotte, a Jain Study Center in Garner, and a Hindu temple in Morrisville. The latter is a modest structure dedicated in 1985 by the Hindu Society of North Carolina, whose members hail from different areas of India, North and South. To accommodate the variety of regional and devotional styles, the founding members turned democratic: they voted on which images to enshrine in their new worship center, a practice rarely used in India, where temples tend to install clusters of mythically related deities. This turn to democracy stalled but did not prevent intracommunity conflict. Recently, some Hindus who were born in South India decided that the eclecticism—and even the subtle North Indian bias—of the Morrisville temple did not meet their spiritual needs, so they have begun to construct a second temple in the Raleigh area, in suburban Cary. And on September 3, 1999, five Hindu priests from across the United States presided at a four-day ceremony to install the South Indian temple's primary image, a statue of Sri Venkateswara, the god of wealth and well-being. Soon North Carolina Hindus will be able to claim another major worship center.

The state's Buddhists, both cradle Buddhists and converts, can practice their faith in fifty-five temples and centers. Most important for North Carolina's emerging diversity, sixteen temples in 2001 nurtured Asian American devotees across the state. Southern California's Hsi Lai Temple, the largest Buddhist temple in the western hemisphere, has an affiliated center in the Tar Heel State: the Buddha's Light International Association in Chapel Hill and Cary. Local leaders of that Taiwanese transnational movement founded in 1980 by the Venerable Master Hsing Yun, a Mahayana Buddhist teacher, aim to nurture the state's Chinese devotees and, more broadly, to establish a "Pure Land on Earth," a peaceful and just world community. One hundred fifty members with more modest goals worship on Sundays at Chua Van Hanh. At that expanding Vietnamese temple in a North Raleigh neighborhood, devotees chant the Lotus Sutra in their native tongue and make sense of their exile in America. And the temple helps, as one middle-aged refugee told me in 1994: "At first we were homesick and religion-sick, but now it's better since we have the pagoda." Hundreds of Southeast Asian Buddhists practice at two temples in Greensboro: Chua Quan Am, a Vietnamese Mahayana Buddhist center, and Greensboro Buddhist Center, a ten-acre monastery where three resident monks guide Lao and Cambodian migrants. The state's first Buddhist temple, Wat Carolina Buddhajakra Vanaram, had two Thai monks in residence by 1988. That Theravada Buddhist monastery, with its traditional red curved roof, was built in Bolivia, a small Protestant town in eastern North Carolina, about a thirty-minute drive southwest of Wilmington. The founding president, a lay follower from Bangkok, explained that he began the effort to build the temple "to give people from Southeast Asia a place to worship." And at first the local residents and the congregation at nearby Antioch Baptist Church did not know what to make of the saffron-robed Thai monks and the new Asian-style building. "This area never had to deal with internationals before," the Baptist pastor explained. "Then it was thrust into becoming an international town overnight."[15]

Symbols of the Emerging Diversity

One symbol of the state's transnationalism, and its emerging religious diversity, can be found in an unlikely place, Raleigh's North Carolina Museum of History, which dedicates itself to "preserving state, regional, and local history for future generations." This museum, which was founded in 1902 and moved to a new building in 1994, might be expected to sponsor the fall 1999 exhibition on "North Carolina and the Civil War." But it also installed a more surprising and revealing exhibit for the opening of the new building.

On March 23, 1994, Phramana Somsak Sambimb, a Thai monk from Wat Greensboro, stood before a home altar in a corner of the museum. He placed two white candles on either side of a twenty-inch bronze image of the Buddha, and in the middle he put three sticks of incense and several paper Lotus flowers. The monk chanted, bowing before the Buddha, and after five minutes the domestic altar was consecrated. "That OK," Sambimb announced.[16]

It is hard to know if all visitors to the museum agreed with the Thai monk, but this permanent exhibit signals the state's rising awareness of Asian religions. Buddhists had become visible enough by 1994 that when curator Sally Peterson planned a folklife exhibit on the everyday religious practice of North Carolinians, she felt compelled to include the Buddhist home altar along with Protestant, Jewish, Muslim, Hispanic Catholic, and Hindu artifacts. Peterson and other museum officials "expected a lot more negative criticism than we have actually gotten." And docents report that when they "take people through who happen to be Hindu or Buddhist or Jewish, they're really pleased to see something there." Still, the museum staff has received some criticism on the comment cards they make available to visitors. One Raleigh resident, who was raised as a Buddhist by his Vietnamese mother and American father, wrote in 1994 that the "placement of [the Buddha] statue should be higher. It's sacrilegious to *look down* on an image of Lord Buddha." If that complaint from a local Buddhist only confirms the perceptions of the state's growing religious diversity, another comment card was somewhat more negative. A woman from Burgaw, North Carolina, reported in 1996 that she was "concerned about seeing the Hindu and Budhu [*sic*] being represented." "What percentage are there of these in N.C.?" she asked. In a written response to this visitor, the curator argued that "membership of [Hindus and Buddhists] numbers in the thousands" and that "showing how these historic world religions are represented in North Carolina demonstrates how our state has become an international community." The museum archives do not include any record of the visitor's reaction to the letter, and it is difficult to know how most other North Carolinian visitors respond to the Buddhist home altar. Even if many who have not filled out comment cards are quietly troubled by the inclusion of Asian religious images—or the exhibit's implication that Protestantism is only one of many southern religions—it is still important to note that the exhibit would have been unthinkable at a North Carolina history museum three decades ago. The state's religious landscape is changing, and the varied home altars displayed in Raleigh represent those changes.[17]

The emerging religious diversity of the state and the region is symbolized even more vividly at another site southeast of the Raleigh museum, in Clinton, the Sampson County seat. Economically, politically, and religiously Clinton has been the typical southern town. Its economy has depended on tobacco, vegetable, and hog farming, and it has one of the oldest cotton markets in the state. By 2000 the town included Catholic, Mormon, and Unitarian Universalist churches, as well as three Methodist and four Pentecostal houses of worship.

Thomas A. Tweed

But most residents attend one of Clinton's many Baptist churches. Not far from a prominent Baptist church stands the town's cultural center, the Sampson County Courthouse, which was first built in 1801. On the courthouse lawn stands a Confederate monument, memorializing the South's Civil War dead. As in many other towns in the state and the region, the local chapter of the United Daughters of the Confederacy decided in 1908 to honor the sons of Sampson County who lost their lives. In 1916 town officials unveiled the Confederate memorial. For its chiseled inscription Mrs. Annie Graham Grady, the local president of the United Daughters of the Confederacy, chose lines from "March of the Deathless Dead," a poem by Abram Joseph Ryan (1838–1886), widely recognized as the poet of the Confederacy. The monument's inscription reads:

In Honor of
The Confederate Soldiers of Sampson County
"Who bore the flag of a sacred trust
And fell in a cause, though lost, still just
And died for me and you."
1861–1865[18]

This monument to the Lost Cause, the South's civil religion, stands only two blocks from Clinton's lone Catholic church, Immaculate Conception Parish. And eighty years after local Protestants dedicated the Confederate memorial, the courthouse was the site of another public ritual, a celebration that symbolizes the emerging diversity. Just after noon on the December feast day of Our Lady of Guadeloupe, the patroness of the Americas, several hundred Latinos gathered at Immaculate Conception Church to await the six-hour festival, which would include a procession, mass, and meal. The church that drew the Virgin's devotees was architecturally unspectacular, a small brick and wood structure with four columns at the entrance and a white steeple on top. But that afternoon something unusual happened there and in the streets of that southern Protestant town.[19]

Bishop Joseph Gossman of the Raleigh Diocese and Immaculate Conception's two priests celebrated a mass for seven hundred devotees, almost all of them Latinos, in the town's middle school at two o'clock, and after that they all walked to the cafeteria next door for a traditional meal of pork, tortillas, and beans. But first there was a procession through the streets of Clinton and past the courthouse lawn. At one o'clock, the streets outside the church were lined with cars that had become mobile shrines to Mary. Mothers fussed with their children's traditional Mexican costumes, and men readied the red pickup truck that would carry the image of Our Lady of Guadeloupe. Then, just after one o'clock, the priest, carrying incense, blessed the truck, and the procession began.

With the three Anglo clergymen leading the way, Latinos who have traveled from all over eastern North Carolina to attend wind their way through the streets. Men from the Mexican state of Zacatecas perform a traditional dance as they pass dry cleaners and drug stores. Young children, on their best behavior, sit in the rear of the truck, the Virgin's truck. And the rest of the Latino devotees, many of whom work in nearby fields or the hog-processing plants, march behind, as the women and girls sing hymns to the Virgin in their native Spanish. The cars, which devotees have decorated with streamers and images, follow. When the procession reaches Sampson Middle School auditorium around two o'clock, the mass begins with more singing. Bishop Gossman's sermon, which draws only polite applause, was not the center of the ritual for most participants, even if the clergyman used the occasion to evangelize and apologize. Looking out toward the slanted rows of auditorium seats, he tried to use popular devotion to exhort the people to center Jesus and attend mass. Mary, he told them, leads to Jesus: "Mary shows us how to live and follow her son, Jesus." Then the bishop noted the contemporary cultural context. "All of us have problems," he said, "and you who come from Latin America have many problems. . . . Mary, the Virgin of Guadeloupe, will always be present for you with a mother's love." And, in English, the bishop continued by acknowledging that the diocese had been unprepared for the migration of so many new Catholics: "My special hope is that you who have come recently to this country and our diocese will feel welcome." That drew the only spontaneous and loud applause of the afternoon from the crowd, the only time the people did not await the translation or the interpreter's encouragement. "You are not visitors," the Anglo Catholic leader continued. "You are our brothers and sisters." And then Bishop Gossman got to the apology as he ended: "I wish we could serve you better. Please believe me when I tell you we are trying our best. We will try to do better and better. . . . Let us pray for each other and the happy fiesta of Our Lady of Guadeloupe."[20]

That sermon and the rest of the public ritual had multiple meanings. For interpreters of American Catholicism, the bishop's homily is historically significant since a leader of North Carolina's Catholics acknowledged the church's slow response to the recent Latino migration. It says much about one of the most pressing challenges now facing U.S. Catholicism—a challenge made vivid by the Latino Pentecostal storefront church that stands only a few blocks from Immaculate Conception parish. For many of the Latino devotees, however, the sermon was an interruption in the half-day festival. They endured the bishop's talk but cared more about the singing, praying, and eating. They came to express their needs and their gratitude to the Virgin, to gather with others who speak their language, and to remember the practices of their Latin American homelands. One thirty-six-year-old Mexican-born man from

Jacksonville, North Carolina, offered a common comment. That immigrant, who plans to stay in the United States, came to the Clinton festival to keep Mexican, and Catholic, traditions alive for his children: "I want my seventeen-year-old daughter to know the culture." And there are other meanings. For interpreters of southern religion, and perhaps for the local Protestants who were watching football at home or window-shopping at the mall, another moment in the day's celebrations might have best captured its significance. Near the start of the procession, with the December sun overhead, the Virgin of Guadeloupe approached the courthouse lawn. It was that ritual moment, as she drove past the Confederate memorial, that best symbolized North Carolina's—and the South's—emerging religious diversity. Even this traditional southern Protestant town—with more than its share of tobacco farmers, gun racks, and Baptists—had begun to feel the effects of the post-1965 immigration. Our Lady of Guadeloupe had visited the Confederate memorial in—of all places—Clinton. And by the beginning of the twenty-first century, the same was happening throughout the state and the region. The Buddha had found a home in Atlanta, the Cuban Virgin had been exiled in Miami, and Asian Indian immigrants had enshrined Lord Ganesha in Nashville. The South was becoming more spiritually diverse. And if the region remained disproportionately pious and predominantly Protestant, the usual claims about southern religious homogeneity seemed less sure and more in need of qualification than ever.[21]

Notes

An earlier version of this article was published in *Southern Cultures* 8, no. 2 (2002), 72–93. I am grateful to Elizabeth Miller Buchanan and Chad Seales, my research assistants, who helped in numerous ways, as did those who attended the 1999 DuBose Lectures at the University of the South, where I first presented these ideas in a symposium on religion in the South. I also want to thank others who read earlier drafts, including Christine Heyrman, Charles Lippy, Donald Mathews, Christian Smith, and John Shelton Reed.

1. On religious regions in the United States, see Samuel S. Hill, "Religion and Region in America," *Annals of the American Academy of Political and Social Science* 480 (July 1985): 132–41; Wilbur Zelinsky, "An Approach to the Religious Geography of the United States: Patterns of Church Membership in 1952," *Annals of the Association of American Geographers* 51 (June 1961): 139–93; and Edwin S. Gaustad and Philip L. Barlow, *New Historical Atlas of Religion in America* (New York: Oxford Univ. Press, 2001). On the historical sources of the South's evangelical Protestant dominance, see, for example, Donald G. Mathews, *Religion in the Old South* (Chicago: Univ. of Chicago

Press, 1977); and Christine Leigh Heyrman, *Southern Cross: The Beginnings of the Bible Belt* (New York: Knopf, 1997). H. L. Menken's dismissal of southern religion has been quoted often, including in John Shelton Reed, *The Enduring South: Subcultural Persistence in Mass Society* (Chapel Hill: Univ. of North Carolina Press, 1986), 57; Reed's own comment about the South's "monolithically Protestant" character appears on the same page of that source. Samuel S. Hill Jr.'s observation on the lack of pluralism in southern religion can be found in his *Southern Churches in Crisis* (New York: Holt, Reinhart, and Winston, 1966), xvii. Influential overviews of Southern religion also highlight the region's religious homogeneity and evangelical flavor. The *Encyclopedia of Southern Culture* notes that religious forms in the region are "relatively homogenous" and "evangelicalism's dominance is decisive in making the South the 'religious region' that it is" (Charles Reagan Wilson and William Ferris, eds., *Encyclopedia of Southern Culture* [Chapel Hill: Univ. of North Carolina Press, 1989], 1269–70). And Donald Mathews suggests that "the South's distinctiveness as a region endures partially because of its especially pervasive, conservative Protestantism" ("Religion," in *The Encyclopedia of Southern History,* ed. David C. Roller and Robert W. Twyama [Baton Rouge: Louisiana State Univ. Press, 1979], 1046).

2. Southern Focus Poll, Spring 1998, Institute for Research in the Social Sciences, Univ. of North Carolina, Chapel Hill. On the persistence of regional patterns in the South and elsewhere in the United States, see Roger Stump, "Regional Divergence in Religious Affiliation in the United States," *Sociological Analysis* 45 (Winter 1984): 283–99.

3. As many observers have noticed, evangelical Protestantism has shaped southern cultures in pronounced ways—in music, art, entertainment, dress, and literature. For example, see Susan Ketchin, *The Christ-Haunted Landscape: Faith and Doubt in Southern Fiction* (Jackson: Univ. Press of Mississippi, 1994). The observations by Grant Wacker are found in his article "A Tar Heel Perspective on *The Third Disestablishment,*" *Journal for the Scientific Study of Religion* 30 (1991): 519–25. Wacker was responding to Philip E. Hammond, *Religion and Personal Autonomy: The Third Disestablishment in America* (Columbia: Univ. of South Carolina Press, 1992).

4. Barry A. Kosmin and Seymour P. Lachman, *One Nation Under God: Religion in Contemporary Society* (New York: Harmony Books, 1993), 51–55. See also Martin B. Bradley et al., *Churches and Church Membership in the United States: 1990* (Atlanta: Glenmary Research Center, 1992). Neither Southern Baptists nor evangelicals more broadly constitute a "homogenous religious subculture," as Kosmin and Lachman's phrase seems to suggest. On evangelical diversity, see Donald W. Dayton and Robert K. Johnston, eds., *The Variety of American Evangelicalism* (Knoxville: Univ. of Tennessee Press, 1991); and David Edwin Harrell, ed., *Varieties of Southern Evangelicalism* (Macon, GA: Mercer Univ. Press, 1985). Historians and sociologists have explored the tensions and complexities of Baptist piety in the South. For example, see Paul Harvey,

Thomas A. Tweed

Redeeming the South: Religious Cultures and Racial Identities among Southern Baptists, 1865–1925 (Chapel Hill: Univ. of North Carolina Press, 1997); and Nancy Tatom Ammerman, *Baptist Battles: Social Change and Religious Conflict in the Southern Baptist Convention* (New Brunswick: Rutgers Univ. Press, 1990).

5. A number of studies have noted the mixing of African and European practices, including Mechal Sobel, *The World They Made Together: Black and White Values in Eighteenth-Century Virginia* (Princeton: Princeton Univ. Press, 1987); Jon F. Sensbach, *A Separate Canaan: The Making of an Afro-Moravian World in North Carolina, 1763–1840* (Chapel Hill: Univ. of North Carolina Press, 1998); John Thorton, *Africa and Africans in the Making of the Atlantic World, 1400–1680* (New York: Cambridge Univ. Press, 1992); and Joseph E. Holloway, ed., *Africanisms in American Culture* (Bloomington: Indiana Univ. Press, 1990). For the history of Native Americans in the region, see Charles Hudson, *The Southeastern Indians* (Knoxville: Univ. of Tennessee Press, 1976). The quotation from Joel W. Martin is from his "Indians, Contact, and Colonialism in the Deep South: Themes for a Postcolonial History of American Religion," in *Retelling U.S. Religious History,* ed. Thomas A. Tweed (Berkeley: Univ. of California Press, 1997), 154.

6. Question 39, Southern Focus Poll. As John Shelton Reed points out in *The Enduring South* (100), "non-Southerners (Protestants, at least) are increasingly likely to have had the sort of religious experience that is theoretically central to Southern Protestantism." On this, see also Mark Shibley, "The Southernization of American Religion," *Sociological Analysis* 52 (1991): 159–74. For Christian Smith's observations, see his *American Evangelicalism: Embattled and Thriving* (Chicago: Univ. of Chicago Press, 1998), 89–90.

7. U.S. Bureau of the Census, *Religious Bodies: 1906* (Washington: Government Printing Office, 1910); Edwin S. Gaustad, *Historical Atlas of Religion in America* (New York: Harper and Row, 1962), 48–51; John Santucci, "The Italian American Agricultural Colony and Its German Missionary at St. Helena, North Carolina: A Parish History, 1905–1925," (Ph.D. diss., Univ. of North Carolina at Chapel Hill, 1994).

8. U.S. Bureau of the Census, *U.S. Census of Population: 1960: General Population Characteristics* (Washington, D.C.: U.S. Government Printing Office, 1960). Here and throughout the essay, all population statistics for 2000 are taken from U.S. Bureau of the Census, *U.S. Census of Population 2000: General Population Characteristics,* http://www.census.gov, released April 2, 2001. Other evidence supports the claims about the changing face of immigration in the South. One study by the Immigration and Naturalization Service (INS) immigrant arrival data, which does not include illegal migrants, identified "New Ellis Islands," counties "in which the number of new legal immigrants (1991–98) was equal in size to at least 50 percent of the existing foreign-born population in 1990." Applying this criterion, the study's authors found that the state with the most counties identified as "New Ellis Islands" was Georgia (with 25). And six of

the top ten states were in the South. The three metropolitan areas with the largest increase in legal immigration were southern cities: Nashville, Atlanta, and Louisville. See Steven A. Camarota and John Keeley, "The New Ellis Islands: Examining Non-Traditional Areas of Immigrant Settlement in the 1990s," Washington, D.C.: Center for Immigration Studies, 2001, http://www.cis.org/. On the Sunbelt as a cultural region, see Raymond A. Mohl, *Searching for the Sunbelt* (Knoxville: Univ. of Tennessee Press, 1990). For fifteen brief field studies of the new diversity, see O. Kendall White Jr. and Daryl White, eds., *Religion in the Contemporary South: Diversity, Community, and Identity*, Southern Anthropological Proceedings, No. 28 (Athens: Univ. of Georgia Press, 1995). There are a number of local and regional studies of Catholics in the South. For example, see Jon Anderson and William B. Friend, eds., *The Culture of Bible Belt Catholics* (New York: Paulist Press, 1995); Randall M. Miller and Jon L. Wakelyn, eds., *Catholics in the Old South: Essays in Church Culture* (Macon, GA: Mercer Univ. Press, 1983); Gary Wray McDonough, *Black and Catholic in Savannah, Georgia* (Knoxville: Univ. of Tennessee Press, 1994); Michael J. McNally, *Catholicism in South Florida, 1868–1968* (Gainesville: Univ. Press of Florida, 1982); and J. J. O'Connell, *Catholicity in the Carolinas and Georgia* (New York: D. J. Sadlier, 1879). There also is a substantial scholarly literature on southern Jews, including Leonard Dinnerstein and Mary Dale Palsson, eds., *Jews in the South* (Baton Rouge: Louisiana State Univ. Press, 1973); and Samuel Proctor and Louis Schmier, with Malcolm Stern, eds., *Jews of the South* (Macon, GA: Mercer Univ. Press, 1984). For an excellent comparative study, see Deborah Dash Moore, *To the Golden Cities: Pursuing the American-Jewish Dream in Miami and L.A.* (New York: Free Press, 1994).

9. On the early history of Miami and its southern Protestant character, see Thomas A. Tweed, "An Emerging Protestant Establishment: Religious Affiliation and Public Power on the Urban Frontier in Miami, 1896-1904," *Church History* 64 (Sept. 1995): 412–37. On the Cuban shrine, see Thomas A. Tweed, *Our Lady of the Exile: Diasporic Religion at a Cuban Catholic Shrine in Miami* (New York: Oxford Univ. Press, 1997).

10. *U.S. Census of Population 2000*. On the new immigrants, see Alejandro Portes and Ruben G. Rumbaut, *Immigrant America: A Portrait*, 2nd ed. (Berkeley: Univ. of California Press, 1996). For helpful overviews of the new immigrants and the religions they brought with them, see the reference work prepared under the auspices of the Human Relations Area File, the international research organization and archive in cultural anthropology: David Levinson and Melvin Ember, eds., *American Immigrant Cultures,* 2 vols. (New York: Macmillan, 1997). See also Stephen Warner and Judith G. Wittner, eds., *Gatherings in Diaspora: Religious Communities and the New Immigration* (Philadelphia: Temple Univ. Press, 1998); and Peter Kivisto, "Religion and The New Immigrants," in *A Future for Religion? New Paradigms for Social Analysis,* ed. William H. Swatos (Newbury Park, CA: Sage Publications, 1993), 92–108. All of these works on the new immigrants and several others that have appeared in the last decade,

Thomas A. Tweed

are helpful, but most have overlooked or de-emphasized the South. There are a few exceptions. On Atlanta, see Gary Laderman, ed., *Religions of Atlanta: Religious Diversity in the Centennial Olympic City* (Atlanta: Scholars Press, 1996). On Sri Ganesha Temple in Nashville, see Thomas A. Tweed and Stephen Prothero, eds., *Asian Religions in America: A Documentary History* (New York: Oxford Univ. Press, 1999), 299–303. For a case study of Houston that focuses on Indian and Pakistani immigrants in that city, see Raymond Brady Williams, *Religions of Immigrants from India and Pakistan: New Threads in the American Tapestry* (Cambridge: Cambridge Univ. Press, 1988), 254–75. Another edited volume considers an even wider range of new immigrant congregations in Houston: Helen Rose Ebaugh and Janet Saltzman Chafetz, eds., *Religion and the New Immigrants: Continuities and Adaptations in Immigrant Congregations* (Walnut Creek, CA: Alta Mira Press, 2000). For a brief attempt to survey developments in the region, see Thomas A. Tweed, "New Immigration," in *Encyclopedia of Religion in the South*, 2nd ed., ed. Samuel S. Hill and Charles Lippy (Macon, GA: Mercer Univ. Press, forthcoming). Interpreters have drawn the boundaries of the South in varied ways. Here I use the Gallup Poll's definition: the eleven ex-Confederate states, plus Kentucky and Oklahoma. This is less inclusive than the U.S. census's boundaries, which include Delaware, Maryland, the District of Columbia, and West Virginia. Of course, these mappings of the South, and all others, have their problems since residence by itself does not tell us all we want to know. If the South is a subculture, just as "southerner" marks collective identity, then other measures would be better, such as self-identification. In that view, a southerner is one who self-identifies that way. However, for the sake of simplicity, I take residence in the southern states as the working definition of the South. Those who live there are southerners. For an insightful analysis of the definitional issues, see Reed, *The Enduring South*, 9–19. A North Carolina newspaper ran a story about the Latino migrants, including Juan Salazar Cruz, a Mexican migrant who was sleeping beneath the underpass: Joby Warrick, "For Latin Immigrants, Home is a Bridge," *Raleigh News and Observer*, 23 Nov. 1994.

11. *U.S. Census of Population 2000*. County statistics about Hispanics and Asians can be found through searches by state and county at the U.S. Census Bureau Web site, http://quickfacts.census.gov/qfd/index.html. For an estimate of the (documented and undocumented) Latino migrant farm workers in eastern North Carolina, see Ned Glascock and Jen Gomez, "A Bitter Harvest for Hispanic Workers," *Raleigh News and Observer*, 24 Sept. 1999.

12. "Teaching English as a Second Language," *Raleigh News and Observer*, 29 Dec. 1993; Sumathi Reddy, "Parents Fear Ethnic Shift in Chatham," *Raleigh News and Observer*, 22 Sept. 1999. For an overview of the history of religion in North Carolina, see John R. Woodward, "North Carolina," in *Encyclopedia of Religion in the South*, ed. Samuel S. Hill (Macon, GA: Mercer Univ. Press, 1984), 535–50.

13. "What's Happening: Durham," *Raleigh News and Observer*, 5 June 1998; Joe DePriest, "North Carolina: Zoning Rules Block Path to a New Temple:

Buddhists Had Hoped to Build a Home in Town Known for Christmas," *Charlotte Observer*, 24 June 2001, Gaston regional section; Ned Glasock, "Rally Divides Siler City," *Raleigh News and Observer*, 20 Feb. 2000.

14. Chester Gillis, *Roman Catholicism in America* (New York: Columbia Univ. Press, 1999), 267; Yonat Shimron, "N.C. Dioceses Accommodate Nation's Largest Rise in Hispanics," *Raleigh News and Observer*, 1 May 2000; Kammie Michael, "Catholic Church to Drop Bilingual Service," *Durham Herald-Sun*, 14 Oct. 1996. For overviews of these two Catholic churches and a discussion of the Latino defection, see Susan Bales, "The Sensual and the Local: An Ethnography of First Communion at Holy Cross Church in Durham, North Carolina" (M.A. thesis, Univ. of North Carolina, Chapel Hill, 1998); and Susan Bales, "Immaculate Conception Catholic Church," The Five Faiths Project, University of North Carolina Museum of Art, affiliated with the Harvard Pluralism Project, 1999, http://www.fas.harvard.edu/~pluralism/ affiliates/ackland/immaculate_conception.html. See also her essay in this volume. For a partial listing of the parishes with a Spanish-language mass, see "Liturgias en Espanol," Supplement to the *North Carolina Catholic*, 22 Aug. 1999, 4A. The Siler City Catholic church, St. Julia's, attracts attention on Good Fridays, as Latino parishioners parade through the streets in a reenactment of Christ's passion. See Joyce Clark, "Holy Drama the Latino Way," *Raleigh News and Observer*, 6 Apr. 1999. I borrow the term "parallel congregations" from Paul David Numrich, *Old Wisdom in the New World: Americanization in Two Immigrant Theravada Buddhist Temples* (Knoxville: Univ. of Tennessee Press, 1996), xxii. Other southern dioceses have seen a similar rise in the number of Spanish-language masses. For example, in the Roman Catholic Archdiocese of Atlanta there were four locations that provided Spanish masses in 1990. By 2000, sixty Spanish masses were celebrated at forty churches. On this, see Chad Seales, "Religion, Location, and Identity Construction: Cuban Catholics in Atlanta," (M.T.S. thesis, Candler School of Theology, Emory Univ., 2000), 51.

15. For an overview of Buddhism in the state, see Thomas A. Tweed, ed., *Buddhism and Barbecue: A Guide to Buddhist Temples in North Carolina* (Chapel Hill: The Buddhism in North Carolina Project, 2001). That volume profiled thirty-three Buddhist centers, but by fall 2001 our collaborative project had identified and profiled fifty-five centers. For those profiles and other information, see the Buddhism in North Carolina Web site, http://www.unc.edu/ncbuddhism. On Hsi Lai Temple, and Chinese American Buddhism, see Stuart Chandler, "Chinese Buddhism in America: Identity and Practice," in *The Faces of Buddhism in America*, ed. Charles S. Prebish and Kenneth K. Tanaka (Berkeley: Univ. of California Press, 1998), 14–30; and Tweed and Prothero, eds., *Asian Religions in America*, 331–34. On that Chinese group in North Carolina, see Noel Yuan Lin, "Finding Buddha in the West: An Ethnographic Study of a Chinese Buddhist Community in North Carolina" (M.A. thesis, Univ. of North Carolina at Chapel Hill, 2001). On the Cambodian Buddhists at

Greensboro Buddhist Center, see Barbara Lau, "The Temple Provides the Way: Cambodian Identity and Festival in Greensboro, North Carolina" (M.A. thesis, Univ. of North Carolina at Chapel Hill, 2000). On Vietnamese Buddhism in America, see Cuong Tu Nguyen and A. W. Barber, "Vietnamese Buddhism in North America: Tradition and Acculturation," in *Faces of Buddhism in America,* ed. Prebish and Tanaka, 129-46; and Paul James Rutledge, *The Vietnamese Experience in America* (Bloomington: Indiana Univ. Press, 1992). The quotation from the devotee at the Raleigh temple is from my fieldwork interview with "DCN" (male, aged forty-nine), Chua Van Hanh, Raleigh, NC, 26 June 1994. Other sources referenced here are Christopher L. Lombardi, "Buddhist Celebration at Wat Buddhajakra Vanaram," *Carolina Asian News,* Dec. 1991, 15; and Debbie Moore, "A Separate Peace: Burgeoning Belief Brings Buddhists to Bolivia," *Raleigh News and Observer,* 18 Sept. 1988.

16. Stephan Hoar, "Buddhist Exhibit Reflects Diversity," *Raleigh News and Observer,* 24 Mar. 1994.

17. The comments about staff expectations and docent observations are taken from a taped interview in the author's files: Sally Peterson, curator, North Carolina Museum of History, interview by Elizabeth Miller Buchanan, 8 Nov. 1999, North Carolina Museum of History, Raleigh. The visitor responses are archived as follows: R.B. (resident of Raleigh), comment card, 31 July 1994, North Carolina Museum of History Archives; and P.O. (resident of Burgaw, North Carolina), comment card, 21 July 1996, North Carolina Museum of History Archives. I determined the religious affiliation of the cradle Buddhist who wrote a comment card in a telephone conversation: R.B., interview by author, 15 Nov. 1999. For the curator's response to the female visitor's comment card, see Sally Peterson to P.O., 22 July 1996, North Carolina Museum of History Archives. It is interesting to note that P.O., the woman who complained about the presence of Buddhists, also expressed concern about "the lack of representation of Greek Orthodox and Russian Orthodox." Neither Buddhists nor Eastern Orthodox have been highly visible in North Carolina's religious history before the 1970s. Only two comment cards written between April 1994 (when the exhibit opened) and November 1999 recorded negative reactions to the Buddhist altar. The curator reports that she has received slightly more complaints from Catholics, and three comment cards criticize the installation of a Mexican home altar. One Anglo Catholic from Siler City, the town with the dramatically increasing numbers of Latinos, complained that "I was left with the impression that all Catholics in NC must be either Latin in origin or suffer from exceptionally bad taste by turning their automobiles into a Shrine of Tackiness. In the future please see that we treat *all* religions with the dignity they deserve as protected by the Constitution" (M.A. [resident of Siler City, North Carolina], comment card, 21 June 1994, North Carolina Museum of History Archives). A Catholic visitor from Annandale, New Jersey, echoed those sentiments. "Your treatment of Catholicism is, in my opinion, totally unacceptable. You have chosen one *very*

limited, not to mention superstitious, view of a world-wide religion. While it may be P.C. to include Hispanic Latinos in your N. Carolina history, it would behoove you to do it separate from a 'religion.' It is just insulting" (J.S. [resident of Annandale, New Jersey], comment card, 30 July 1997, North Carolina Museum of History Archives).

18. Cora Bass, *Sampson County Yearbook, 1956-57* (Clinton: Bass Publishing Co., 1957.), 84. On the Confederate memorial, see Mrs. S. L. Smith, for the United Daughters of the Confederacy, North Carolina Division, *North Carolina's Confederate Monuments and Memorials* (Raleigh: Edwards and Broughton, 1941), 117–18. For the Ryan poem, see Joseph Abram Ryan, "The March of the Deathless Dead," *Poems: Patriotic, Religious, Miscellaneous* (New York: P. J. Kennedy, 1898), 76–77. For biographical information on Ryan, see John A. Garraty and Mark C. Carnes, eds., *American National Biography,* vol. 19 (New York: Oxford Univ. Press, 1999), 139–40.

19. On the South's civil religion, see Charles Reagan Wilson, *Baptized in Blood: The Religion of the Lost Cause, 1865–1920* (Athens: Univ. of Georgia Press, 1980). My account of the Our Lady of Guadeloupe Festival is taken from my field notes, 8 Dec. 1996, Immaculate Conception Church, Clinton, NC. For a journalist's description, see Ben Stocking, "Hispanic Culture Comes to Downtown Clinton," *Raleigh News and Observer,* 9 Dec. 1996.

20. Author's field notes, 8 Dec. 1996, Festival Mass, Sampson Middle School, Clinton, NC.

21. Author's field notes, 8 Dec. 1996, Immaculate Conception Church, Clinton, NC.

Thomas A. Tweed

CHAPTER 8

THE FLOWERING OF INTEREST IN
SOUTHERN JEWISH HISTORY AND ITS
INTEGRATION INTO MAINSTREAM HISTORY

THIRTY YEARS AGO THE LATE ARNOLD SHANKMAN ENTITLED AN ARTICLE "Southern Jews: People in Need of a History." He lamented, "From 1733 to 1973, nearly 250 years, the bulk of that which can be labeled Southern Jewish history has been filiopietistic, inaccurate, or irrelevant. Even worse it has been almost non-existent." Shankman identified Bertram Korn, Jacob Rader Marcus, Leonard Dinnerstein, Harry Golden, and Stanley F. Chyet as a "tiny handful of scholars . . . [who were] getting lonely" as they explored primary documents. Nonetheless, he found some hope in a few manuscripts just then appearing.[1] When I was lured into researching southern Jewish history by the editor of what was then the *Atlanta Historical Journal* about five years after Shankman's article appeared, the field remained in its infancy.[2] In 1979, although adding to Shankman's list, Chyet could write, "[W]ith some few exceptions, these studies have been episodic or they have focused on the Old South. . . . What has resulted is a certain provincialism in the presentation of Southern Jews and Southern-Jewish history."[3] Although some good works had appeared, only a few scholars, particularly Louis Schmier, were actively involved on a regular basis.[4] Today an incomplete bibliography is more than one hundred pages long, and a mini-library has appeared since 1996.[5] Accounting for this burgeoning interest as reflections of a matrix between history and culture and fostering integration of the specialty into broader courses are two purposes of this essay.

Understanding the rising interest requires both macro and micro approaches. The movement of America and American history toward pluralism has been influenced by various factors, including, on the broadest level, the criticism of government and society that prevailed during the 1960s, especially through the African American civil rights struggle, and, on the popular level, the interest in such works as Alex Haley's *Roots*. Rejecting an elitist approach, historians emphasized the "new social history" and "history from the bottom up." Almost simultaneously, immigration and ethnic history flourished across academic disciplines as the country and its historians, to borrow from Daniel Patrick Moynihan and Nathan Glazer, gradually moved "beyond the melting pot." To simplify, the civil rights movements facilitated the freedom of minority groups and their scholars to explore America's ethnic pasts. This is not to argue that this had not been done before but, rather, that this pluralistic image of history had now gained wide-scale acceptance.[6]

American Jewry and American Jewish history were impacted by and benefited from these and other trends. The latter included a changing sense of identity that rose dramatically in response to Israeli wars in 1967 and 1973, when fear for the survival of the Jewish state mingled with pride in its success. This, coupled with a declining anti-Semitism, encouraged many American Jews to feel more comfortable demonstrating for such causes as the plight of Russian Jews.

Parallels with African American history abound. The Americanization of the Holocaust, with its dual image of Jew as victim and as Warsaw ghetto fighter, reverberated much as the study of slavery stressed victimization but also survival and insurgency. Even as blacks and Jews seemingly came into conflict and partially broke ranks, resurgent American Jewish identity and pride mirrored those same forces among African Americans.

Into this environment came young Jewish historians, especially second- and third-generation descendents of East European immigrants, who benefited from the opening of the academy to them as students, teachers, and researchers. During the last thirty-five years, the work of these and others contributed to a flourishing of American Jewish history and the creation of numerous Jewish studies programs that, to some extent, were again facilitated by and found parallels in the dramatic rise in interest in African American history and the creation of black studies programs.

Still, concern for southern Jewish history increased only slowly during the late 1970s and into the 1980s. Two important anthologies, a number of articles, and a smattering of books from a very few presses did appear.[7] Nonetheless, the number of researchers deeply involved and the consciousness within the field of American Jewish history of southern brethren remained very limited.[8] It is always dangerous to speculate why something did not occur, but a few factors may be considered. First, the number of Jews in the region has always been small. Estimates usually suggest slightly over 1 percent of the total population. Although Charleston and then New Orleans showed relatively large concentrations of Jews before the Civil War, during the twentieth century major concentrations in Miami developed only since World War II and in Atlanta and other Sunbelt cities only since the 1970s.[9] During the twentieth century, also, the number of Jews and Jewish communities in small towns, a staple of the nineteenth- and early-twentieth-century experience, dramatically declined. Thus, relatively few people were directly concerned with the recording of their own history.[10] Second, although I may be guilty of circular reasoning, the number of Jewish studies programs and scholars interested in the Jewish experience working in the South lagged behind the Northeast. Few teachers and few programs meant that few graduate students entered the field, and few scholars could find academic recognition or employment through research in the area. A critical mass had to be achieved.

Because of the small Jewish population, the field itself could be viewed as peripheral in comparison to the history of the far larger and more powerful communities in the Northeast. This is reflected in the title of Eli Evans's *The Provincials: A Personal History of Jews in the South*.[11] Southern Jews, in essence, were colonists in relation to Jews in New York City and other northern enclaves. Melvin Urofsky observed, "[I]t appears that the Southern-Jewish experience differed both qualitatively and quantitatively from that of Northern Jewry. . . . the Jews in the South always remained a minority, at times an almost invisible minority. They did not affect the South so much as they imbibed its values and became part of it."[12] Like southerners generally, Jews could be viewed as exotic. Yet, because their history also differed somewhat from that of southern Christians who were also perceived as deviant, their distinctiveness and marginality are exaggerated even more. Historians continue to debate the relative impact the South had on its Jewish residents, and they on it.[13]

How can one explain the groundswell of the last decade?[14] Again several factors may be at work. The Sunbelt effect impacted greatly on the movement of Jews from the North to the South. Today south Florida trails only New York and Los Angeles in the size of its Jewish community, and Atlanta, with an estimated one hundred thousand Jews, also serves as a regional and national hub.[15] These Jews directly confront the question "Have there really been Jews in the South?" A generation of southern Jews growing older uses its resources in an attempt to answer that question and to preserve what in many areas are the records of a dying past. This again serves as a micro-category of the growing interest in the region as the South exerts influence on the national government and culture.[16]

Two parallel but nonetheless intertwined phenomena both contributed to the groundswell and benefited from it. The first reflects popular history and culture. Evans's book has proven to be so popular that it was recently reprinted as a twenty-fifth anniversary edition.[17] Evans emphasizes how a peculiar people adapted to a very peculiar southern environment. Equally, if not more significant, have been the plays of Alfred Uhry. Starting with *Driving Miss Daisy,* which became a movie, and continuing with *Last Night at Ballyhoo,* commissioned for the 1996 Summer Olympics in Atlanta, followed by *Parade,* Uhry's plays have won numerous awards and captivated the country.[18] Uhry's themes of ambiguity, alienation, marginality, and persecution highlight an ironic view of the experiences of Jews in the South.

Uhry pinpoints not only some of the major themes of what I will call the "mint julep school" but also of its critics. The only major Jewish character in his plays that is not a descendent of Central European (mostly German) Reform Jews is the foil to them in *Last Night at Ballyhoo.* If Irving Howe's *World of Our Fathers* creates a New York Jewry of East Europeans, the major thrust of southern Jewish history has created a world inhabited by German Jews who came to the South and achieved acceptance as they accepted southern mores, eschewed religious observance, and contributed to southern society.[19] Although none of these generalizations are incorrect in themselves, they have had the effect of emphasizing the distinctive and exotic and stifling a more complex reality. Rather than starting with the questions "How did Jews in the South live?" and "How can the history of Jews across the country be compared and contrasted?" they ask first, "What are the differences between Jews in the North and Jews in the South?"[20]

Evans's books and Uhry's plays deserve credit for hastening the popular and scholarly waves of which they are parts. Institutional structures have contributed to the groundswell of interest as well. The most important of these are the Southern Jewish Historical Society (SJHS) and the Goldring/Woldenberg Institute for Southern Jewish Life in Mississippi.

A short lived SJHS was established during the mid-1950s. Under the leadership of Saul Viener and others, it held a few meetings and published short articles in a journal. In 1976 Viener and Melvin I. Urofsky, among others, convened a conference in Richmond with the support of the American Jewish Historical Society. From this conference came a society that meets on an annual basis for scholarly presentations; sponsors book and article awards, grants programs, and a Web site; has published two anthologies; and, since 1998, produced a peer-reviewed annual journal, *Southern Jewish History.* Although having to balance the concerns of interested laypeople with those of scholars, the society has performed the important missions of fostering scholarship and nurturing a scholarly community framework.

The Museum of the Southern Jewish Experience grew out of the Henry S. Jacobs Camp that brings Jewish children together from throughout the South and is itself one way of networking and preserving Jewish identity. The brain-

Mark K. Bauman

child of Macy B. Hart, the museum was established in 1989 to preserve the records of rapidly disappearing small-town Jewry. In 2000 it came under the auspices of a new Goldring/Woldenberg Institute for Southern Jewish Life. With an extensive endowment and staff, the museum and institute have preserved objects and records and sponsored conferences, exhibits, photographic projects, and an extensive interview program. Besides publishing a newsletter, the institute is supporting a program to provide circuit-riding educators to declining communities, as well as new book and film series.[21]

Numerous other examples illustrate popular interest. Jewish historical societies with regular conferences sprang up in Texas (established 1980), North Carolina (established 2003), and South Carolina (established 1994). By 2003 at least twenty-one archives, museums, and societies specializing in southern Jewry appeared in the region. In 1990, Mosaic, a pioneering exhibit that portrayed the Florida Jewish experience and was organized by Henry A. Green and Marcia K. Zerivitz, began traveling the state.[22] This contributed to the creation of the Sanford L. Ziff Jewish Museum of Florida, which opened in 1995.[23] The Atlanta Jewish Federation sponsored exhibits celebrating 250 years of Jewish life in Georgia (1983) and 150 years of Atlanta Jewish history (1994), while the Jewish Historical Society of South Carolina, the McKissick Museum of the University of South Carolina, and the College of Charleston sponsored "A Portion of the People: Three Hundred Years of Southern Jewish Life" (2002), which continues as a traveling exhibit today. Atlanta's Ida Pearle and Joseph Cuba Archives and Genealogy Center of the William Breman Jewish Heritage Museum (established 1994), under the direction of Jane Leavey, boasts of being the largest museum and archive south of Cincinnati devoted to the subject. It houses an extensive oral history collection begun in the late 1970s.[24] PBS documentaries have appeared on Jewish life in the Mississippi Delta, Louisiana, and Texas; and Bill Aron's photographs are exhibited regularly.[25] Reaching centennial and later anniversaries, congregations have sponsored illustrated histories.[26]

Memoirs, diaries, and historical fiction have flourished in this mixed popular and scholarly environment.[27] One of the earliest and most insightful diaries is that of Clara Solomon, a New Orleans teenager during the Civil War whose account sheds substantial light on the impact of the war on Jews, how they were integrated and yet apart from the community, the roles of women, and relations between the family, their slave, and servant.[28] A diary by Helen Jacobus Apte details the life of an affluent Jewish woman of German descent in Florida and Georgia during the early twentieth century. It illustrates the limited roles of women of the era and the ups and downs of the cigar and other businesses.[29] The most noteworthy of the spate of memoirs is by Edward Cohen, who recalls his family and his years growing up in Mississippi. One of the striking aspects of this and other memoirs and recent works of fiction is that several depict East European enclaves during the twentieth century where Jews accommodate but remain in ethnic clusters and participate in occupations and recreational activities not very unlike their northern brethren.[30] Fictionalized family memoirs by Stella Suberman and Leta Weiss Marks describe acceptance but also the difficulties of the isolated small-town Jewish merchant in Tennessee and the mixture of acculturation, acceptance into Huey Long's Louisiana, and the cosmopolitan outlook of a distinguished New Orleans family, respectively.[31] Some of the memoirs and novels address the impact of the Holocaust and civil rights movement. Others relate to a southern Jewish literary tradition.[32]

Most memoirs and novels have been written by individuals born in the South who spent most of their adult lives in the North. Seemingly, as American Jews have found the South, transplanted southerners have drawn their identities from within their memories of family and region. In essence, northerners with southern roots have become professional southern Jews.[33] It is difficult to gauge how much this is reflected in the mixed message of nostalgia for and rejection of southern mores that marks these works. Perhaps this mélange of institutions and media, too, is part of a clarion call for a distinctive southern Jewishkeit quickly departing the scene. Jews associated with the South appear to feel an urgent need to forge an identity of place by recording their history.

The rise of academic interest brings substance to the popular side, particularly through presentations, publications, and personal interaction. But organizations such as the Southern Jewish Historical Society also foster the academic arena by providing incentives and a venue for papers and writing, as well as furnishing mechanisms for networking. The increase in consciousness has also engaged students who would not otherwise have pursued such research. Students now undertake honors papers, theses, and dissertations on southern Jewish topics in Jewish studies programs, American studies programs, and history departments throughout the country and even overseas. The College of Charleston, Emory University, Hebrew Union College, the University of Virginia, Duke University, and the University of North Carolina at Chapel Hill are among the schools offering courses in southern Jewish history.[34]

While an enormous amount of research remains to be done, several key areas have begun to be addressed. Numerous studies have appeared for individual cities and states. Unfortunately, few have achieved the sophistication of Steven Hertzberg's history of the Atlanta Jewish community,[35] and many are best described as chronicles.[36] Nevertheless, the general outlines of southern Jewish history are beginning to come into focus. During the colonial era, Jews

Mark K. Bauman

participated in an Atlantic economic and religious web. They settled in port cities as businesspeople and some traveled inland as traders. This pattern was partly repeated by succeeding waves of immigrants. During the nineteenth century and into the twentieth in disproportionate number, Jewish peddlers provided goods to a rural region and gradually settled in towns and cities as merchants. During the New South era, migrants from the North and immigrants from Central Europe and then from Eastern Europe augmented the earlier inhabitants, and department stores burgeoned. Where cities and towns thrived, Jews remained; when cities and towns declined or when economic, social, and/or religious opportunities seemed better elsewhere, they migrated. Recently, attention has been paid to Jewish life in small towns during the twentieth century. This writing offers insight into the mostly neglected role of the East European immigrants who largely replicated the experiences of their predecessors in this milieu.[37] Although most of our theological knowledge comes from congregational, city, and state histories, the number of rabbinic biographies is encouraging.[38] Although Protestantism greatly influenced nineteenth-century Reform, almost nothing has been written concerning theological interaction between practitioners of the two.[39]

Much of the economic, demographic, and institutional history derives from the city and state studies as well as from congregational histories. Nonetheless, some specialized studies are noteworthy. In one of the best of these, Eliot Ashkenazi probes the networks that Jewish wholesalers, peddlers, and shopkeepers forged to fill important economic niches in the region.[40] Numerous communities conducted population surveys shortly after World War II and again during the 1980s and 1990s. Few of these have been analyzed for the historian.[41] Again with few exceptions, one has to scour state and local histories for discussion of Jewish social service agencies.[42] Although of great importance to our understanding of changes in religious practice, social services, and activism, the roles of Jewish women in the South are just beginning to be discussed. As in smaller communities elsewhere, their roles appear pivotal.[43] A consensus is forming that as middle- and upper-class merchants in southern cities, Jews owned slaves and participated in the slave trade in similar proportions to non-Jews in the same class. They also actively supported the South during the Civil War.[44] As interest in African American–Jewish relations has increased, much has appeared on the often ambivalent interaction between the two in the South. The literature treats the relationship between Jewish business people and black customers and employees and the images each had of the other, as well as the Jewish role, or lack thereof, in the civil rights struggle.[45]

In terms of interaction between Jews and non-Jewish whites since the pioneering research of John Higham and Leonard Dinnerstein, emphasis has been placed on the acceptance Jews received in the South relative to Europe and elsewhere in America, at least until the Populist era.[46] One of the assumptions has been that the presence of widespread racism against African Americans shielded Jews, who also posed little threat because of their small numbers and because they accommodated themselves to the dominant culture and did not compete with other groups occupationally.[47] Ambiguity is reflected in this as in many areas. Jews in the South, for the most part, did succeed economically and played important roles in government as well.[48] They served as mayors of numerous southern cities and represented constituents in city councils, state legislatures, and the U.S. Congress, winning usually regardless of religion. Nonetheless an underlying theme of tolerance, as opposed to outright acceptance, clouds the picture. Anti-Semitism is too close to the surface and occurs too often to downplay. Southern Jews were integrally involved in national advocacy for Jewish acceptance and protests against anti-Semitic incidents.[49] If anti-black racism shielded Jews, as some argue, how can one make sense of the fact that the times of greatest prejudice against each coincided, and that outbreaks of persecution against African Americans typically sparked anti-Jewish incidents?[50]

Toward an Integration of Jewish History into the Religious History of the South

Thus far I have attempted to address the rising interest in southern Jewish history and to offer an introductory bibliography. Rather than addressing the issue of why it is important to study southern Jewish history, I will now deal with why and how to integrate it into southern history and southern religious studies in particular.[51] Many of the reasons for integration are obvious. Historians recognize the responsibility to record the histories of minorities as well as majorities. Doing so illustrates the diversity and complexity of the South. By exploring the history of Jews and other minorities, one can use the comparative perspective to gain a better understanding of these groups and the majority culture.

More specifically, there is little doubt that the region's environment had an immense impact on the peoples who inhabited it. Yet the picture can appear overly deterministic if black and white are the only categories employed. Although Jews were influenced by living in the South, I am struck by their divergence from the norm in terms of how they adjusted.[52] To offer a few examples: Whereas the majority of African Americans and whites were wedded to a rural, agricultural system, Jews lived as urban merchants. Whereas the region's population is often depicted as undereducated, parochial, and staunchly conservative, southern Jews are characterized by relatively high levels of education, a cosmopolitan perspective, and liberal bent. Whereas the majority religion is defined by evangelicalism, Judaism in the South is demarcated by its secularization and emphasis on a Jewish social gospel. However problematic the feminization of nineteenth-century white Protestantism is, the argument can certainly be made for the feminization of southern Judaism. The impact of the Civil War, Reconstruction, the rise of the New South and Populism, industrialization, and the civil rights movement differed decidedly from one group to another. Thus, by integrating Jews and other ethnic groups into the story of the South, the historian can better understand the impact of cultural baggage on the choices people made.

Integrating the religious history of Jews in the South by emphasizing similarities with white Protestants is problematic.[53] Instead, three variables may be addressed: the contrasts between white Protestants and Jews, the reasons for their diverse responses, and the impact they had on each other. The following is a rough outline of Jewish religious history in the South with some suggestions to assist in this endeavor.

During much of the colonial era, the small number of Jews in the South tried to maintain Jewish tradition but those outside the port cities found this most difficult. Often subject to de jure discrimination, but usually in fact tolerated if not welcomed, these Jews formed two of the first five congregations in America. These Savannah and Charleston congregations, like their counterparts in New York, Newport, and Philadelphia, conformed to the Sephardic rite of the Spanish and Portuguese homes of the most distinguished of their congregants. International in outlook and association, they remained in contact with and were assisted by fellow Jews and congregations in London, Amsterdam, and the Caribbean. Although overcome by Jews from central Europe during the early nineteenth century, the more prestigious Sephardim left their mark on congregational practices and ritual.

These Jews had departed lands in which they were singled out for persecution by Catholic Inquisitors, and/or they emigrated, after short sojourns, from Holland and England, where they were part of government-sanctioned communities. The relative tolerance and voluntarism the Jews found in America, coupled with their sparse numbers, contributed to substantial intermarriage before the Revolution in remote areas and in the towns and cities in later decades.[54] While Protestants experienced revivalism, Jewish religious practice and even membership declined with each generation. Unlike Protestants, they did not bring clergy with them. Groups of at least ten men could practice sacred rituals without professional functionaries, and America was not viewed as a congenial destination for European rabbis. The first ordained rabbi to come to America was Abraham Rice, who had a short and mixed career during the late Jacksonian era in Baltimore. Thus, education and the maintenance of tradition were left up to individuals, and the lures of the secular world contributed to the decline.[55]

As Protestant America experienced the Second Great Awakening, Jewish practices, participation, and spirituality were sorely challenged. Yet, before the 1870s, Judaism, unlike Protestantism, did not split into competing denominations. On the other hand, to accommodate a laity gradually departing from tradition and attempting to find acceptance in the eyes of the majority, Jews, starting in Charleston in the 1820s and 1830s, experimented with reform. More decorum in the service, the use of a choir and organ, mixed seating of men and women, and the participation of those who no longer kept the Sabbath or who intermarried were fought over amidst the processes of modernization and acculturation.[56] These changes were confined neither to the South nor to America. Rather, they reflect transatlantic forces led by the Germanic states toward middle-class norms in more tolerant and voluntaristic societies.

Although reform in America began in the South, key learned laymen in Richmond and New Orleans supported continuity. In Richmond one of those laymen mentored Isaac Leeser, who moved on to pulpits in Philadelphia. There he championed tradition against the moderate reformer Isaac Mayer Wise and the radical reformer David Einhorn, who served a Baltimore congregation, the first in America begun under the banner of Reform. Nonetheless, even Leeser was affected by the pull of accommodation to American Protestantism. At the behest of the women of the congregation, led by Rebecca Gratz, Leeser introduced the sermon for edification. Prior to this, rabbinic functionaries gave few discourses, and these were explanation of texts for education rather than for spiritual messages.

Indeed, women had such a decided impact on nineteenth-century southern Jewry that one can speak about a feminization of Judaism in the region mirroring that of the country at large. Many elements of Reform were geared toward and influenced by women. Men were departing the pews for the Saturday business so important in the United States, while women, traditionally limited to home observance, were taking their places. The middle-class lifestyle that included servants (in the South, often slaves) and the Protestant model also contributed to their greater participation. Rebecca Gratz of Philadelphia was the most important women's institution builder of mid-nineteenth-century American Jewry. Borrowing from tradition and the models of Jewish men and Protestant women, Gratz organized Jewish Sunday schools, homes for women and orphans, and ladies' Hebrew benevolent societies that were copied throughout the antebellum South, largely through a women's network. Unlike in Europe but common to Christian America, religious education and much of a growing philanthropic empire fell within the purview of women under the supervision of male rabbis and laymen. Jewish women raised money to endow the rabbinic position at Savannah's Mickve Israel.

Clearly Charleston and later New Orleans served as major centers of American Jewish life. As Charleston declined economically during the 1820s and thereafter, its highly educated, professional Jewish community members provided seeds, sustenance, and leadership for Jewish communities elsewhere.[57] Penina Moise, the first American Jewish poetess, composed hymns for Charleston's Beth Elohim and poems on Jewish and southern causes.

Still, moral fervor (or the absence thereof) drew neither many women nor their husbands into broader social reforms, including abolition. With their strong Christian bases, Jews were not welcomed into these reform movements. And conversion of others into Judaism was a sticking point rather than a priority. More often Jews were objects of Protestant missionary activities, and the creation of separate philanthropic institutions partly illustrated reactions to these efforts. Jews responded to certain secular needs, such as assistance for yellow fever or flood victims, but more frequently concentrated on parochial survival.

The latter included overseas relief and responses to incidents of anti-Semitism. Responses to international events and an inability to influence American policy contributed to the first successful short-term attempt to unify American Jews. The Board of Delegates of American Israelites came into existence in 1858. Southern Jews were deeply involved in its formation and leadership. That Jews came together across the country on the eve of the Civil War and that the organization continued after the war with little disruption contrasts with the histories of Baptist, Methodist, and Presbyterian churches that split along sectional lines during the 1830s and 1840s. While Jews were divided much like fellow Americans before and during the war, strong ties of religion, family, and business seem to have ameliorated any lingering sectional animosity. Although Jews apparently participated in and benefited from slavery and the slave trade in approximately proportional numbers to other Americans in the same demographic cohort, they were, as urban-oriented business people, less wedded to the system and could more readily adjust to changes after the war. Moreover, a high percentage of the Jews in the South arrived in the decades immediately preceding the war. Although typically loyal to the section of their adoption, these individuals reacted somewhat differently than the scions of families that had spent generations in the South. For these Jews, the issues that were so important to more entrenched southerners may have seemed less pressing.

Many of these factors were magnified after the war. Interaction between Jews across sectional lines seemed to have resumed automatically. Highly mobile, Jews readily moved across regions. Numerous migrants from the North augmented the sparse numbers of southern Jews. A boom took place in the creation of southern congregations, benevolent societies, cemetery associations, fraternal orders, and schools, often nurtured by Leeser and, especially after Leeser's death in 1868, by Wise. Fraternal orders begun before the war flourished afterward. Lacking competing denominational splinter groups, cooperation and integration were the rule. The 1870s through the 1890s witnessed a synagogue building boom with architecture and dedication programs geared toward gaining acceptance from the Protestant elite. In the Bible Belt, where church membership was normative, Jews joined congregations more than elsewhere.

Yet southern Judaism, as a part of American Judaism, also experienced tension and division. Congregations tore asunder and hired and fired rabbis frequently as traditionalists battled reformers. By the mid-1890s, however, southern congregations seemed to have accepted the Pittsburgh Platform of 1885 and Reform in disproportional numbers, many becoming bastions of classical Reform. In contrast to evangelical Protestants in the region who opted for revivalism and fundamentalism, southern Jews of central European descent swung toward a less spiritual and ceremonial religion with a prophetic social justice agenda, associated on the national arena with Isaac Mayer Wise and akin to the Protestant social gospel. Contrary to the view of southern Jews on the periphery, Jews in the region provided leadership on the road to Reform, and an early southern association provided a model and impetus to the creation of the movement's Central Conference of American Rabbis.[58] Borrowing from Protestantism, congregations replaced the male bar mitzvah with the confirmation for boys and girls, and some rabbis introduced Sunday services. Prior to the advent of public schools, to supplement their income and maintain multiple identities, many rabbis ran English-Hebrew-German academies.

And yet many reform efforts of both fundamentalists and modernists proved anathema to Jews. Christian Sabbatarianism translated into Sunday blue laws that forced Jews to either break their own Sabbath or refrain from business on both Saturday and Sunday. The rise of public schools meant that Jews had to contend with New Testament Bible readings, the use of Shakespeare's *Merchant of Venice* as an assignment, and not being given excused absences on Jewish holidays.[59] Missionary and prohibitionist activities often targeted Jews and their businesses.[60] The North Georgia Conference of the Methodist Episcopal Church, South, for example, licensed a convert from Judaism to proselytize Jews during the 1890s. Attacks of groups like the Men and Religion Forward movement in Atlanta against red-light districts were directed at Jewish liquor vendors and saloon keepers as well as at blacks. Although the anti-Semitic tendencies of Populists are debatable, as anti-black racism reached its nadir during the 1890s

Mark K. Bauman

and early twentieth century, so too did anti-Jewish prejudice. The dramatic rise of the industrial revolution with its dislocation of rural Americans required more than one convenient scapegoat, and Jewish businesspeople felt the brunt from both lower- and upper-class elements of the Protestant majority. The lynching of Leo Frank in Atlanta in 1915 and the rise of the modern Ku Klux Klan were not unrelated coincidences.[61] Nor was Frank the only Jew murdered in the South because of religious prejudice, although the Anti-Defamation League of B'nai B'rith organized in response to the Frank incident. Somewhat ironically, a proto-Zionism was advanced by some Christian millennialists even as the majority of Reform Jews eschewed the concepts of a messianic age and return to Israel.

Not all was negative. Jews continued to be relatively tolerated compared to African Americans and to Jews in Czarist Russia. Their rise economically continued. Although not accepted socially, they held elective political positions and contributed to the arts, culture, and education. Jewish women, in particular, through the National Council of Jewish Women (1893) and other club efforts, forged liaisons with their Christian counterparts.

When Wise's Hebrew Union College began training an American rabbinate in earnest during the last decades of the nineteenth century, many graduates traveled to the welcoming climate of the region and helped cement the move toward Reform. Although some rabbis readily crossed regional lines for career advancement, many entered pulpits they would serve for decades. Typically these rabbis accepted roles as "ambassadors to the Gentiles" or as Jewish community representatives. Stressing ecumenism and universalism, some rabbis' services were solicited by Universalist and Unitarian churches, and some Jews became practitioners of Christian Science although frequently continuing their association with the Jewish community.[62] As religious observance eroded among the laity, rabbis became the surrogate Jews.

The seemingly unified face of southern Jewry was short-lived. The Russian pogroms and anti-Semitic policies begun in 1881 fostered the onslaught of East European immigration. Although most of these immigrants sought opportunities in the industrial metropolises, many ventured south. Galveston often served as the southern Ellis Island of this group as Jews of the North sponsored the Industrial Removal Office, Galveston Movement, and Hebrew Immigrant Aid Society. Widespread fear of an outbreak of anti-Semitism in response to the wave of immigrants hitting the shores of New York led to the desire to disperse Jews into the interior of the country. Far more came of their own volition through the magnet of chain migration, however, than under community auspices.[63]

The immigrants brought with them their traditional practices, Yiddish culture, and ultimately a strong dose of Zionism. They created their own congregations, burial, and benevolent associations much as their predecessors had done. Like their brethren in the North, some debated the merits of socialism and communism and organized Farband/Arbeiter Rings. Except in industrial cities like Baltimore, or for a short while as cigarette and cigar rollers in Tampa or Raleigh, East European Jews who ventured south replicated the peddler–small shopkeeper experience of those who came before and did not enter factory doors as workers. As a result, few Jews in the South were directly involved in labor union activity, and the radical debates remained intellectual pursuits as opposed to practical considerations. Arbeiter Ring schools fostered Yiddish culture more than socialist ethics.[64]

The Jews of Central European descent initially welcomed and assisted the newcomers. Yet the assistance, especially as the numbers increased dramatically, tended to be patronizing. This reflected differences of class, education, culture, language, and religion, as well as the growing fear of an anti-Semitic backlash. The establishment of Jewish education alliances with classes in English, American cooking, vocational education, and even hygiene, following the social settlement model and usually taught by members of the National Council of Jewish Women, responded to the call for rapid acculturation. Often resentful, the newcomers accepted the aid out of necessity. Although calls for immigration restriction were not as loud in the South as elsewhere, Jews unified in their opposition to such legislation.

Such assistance was not new. *Tzedekah*, or righteous giving, is an integral part of Jewish precepts much as charity is to Christians and Muslims. The first major American Jewish philanthropist, Judah Touro of New Orleans, endowed many institutions throughout the country through his will. One of the major female benefactors of the nineteenth century also hailed from the South. A nurse and spy for the Confederacy during the Civil War, the German-born Texan Rosanna Dyer left a quarter of a million dollars to various organizations when she died in a Mississippi riverboat explosion in 1866.

The first organized Jewish charities in America and the South were specialized and geared to the assistance of people with the same national origins. The New Orleans Widows and Orphans Society (1855), greatly influenced by recurring outbreaks of yellow fever, is a case in point. Male and female Hebrew benevolent societies provided mutual aid for members as well as charity for non-members. During the 1880s regional Hebrew orphan homes sponsored by district B'nai B'rith lodges sprang up in cities around the country including Atlanta.

The declining needs of the earlier nineteenth-century immigrants and their descendents and the rising need of the newcomers contributed to the transformation of Jewish social services and indeed the structure of the Jewish community. The first citywide federation of Jewish charities was established in

Boston in the 1880s with communities in the South following during the early 1900s. These federations combined free-loan associations, free kindergarten and social settlements, Jewish education alliances, and National Council of Jewish Women efforts under one umbrella. They were designed to eliminate duplication of services and fundraising efforts, and to make giving more "scientific" and "rational." They gradually replaced "friendly visitors" with professional social workers. Although East Europeans and new Sephardic immigrants from the declining Ottoman Empire were brought into federation boards and eventually forged ties across national boundaries, federation efforts also often translated into social control over the efforts of the new immigrants. The federations also influenced the roles of rabbis. Although Reform rabbis typically spearheaded the creations of federations and served as federation officers, the professional heads of federations eventually usurped rabbinic power outside of the congregation. Federations were charter members of community chests, forerunners of the United Way, and these solicited federation personnel for leadership positions.

The Balkan Wars and World War I led to immense suffering for Jews in Europe. National relief efforts had their local counterparts and ushered in altered priorities for American Jewish communities. During the 1920s immigration restriction legislature essentially closed the nation's doors to Jews from Eastern Europe. Acculturation and the rise into the middle class, slowed only temporarily by the Great Depression, accelerated, and with these trends, domestic relief needs declined. Thus, with the rise of Hitler and persecution of German Jews, giving was focused overseas. Beginning in the 1920s but especially in the mid- to late 1930s, federations were again reorganized with the creation of separate yet coordinated fundraising and planning arms, and an arm to combat intolerance at home and abroad. The new structure and priorities also reflected the coming of age of the East European Jews who now worked as equals with their predecessors.

After World War II, assistance to Holocaust survivors, especially in their adjustment to America, followed a familiar pattern. But the limited number of survivors entering the South did not strain resources. Federations in major cities stressed scientific planning, research, Jewish demographic studies, and the use of experts as a huge building boom of Jewish community centers, old-age homes, synagogues, and religious educational institutions was launched. Southern cities housed regional offices of all of the major national Jewish defense organizations. At a 1938 meeting in Columbus, Ohio, the Reform rabbinate endorsed the creation of a Jewish homeland. Although some Reform rabbis and laypeople, a significant percentage of whom were from the South, rejected this reversal of policy and subsequently created the American Council for Judaism, efforts to assist the creation of Israel and then the infant state's fight for survival unified the Jewish community as nothing since the Mortara case. Now identity could be defined by association with Israel as it had been before by religion, nationality, social association, history, suffering, and peoplehood.

Parallels exist between Jewish and African American self-help efforts, especially among women, and similarities can be drawn with pan-national movements among African Americans and Irish Catholics. Christian missionary efforts also met needs of brethren overseas. Yet the amount of overseas aid required and its impact on American Jewry made the experience far more dominant if not unique.

The same cannot be said about twentieth-century structural innovations in small communities and in states with few Jews where outreach was essential. Here Jews accepted the lead of Methodists by introducing circuit-riding rabbis. They also used students from Hebrew Union College and, to a lesser extent, the Jewish Theological Seminary for High Holidays and to conduct services monthly in a fashion similar to Methodist "supplies." Reform and Orthodox rabbis, congregations, and/or benevolent societies in large cities or regional centers offered assistance to Jews in outlying communities. These included conducting periodic services and life-cycle events and offering expertise and mediation on such issues as kashrut and divorce. State rabbinic associations formed in Texas and North Carolina, among other states, to nurture the few and far flung rabbis, and Arkansas's state Federation of Jewish Charities assumed the role of local units. The North Carolina Association of Jewish Women boasted of being the first organization bringing together people across denominational divisions. In fact, cooperation between German Reform and East European Orthodox assumed various guises in communities with small Jewish populations. Sometimes they shared buildings and rabbis. These are examples of what may be called "survival mechanisms."

Larger communities supported more specialized and separated groups. Montgomery and Atlanta hosted Sephardic congregations begun early in the twentieth century by Jews from Greece and Turkey. Ladino, a mixture of Hebrew and Spanish, differed from the Yiddish and German of their predecessors. The Sephardim so differed in food preferences, songs, and other traditions that earlier comers sometimes questioned whether they were Jewish. Nonetheless, these Jews also obtained assistance and gradually gained acceptance through federation activities and as they advanced economically and educationally. Their ties to the Ottoman Empire also set them apart, although they crossed national and denominational boundaries on behalf of Zionism.[65]

East European Jews in Atlanta, Memphis, New Orleans, and other cities clustered residentially like their northern counterparts. Such clusters supported kosher butchers and other ethnic specialists, but with fewer rabbis and less money involved, conflict over supervision of (and the resultant income from) such establishments was lessened. In such places congregations named Anshe (or Anshi) S'fard emerged with adherents from Poland, the Ukraine, Hungary, and Romania. Quite small, these often ultra-Orthodox/Hassidic synagogues claimed adherence to the liturgy of the sixteenth-century rabbi and mystic Isaac Luria of Tsefat, Palestine. They came closer to Protestant fundamentalism in ritual and spirituality than most other Jewish congregations. But this was a small minority. More common were congregations established along landsleit lines and, with the process of acculturation, the gradual creation of less observant congregations among East Europeans. Although a few experimented with Conservatism around World War I, many Orthodox congregations in the South accepted Conservative affiliation during the 1940s and 1950s.

While fundamentalism dominated the image of black and white southern Protestantism, the tendency in Judaism was toward secularization. This changed somewhat after World War II. Some new Orthodox congregations were begun by more traditional East Europeans. During the 1950s and 1960s, many Reform congregations, reacting to the greater acceptance of pluralism in American society, the entrance of second generation East Europeans into the Reform rabbinate, and the loss of members, reintroduced ritual and spirituality.

Still, some Reform rabbis and a small but disproportionate number of laypeople, following a tradition begun during the 1890s, continued their prophetic mission by advocating an end to segregation, even though fear of retaliation and an anti-Semitic backlash quieted most. Rabbis joined ministers and priests in speeches for brotherhood under the auspices of the National Council of Christians and Jews and joined citywide ministerial associations.[66]

The last four decades of the twentieth century witnessed the movement of Jews from small southern towns and from the North into the burgeoning southern cities, suburbs, and college towns. This migration was augmented with Jews from Cuba, Iran, Russia, and Israel, some of whom formed their own infrastructure.[67] Congregations and institutions continued their move away from the inner cities, and the number of congregations and their religious practices multiplied. Citywide rabbinical associations were created. Communities ranging from Chabad Lubavitcher to Reconstructionist gay and lesbian congregations dotted the landscape along with Jewish day schools. At the dawn of the twenty-first century, the varieties of Jewish institutions and religious practices testify to the growing pluralism and tolerance of American society. Yet Jewish community leaders bemoan declining rates of affiliation and increasing rates of intermarriage, trends attributable to the same forces. Perhaps at no previous time have large southern Jewish communities so resembled their counterparts in the northern industrial cities and, simultaneously, mirrored the fragmentation of Protestant denominationalism.

By no means complete, this religious history of Jews in the South is a work in progress designed to illustrate certain specific forces and how the material available can and should be integrated into courses in religion in southern and American history. Coupled with the citations, it will also, I hope, nurture dialogue among historians interested in the varieties of religious experience and the challenges that comparative analysis pose.

Notes

This article was inspired by the feedback the author received to a presentation he gave at a conference on religion in the South at Emory University, November 1999. He greatly appreciates the encouragement of Gary Laderman, one of the conference organizers.

1. Arnold Shankman, "Southern Jews: People in Need of a History—An Historian's View," *Jewish Currents* (Dec. 1973), 16. Samuel Proctor and Malcolm Stern should be added to Shankman's list although southern Jewish history was a segment of their broader interests. See, for example, Proctor, "Pioneer Jewish Settlement in Florida, 1765–1900," in *Proceedings of the Conference on the Writing of Regional History in the South, with Special Emphasis on Religious and Cultural Groups* (Miami: n.p., 1956); Proctor, "Jewish Life in New Orleans, 1718–1860," *Louisiana Historical Quarterly* 40 (Apr. 1957): 110–32; Stern, "New Light on the Jewish Settlement of Savannah," *American Jewish Historical Quarterly* (hereafter *AJHQ*), vol. 52 (1962–63): 169–99; Stern, "The Sheftall Diaries: Vital Records of Savannah Jewry (1733–1808)," *AJHQ* 54 (1964–65): 243–77. See also James Lebeau, "Profile of a South Georgia Community: Waycross, Georgia," *AJHQ* 58 (June 1969): 429–44.

2. See the special issue on Jews in Georgia, including Mark K. Bauman, "Centripetal and Centrifugal Forces Facing the People of Many Communities: Atlanta Jewry from the Leo Frank Case to the Great Depression," *Atlanta Historical Quarterly* 23 (Fall 1979): 25–54.

3. Stanley F. Chyet, "Reflections on Southern Jewish Historiography," in *"Turn to the South": Essays on Southern Jewry*, ed. Nathan M. Kaganoff and Melvin I. Urofsky (Charlottesville: Univ. Press of Virginia, 1979), 15.

4. Important articles that appeared prior to Shankman's December 1973 piece in *Jewish Currents* include Janice O. Rothschild [Blumberg], "Pre-1867 Atlanta Jewry," *AJHQ* 62 (Mar. 1973): 242–49; Leonard Dinnerstein and Mary Dale Palsson, eds., *Jews in the South* (Baton Rouge: Louisiana State Univ. Press, 1973); Arnold Shankman, "A Temple is Bombed—Atlanta, 1958," *American Jewish Archives* (hereafter *AJA* or *AJA Journal* for recent volumes), vol. 23 (Nov. 1971): 125–53; Shankman, "Atlanta Jewry, 1900–1930," *AJA* 25 (Nov. 1973): 131–55; Will F. Holmes, "Whitecapping: Agrarian Violence in Mississippi, 1902–1906," *Journal of Southern History* (hereafter *JSH*), vol. 25 (May 1969):

165–85; Holmes, "Whitecapping in Mississippi, Agrarian Violence in the Populist Era," *Mid-America* 55 (Apr. 1973): 134–48; Allen Tarshish, "The Charleston Organ Case," *AJHQ* 54 (1965): 411–49; and Myron Berman, "Rabbi Edward Nathan Calisch and the Debate Over Zionism in Richmond, Virginia," *AJHQ* 62 (Mar. 1973): 295–305. Of subsequent work, see also Myron Berman, *Richmond's Jewry, 1769–1976: Shabbat in Shockoe* (Charlottesville: Univ. Press of Virginia, 1979); Solomon Breibart, *The Rev. Mr. Gustavus Poznanski: The First American Jewish Reform Minister* (Charleston: Kahal Kadosh Beth Elohim, 1979); Mark H. Elovitz, *A Century of Jewish Life in Dixie* (University: Univ. of Alabama Press, 1974); Eli N. Evans, *The Provincials: A Personal History of Jews in the South* (New York: Atheneum, 1973); Harry Golden, *Our Southern Landsman* (New York: G. P. Putnam's Sons, 1974); Steven Hertzberg, *Strangers within the Gate City: The Jews of Atlanta, 1845–1915* (Philadelphia: Jewish Publication Society, 1978); Hertzberg, "The Jewish Community of Atlanta from the End of the Civil War Until the Eve of the Frank Case," *AJHQ* 62 (Mar. 1973): 250–85; Hertzberg, "Unsettled Jews: Geographic Mobility in a Nineteenth-Century City," *AJHQ* 67 (Dec. 1977): 125–39; Kaganoff and Urofsky, eds., *"Turn to the South"*; Abraham D. Lavender, ed., *A Coat of Many Colors: Jewish Subcommunities in the United States* (Westport, CT: Greenwood, 1977); Patricia A. Smith, "Rhoda Kaufman: A Southern Progressive's Career, 1913–1956," *Atlanta Historical Bulletin* 18 (Spring–Summer 1973): 43–50; Morris Speizman, *The Jews of Charlotte* (Charlotte, NC: McNally and Loften, 1978). For examples of Louis Schmier's work, see "Helloo! Peddler Man! Helloo!" in *Ethnic Minorities in Gulf Coast Society,* ed. Jerrell Schopner (Pensacola: Historic Pensacola Preservation Board, 1979); and "A Jewish Peddler and His Black Customers," *AJH* 73 (Sept. 1983): 56–70.

5. Eric L. Goldstein and Marni Davis, eds., "Southern Jewish History: A Research Guide to Archival Sources and a Bibliography of Published Works" (Atlanta: Emory Univ., 2001). This is a manuscript bibliography developed originally for use in a graduate seminar on the subject by Eric L. Goldstein at Emory University in the spring of 2001. A copy graciously provided by Goldstein greatly facilitated the writing of this essay.

6. In 1979 Melvin I. Urofsky commented on what he perceived as an increased interest in Southern Jewish history at that time. He noted two causal factors: "the rediscovery of ethnicity, with blacks, Irish, Italians, Chicanos, Poles, and, of course, Jews seeking to sketch out the details of their group's communal life in the United States," and "the final emergence of the South as a major region and influence in contemporary America" ("Preface: The Tip of the Iceberg," *Turn to the South,* xi).

7. The University of Alabama Press, with its Judaic Studies Series, is conspicuous.

8. One important exception was a special issue (vol. 73, Sept. 1983) of *American Jewish History* devoted to Georgia Jewish history. (The successor to *AJHQ,* this journal will hereafter be referred to *AJH.*) Integration of southern Jewish experience into southern and American history is even more limited. For example, to

the best of my knowledge, only one article has appeared in the *Journal of Southern History*—Joshua D. Rothman, "'Notorious in the Neighborhood': An Interracial Family in Early National and Antebellum Virginia," *JSH* 67 (Feb. 2001): 73–114—and only one in the *Journal of American History:* Nancy MacLean, "The Leo Frank Case Reconsidered: Gender and Sexual Politics in the Making of Reactionary Populism," *JAH* 78 (Winter 1991): 917–48. Some articles give insight without concentrating on southern Jewry. See, for example, Gary Gerstle, "Liberty, Coercion, and the Making of Americans," *JAH* 84 (Sept. 1997): 524–58 and responses.

9. Charleston boasted the largest Jewish population in the United States during the first decades of the nineteenth century, and New Orleans had the fifth-largest Jewish contingent in 1860.

10. Eli Evans suggests the causes for the lack of southern Jewish historical writing include fear of being persecuted as a minority and a "deep-seated inferiority complex—the feeling that the only part of American Jewish history that mattered was the story of the immigrants and their rise to greatness in New York and the East. The Jews who went to the South were outside of the mainstream, unimportant even in their own eyes. . . . They were down in Dixie making history where it didn't matter" (Evans, *The Lonely Days Were Sundays: Reflections of a Jewish Southerner* [Jackson: Univ. Press of Mississippi, 1993], 31).

11. The only other synthesis reflects this same marginality. See journalist Harry Golden's *Our Southern Landsman.* Stanley Chyet also discussed provincialism in both American and southern Jewish historiography. He concludes, "[I]t may be said without exaggeration that historiographically Southern Jewry—a group whose communal roots go back to at least the early 1700s—has had to endure something of a shadow existence since the Civil War. It is time for a true Southern-Jewish historiography to begin taking shape." See Cheyet, "Southern Jewish Historiography," 15–16, 20 (quotation).

12. Urofsky, "Introduction," *Turn to the South*, xii. In the preface to the same volume (ix), Lawrence H. Fuchs commented, "To be a Jew in the American South is to be affected by the culture of the South." In the foreword to *Jews of the South* (viii), Jacob Rader Marcus asked, "Is there a special Southern Jewish regional history, a distinctive Southern Jewish psyche, mind-set, ethos?"

13. For a controversial perspective, see Mark K. Bauman, *The Southerner as American: Jewish Style* (Cincinnati: American Jewish Archives, Brochure Series 19, 1996).

14. For an essay that introduces some of these forces, see Stephen J. Whitfield, "In the High Cotton: Review Essay," *Southern Jewish History* (hereafter *SJH*), vol. 4 (2001), 123–44.

15. See, for example, Deborah Dash Moore, "Jewish Migration to the Sunbelt," in *Shades of the Sunbelt: Essays on Ethnicity, Race, and the Urban South*, ed. Randall M. Miller and George Pozetta (Westport, CT: Greenwood, 1988).

16. See, for example, Peter Applebome, *Dixie Rising: How the South is Shaping American Values, Politics, and Culture* (New York: Times Books, 1996); and John Egerton, *The Americanization of Dixie: The Southernization of America* (New York: Harper's Magazine Press, 1974).

17. That edition was published in 1997 by Atheneum.

18. Alfred Uhry, *Driving Miss Daisy* (New York: Three Communications Group, 1987); Uhry, *The Last Night at Ballyhoo* (New York: Three Communications Group, 1997); Original Broadway Cast Recording, *Parade,* music and lyrics by Jason Robert Brown and co-conceived by Harold Prince, book by Uhry, RCA Victor 63378. For a literary, historical analysis, see Sharon Teitelbaum, "Staging the Atlanta Jew: A Theatrical Representation of the Atlanta Jewish Community in the Plays of Alfred Uhry" (honors thesis, Wesleyan Univ., 2000); Eliza R. L. McGraw, "Driving Miss Daisy: Southern Jewishness on the Big Screen," *Southern Cultures* (Summer 2001): 41–59. Deeper insights than those found in *Driving Miss Daisy* can be drawn from Roy Hoffman, *Almost Family* (Tuscaloosa: Univ. of Alabama Press, 1983). This is the best fictional volume for understanding the relationship between Jews and African Americans in the twentieth-century South as they attempt to cope with the dominant society. For a historical account of the Ballyhoo-type phenomenon, see Carolyn Lipson-Walker, "'Shalom Y'all: The Folklore and Culture of Southern Jews" (Ph.D. diss., Indiana Univ., 1986). Lipson-Walker emphasizes the folkways that Jews adapted to the South. For a less historically accurate drama about the Frank case than *Parade,* see David Mamet, *The Old Religion* (New York: Free Press, 1997). For a good review, see Melissa Fay Greene, "The Old History-as-Fiction Gambit: Leo Frank as a Fictional Character," *Georgia Historical Quarterly* (hereafter *GHP*), vol. 82 (Spring 1998): 73–83. The historiography of the Leo Frank case is immense. Steve Oney's *And the Dead Shall Rise: The Murder of Mary Phagan and the Lynching of Leo Frank* (New York: Pantheon, 2003) supercedes Leonard Dinnerstein's *The Leo Frank Case* (New York: Columbia Univ. Press, 1968), long considered the classic study. For a controversial analysis of the literature emphasizing its changing meaning and negative relationship to black-Jewish affairs, see Jeffrey Melnick, *Black-Jewish Relations on Trial: Leo Frank and Jim Conley in the New South* (Jackson: Univ. Press of Mississippi, 2000).

19. See Irving Howe, *World of Our Fathers* (New York: Harcourt Brace Jovanovich, 1976), and the special issue of *AJH* 88 (Dec. 2000) analyzing it.

20. Evans, *The Lonely Days,* 4, posits the second question about comparison across the country.

21. Wendy Machlovitz, *Clara Lowenburg Moses: Memoir of a Southern Jewish Woman* (Jackson: Museum of the Southern Jewish Experience, 2000).

22. See Henry Green and Marcia Kerstein Zerivitz, *Mosaic: Jewish Life in Florida* (Coral Gables: n.p., 1991).

23. The museum also sponsored a guidebook—Rachel B. Heimovics and Marcia Zerivitz, *Florida Jewish Heritage Trail* (Miami: Florida Dept. of State, Div. of Historical Resources, 2000)—in addition to various popular education programs.

24. On Atlanta, see Jane D. Leavey, *Creating Community: The Jews of Atlanta from 1984 to the Present* (Atlanta: Atlanta Jewish Federation, 1994); Mark K. Bauman and Doris H. Goldstein, *The Jews of Atlanta: 150 Years of Creating Community* (Atlanta: Atlanta Jewish Federation, 1994). On South Carolina, see Theodore Rosengarten and Dale Rosengarten, eds., *A Portion of the People: Three Hundred Years of Southern Jewish Life* (Columbia: Univ. of South Carolina Press, 2002). The Jewish Museum of Maryland has also been quite active with exhibits. See the must-read catalog for those interested in the small town Jewish experience: Karen Falk and Avi Y. Dector, eds., *We Call This Place Home: Jewish Life in Maryland's Small Towns* (Baltimore: Jewish Museum of Maryland, 2002). Sherry Blanton also curated an exhibit in Anniston, Alabama, "Lives of Quiet Affirmation: An Alabama Jewish Community." See also exhibits at the Beth Ahabah Museum and Archives, Richmond, Virginia, and Melvin I. Urofsky, *Commonwealth and Community: The Jewish Experience in Virginia* (Richmond: Virginia Historical Society, 1997).

25. Documentaries include Mike DeWitt, *Delta Jews: A Film About Jews in the Land of the Blues* (1998); Brian Cohen, *Pushcarts and Plantations: Jewish Life in Louisiana* (1998); and Cohen, *At Home on the Range: Jewish Life in Texas* (1997). Bill Aron's book *Shalom Y'all: Images of Jewish Life in the American South* (Chapel Hill: Algonquin Books, 2003) is the catalog for an exhibit of the same name that took place at the Skirball Museum, Los Angeles, 2002–2003.

26. The best of these include Hollace A. Weiner, *Beth-El Congregation, Fort Worth, Texas* (Fort Worth: Beth-El Temple, 2002); Gerry Cristol, *A Light in the Prairie: Temple Emanu-El of Dallas, 1872–1997* (Fort Worth: Texas Christian Univ., 1998); Susan Gross, *Wings Toward the South: The First Hundred Years of Congregation Agudath Achim* (Shreveport, LA: Congregation Agudath Achim, 1999); Janice O. Rothschild [Blumberg], *As but a Day: To a Hundred and Twenty, 1867– 1987,* rev. ed. (Atlanta: Hebrew Benevolent Congregation, 1987); and Belinda Gergel, *In the Pursuit of the Tree of Life: A History of the Early Jews of Columbia, South Carolina, and the Tree of Life Congregation* (Columbia: Tree of Life Congregation, 1996). Unfortunately, most books in this genre lack analysis and depth.

27. For an excellent earlier survey of southern Jews in literature, see Stephen J. Whitfield, *Voices of Jacob, Hands of Esau: Jews in American Life and Thought* (Hamden, CT: Archon Books, 1984). Reflecting the meteoric rise in output, an article I wrote in 1998—"Judaism," in *The Companion to Southern Literature,* ed. Joseph M. Flora and Lucinda H. MacKethan (Baton Rouge: Louisiana State Univ. Press, 2001)—became obsolete before publication.

28. Eliot Ashkenazi, ed., *The Civil War Diary of Clara Solomon: Growing Up in New Orleans* (Baton Rouge: Louisiana State Univ. Press, 1995). See also Spencer King Jr., "Fanny Cohen's Diary of Sherman's Occupation of Savannah," *Georgia Historical Quarterly* 41 (Dec. 1958): 407–16; Raphael Jacob Moses, *Last*

Order of the Lost Cause: The Civil War Memoirs of a Jewish Family from the "Old South," ed. Mel Young (Lanham, MD: Univ. Press of America, 1995); Phoebe Yates Pember, *A Southern Woman's Story: Life in Confederate Richmond*, ed. Bell I. Wiley (Jackson, TN: McCowat-Mercer Press, 1959); Louis Schmier, ed., *Reflections of Southern Jewry: The Letters of Charles Wessolowsky* (Macon, GA: Mercer Univ. Press, 1982); Saul Viener, "Rosena Hutzler Levy Recalls the Civil War," *AJHQ* 62 (Mar. 1973): 306–13; Archie P. McDonald, ed., *Hurrah for Texas! The Diary of Adolphus Sterne, 1838–1851* (Waco, TX: Texian Press, 1969); and Patricia Spain Ward, *Simon Baruch: Rebel in the Ranks of Medicine, 1840–1921* (Tuscaloosa: Univ. of Alabama Press, 1994).

29. Helen Jacobus Apte, *Heart of a Wife: The Diary of a Southern Jewish Women*, ed. by Marcus Rosenbaum (Wilmington: SR Books, 1998). See also Richard E. Sapon-White, "A Polish Jew on the Florida Frontier and in Occupied Tennessee: Excerpts from the Memoirs of Max White," *SJH* 4 (2001): 93–122; Mark K. Bauman, "The Youthful Musings of a Jewish Community Activist: Josephine Joel Heyman," *Atlanta History* 39 (Summer 1995): 46–59; Myron Berman, ed., "Joseph Joel: My Recollections and Experiences in Richmond, Virginia, U.S.A.," *Virginia Magazine of History and Biography* 87 (1979): 344–56; Emily Sims Bingham, "Mordecai: Three Generations of a Southern Jewish Family, 1780–1865" (Ph.D. diss., Univ. of North Carolina, 1998); Rachel Mordecai Lazarus, *The Education of the Heart: The Correspondence of Rachel Mordecai Lazarus and Maria Edgeemood* (Chapel Hill: Univ. of North Carolina Press, 1977); Cynthia Betty Levy, "'You Can't Imagine This Life': Diaries and Letters of a Southern-Jewish Grande Dame, Josephine Joel Heyman, 1901–1993" (Ph.D. diss., Louisiana State Univ., 1999); Wendy Machlowitz, ed., *Clara Lowenburg Moses: Memoir of a Southern Jewish Woman* (Jackson, MS: Museum of the Southern Jewish Experience, 2000); and Emanuel Feldman, *Tales Out of a Shul: The Unorthodox Journal of an Orthodox Rabbi* (New York: Shaar Press, 1997). The last is the only autobiography of an Orthodox rabbi in the South. For an account of a labor union attorney and Democratic Party leader, see Cliff Kuhn, "'We Lived That Way': An Oral History Interview with Joe Jacobs," *Atlanta History* 36 (1993): 54–67.

30. Edward Cohen, *The Peddler's Grandson: Growing Up Jewish in Mississippi* (Jackson: Univ. Press of Mississippi, 1999); Stanley Ely, *In Jewish Texas: A Family Reunion* (Fort Worth: Texas Christian Univ. Press, 1998); and Evans, *The Lonely Days*. Two lesser-known memoirs depicting life in Charleston during the twentieth century are Arthur V. Williams, *Tales of Charleston, 1930s* (Charleston: College of Charleston Library and Jewish Historical Society of South Carolina, 1999); and Henry Yaschik, *From Kaluszyn to Charleston: The Yaschik Family in Poland, Argentina, and South Carolina* (Charleston: privately published, 1990).

31. Stella Suberman, *The Jew Store: A Family Memoir* (Chapel Hill: Algonquin Books, 1998); Leta Weiss Marks, *Times Tapestry: Four Generations of a New Orleans Family* (Baton Rouge: Louisiana State Univ. Press, 1997). Eli Evans

describes Belva Plain's *Crescent City,* a romance novel set in Civil War–era New Orleans, as an unsuccessful Jewish version of *Gone With the Wind;* see Evans, *The Lonely Days,* 72–74. Other novels include Judy Goldman, *The Slow Way Back: A Novel* (New York: HarperCollins, 1999), and Tova Mirvis, *The Ladies Auxiliary* (New York: W. W. Norton, 1999). For scholarly treatments, see Emily Angel Baer, "Breaking Patterns, Creating Patterns: Images of the Pinch of Memphis, Tennessee, 1900–1948" (Ph.D. diss., Memphis State Univ., 1992); Mark K. Bauman, "Factionalism and Ethnic Politics in Atlanta: German Jews from the Civil War Through the Progressive Era," *Georgia Historical Quarterly* 82 (Fall 1998): 533–58; and Ronald Bayor, "Ethnic Residential Patterns in Atlanta, 1880–1940," *Georgia Historical Quarterly* 63 (Winter 1979): 435–46.

32. Benjamin Hirsch, *Hearing a Different Drummer: A Holocaust Survivor's Search for Identity* (Macon, GA: Mercer Univ. Press, 2000); Abram Korn, *Abe's Story: A Holocaust Memoir,* ed. by Joseph Korn (Atlanta: Longstreet, 1995). See also Pat Conroy, *Beach Music* (New York, Bantam Books, 1995). One of the best books to personalize the Holocaust through the story of one family is Lawrence Powell, *Troubled Memory: Anne Levy, The Holocaust, and David Duke's Louisiana* (Chapel Hill: Univ. of North Carolina Press, 2000). See also Powell, "When Hate Came to Town: New Orleans Jews and George Lincoln Rockwell," *AJH* 85 (Dec. 1997): 393–420. Examples that treat the civil rights movement include Marvin Caplan, *Farther Along: A Civil Rights Memoir* (Baton Rouge: Louisiana State Univ. Press, 1999); James C. Cobb, ed., *The Mississippi Delta and the World: The Memoirs of David L. Cohn* (Baton Rouge: Louisiana Univ. Press, 1995); and Morris B. Abram, *The Day is Short: An Autobiography* (New York: Harcourt Brace Jovanovich, 1982). On Jewish and African American relations, see also James McBride, *The Color of Water: A Black Man's Tribute to His White Mother* (New York: Riverhead Books, 1996); Hugh Pearson, *Under the Knife: How a Wealthy Negro Surgeon Wielded Power in the Jim Crow South* (New York: Free Press, 2000); and Alice Walker, *Meridian* (San Diego: Harcourt Brace Jovanovich, 1976). Of related interest is Gwendolyn Midlo Hall, *Love, War, and the 96th Engineers (Colored): The World War Two Diaries of Captain Hyman Samuelson* (Champaign: Univ. of Illinois Press, 1995). Works relating to southern Jewish literature include Louis Rubin Jr., *The Golden Weather* (New York: Atheneum, 1961; reprint, Baton Rouge: Louisiana State Univ. Press, 1995); and Ralph Melnick, *The Life and Work of Ludwig Lewisohn,* 2 vols. (Detroit: Wayne State Univ. Press, 1998).

33. Eli Evans reflects that he wrote *The Provincials* as an outgrowth of investigating his family's history. His experience with oral history "was linked with my discovery of self" (Evans, *The Lonely Days,* 11).

34. The instructors and schools are Dale Rosengarten, Theodore Rosengarten, and Jack Bass at the College of Charleston; Eric Goldstein at Emory University; Gary P. Zola at Hebrew Union College; Marcie Ferris at the University of North Carolina; Leonard Rogoff at Duke University; and Phyllis Leffler at the University of Virginia.

35. Hertzberg, *Strangers within the Gate City.* See also Wendy Lowe Bessman, *A Separate Circle: Jewish Life in Knoxville, Tennessee* (Knoxville: Univ. of Tennessee Press, 2001); Canter Brown Jr., *Jewish Pioneers of the Tampa Bay Frontier* (Tampa, FL: Tampa Bay History Center, 1999); Mark Elovitz, *A Century of Jewish Life in Dixie: The Birmingham Experience* (University: Univ. of Alabama Press, 1974); Bertram W. Korn, *The Jews of Mobile, Alabama, 1763–1841* (Cincinnati: Hebrew Union College Press, 1970); Korn, *The Early Jews of New Orleans* (Waltham, MA: American Jewish Historical Society, 1969); Deborah Dash Moore, *To the Golden Cities: Pursuing the American Dream in L.A. and Miami* (New York: Free Press, 1994); Stephen J. Whitfield, " Blood and Sand: The Jewish Community of South Florida," *AJH* 82 (1994): 73–96; Whitfield, "Florida's Fudged Identity," *Florida Historical Quarterly* 71 (Apr. 1993): 413–435; Mark I. Greenberg, "Creating Ethnic, Class, and Southern Identity in Nineteenth Century America: The Jews of Savannah, 1830–1880" (Ph.D. diss., Univ. of Florida, 1997); Bobbie S. Malone, "New Orleans' Uptown Jewish Immigrants: The Community of Congregation Gates of Prayer, 1850–1860," *Louisiana History* 32 (Summer 1991): 239–78; James W. Hagy, *This Happy Land: The Jews of Colonial and Antebellum Charleston* (Tuscaloosa: Univ. of Alabama Press, 1993); Fedora Small Frank, *Five Families and Eight Young Men: Nashville and Her Jewry, 1850–1861* (Nashville: Tennessee Book Company, 1962); Frank, *Beginnings on Market Street, Nashville and Her Jewry, 1861–1901* (Nashville: Fedora S. Frank, 1976); Rob Spinney, "The Jewish Community in Nashville, 1939–1949," *Tennessee Historical Quarterly* 52 (1993): 225–41; Myron Berman, *Richmond's Jewry, 1769–1976: Shabbat in Shockoe* (Charlottesville: Univ. of Virginia Press, 1979); Eric Goldstein, *Traders and Transports: The Jews of Colonial Maryland* (Baltimore: Jewish Historical Society of Maryland, 1993); and Gilbert Sandler, *Jewish Baltimore: A Family Album* (Baltimore: Johns Hopkins Univ. Press, 2001). For a survey, see Leah Elizabeth Hagedorn, "Jews and the American South, 1858–1905," (Ph.D. diss., Univ. of North Carolina, 1999).

36. Works of varying quality include Caroline Gray LeMaster, *A Corner of the Tapestry: A History of the Jewish Experience in Arkansas, 1820s–1990s* (Fayetteville: Univ. of Arkansas Press, 1994); Malvina W. Liebman, *Jewish Frontiersmen: Historical Highlights of Early South Florida Jewish Communities* (Miami Beach: Jewish Historical Society of South Florida, 1979); Saul Rubin, *Third to None: The Saga of Savannah Jewry, 1733–1983* (Savannah, GA: Congregation Mickve Israel, 1983); Morris Speizman, *The Jews of Charlotte* (Charlotte, NC: McNally and Loftin, 1978); Leo and Evelyn Turitz, *Jews in Early Mississippi, 1840–1900* (Jackson: Univ. Press of Mississippi, 1983); Natalie Ornish, *Pioneering Jewish Texans: Their Impact on Texas and American Jewish History for Four Hundred Years, 1590–1990* (Dallas: Texas Heritage Press, 1989); Ruthe Winegarten and Cathy Schecter, *Deep in the Heart of Texas: The Lives and Legends of Texas Jews* (Austin, TX: Eaken Press, 1990); Isaac M. Fein, *The Making of An American Jewish Community: The*

History of Baltimore Jewry from 1773 to 1920 (Philadelphia: Jewish Publication Society, 1971); and Selma Lewis, *A Biblical People of the Bible Belt: The Jewish Community of Memphis, Tennessee, 1840s–1960s* (Macon, GA: Mercer Univ. Press, 1998).

37. Terry Barr, "A Shtetl Grew in Bessemer: Temple Beth-El and Jewish Life in Small-Town Alabama," *SJH* 3 (2000): 1–44; Leonard Rogoff, *Borderlands* (Tuscaloosa: Univ. of Alabama Press, 2001); Rogoff, "Synagogue and Church History: A Congregational History of North Carolina," *SJH* 1 (1998): 43–81; Deborah Weiner, "The Jews of Clarksburg: Community Adaptation and Survival, 1900–1960," *West Virginia History* 54 (1995): 59–77; Weiner, "The Jews of Keystone: Life in a Multicultural Boomtown," *SJH* 2 (1999): 1–23; Lee Shai Weissbach, "Stability and Mobility in the Small Jewish Community: Examples from Kentucky History," *AJH* 79 (Spring 1990): 355–75; Weissbach, "Kentucky's Jewish History in National Perspective: The Era of Mass Migration," *Filson Club Historical Quarterly* 69 (1995): 255–74.

38. For Reform rabbis, see Mark K. Bauman and Arnold Shankman, "The Rabbi as Ethnic Broker: The Case of David Marx," *Journal of American Ethnic History* 2 (Spring 1983): 51–68; Myron Berman, "Rabbi Edward Nathan Calisch and the Debate Over Zionism in Richmond, Virginia," *AJHQ* 62 (Mar. 1973): 295–305; Janice Rothschild Blumberg, *One Voice: Rabbi Jacob M. Rothschild and the Troubled South* (Macon, GA: Mercer Univ. Press, 1985); Solomon Breibart, *The Rev. Gustavus Poznanski: First American Jewish Reform Minister* (Charleston, SC: n.p., 1979); Mark Cowett, *Birmingham's Rabbi: Morris Newfield and Alabama, 1895–1940* (Tuscaloosa: Univ. of Alabama Press, 1986); A. Stanley Dreyfus, *Henry Cohen: Messenger of the Lord* (New York: Bloch Publishing Company, 1963); Israel Goldman, "Henry W. Schneeberger: His Role in American Judaism," *AJHQ* 57 (Dec. 1967): 153–90; Henry M. Green, *Gesher VaKesher/Bridges and Bonds: The Life of Leon Kronish* (Atlanta: Scholars Press, 1996); Berkley Kalin, "Rabbi William H. Fineschriber: The Memphis Years," *West Tennessee Historical Society Papers* 25 (1971): 47–62; Bobbie S. Malone, *Rabbi Max Heller: Reformer, Zionist, Southerner* (Tuscaloosa: Univ. of Alabama Press, 1997); Karl Preuss, "Personality, Politics, and the Price of Justice: Ephraim Frisch, San Antonio's 'Radical' Rabbi," *AJH* 85 (Sept. 1997): 263–88; William Warren Rogers Jr., "In Defense of Our Sacred Cause: Rabbi James K. Gutheim in Confederate Montgomery," *Journal of Confederate History* 7 (1991): 113–22; Hollace Ava Weiner, "The Mixers: The Role of Rabbis Deep in the Heart of Texas," *AJH* 85 (Sept. 1997): 289–332; and Weiner, *Jewish Stars in Texas: Rabbis and Their Work* (College Station, TX: Texas A&M Univ. Press, 1999). See also Julian B. Feibelman, *The Making of a Rabbi* (New York: Vantage Press, 1980). For Orthodox rabbis, see Mark K. Bauman, *Harry H. Epstein and the Rabbinate as Conduit for Change* (Rutherford, NJ: Associated Univ. Presses for Fairleigh Dickinson Univ. Press, 1994); Nathan M. Kaganoff, "An Orthodox Rabbinate in the South: Tobias Geffen, 1870–1970," *AJH* 73 (Sept. 1983): 56–70; Israel Tabak, "Rabbi Abraham Rice of Baltimore: Pioneer of Orthodox

Judaism in America," *Tradition* (Summer 1965): 100–20; and Joel Ziff, ed., *Lev Tuviah: On the Life and Work of Tobias Geffen* (Newton, MA: privately published, 1988).

39. John C. English, "John Wesley and his 'Jewish Parishioners': Jewish-Christian Relations in Savannah, Georgia, 1736–1737," *Methodist History* 36 (1998): 220–27; Scott Langston, "Interaction and Identity: Jews and Christians in Nineteenth Century New Orleans," *SJH* 3 (2000): 45–82.

40. Elliott Ashkenazi, *The Business of Jews in Louisiana, 1840–1875* (Tuscaloosa: Univ. of Alabama Press, 1988); Ashkenazi, "Jewish Commercial Interests Between North and South: The Case of the Lehmans and Seligmans," *AJA* 43 (1991): 25–40. See also Thomas Clark, "The Post-Civil War Economy in the South," *AJHQ* 55 (1966): 424–33; Bennett H. Wall, "Leon Godchaux and the Godchaux Business Enterprise," *AJHQ* 66 (Sept. 1976): 50–66; Burton Alan Boxerman, "The Edison Brothers, Shoe Merchants: Their Georgia Years," *Georgia Historical Quarterly* 57 (Winter 1973): 511–25; George S. Bush, *An American Harvest: The Story of the Weil Brothers Cotton* (Englewood Cliffs, NJ: Prentice-Hall, 1982); Don M. Coerver and Linda D. Hall, "Neiman-Marcus: Innovators in Fashion and Advertising," *AJHQ* 66 (Sept. 1976): 123–36; Gary Fink, *The Fulton Bag and Cotton Mills Strike of 1914–1915: Espionage, Labor Conflict, and New South Industrial Relations* (Ithaca, NY: Cornell Univ. Press, 1993); Walda Katz Fishman, "Jews and the New Orleans Economic and Social Elite," *Jewish Social Studies* 44 (Summer–Fall 1982): 291–97; Gary R. Freeze, "Roots, Barks, Berries and Jews: The Herb Trade in Gilded-Age North Carolina," *Essays in Economic and Business History* 13 (1995): 107–27; Jacqueline Dowd Hall, "Private Eyes, Public Women: Images of Class and Sex in the Urban South, Atlanta, Georgia, 1913–1915," *Atlanta History* 36 (Winter 1993): 24–39; Richard A. Hawkins, "Lynchburg's Swabian Jewish Entrepreneurs in War and Peace," *SJH* 3 (2000): 45–81; Harold Hyman, *Oleander Odyssey: The Kempners of Galveston, Texas, 1854–1980s* (College Station, TX: Texas A&M Univ. Press, 1990); Leonard Rogoff, "Jewish Proletarians in the New South: The Durham Cigarette Rollers," *AJH* 82 (1994): 141–58; Leon Joseph Rosenberg, *Sangers': Pioneer Texas Merchants* (Austin: Texas State Historical Association, 1978); and Deborah R. Weiner, "Middlemen of the Coalfields: The Role of the Jews in the Economy of Southern West Virginia Coal Towns," *Journal of Appalachian Studies* 4 (Spring 1998): 29–56. A popular account is Leon Harris, *Merchant Princes: An Intimate Portrait of the Jewish Families Who Built Great Department Stores* (New York: Harper & Row, 1979).

41. An exception is the work of Ira M. Sheskin. See, for example, Sheskin, "The Dixie Diaspora: 'Loss' of the Small Southern Jewish Community," *Southwestern Geographer* 40 (May 2000): 52–74. Steven Hertzberg explored mobility patterns in *Strangers within the Gate City* and in "Unsettled Jews." For an excellent sociological study, see Solomon Sutker, "The Role of Social Clubs in the Atlanta Jewish Community," in *The Jews*, ed. Marshall Sklare (Glencoe, IL: Free Press, 1958).

42. See Mark K. Bauman, "The Emergence of Jewish Social Service Agencies in Atlanta," *Georgia Historical Quarterly* (Winter 1985): 488–508; Bauman, "The Transformation of Jewish Social Services in Atlanta, 1928–1948," *AJA Journal* 53 (2001): 83–111; and Mike Gettinger, *Coming of Age: The Atlanta Jewish Federation, 1962–1982* (Hoboken, NJ: KTAV Publishing House, 1994).

43. Mark K. Bauman, "Southern Jewish Women and Their Social Service Organizations," *Journal of American Ethnic History* 22 (2003): 34–78; Mark I. Greenberg, "Savannah's Jewish Women and the Shaping of Ethnic and Gender Identity, 1830–1900," *GHQ* 82 (Winter 1998): 751–74; Beth Wenger, "Jewish Women of the Club: The Changing Public Role of Atlanta's Jewish Women (1870–1930)," *AJH* 76 (Mar. 1987): 311–33; Wenger, "Jewish Women and Voluntarism: Beyond the Myth of Enablers," *AJH* 79 (Autumn 1989): 16–36; Wenger, "Southern Lady and the Jewish Woman: The Early Organizational Life of Atlanta's Jewish Women" (honors thesis, Wesleyan Univ., 1985); Wenger, "Jewish Women and Voluntarism: Beyond the Myth of Enablers," *AJH* 79 (Autumn 1989): 16–36; Deborah Weiner, "Jewish Women in the Central Appalachian Coal Fields, 1890–1960: From Breadwinners to Community Builders," *AJA Journal* 52 (2000): 10–33.

44. Robert N. Rosen, *The Jewish Confederates* (Columbia: Univ. of South Carolina Press, 2000), has a complete bibliography including sources on Judah P. Benjamin and David Yulee Levy. An attorney and plantation owner, Benjamin served in the U.S. Senate and then in the Confederate cabinet. Levy was the first congressman from Florida and the first Jew to serve in that body. He developed land tracts and railroads. Neither practiced Judaism as adults and both intermarried. See also Moses Elias Levy, "A Plan for the Abolition of Slavery, Consistent with the Interests of All Parties Concerned (London, 1928)," ed. Chris Monaco, *AJA Journal* 60 (1999): 109–54; Chris Monaco, "Moses E. Levy of Florida: A Jewish Abolitionist Abroad," *AJH* 86 (Dec. 1998): 377–96; and Monaco, "A Sugar Utopia on the Florida Frontier: Moses Elias Levy's Pilgrimage Plantation," *SJH* 5 (2002): 103–40.

45. Mark K. Bauman and Berkley Kalin, eds., *Quiet Voices: Southern Rabbis and Black Civil Rights, 1880s to 1990s* (Tuscaloosa: Univ. of Alabama Press, 1997); Clive Webb, *Fight against Fear: Southern Jews and Black Civil Rights* (Athens: Univ. of Georgia Press, 2001). These works provide complete bibliographies, and Bauman's introduction to *Quiet Voices* provides a historiographical essay. See also S. Jonathan Bass, *Blessed Are the Peacemakers: Martin Luther King, Jr., Eight White Religious Leaders, and the "Letter from Birmingham Jail"* (Baton Rouge: Louisiana State Univ. Press, 2000); David Goldfield, "Sense of Place: Blacks, Jews, and White Gentiles in the American South," *Southern Cultures* 3 (1997): 58–79; Cheryl Greenberg, "The Southern Jewish Community and the Struggle for Civil Rights," in *African Americans and Jews in the Twentieth Century,* ed. V. P. Franklin et al. (Columbia: Univ. of Missouri Press, 1998); Greenberg, "Negotiating Coalitions: Black and Jewish Civil Rights Agencies in the Twentieth Century," in *Struggles in the Promised Land,* ed. Jack Saltzman and

Cornel West (New York: Oxford Univ. Press, 1997); Raymond A. Mohl, *South of the South: Jewish Activists and the Civil Rights Movement in Miami, 1945–1960* (Gainesville: Univ. Press of Florida, 2004); Adam Mendelsohn, "Two Far South: Rabbinical Responses to Apartheid and Segregation in South Africa and the American South," *SJH* 6 (2003); and Debra L. Schultz, *Going South: Jewish Women in the Civil Rights Movement* (New York: New York Univ. Press, 2001). Patricia Spain Ward, *Simon Baruch: Rebel in the Ranks of Medicine, 1840–1921* (Tuscaloosa and London: Univ. of Alabama Press, 1994), provides the story of an important physician born in Poland but who spent several years in Camden, South Carolina, before moving to New York City. On views of Jews, see Arnold Shankman, *Ambivalent Friends: Afro-Americans View the Immigrant* (Westport: Greenwood Press, 1982), as well as Leonard Rogoff, "Is the Jew White? The Racial Place of the Southern Jew" *AJH* 85 (Sept. 1997): 195–230.

46. John Higham, *Send These to Me: Jews and Other Immigrants in Urban America* (New York: Atheneum, 1975); Leonard Dinnerstein, *Uneasy at Home: Anti-Semitism and the American Jewish Experience* (New York: Columbia Univ. Press, 1987). See also Edward S. Shapiro, "Anti-Semitism Mississippi Style," in *Anti-Semitism in American History*, ed. David A. Gerber (Urbana: Univ. of Illinois Press, 1986): 129–51

47. For an excellent bibliography, see Howard Rabinowitz, "Nativism, Bigotry, and Anti-Semitism in the South," *AJH* 72 (Mar. 1988): 437–51. See also Leonard Dinnerstein, *Anti-Semitism in America* (New York: Oxford Univ. Press, 1994).

48. There is an ongoing debate over whether Jews made such gains because of their acceptance of southern mores or because their proclivity to business and service earned them such places. See Mark I. Greenberg, "Creating Ethnic, Class, and Southern Identity in Nineteenth Century America: The Jews of Savannah, 1830–1880" (Ph.D. diss., Univ. of Florida, 1997); Greenberg, "Becoming Southern: The Jews of Savannah, Georgia," AJH 86 (Mar. 1998): 55–75; and Mark K. Bauman, "Victor H. Kriegshaber, Community Builder," *AJH* 79 (Autumn 1989): 94–110. There is a small but growing literature on Jews who served as mayors, especially during the 1890s. See, for example, Margaret Armbrester, *Samuel Ullman and "Youth": The Life, the Legacy* (Tuscaloosa: Univ. of Alabama Press, 1993); Armbrester, "Samuel Ullman [1840–1924]—Birmingham Progressive," *Alabama Review* 47 (Jan. 1994): 29–43; Cantor Brown Jr., "Philip and Morris Dzialynski: Jewish Contributions to Rebuilding the South," *AJA* 44 (1992): 517–40; and Mark I. Greenberg, "Tampa Mayor Herman Glowgowski: Jewish Leadership in Gilded Age Florida," in *Florida's Heritage of Diversity: Essays in Honor of Samuel Proctor,* ed. Mark I. Greenberg, William Warren Rogers, and Cantor Brown Jr. (Tallahassee, FL: Sentry Press, 1997).

49. See, for example, Mark K. Bauman, "Variations on the Mortara Case in Mid-Nineteenth-Century New Orleans," *AJA Journal,* forthcoming.

50. See, for example, Melissa Fay Greene, *The Temple Bombing* (Reading, Mass.: Addison-Wesley, 1996); Jack Nelson, *Terror in the Night: The Klan's Campaign*

Against the Jews (New York: Simon & Schuster, 1993); and Rosalind Benjet, "The Ku Klux Klan and the Jewish Community of Dallas, 1921–1923," *SJH* 6 (2003). In *The Lonely Days* (110), Eli Evans astutely observes, "It was always an axiom of Jewish life in the South that racial trouble meant heated passions and a dangerous atmosphere that was 'bad for the Jews.' The opposite was true, too; if blacks were making progress, so were Jews."

51. See Gary P. Zola, "Why Study Southern Jewish History?" *SJH* 1 (1998): 1–21.

52. See Bauman, "Southerner as American," and the excellent article by Abraham Peck, "'That Other Peculiar Institution': Jews and Judaism in the Nineteenth Century South," *Modern Judaism* 7 (Feb. 1987): 99–114.

53. Although contrasts are emphasized here, the Central European Jewish religious experience in America was tremendously influenced by High Church Protestantism. As indicated here and elsewhere, many of the ritual reforms and practices and organizational structures, from this perspective, reflect transatlantic middle- and upper-class tendencies as well as attempts by Jews to emulate and be accepted by their urban and business-class Protestant counterparts. Thus, this insight would reinforce those who see class differences reflected in southern religious history and stress that all did not follow the evangelical-fundamentalist banner. Ultimately, the Jewish experience should also be compared and contrasted with that of other minorities, including Catholics and African Americans.

54. Several congregations actually sent letters to Washington and Jefferson soliciting the presidents' views on separation of church and state and freedom of religion, and they consequently received favorable responses.

55. Leon Jick, *The Americanization of the Synagogue* (Hanover, NH: Brandeis Univ. Press–Univ. Press of New England, 1976); Michael A. Meyer, *Response to Modernity: A History of the Reform Movement in Judaism* (New York: Oxford Univ. Press, 1988).

56. Gary Phillip Zola, *Isaac Harby of Charleston, 1788–1828: Jewish Reformer and Intellectual* (Tuscaloosa: Univ. of Alabama Press, 1994); Zola, "The First Reform Prayer Book in America: The Liturgy of the Reformed Society of Israelites," in *Platforms and Prayer Books: Theological and Liturgical Perspectives on Reform Judaism,* ed. Dana Evan Kaplan (Lanham, MD: Rowman & Littlefield, 2002), 99–117.

57. On the movement of people and ideas, see Mark K. Bauman, "Perspectives: History from a Variety of Vantage Points," *AJH* 90 (Mar. 2002): 3–12. This entire issue of *AJH* is devoted to Leon Jick's *Americanization of the Synagogue.*

58. Gary P. Zola, "Southern Rabbis and the Foundation of the First National Association of Rabbis," *AJH* 85 (Dec. 1997): 353–73. Zola posits the impact of a rabbi in the South on early Reform Zionism in "Reform Judaism's Pioneer Zionist: Maximilian Heller," *AJH* 85 (1997): 353–72.

59. One of the few articles on Jewish educators is Arlene G. Rotter, "Climbing the Crystal Stairs: Annie T. Wise's Success as an Immigrant in Atlanta's Public

School System (1872–1925)," *SJH* 4 (2001). See also Francis J. Froelicher, Jr., ed., "The Beginnings of Park School: The Personal Account of Hans Froehlicher," *Maryland Historical Magazine* 90 (1995): 44–55; and Tom Keating, *Saturday School: How One Town Kept Out the "Jewish," 1902–1932* (Bloomington: Phi Delta Kappa Educational Foundation, 1999). This last work focuses on Decatur, Georgia.

60. For a twentieth-century view of such activities, see Eliza Russi Lowen McGraw, "How to Win Jews for Jesus: Southern Jewishness and the Southern Baptist Convention," *Mississippi Quarterly* (Spring 2000): 209–22.

61. Leo Frank, who had been raised in New York, managed a pencil factory in Atlanta. He was accused, tried, and convicted of murdering one of his young employees, Mary Phagan. The evidence against him was flimsy, especially the changing testimony of Jim Conley, an African American janitor. The trial and subsequent press coverage was tainted by anti-Semitism. After Governor John Slaton, who believed Frank innocent, commuted his sentence to life in prison, a group of men took Frank from the penitentiary to Phagan's home in Marietta and lynched him. The incident contributed to the rise of the Knights of Mary Phagan, precursor of the Ku Klux Klan.

62. Ellen M. Umansky, "Christian Science, Jewish Science, and the Writings of Alfred Geiger Moses," *SJH* 6 (2003).

63. Hollace Ava Weiner, "Removal Approval: The Industrial Removal Office Experience in Fort Worth, Texas," *SJH* 4 (2001); Bernard Marinbach, *Galveston: Ellis Island of the West* (Albany: State Univ. of New York Press, 1983).

64. Unfortunately, the roles of these people in the cities, in Zionism, in Yiddish culture, in the re-emergence of traditional practices, and in the Conservative movement have received scant study. Beyond notice in city and state accounts, one has to go to the few congregational histories. See, for example, Doris Goldstein, *From Generation to Generation: Congregation Ahavath Achim, 1887–1987* (Atlanta: Ahavath Achim Synagogue, 1987); and Kenneth W. Stein, *A History of Ahavath Achim Congregation, 1887–1977* (Atlanta: Standard Press, 1978). One exception is Mark K. Bauman, "Rabbi Harry H. Epstein and the Adaptation of Second-Generation East European Immigrants in Atlanta," *AJA* 42 (Fall–Winter 1990): 133–46.

65. Studies of the Sephardic Jews who came from the declining Ottoman Empire during the early twentieth century to settle in Atlanta and Montgomery include Sol Beton, ed., *Sephardim and a History of Congregation Or VeShalom* (Atlanta: Congregation Or VeShalom, 1981); and Yitchak Kerem, "The Settlement of Rhodian and Other Sephardic Jews in Montgomery and Atlanta in the Twentieth Century," *AJH* 85 (Dec. 1997): 373–92.

66. See, for example, Harry E. Moore, Jr., "The National Conference of Christians and Jews in Memphis, 1932–1989," *West Tennessee Historical Society Papers* 45 (1991): 48–67.

67. An excellent folklore-sociological study tracing changing and multiple identities is Caroline Bettinger-López, *Cuban-Jewish Journeys: Searching for Identity, Home, and History in Miami* (Knoxville: Univ. of Tennessee Press, 2000). See also Abraham D. Lavender, "Sephardic Political Identity: Jewish and Cuban Interaction in Miami Beach," *Contemporary Jewry* 14 (1993): 116–32. For other studies of blurred identity, see Bryan Stone, "'Ride 'em Jewboy': Kinky Friedman and the Texas Jewish Mystique," *SJH* 1 (1998): 23–42; and Seth Wolitz, "Bifocality in Jewish Identity in the Texas-Jewish Experience," in *Jewries at the Frontier: Accommodation, Identity, Conflict,* ed. Sander L. Gilman and Milton Shain (Urbana and Chicago: Univ. of Illinois Press, 1999), 185–208.

CHAPTER 9

SWEET TEA AND ROSARY BEADS: AN ANALYSIS OF SOUTHERN CATHOLICISM AT THE MILLENNIUM

AS I WALK DOWNSTAIRS INTO BLESSED SACRAMENT CATHOLIC SCHOOL'S kindergarten classroom, where the parish's Faith Formation classes are held each Sunday, I hear a cacophony of children's voices rising to greet me. By the time I reach the bottom stair the voices have quieted. I turn the corner to see forty children in a circle holding hands preparing for opening prayer. I join the circle between a seven-year-old Anglo girl with long blonde hair and a seven-year-old Latina with short, dark brown hair, both preparing for their First Eucharist. Throughout the circle, Latino and Anglo children hold hands before they make the sign of the cross. Then their teacher, Ann, moves into the center of the circle and asks the children to raise their right hands. Once they have differentiated their right from their left—not always an easy task at age seven—she offers the class a baseball mnemonic to remember how to make this all-important gesture. "Home plate," Ann says as she touches her head. "Pitcher's mound," she says as she moves her hand to the center of her chest. Then she moves her hand over to her left shoulder, saying "third base," then "first base," as she touches her right shoulder. After the sign of the cross, the children all bow their heads to say the "Our Father." Some of the children say it with a Southern drawl, while others have a New Jersey accent. About half the class says it in Spanish and the other half in English.[1] Although in many ways this prayer circle mirrors rituals in other Faith Formation classes around the country, this one is noteworthy because it happens in the South, which until recently had been insulated from the waves of immigration that transformed the North.

This insulation is now disappearing, and the effect on the southern Catholic Church has been profound. Prayer circles like the one in which I participated are playing an important role in managing this change. Considering the changes at Blessed Sacrament Parish in Burlington, North Carolina, and in its Diocese (the Diocese of Raleigh) reveals much about the recent developments in Catholicism in the South: how the parishioners see their church as responding to, and being shaped by, the surrounding Protestant "Bible-Belt" culture; and how it has changed with the coming of Catholic migrants from the North and, more recently, Latin America.[2] To understand how parishioners and their priests feel about these changes, I did fieldwork at two parishes in the Raleigh Diocese—Holy Cross Catholic Church, an African American congregation in Durham, North Carolina, and Blessed Sacrament, an Anglo and Latino parish—as well as some short-term work with other churches in the area. I explored how these demographic shifts have shaped the southern Catholic Church in North Carolina and surrounding states, particularly outside those regions of original Catholic settlement, both in terms of how the Catholic Church has been accepted into the wider southern religious community and its struggles to incorporate a growing Latino Catholic population.[3]

The story of southern religion has been primarily a Protestant one. The annals of southern religious history include an ever-growing number of studies on white and black Baptists, Methodists, and Pentecostals, but few on southern Catholicism outside Texas, Louisiana, and other places of early Catholic settlement. The works that are available generally focus on the early days when Baltimore, Maryland, was the center of the Catholic Church in America, and on the Church's attitude towards slavery, Reconstruction, and segregation.[4] In part, this lack of scholarly work on Catholics in the South reflects the relative paucity of Catholics in the region. In 1820, at the time Irish immigrants began flooding parishes in the North, the number of Catholics in Georgia and the Carolinas only warranted the creation of a single diocese, the Diocese of Charleston.[5] Twenty years later, nearly three hundred thousand Irish had joined parishes in the Northeast, while North Carolina claimed only five Catholic churches.[6]

Without the influx of European immigrants, the southern Catholic Church grew slowly until the late 1960s when northerners came south to enjoy the benefits of the Sunbelt. The pace grew even more rapidly when the Latino migration, primarily from Mexico, began in the 1990s. Indeed, one could argue that the Catholic Church is thriving in the South at the beginning of the twenty-first century, having almost tripled its population in the region since 1970.[7] In the Atlanta Diocese, for instance, the number of Catholics has doubled in the past decade, though the general population grew by only 25 percent.[8] Likewise, in Mississippi one parish went from one Spanish mass a month to two Spanish masses a week in less than four years.[9] The director of religious education commented on the non-Hispanic growth she had witnessed in the past five years, stating that there has "been a tremendous amount of growth in this area which has tended to bring people from other places like Ohio, where they might have more Catholics. . . . We're the only Catholic Church for two and a half counties."[10] While not every diocese has experienced this degree of growth, many rural and urban dioceses in the South are struggling to build new churches to house their swelling populations, and more and more children—like those I held hands with on that Sunday—learn how to make the sign of the cross on Sunday mornings and weekday afternoons in Catholic Churches and during the day at hundreds of parochial schools in the South. As their parishes become more vibrant, with more parishioners, programs, and projects, many of these children, both Anglo and Latino, realize only slowly that, according to many of their Protestant neighbors as well as many scholars of religious studies, sweet tea and rosary beads do not easily go together.

Building Relationships Between Protestants and Catholics

From my interviews with almost thirty seven- and eight-year-olds at both Blessed Sacrament and Holy Cross, I found that the children make few distinctions between their religious practices and those of their Protestant friends. If, however, these children's experiences follow those of previous generations of southern Catholics, the distinctions between the two faiths will become very clear as the children age—for example, as their Protestant friends describe their conversions or baptismal experiences. If the Protestant South's perception of the South remains as it has been for generations, the young Catholics with whom I spoke will face continuing scrutiny as their friends question their Christian identity. Adult southern Catholics, for instance, often recount how their Protestant friends' conversion testimonies would end with the dreaded question, "Have you been saved?" Saved? Many older Catholics remember struggling with just how to approach this question. One middle-aged Anglo woman described the struggle this way: "'Are you saved?' . . . doesn't translate well into a Catholic context. Well, yes, I have been sanctified through baptism, and I am on my way to finding Jesus Christ, but that's not the same as being 'saved.'"[11] Unlike this woman, children do not usually have the facility with words or the understanding of their faith necessary to provide such nuanced answers. When they try to explain why they have not been saved, their non-Catholic friends often reply that they are "going to Hell," or at least that the state of their souls is in question. For this reason, adult southern Catholics often remember that as children they learned that the larger religious community did not see them as Christians. The director of faith development at Blessed Sacrament recalled when a Protestant friend, Joanne, asked her, "Are you a Catholic or a Christian first?" Although she tried to convince her friend that Catholics were Christians, Joanne "was insistent."[12]

Being perceived as non-Christian, as something foreign, had far-reaching social implications. These Catholics remember that as children they were not only taunted about the state of their souls, they also were ostracized. One forty-four-year-old North Carolina native recalled that the neighborhood children "would come to the screen door, [and] here we all were on our knees saying the rosary. The kids [would] come up to the door and say, 'Well, my parents don't want me to play with you.'"[13]

Often, these confrontations went beyond schoolyard arguments and individual feelings of isolation to community-wide exclusion. Unlike in the Northeast and Midwest, where the large numbers of Catholics meant that they had their own social clubs, youth organizations, and neighborhood groups, in the South (where as recently as 1995 fewer than four in one hundred people were Catholic) Catholics were excluded from much of the networking and many community events.[14] One fifty-year-old Anglo man from a small town in South Carolina described the institutional exclusion this way: "A lot of the social events were routed through the town's churches, and since 99 percent of the churches were Protestant, well, Catholics weren't included."[15]

To combat this exclusion, southern Catholic churches have made a great effort to connect with their Protestant neighbors, especially after Vatican II encouraged building ecumenical relationships. In an essay in *The Culture of Bible Belt Catholics*, Jon Anderson argues that southern Catholics have had to work hard for community acceptance, to make others see them as "just another church."[16] Recently, local parishes and many Catholic congregations throughout the South have begun to focus on ecumenical activities with the hope that their interactions will allow the local Protestant majority to see their parishioners as brothers and sisters in Christ, rather than as resident aliens in a Protestant homeland. The priests with whom Anderson spoke emphasized their roles in local committees. Similarly, many priests in the Raleigh Diocese I interviewed also highlighted the Church's need to be seen as part of the community and its associations. One of the pastors of Immaculate Conception Church in Durham explained: "Because being Catholic [here] is a bit suspect . . . we make more of an effort to be involved in the work of the city, and with other churches in the city. And we're more inclined or make more of an effort to do that lest we seem somehow disinterested or think that we're superior, I suppose."[17] Lay leaders, as well as priests, often emphasized to me the connections their church had with local civic organizations. Louise, a sixty-year-old African American woman, for instance, proudly outlined some of Holy Cross's most recent efforts at community outreach: "We've become more a part of the community outside of Holy Cross, to the community of Durham. We take part in Churches in Action. That's where all the churches come together for the welfare of the people of Durham. We participate in activities, like we just finished the Crop Walk," a community-wide event that raises money to fight world hunger.[18]

At the parish level, Holy Cross has sought to foster this acceptance, in part, through a fundraiser called the "Rib Joint." Each week of home football games at nearby universities, volunteers set to work seasoning 200 pounds of catfish and marinating 250 pounds of chicken and 2,000 pounds of ribs, all of which would be cooked and sold on the lawn beside the church during the coming weekend. The reason for all of this work on the Rib Joint, one of the founders explained, was that "this being a particularly Protestant belt, most folks are Baptist so we've done a lot of work with the Rib Joint just getting people on the grounds and meeting folks to see that Catholics can be real people too."[19] These efforts at making Catholics legitimate and familiar may mean that the children at Holy Cross, as well as their counterparts at Blessed Sacrament and other parishes in the South, will face less questioning and suspicion than previous generations of southern Catholics have faced. As Catholic churches begin to build these relationships through traditional southern means such as Church barbeques, they must also grapple with how to attract and support the influx of many northern transplants and Latino migrant parishioners.

Including Northern Catholic Transplants into the Southern Church

Most parishes in North Carolina served fewer than one hundred families before the development in the late 1960s of Research Triangle Park, a light industrial center that is located between Raleigh and Durham. The Triangle attracted technical and research firms from across the country, such as Bell Telephone and later GlaxoSmithKline to North Carolina. Many people from the Northeast, including many Catholics, moved to the South with these corporations. The churches these Catholics found often differed greatly from the ones they left behind. Unlike northern parishes, which tended to be extremely large and sometimes impersonal, these southern Catholic Churches had small congregations with familial atmospheres.[20] When northerners came to southern parishes, the slower pace of the mass, the extended length of the homily, and the parishioners' inclination to talk after mass often surprised them. One Anglo mother recalled, "Where I grew up in Maryland the churches were huge, and it was a drag race to see who could get out of the parking lot . . . and here people hang out and nobody is in a big hurry to leave."[21] While the slower pace of southern life may have frustrated some transplanted northerners, they seemed to hope that the southerners' deep commitment to religion would keep their children coming to church. As Martha, originally from Pennsylvania, said, "Hopefully, just being in the South . . . [where] the other religions . . . don't really seem to mind going to church, hopefully that will rub off [on the kids]."[22]

While northern parents hope that being in the South eventually will cultivate religious commitment in their children, as religious historian Samuel Hill predicted and my interviews confirm, living in the religiously committed South already has had its effect. Joseph, a thirty-eight-year-old member of Blessed Sacrament who moved to Burlington, North Carolina, from New Jersey said, "I felt kind of weird cutting my grass on Sunday . . . Sunday is the Lord's day [on which here in the South] you don't do anything. You relax and serve Him."[23] To fit in with his neighbors, Joseph, like many other northern transplants, has begun to go to mass each Sunday. Interactions with evangelicals have also caused other people to return to the Catholic Church after visiting a neighbor's Protestant church. Elizabeth's parents, for instance, returned to Blessed Sacrament after going to First Baptist Church at a friend's suggestion. After spending more than a year at the Baptist church, Elizabeth and her family have returned to the Catholic Church so that she and her brothers could receive the sacraments and her parents could honor their promise to rear the children Catholic.[24] Being among religiously committed Protestants has not only had some effect on northern Catholic's mass attendance, it also has caused some parishioners to consider more what it means to be Catholic and their degree of commitment to the Church. One of the pastors at Immaculate Conception explained: "Because in the North being a Catholic is somewhat commonplace, you . . . lose your identity because you don't have to think about it—being Catholic. Lots of people are Catholic. You don't have to explain it. But down here lots of people are puzzled about that [and] you are forced to think, well, who are you?"[25] Northern Catholic parents must answer this question for themselves just as they and their churches help the children wrestle with these issues of identity.

The Research Triangle attracted northern Catholics to the Bible Belt in such numbers that almost all the Anglo children at Blessed Sacrament and Holy Cross travel to the Northeast to visit their relatives. When asked who was coming to see her at First Communion, Brittany, like many of the children with whom I spoke, replied, "My godparents and my grandma from New Jersey. I don't know if my other cousins from Pennsylvania are coming too."[26] For these children, northern and southern Catholic worlds meet when the children hear from their northern relatives about life growing up in predominately

Catholic neighborhoods, while these children experience life in the South as a religious minority. Further, with the absence of Catholic neighborhoods in the South and increased geographic and social mobility, a Catholic child with a non-Catholic parent is not uncommon. Some children, like Shannon, alternated between Faith Formation classes at Blessed Sacrament, where her father's family have been parishioners for more than forty years, and Sunday school at her mother's Protestant church so her family could go to church together each Sunday—and so she could see that her parents honored each other's view of God.[27] Unlike their northern Catholic parents, who most likely learned about the church in older ethnic parishes, these children are learning the catechism with a Southern accent that is often made more pronounced through the influence of a non-Catholic parent.

This accent is most marked in their heightened concern about their relationship with Jesus. In the South, as in other parts of the country, catechists teach children preparing for their First Communion that they will receive the person of Jesus under the appearance of the bread and wine, according to the doctrine of transubstantiation. While children interpret these words in various ways, in the South many of them put great emphasis on the relational aspects of this encounter in ways that recall Protestant discussions of their personal relationship with Christ. For Maureen at Holy Cross, for instance, First Communion was when "you get to eat a little bit from the Last Supper from Jesus, and Jesus is happy for you."[28] Her mother commented on this emphasis on a personal relationship with Jesus as well as the atmosphere of the church, saying, "It's very different being here. I think there is a lot of Protestant or Baptist influence in the church."[29] Similarly, all the children I spoke with at Blessed Sacrament talked about getting "closer to Jesus" by having him know them in a different and more personal way. The catechists reinforced the children's emphasis on the immediacy of their relationship with Jesus by drawing pictures of Jesus playing with them and having Jesus give them bear hugs.[30] The combination of the "Jesus and me of the Bible-Belt," as Father Barry at Holy Cross phrased it and Catholicism as their workbooks taught it, reflects the trans-regional Catholicism that these children experience.

Some scholars have argued that southern Catholics know little about their Protestant neighbors' religious practices and have not been influenced by them. In the area encompassed by the Raleigh Diocese, however, Catholics and Protestants, whether originally from the North or the South, are meeting, talking, and rearing families.[31] On Palm Sunday 2001 this contact occurred institutionally when the parishioners from the 10:30 A.M. English-language mass at Blessed Sacrament joined members of the Presbyterian church across the street for the blessing of the palms before proceeding to their respective churches to continue their worship.[32] Such exchanges make Catholics seem less exotic to

Protestants, thereby strengthening interdenominational relations. Outside observers would have had difficulty distinguishing the Catholics from the Protestants in this group, as they would on most Sundays before the mass begins. In contrast to traditional Latino masses, few people say the rosary before or during the liturgy, there are no lighted candles or offerings to the Virgin near the altar, and parishioners do not bring objects for the priests to bless. The Catholicism that Latinos bring with them to the South seems foreign in many ways to both Protestants and many native southern Catholics alike.

Examining Latino Catholicism's Impact on Anglo Southern Parishes

The influx of Catholics into the South from both the Northeast and Latin America has nudged the southern Catholic Church to struggle with two distinct levels of integration. As I have noted, the increased presence of the Catholic Church in the South (resulting in large part from the migration of northern Catholics) has led to more interactions between southern Catholics and southern Protestants. These interactions have enabled many in both groups to see each other as fellow Christians. However, at a second level, the integration of Latinos within the Catholic Church has been much more challenging, and it has yet to be fully resolved. Although Texans have a longstanding and unbroken Hispanic heritage, the weaving of Latinos into the fabric of some southern urban and rural areas presents some new challenges. For the first time, many parishes in the South outside Texas and Florida must contend with large numbers of people who do not speak English or understand the workings of American culture.

The Latino population in Durham, North Carolina, for instance, has grown from a barely visible minority to a group whose strong presence in the area is evident in the rapid increase in Mexican restaurants, Latino markets, and bilingual signs. Hispanics, chiefly from Mexico, began coming to North Carolina in the early 1990s to work in construction, food services, and other industries that grew in response to the population boom in the Research Triangle (Durham, Raleigh, and Chapel Hill) and the outlying areas. Although the number of Latinos currently living in the Research Triangle is difficult to measure because of their immigration status and their high degree of mobility, the 2000 census counted 378,963 Latinos in North Carolina, an increase of more than 550 percent in the last decade.[33] While other parishes throughout the U.S. have had a great increase in Latino parishioners, migrants to North Carolina and other southeastern states, unlike those who settle in the borderlands of the Southwest, find churches with little knowledge of Latino religion and culture. Like

Susan Ridgely Bales

the earlier European immigrants to the North, however, many of these Latinos have turned to the Catholic Church to help them maintain their traditions and learn the customs of their new home.[34] What they have found in their parishes in their new neighborhoods varies greatly. In the Southwest and Florida, there are many Spanish-speaking parishes that center Latino culture in their masses.[35] In most other places in the South, however, these parishioners have entered small parishes that were largely unprepared for their arrival. In recent years, therefore, parish councils throughout the Raleigh Diocese, and many other southern dioceses, have spent much time trying to develop a plan that incorporates their new Latino members into the parish in a way that honors both Hispanic and Anglo religious traditions.

The speed and size of this migration, together with the relative lack of existing resources, have created serious challenges. Churches have been stretched to find space within their sanctuaries and classrooms for their new parishioners as well as to meet their spiritual and physical needs. While most churches are devising ways to accommodate the swelling number of worshippers—even if it means holding rituals in unorthodox places like school cafeterias while they build new sanctuaries—finding room for new cultures and, even more importantly, new languages can be more difficult. Holy Cross, once known as the home of Hispanic Catholics in Durham, is now one of the thirty-four churches, of eighty-eight in the diocese, that does not have at least one Spanish mass.[36] As Thomas A. Tweed mentions in his contribution in this volume, Holy Cross suspended its Spanish masses in October of 1996.[37] Father Bruce Bavinger began Holy Cross's Hispanic ministry in 1988 at the request of the Latinos themselves. Eight years later, however, when Father Bruce's tenure at Holy Cross ended and his replacement did not know Spanish, the parish board voted to end its Spanish masses. Although the church said it canceled its Spanish masses in part to integrate the Hispanics into the larger English-speaking parish, most of the Latino parishioners at Holy Cross interpreted this cessation as a call for their departure. The majority of the Latino immigrants who had made Holy Cross their home walked out of the church in October 1996, taking their statue of Our Lady of Guadeloupe with them. After they left, many of these Latino Catholics and others who came to the region after them chose to attend Immaculate Conception Parish, only a few miles from Holy Cross. As a result of this shift, membership at Immaculate Conception rose from approximately twenty-three hundred in 1992 to approximately thirty-two hundred in 1998 as more and more Latino Catholics— approximately six hundred as of July 31 of that year—found their way to this church.

While dramatic events such as those at Holy Cross are the exception, many Catholic churches in North Carolina are struggling with how to meet the many needs of their increasingly diverse parishioners. In many parishes, the two communities—Anglo and Latino—exist as parallel congregations, divided primarily along the lines of language and, to a lesser extent, by ethnicity. In these parishes, the parishioners use the same facilities but rarely meet together.[38] Other churches are working hard to create a single community— either by having only bilingual masses or by having Spanish and English masses as well as bilingual events to bring the parish together. For the parishes that hope for one multicultural community, maintaining the balance between the spiritual and communal needs of their Anglo and Latino parishioners presents more challenges than simply adding masses and expanding social services. It also means that the churches must work to bring Latinos into the parish's decision-making bodies and encourage Anglos to be receptive to Latinos' viewpoints. Thus far, there have not been many inclusive parish councils that allow the church to represent both communities. Instead, the Anglo community and its impression of what the Latinos need dominate. This inequality in exchange comes in large part from lack of understanding. Few Catholic Churches in the South have had the time or the resources to educate Anglo and Latino parishioners in parallel congregations about each other's customs so that each might be able (and willing) to participate in the celebrations of the other. These tasks are somewhat easier for city parishes with a large rural component, like Blessed Sacrament, and strictly rural parishes that have had Hispanic ministries to migrant workers for many years before the demographic shift of the nineties. For example, unlike those Catholic churches in Durham that had only one or two Latino families before 1993, Blessed Sacrament already included Spanish-speaking administrators, who understood many of the Latino community's social needs and their religious traditions, on its parish staff. Most of the parishioners involved in Blessed Sacrament's Hispanic ministry have been at that task since it began in 1982. At that time their main goals were to provide at least one Spanish mass a month and to ensure that these migrant workers had adequate clothing and housing. In the subsequent twenty years, that ministry has grown in the number of parishioners it serves by more than 400 percent, according to its director.[39] Today, Blessed Sacrament has two Spanish masses a week to accommodate all of its parishioners. This increase in Spanish masses, one Latina commented, meant that she and the other Latinos in the church "ha[d] made our mark."[40]

That influence on Catholicism in North Carolina extends far beyond the number of Spanish masses; Latino religious customs and commitments have transformed parish life. Many Anglos have welcomed some of the Hispanic influences in the Sunday celebration but have resisted some para-liturgical devotions, which they dismiss as remnants of pre–Vatican II Catholicism. For the clergy and lay religious educators, both Anglo and Latino, this tension between the desire to accept Latino culture and the concern to conform to the mores of the American Church has meant that the Latinos have relinquished the church's involvement in some of their traditions and have also accepted some American religious practices. This has often led to prohibiting use of lighted candles, which are particularly important in Hispanic devotion, as well as to many conversations about altering (or even discontinuing) *quinceaños* celebrations and other para-liturgical events. Father John Heffernan at Immaculate Conception, for instance, said, "We are people who are very open to the culture and religious experience that people bring. Yet, it's appropriate as well to sort out, well, what's good from what the people bring and what's good from what we have and come to a melding and a better experience for us."[41] These decisions about how to bring the two cultures together, however, rest largely with Anglos because they predominate on parish councils (although almost all churches with Latino parishioners have Hispanic representation in church government) and because many Anglos and Latinos see Anglos as the core members of the parish. One Latina, who has lived in Burlington for sixteen years, described the Anglo standing in the parish this way: "I feel like we were the second and they're the first."[42] For some Latinos, it seems, this limited sense of belonging obstructs their involvement in the inner workings of the parish. Although she put her relationship with the church in this hierarchical way, she did see that things had been changing in recent years, stating, "The Spanish groups are getting more involved. It's a lot of progress."[43]

Along with volunteering to work with the religious education program, many of these Spanish groups have been working hard to ensure that Mexican traditions (the traditions of most Hispanic parishioners) continue in their parish by incorporating these celebrations into the life of the parish. With the persistence and guidance of a vocal and growing Latino lay-elite and clergy, who are beginning to become involved in many parishes, some southern Catholic churches are now facilitating celebrations for many important cultural and religious events such as la Fiesta de Guadalupe and la Via Crucis. Under the direction of Blessed Sacrament's first Latino priest, for instance, the parish held its inaugural Via Crucis on April 13, 2001. In the parking lot facing the large Presbyterian church next door, Jesus (played by a lanky, bearded Latino youth dressed in an off-white tunic) stood on a stage with Pontius Pilate (played by another bearded but slightly stouter Latino wearing cardboard armor) while a group of young Latinos in tunics and veils looked on from the blacktop as they ritually reenacted the original stations of the cross.[44] Alma de Niño, Blessed Sacrament's chapter of Grupo Juvenil Latino (the Hispanic young adult group), staged this procession, which attracted more than three hundred people, primarily but not exclusively Latinos, to follow the cross through the streets of Burlington. This public expression of Hispanic piety served to reinforce the Latino presence in the community, as well as to reassure Latino adults that their children would carry on ancestral spiritual traditions in their new home. In their conversations at the procession's conclusion, for instance, the majority of parishioners mentioned that having the youth prepare and present the Via Crucis made it better than the more publicized (and adult-led) ritual in Siler City, North Carolina.[45]

Incorporating Parishes through Children's Participation

Unfortunately, since few Anglos attend these Latino events, such celebrations cannot form the basis of Anglo-Latino exchange. Since the church cannot require its parishioners to go to such events, most parishes rely on one area of participation they can control—children's religious education. As the director of religious education at Immaculate Conception noted, "We mostly work at integration through the children because usually the children can speak both Spanish and English while the parents speak only Spanish."[46] The children not only bridge the language gap between the two cultures, but through their joint participation in Faith Formation classes, religious educators and others hope that Latino children will develop friendships with their southern Anglo classmates as they learn the Church's doctrine and American customs from their catechists. Using mnemonics from an American pastime like baseball to teach the sign of the cross, which I noted at the start of the chapter, is only one example of a learning technique that blends American culture with Catholic doctrine.

The children's function as cultural and spiritual mediators extends far beyond their own friendships and education. Blessed Sacrament and many other parishes in the South hope that these children will also bring their parents together into one community. At Blessed Sacrament, the First Communion workshop was the most successful event in bringing Anglo and Latino parents together. There, the parents worked side by side, helping the children make their First Communion banners, bake bread, and learn songs.[47] As the parents worked together in the workshop and other activities, the director of religious education hoped that they would get to know one another and begin to interact at non-scheduled times and that through their socialization the Latino parents would begin to feel comfortable getting involved in parish activities.[48] While this kind of broader exchange has not yet developed, some children from Mexico and North Carolina have begun voluntarily to stand next to each other, hold hands, and call each other friend in the prayer circle. This southern parish and others like it may edge their parallel congregations closer together even if the two spiritual "lines" never fully meet. Moreover, if

Latino growth continues, many southern Catholic parishes will have Spanish-speaking majorities. And salsa will become as ubiquitous as sweet tea at the church picnics.

Notes

I would like to thank the parishioners of Blessed Sacrament and Holy Cross, as well as the clergy and staff of Immaculate Conception, for sharing their feelings with me about their parishes and how they are changing in response to their new parishioners. I hope that they all find themselves faithfully represented here. I also want to thank Thomas A. Tweed, Stephanie Cobb, and Mary Key for reading earlier drafts of this chapter.

1. Field notes, Faith Formation class, Blessed Sacrament Catholic Church, Burlington, North Carolina, 1 Oct. 2000.

2. Here, I am using the term "South" as the Gallup Poll defines it: the eleven ex-Confederate states plus Oklahoma and Kentucky. The developments that I discuss, however, do not include those areas of Texas and Florida that have historically had substantial Latino populations. Therefore, they are not in the midst of the recent transformations discussed in the text.

3. Of course, the effects of these migrants have not been uniform across the South. While some areas have felt little impact, others are seemingly over-whelmed by the arrival of new parishioners.

4. For discussions of the early Church in the South, see Randall M. Miller and Jon L. Wakelyn, eds., *Catholics in the Old South: Essays on Church and Society* (Macon, GA: Mercer Univ. Press, 1983). For more on the Catholic Church's discussion about slavery and segregation, see William A. Osborne, *"The Segregated Covenant": Race Relations and American Catholics* (New York: Herder and Herder, 1967); John T. Gillard, *Colored Catholics in the United States* (Baltimore: Josephite Press, 1941); John T. McGreevy, *Parish Boundaries: The Catholic Encounter with Race in the Twentieth-Century Urban North* (Chicago: Univ. of Chicago Press, 1996); and Edward D. Reynolds, S.J., *Jesuits for the Negro* (New York: The American Press, 1949).

5. Gerald L. Lewis, "The Diocese of Raleigh: An Overview," Catholic Diocese of Raleigh Web site, http://www.dioceseofraleigh.org/html/history1.html, 1.

6. Ibid.; Jay P. Dolan, *The American Catholic Experience: A History from Colonial Times to the Present* (Notre Dame: Univ. of Notre Dame Press, 1992), 128.

7. Helen Ellis, "Loyola to Create Center for Study of Catholicism in the South," *Loyola Today,* 19 Jan. 2001, accessible online at Loyola University (New Orleans) Web site, http://www.loyno.edu/newsandcalendars/loyolatoday/2001/01/newcenter.html. For statistics on Catholics in the United States in

2000, see the Glenmary Research Center Web site, http://www.glenmary.org/grc/RCMS_2000/Catholic_findings.htm.

8. Arthur Jones, "Hispanic Catholics Ignored," *National Catholic Reporter* 36 (11 February 2000): 3–4.

9. Danny Duncan Collum, "Unexpected Guests: Glenmary Missions Learn to Welcome Spanish-Speaking Newcomers," *Glenmary Challenge* Autumn 2000, accessible at Glenmary Home Missioners Web site, http://www.glenmary.org/challenge/Autumn00/guests/guests.htm.

10. Director of religious education, Immaculate Conception Church, Durham, NC, interview by author, 27 Jan. 1999. All names have been changed except for those of the most visible members of the parish, such as the priests and directors of religious education.

11. Forty-five-year-old Anglo woman, interviewed by author, Blessed Sacrament Catholic Church, Burlington, NC, winter 2000.

12. Director of religious education, Blessed Sacrament Catholic Church, Burlington, NC, interview by author, 13 Feb. 2001.

13. Forty-four-year-old Anglo woman, Blessed Sacrament Catholic Church, Burlington, NC, interview by author, 14 Jan. 2001.

14. Jon W. Anderson, "An Ethnographic Overview of Cultural Differences of Bible Belt Catholics," in *The Culture of Bible Belt Catholics*, ed. Jon W. Anderson and William B. Friend (New York: Paulist Press, 1995), 11.

15. Quoted in Sam Boykin, "Growing up Catholic in the South: Bob Jones Controversy reopens Old Wounds" *Raleigh Spectator*, Apr. 12–18, 2000, 11.

16. Jon W. Anderson, "Catholic Imagination and Inflections of 'Church' in the Contemporary South," in *Bible Belt Catholics*, ed. Anderson and Friend, 86.

17. Father John Heffernan, O.F.M., Immaculate Conception Catholic Church, Durham, NC, interview by author, 17 Jan. 1998.

18. Sixty-year-old African American woman, Holy Cross Catholic Church, Durham, NC, interview by author, 11 Apr. 1999.

19. Fifty-five-year-old African American man, Holy Cross Catholic Church, Durham, NC, interview by author, 2 April 1999. Even for those Protestants who never stop, the Rib Joint has served to tie Holy Cross to the wider community. An older white Baptist man and lifetime resident of Durham, for instance, when he heard the name Holy Cross asked, "Oh, is that the little church on Alston Avenue with the grills on the front lawn?"

20. For more on the familial atmosphere and the importance of the family metaphor, see Anderson and Friend, eds., *Bible Belt Catholics*, and Gary Wray McDonough, *Black and Catholic in Savannah, Georgia* (Knoxville: Univ. of Tennessee Press, 1994).

21. Forty-five-year-old Anglo woman, Holy Cross Catholic Church, Durham, NC, interview by author, 8 Feb. 1998.

Susan Ridgely Bales

22. Forty-year-old Anglo woman, Chapel Hill, NC, interview by author, 19 Mar. 2001.

23. Thirty-eight-year-old Anglo man, Blessed Sacrament Catholic Church, Burlington, NC, interview by author, 12 Nov. 2000; Samuel S. Hill, "Religion and Region in America," *Annals of the American Academy of Political and Social Science* 480 (July 1985): 140–41.

24. Anglo man, Blessed Sacrament Catholic Church, Burlington, NC, conversation with author, 11 Nov. 2001.

25. Father John Heffernan, Immaculate Conception, Durham, NC, interview by author, 17 Jan. 1999.

26. Seven-year-old Anglo girl, Blessed Sacrament Catholic Church, Burlington, NC, interview by author, 18 Mar. 2001.

27. Thirty-nine-year-old Anglo woman, telephone interview by author, 29 Jan. 2001.

28. Seven-year-old Anglo girl, Holy Cross Catholic Church, Durham, NC, interview by author, 13 Apr. 1997.

29. Forty-five year-old Anglo woman, Holy Cross Catholic Church, interview by author, Durham, NC, 8 Feb. 1998.

30. Second-grade Faith Formation lesson, Blessed Sacrament Catholic Church, Burlington, NC, 22 Apr. 2001.

31. For an argument about the lack of Protestant influence in the Catholic church, see Anderson and Friend, eds., *Bible Belt Catholics.*

32. Blessed Sacrament Sunday bulletin, 1 Apr. 2001.

33. Maureen Fan, "Triangle Takes the Lead," *Mercury News,* 7 July 2001, http://www0.siliconvalley.com/docs/news/depth/raleig070801.htm (last accessed July 2001).

34. For more information about the Catholic Church's role in the lives of earlier European migrants, see Jay P. Dolan, *The Immigrant Church: New York's Irish and German Catholics, 1815–1865* (Baltimore: Johns Hopkins Press, 1975); and Dolores Liptak, R.S.M., *Immigrants and their Church* (New York: Macmillan, 1989).

35. For historical overviews of Latinos in the U.S. Catholic Church, see Jay P. Dolan, *Hispanic Catholic Culture in the U.S.: Issues and Concerns* (Notre Dame: Univ. of Notre Dame Press, 1994); and Timothy Matovina and Gerald E. Poyo, eds., *¡Presente! U.S. Latino Catholics from Colonial Origins to the Present* (New York: Orbis Books, 2000). For more information on traditional Latino Catholic practices and their impact on the United States, see Anthony M. Stevens-Arroyo and Ana María Díaz-Stevens, eds., *An Enduring Flame: Studies on Latino Popular Religiosity* (New York: Blinder Center for Western Hemisphere Studies, 1994); Ana María Díaz-Stevens and Anthony M. Stevens-Arroyo, eds., *Recognizing the Latino Resurgence in U.S. Religion: The Emmaus Paradigm*

(Boulder, CO: Westview Press, 1998); and Peter Casarella and Raúl Gómez, S.D.S., *El Cuerpo De Cristo: The Hispanic Presence in the U.S. Catholic Church* (New York: Crossroad Publishing Co., 1998).

36. For Spanish masses in the Catholic Diocese of Raleigh, see the listing on the diocesan web site, http://www.dioceseofraleigh.org/sites/hispanic_ministry/mass/mass_times.html

37. Kammie Michael, "Catholic Church to Drop Bilingual Service," *Durham Herald Sun,* 14 Oct. 1996.

38. I borrow the term "parallel congregations" from Paul David Numrich, *Old Wisdom in the New World: Americanization in Two Immigrant Theravada Buddhist Temples* (Knoxville: Univ. of Tennessee Press, 1996), xxii.

39. Fifty-five-year-old Latina, Blessed Sacrament, Burlington, NC, interview by author, 28 Jan. 2001.

40. Fifty-year-old Latina, Blessed Sacrament Catholic Church, Burlington, NC, interview by author, 8 Apr. 2001.

41. Father John Heffernan, O.F.M., Immaculate Conception Catholic Church, Durham, NC, interview by author, 17 Jan. 1999.

42. Forty-year-old Latina, Blessed Sacrament Catholic Church, Burlington, NC, interview by author, 29 April 2001.

43. Ibid.

44. Field notes, Via Crucis, Blessed Sacrament Catholic Church, 13 Apr. 2001.

45. Ibid.

46. Director of religious education, Immaculate Conception Catholic Church, Durham, NC, interview by author, 27 Jan. 1998.

47. Field notes, First Communion Workshop, Blessed Sacrament Catholic Church, Burlington, NC, 7 Apr. 2001.

48. Director of religious education, Blessed Sacrament Catholic Church, Burlington, NC, interview by author, 13 Feb. 2001.

Steven W. Ramey

CHAPTER 10

TEMPLES AND BEYOND: VARIETIES OF HINDU EXPERIENCES IN THE SOUTH

WITH A CLEAR BLUE SKY ABOVE, THE EAST ROSWELL COMMUNITY PARK IN metropolitan Atlanta provided a typical suburban venue for any spring picnic or game of softball, but this was not the typical Sunday afternoon in the American South. As I opened the glass door to the community building, the smell of incense filled my nostrils, and a jumbled line of shoes sat against the wall. For about two hundred Hindus, the institutional-grade carpet had become sacred ground.

The Sindhi Sabha of Georgia, an organization of Hindu families who trace their heritage to Sindh (a region that is now in Pakistan), met in the community building in this park to celebrate Cheti Chand, the Sindhi Hindu New Year, in March 2000. Guests had arrived from around Atlanta as well as other parts of Georgia and even Alabama and Tennessee. The community room had tables for the dinner and a small stage for the musicians. On a pedestal in front of the stage was a two-foot-high statue of Jhule Lal, the god whom Sindhis particularly revere because he appeared in Sindh to protect Hindus. The statue was sitting on a foil-covered aeronautical chariot that had images of other Hindu deities on its sides.

After many people had arrived and were chatting at the tables, several musicians from Chattanooga played traditional Sindhi devotional music, including Hindu *bhajans* and Islamic *ghazals*. Their selection of devotional songs from both traditions and their commentary reflected the religious diversity and interconnections of Sindhi traditions, where the boundaries between

Hinduism, Sufism (Islamic mysticism), and Sikhism (a religious movement that began in fifteenth-century India) were highly permeable. With recorded music praising Jhule Lal in the background, the president of the Sabha processed into the room with a silver tray of traditional offerings on her head and several people following her. As she began to circumambulate Jhule Lal's image, many of us joined the mass of bodies, some walking, some dancing with sticks, and some parents prodding their children to participate. Many people took turns placing the tray of offerings on their heads, at least for a brief moment. Following this worship, the group prayed to the goddess Lakshmi for her blessings. The afternoon concluded with the installation of officers of the Sabha for the next year and a delicious meal of home-cooked Indian dishes.

This religious festival is one of the many signs of the growing religious diversity of the South. Throughout the South, from Richmond, Virginia, to Tampa, Florida, to Houston, Texas, many large and medium-sized cities have one or more Hindu temples. The diversity in this region and among Hindus themselves is far greater, however, than the publicly visible temples suggest. Much of the religious life of Hindus functions beyond the temples, with family practices in the home as well as community gatherings in homes or rented facilities. To comprehend the diverse Hindu presence in the South, it is imperative to consider both the array of temples in the region and the variety of associations and activities beyond the temples, such as this festival.

In this essay I will approach Hindu experiences from only two of the numerous perspectives necessary to develop a full understanding. I will first focus on the variety of institutions and activities that Hindus have considered important enough to establish in the American South. To survey this variety, I will discuss the development of organizations, including temples, other religious centers, and associations related to India, as well as the relationships among them, in one metropolitan area, the North Carolina Triangle. I will then highlight some similarities and differences between the Hindu activities in the Triangle and in several other cities in the region. To place the institutional survey in the context of lived experiences, I will focus on the practices of a Hindu family to illustrate one way that a family can incorporate a variety of these activities in temples and beyond the temples into their religious lives.

Besides demonstrating the diversity of activities in and beyond the temples, the activities that I discuss raise several other interesting points that I will touch on only briefly. Most notably, Hindu experiences and organizations intersect with the activities of other religious communities of India, including Sikhism, Jainism, and Islam. While many Hindus commonly participate in Sikh, Jain, or Muslim activities in India, the experience of being in a foreign land adds new dimensions to the cooperation between organizations and the cross-tradition participation of individuals. Other developments in the context of the American South include constructing social halls along with the temples, coordinating the schedule of some religious events with the American calendar, and heightening the emphasis on the unity of all divine figures in the Supreme Being. While these adaptations are not unprecedented in India, they occur more frequently in the American South.

The Religions of India

Before addressing the specifics of Hindu experiences in the American South, I will present, for readers unfamiliar with India, a brief introduction to the religious traditions that I am discussing. The diverse Hindu practices in the American South represent only a part of the conglomeration of religious texts, activities, and ideas that constitute the broad religious tradition typically called Hinduism. Many Hindus identify the Vedas, ancient collections of primarily poetry and ritual instructions, as the foundation of their religious traditions, and priests recite Vedic hymns in many rituals. On the personal level, however, people's understanding of the world and their own devotional activities draw more on other texts and practices within Hinduism than the Vedas. People commonly select personal deities from the array of Hindu and sometimes non-Hindu gods and goddesses, expressing their devotion by reciting a text about that deity, giving water, light, and food to an image in which they have invited the deity to reside, or celebrating a festival related to that deity. Some Hindus also follow the teachings of a guru (teacher) whom they recognize as divine. Drawing on Hindu schools of philosophy, many Hindus explain the plethora of deities with the assertion that everything is a component of the ultimate; therefore, all names of divine figures represent a single Supreme Being.

The religious diversity of India extends well beyond the conglomeration of practices that we call Hinduism. Jains follow the teachings of Mahavir Jain, a teacher from the sixth century B.C.E., whom they identify as the twenty-fourth *Tirthankar* (highly developed soul who becomes divine) of Jainism. His teachings include a strong commitment to *ahimsa* (non-violence) toward all living beings. Sufism, the mystical component of Islam, has a strong presence in India along with orthodox Islam. Sufi saints emphasize the experience of Allah through various meditation techniques beyond the dictates of Islamic law and often express their mystical experiences in poetry. The saints themselves have become figures with spiritual powers, attracting many Indians from various religious communities to pray at their graves. Sikhism began in northwest India with the teachings of Guru Nanak, who advocated a focus on the name of the divine over ritual service to images of deities. A succession of nine gurus expounded on Nanak's teachings until Guru Gobind Singh declared the Adi Granth, a compilation of the poetry of Sikh gurus and other Hindu and Muslim religious figures, as his successor. Sikhs today serve the Adi Granth as their guru and study its teachings. As I will demonstrate later, these other religious traditions of India impact the experiences of many Hindus in the United States.

Institutional Survey

Distinctive regional traditions and sectarian practices contribute to the diversity within Hinduism. Certain regions and even local groups emphasize particular deities over others, and standards for ritual conduct and festivals vary considerably across the vast territory of India. The variety of temples and organizations that Indian Americans have established in the South arises from this diversity and the various ways Indian Americans adapt their practices to a new context.

Some groups have followed a pan-Indian philosophy, emphasizing the unity of all Indian Americans and attempting to create institutions that can incorporate the diversity of India. The emphasis on unity, which some nationalist groups in India also extol, provides the immigrant minority greater strength in numbers. Other groups, however, have emphasized the specific traditions of a region or sectarian community in an attempt to draw closer to an experience of India. With these differing emphases, the temples in the South fall into three general categories, pan-Indian, regional, and sectarian.[1]

These general categories, however, overlap considerably. Some temples with a pan-Indian philosophy contain a dominant regional group, which creates dissatisfaction among people from other regions of India, while some temples with a regional or sectarian emphasis attract people outside their group. Similarly, Indian American associations outside the temples often work alongside established temples, using their facilities and supporting temple activities, even if the association is pan-Indian and the temple regional, or vice versa. Furthermore, many people participate in both regional and pan-Indian organizations, even espousing both philosophies in varying circumstances. Though the boundaries between these categories are fluid in India, the experience of being in the South increases the fluidity between the categories because the options available to individuals (in terms of religious activities) and groups (in terms of resources available for their support) are more constrained.

Variety of Activities in the Triangle

The Triangle metropolitan area of North Carolina provides an excellent location for this survey because it has one temple that falls, generally, into each of the three categories. The largest Hindu organization in the Triangle, the Hindu Society of North Carolina, follows a pan-Indian philosophy, while the newest temple, the Shri Venkateswara Temple, follows a specific tradition from South India. New Goloka, the third temple, is a part of the Krishna Consciousness Movement, commonly called Hare Krishnas.

In the 1970s several Hindu families met in homes to conduct rituals, led by an engineer from a Brahmin (priest) family. Although he received a European education instead of a traditional Brahmin education (which emphasizes the Vedas and ritual practices), he served as a volunteer priest for the Hindu Society of North Carolina for several decades. By 1980 the community had outgrown home meetings and purchased a building in Raleigh, formerly used by the Jehovah's Witnesses, which they made into a temple with meeting rooms.

In 1986 the rapidly growing community completed the construction of a temple on land they had purchased in Morrisville, a small town near the center of the Triangle. Their initial application for a building permit faced some opposition, which they attributed to conservative southern Protestants. The volunteer priest responded to the opposition by asserting that the community would not attempt to convert non-Hindus. In an ironic twist, a neighbor to the proposed temple, who expresses his southern Christian identity by flying several flags decorated with crosses and an American flag in his front yard, supported the temple's application, facilitating the town's approval of it. This neighbor has continued to assist the Hindus at the temple by providing security for the building and keeping a key so that people can enter after hours. On one occasion, when the volunteer priest accidentally triggered the alarm system at the temple, this neighbor met him at the door, carrying his shotgun to help protect the temple.

The Hindu Society's temple, called the Hindu Bhavan, is a single-story, yellow-brick structure with a flat roof. Except for the white, Indian-style arches on the front porch, the building resembles the industrial and office park–style buildings that are mixed with residences in this area. Upon entering the temple, the visitor comes into a large meeting room with a stage and a kitchen on the left side. Looking to the far end of the assembly room, the visitor's eyes reach the sanctum where five *murtis* (statues, literally "bodies" in Sanskrit) of deities sit on a marble platform along the back wall. The deities always wear matching clothes, usually trimmed in gold. For special occasions, the temple orders new clothes for the deities from a tailor in India who has the measurements for each murti. The hallway behind the sanctum allows visitors to circumambulate the sanctum and provides access to the office and several small rooms.

When they built this temple, the community democratically selected the deities they would install in the sanctum, a process that reflects the diffuse nature of the financial support of the temple and its pan-Indian philosophy. The deities receiving the most votes, the couple Krishna and Radha, sit in the center of the sanctum, with several deities popular in various regions across India on either side. Several years later, the community added other deities some members considered important, including Mahavir Jain and Shri Venkateswara, a popular manifestation of Vishnu from South India. The inclusion of Mahavir Jain reflects the activity of the Jain Study Circle of North Carolina at the Hindu Bhavan. While both the Hindus and the Jains recognize the distinctiveness of their traditions, they cooperate out of a need to combine their resources, an interest in pan-Indian unity, and the inclusion of Jainism within the broader definition of Hindu practices that some Hindus assert.

The democratic emphases of this temple correlate with the ritual openness that the community maintains. The Hindu Bhavan is open every morning and evening for people to pray and conduct personal rituals. Unlike other temples in the Triangle and many temples in India, where only trained priests or initiated members serve the deities, the sanctum at the Bhavan is open so that anyone can present offerings and touch the murtis of the deities. This arrangement has not only been necessary in the absence of a full-time priest who would be present whenever the temple is open, but it also reflects the ideals of some leaders to allow everyone to access the deities. Since the volunteer priest expressed a desire to retire in 2000, the community has pursued the employment of a full-time priest. How the access to the sanctum will change if the community hires a priest remains to be seen.

The schedule at the Bhavan also reflects the diversity within this community. While some people gather on Sunday mornings at the temple, other groups meet weekly on the traditional day of a particular deity. For example, devotees of Hanuman (the monkey-faced deity who is especially worshipped on Tuesdays) gather at the Bhavan every Tuesday evening to recite Hanuman's praises. While the Sunday gatherings suggest an Americanization or southern Protestantization of Hindu practice, the gatherings at other times demonstrate the various ways Hindus have adapted to the South.

Another component of the pan-Indian philosophy of the Hindu Bhavan is the celebration of various regional festivals. Within the Triangle, numerous Indian regional associations, such as the Triangle Area Telugu Association and the Triangle Gujarati Association, operate in conjunction with the Hindu Bhavan. They often organize their regional festivals at the Bhavan and invite the entire Indian American community to attend to foster pan-Indian unity. For these festivals, hundreds of people pack the temple for the special rituals, cultural performances by the children, and dinner. For festivals that are significant in several regions of India, the temple organizes the festival, while some regional associations organize their own celebration of the festivals at another time, either at the Bhavan or in another rented facility. In these ways, several regional associations at times work with the Bhavan to promote pan-Indian unity, while at other times the same associations foster regional identification, almost in opposition to pan-Indian unity.

These festivals provide clearer examples of adaptations to a new context. The temple and the various associations typically schedule the events on weekends near the date of the Indian holiday to accommodate the American work schedule. The programs, with cultural performances and a meal, provide cultural preservation and socialization for an immigrant minority.

Beyond the festivals, various organizations conduct classes and events at the Bhavan. For example, the Telugu Association conducts a special ritual for Vishnu one Friday each month, while the Maharashtrian Mandal organizes classes to teach Marathi, their regional language, to children. Other groups provide religious education for children or teach traditional dances while a few focus on yoga and other practices, primarily for adults. With the continued growth of the community, the Hindu Bhavan has found it difficult to schedule all of the festivals, meetings, and classes in the original temple. Near the end of 2000, they opened a larger social hall with adjacent classrooms that provides additional space for the community. Numerous temples in the South have similar facilities that are not commonly associated with temples in India. Attaching classrooms, auditoriums, and dining facilities highlights the cultural and social functions of these institutions beyond the traditional functions of Hindu temples.

The arrangements at the Bhavan contain their own tensions. One member, for example, spoke glowingly about the pan-Indian philosophy, while she also emphasized her regional association's celebration of a festival over the pan-Indian celebration of the same festival. Language also creates tensions. The Hindu Bhavan uses both English and Hindi in many of its programs, unless the program relates directly to a regional group that does not speak Hindi. Since Hindi-speakers are the largest language group in India, the selection of Hindi over other Indian languages can be justified. However, since the primary leaders of the community are from Hindi-speaking North India and the style of the central murtis is North Indian, the Hindu Bhavan, while attempting to unite the Indian American community, in some senses has a regional, North Indian focus. In fact, some regular members, particularly from South India, have expressed feelings of alienation because of the North Indian dominance.

The ritual openness also has not united the community. Some of the members have expressed a desire to limit access to the murtis to specially trained priests. As an outgrowth of these concerns, a group organized another temple with a South Indian focus. In January 1999 they broke ground for a new temple, to be dedicated to Shri Venkateswara, only a few miles from the Hindu Bhavan. The supporters of the Shri Venkateswara Temple clearly stated that they wanted to continue to support the Hindu Bhavan as a cultural and social center, and they honored the founders of the Bhavan at the ground-breaking ceremony. Such connections have continued as the organizers of the new temple have used the Hindu Bhavan's facilities for their fund-raisers.

However, the organizers of the new temple have also made their dissatisfaction with the Hindu Bhavan's rituals clear, as they declared that the new temple will be a "proper" Hindu temple. Each deity in the Shri Venkateswara temple, when its construction is complete, will reside in a separate shrine within a larger, open room. Only specially trained priests, brought to the United States from India, will enter a sanctum and touch the murtis. These priests will conduct the rituals according to the ritual codes, the *Agama Sasthras,* that are also used in the Shri Venkateswara temple at Tirupati in South India. At the installation of the images for the temporary temple on August 29, 1999, a leader specifically declared that everyone should remain quiet so that the procedures could proceed "as they would be done at Tirupati."

Selecting Shri Venkateswara as the presiding deity and committing to the use of the *Agama Sasthras* enable the organizers to establish an important relationship to the temple in Tirupati. The temple in Tirupati loans money to new temples and assists in procuring the services of traditional artisans who carve the ornate temple towers if the new temple follows these practices of Tirupati.[2] Beyond the assistance with the construction, the connection with this temple in India creates a certain legitimacy for the new temple, as the various Shri Venkateswara temples in the United States quickly become pilgrimage sites like their namesake in India.

In the context of the American South, minor accommodations are necessary, even when organizers want to maintain a particular ritual tradition. When they conducted a special ritual for the ground breaking in January 1999, several volunteers worked tirelessly to prepare both the house that serves as the temporary temple and the site for the new temple. Either through oversight or because of the limited time for preparation, the traditional clay bricks for the fire ritual were not available, so the priests used a disposable aluminum roasting pan instead. Later that year, when they installed the new images for the temporary temple, the trustees of the temple took an oath that concluded with the phrase "So help me Lord Venkateswara." The Americanness of this adaptation became even more obvious when one of the trustees misspoke, say-

Steven W. Ramey

ing, "So help me God." He quickly corrected his error by asserting that Lord Venkateswara is God, drawing on the Hindu assertion that all divine figures are One.

While the new temple draws most of its leadership from people originally from South India and the selection of deities and ritual codes makes this temple a regional temple, the organizers have clearly stated that they want the temple to serve all Hindus. The extent to which non–South Indians will concentrate their religious activities at the Shri Venkateswara temple instead of the Hindu Bhavan has yet to be seen. However, some pan-Indian organizations have scheduled children's classes at the new temple's temporary building, partly because the Hindu Bhavan could not accommodate them before the new social hall opened. These interactions demonstrate again the limits of the general categories I have used, as regional temples often work with pan-Indian associations and attract devotees from other regions.

Members of the International Society of Krishna Consciousness (ISKCON) established the other temple in the Triangle. ISKCON is a sectarian organization based on the teachings of Swami Prabhupada, who arrived in the United States in 1965 to bring a tradition of devotion to Lord Krishna that has been present in India for centuries. In 1982 a European American follower of Swami Prabhupada established a Krishna Consciousness center, called New Goloka, on the northwest edge of the Triangle, outside the small town of Hillsborough. The community includes a farm and residences for some of those initiated into ISKCON. The temple itself is located in a geodesic dome and includes a life-size murti of Swami Prabhupada facing an altar that contains murtis of Krishna and Radha. The initiated members of the community serve Krishna and Radha in the temple each day, offering music, food, and light to them. They also serve the people outside their community, including distributing sanctified food regularly on the campuses of several universities.

The majority of the initiated members of New Goloka are European Americans. On many Sunday evenings, several Indian Americans participate in the *sankirtan*, the largest community gathering at New Goloka, which includes chanting and dancing before Lord Krishna, a lecture reiterating Prabhupada's teachings, and a feast. When I talked with several participants in spring 1998, one Indian American expressed a strong commitment to the philosophy of ISKCON and was especially devoted to Lord Krishna. Other Indian Americans, however, attended this particular temple for less sectarian reasons, such as its proximity to their homes.

While these three temples provide very different options for Indian Americans in the Triangle and operate in conjunction with various regional associations, they do not exhaust the Hindu activities in the area. The organizations that conduct some of the regional festivals at the temples also organize religious festivals outside the temple's facilities. Similarly, Hum Sub, one of several pan-Indian associations, organizes events and classes related to various regions and traditions of India, including a summer Sanskrit camp for children at a local park. Followers of Satya Sai Baba meet regularly in homes to view a tape of this holy man's teachings and worship him as a divine figure. Other formal and informal groups meet in homes to study a text such as the Bhagavad Gita or to conduct specific religious activities. People will also sponsor a reading of the entire Adi Granth, the central text of Sikhism, or a concert of devotional or classical Indian music in their homes.

Also beyond the temples, the Islamic mosques throughout the Triangle and the two Sikh gurdwaras in the city of Durham, attract many Indian Americans. These other religious centers impact the variety of activities for Hindus, as some Hindus visit a gurdwara or a mosque in addition to praying at a temple while a few Sikhs and Muslims visit one of the temples. Some Indian Americans who visit other religious centers are accompanying friends on special occasions, while others attend regularly for their own personal religious activities. Such cross-tradition participation occurs in India as well and demonstrates the permeability of the boundaries between Hinduism, Jainism, Islam, and Sikhism in the experiences of many people from India. The context of the United States, with the limited number of Indian religious centers, encourages such participation for some people in the community.

Temples and Beyond across the South

While this discussion of religious organizations in the Triangle highlights the overlapping nature of the general categories of pan-Indian, sectarian, and regional organizations, most temples and associations in the South fit one of the categories best. The Hindu Community Center outside Knoxville, Tennessee, and the Hindu Temple and Cultural Center near Columbia, South Carolina, are two of the pan-Indian temples in the South, while the Hindu Temple of Atlanta (Sri Venkateswara) and the Shakti Mandir, also in Atlanta, have a greater regional emphasis. The ISKCON temples and the Swaminarayan temples throughout the region are all examples of sectarian temples, many of which emphasize a specific region also.

Despite these categories, each temple presents a unique solution to some of the challenges of developing Hindu traditions in the South and exhibits unique relationships with other temples. In Nashville, Tennessee, the Shri Ganesh temple is the only temple. Architecturally and ritually, it follows South Indian traditions with separate shrines decorated with intricate carvings of divine figures and access to the shrines limited to specially trained priests. Perhaps because it must serve the entire Indian American community, the temple is dedicated to Ganesh, a deity who is popular throughout India.

In Greenville, South Carolina, a group of both Hindus and Jains organized the Vedic Center and, therefore, emphasized a pan-Indian philosophy, including images of several Hindu deities along with Mahavir Jain in the sanctum. Like the Hindu Bhavan, the temple does not have a full-time priest. Families volunteer to be responsible for the nightly worship once each month.

Charlotte, North Carolina, has two established Hindu temples. The followers of Swaminarayan built a temple using volunteer labor from Swaminarayan communities across the country. The other temple in Charlotte, the Hindu Center, follows a pan-Indian philosophy. In addition to having a full-time priest to lead rituals, various regional associations meet regularly in the temple and organize the rituals according to their own style. For Diwali (the Hindu festival of lights) in 1999, the Sindhi Sabha organized special religious and cultural activities and prepared a full meal for the entire community. The Sikh community in Charlotte uses the social hall at the Hindu Center, not the temple itself, for their meetings and religious events until they can build a gurdwara in the area. As of 2001, they had purchased land for their gurdwara, but construction had not commenced.

Atlanta, Georgia, has the widest array of Indian temples and organizations in the South. The first temple that Indian Americans constructed in the area was a pan-Indian temple as a part of the Indian Cultural and Religious Center (ICRC) in Smyrna. In addition to a temple room with a range of deities served by a priest, the center included a room for a Sikh gurdwara, an Indian Islamic mosque, and an Indian Christian church. As these communities have grown, all but the temple have moved into their own facilities. The Sikhs built a gurdwara in Stone Mountain, on the east side of Atlanta, and have established a second gurdwara on the north side of the city. Numerous mosques dot the city, and various Indian Christian churches conduct worship in Indian languages. The auditorium of the ICRC continues to promote pan-Indian ideals and serves as a venue for larger festivals, including the Durga Puja organized by the Bengali Association of Greater Atlanta in 1999, along with Christmas and the Muslim festival Id Ul Adha. These last two celebrations are sponsored by the parent organization of the ICRC as part of its pan-Indian philosophy.

The other temples in Atlanta have a regional or sectarian focus. The Greater Atlanta Vedic Temple in northeast Atlanta (Lilburn) follows the Arya Samaj reformist Hindu philosophy, which rejects the worship of deities' images. On Sundays the community, dominated by North Indians, conducts weekly rituals following their understanding of original Vedic practice. The Swaminarayan temple in east Atlanta serves the predominantly Gujarati followers of the Swaminarayan sect, while the Shakti Mandir in southeast Atlanta contains murtis of the goddess in various forms and also serves the large Gujarati community. New Panihati Dhama is an ISKCON temple, located near downtown Atlanta, which follows a similar schedule to that at New Goloka and includes Indian Americans, European Americans, and African Americans among its initiated members and regular worshippers. The newest temple in the area is the Hindu Temple of Atlanta, located in Riverdale, south of Atlanta. Shri Venkateswara resides in the central shrine of this temple, and the priests follow the same ritual code as in the other Shri Venkateswara temples. While dominated by South Indians, people from a variety of regions visit this temple.

Beyond these temples and other religious centers, the Indian American community in Atlanta has a wide array of associations. Several associations promote pan-Indian relationships, including the Indian Professionals Network, Indian Development and Relief Fund, and Indian Classical Music Society. Most regions of India, from Punjab to Tamil Nadu to Bengal, have one or more associations that organize cultural, social, and religious activities. A few caste groups have organizations, and several sectarian movements within Hinduism, such as the Brahma Kumaris and the Sadhu Vaswani Mission, have separate associations in the city. Many of these associations celebrate festivals and conduct religious events periodically.

While Atlanta has the largest concentration, such organizations and religious centers operate in most medium and large cities throughout the South. In cities without an established temple, Indian Americans frequently have an association that organizes occasional festivals, and families conduct special rituals in their homes. For Indian Americans in Asheville, North Carolina, for example, the closest temple is in Greenville, South Carolina, about an hour away. Some families travel to that temple occasionally, while the Asheville association meets several times a year. These arrangements resemble the activities in the Triangle before the Hindu Society of North Carolina established its first temple. In the future, Indian Americans in many cities without a temple will construct one as their communities grow.

The variety of organizations throughout the South reveal the dynamic nature of Hinduism in the region. Indian Americans have committed significant resources to establish Indian religious activities, adapting their traditions in numerous ways. The communities have fostered cooperation between various religious groups to maximize their presence and activities as an immigrant community, even as some groups focus on re-creating a specific tradition.

Variety of Activities in One Family

This survey of religious organizations presents only a portion of the story. Hindus incorporate these various religious activities into their lives in numerous combinations. Beyond the interactions between organizations, individuals participate in a variety of groups according to their own familial traditions, the options in their geographical area, and personal interests. Components of Hindu philosophy support an inclusiveness that views various traditions as different paths to the same goals. With this view, it is even common for people to participate in activities that others commonly identify as components of distinct religious traditions, such as Hinduism, Sikhism, Buddhism, and Islam. These patterns of participation counter a common assumption, prevalent within Christian traditions, that having a commitment to a specific aspect of a religious tradition excludes participation in other traditions. To provide one example of the possibilities of participating in various groups, I will focus on how one family in metropolitan Atlanta weaves various religious practices, both within the plethora of organizations in Atlanta and within their home, into their lives.

This family consists of a couple, whom I will call Ram and Satya, who both work in professional careers. They have a daughter and a son who are both completing doctorates, one of whom lives in Atlanta while the other visits periodically. The family has lived in Atlanta since the mid-1970s and has viewed the growth of the Indian American community and many Indian religious organizations in the area.[3]

Satya grew up around Mumbai (Bombay), and Ram grew up in a smaller town in the state of Gujarat. However, both trace their family's heritage to the Sindh. When India was partitioned in 1947, Sindh became a part of Pakistan, leading many Sindhi Hindus, including the families of Ram and Satya, to immigrate to independent India. Ram and Satya emphasize their Sindhi heritage in both their participation in religious activities related primarily to the Sindh (such as Cheti Chand, described in the introduction) and their involvement in other Sindhi activities, such as attending an annual international gathering of Sindhis.

For Ram and Satya, religious practices outside the temples impact their daily lives. Each morning, they open the door of their upstairs linen closet and give devotion to the images of deities sitting on the middle shelf, with stacks of folded pink and orange bath towels on the shelves above and below. In the shadows at the back of the shelf is a carving depicting Guru Nanak, the first of the ten gurus of Sikhism. In the center of the shelf are small murtis of Satya Narayan and his wife Lakshmi, side by side. Other Hindu deities in the shrine include Hanuman, Radha-Krishna, a Shiva lingam, and a picture of Jhule Lal, the Sindhi Hindu deity celebrated at Cheti Chand. In addition to their daily prayers, Satya also encourages her adult children to take the blessings of the deities before they depart following a visit.

The deities and guru they have placed in their household shrine reflect their religious heritage. Satya grew up in a Sindhi household that particularly revered Guru Nanak, as many Sindhi Hindus do. Satya Narayan and his wife Lakshmi are also popular deities among Sindhis, and Satya during her youth prayed specifically to Lord Shiva to bless her with a happy married life. She has continued to honor Shiva for his continued blessing of her family life, but her daughter is unwilling to pray to Shiva in the same manner.

In addition to their daily devotional practices, they observe additional personal practices on certain days. Within Hindu traditions, particular days of the week are special for certain deities (e.g., Mondays for Shiva, Tuesdays for Hanuman, Saturdays for Shani). Satya and Ram honor Shiva especially on Mondays by pouring milk and water over the lingam in their household shrine. They are not vegetarian but express their special devotion to Shiva on Mondays, Hanuman on Tuesdays, and Vidal Bhagwan on Thursdays by not eating meat on those days. Since full-moon days are similarly devoted to Satya Narayan, they also fast from meat on each full moon. At work Satya's colleagues often ask her, "Is this a veggie or non-veggie day?" because of the shifting schedule of full-moon days and other vegetarian days.

Ram and Satya add community religious events to these daily personal practices. They go to either of the two Punjabi Sikh gurdwaras in Atlanta every two or three weeks. There they listen to the devotional songs and the readings from the Adi Granth in Punjabi, a language they do not understand. At the conclusion of the service, they join the others in the *langar,* a communal meal.

As children in India, both of their families typically went to a Sindhi-sponsored gurdwara, called a *tikana*. Tikanas differ from the typical Punjabi Sikh gurdwara in that they include images of Guru Nanak and various Hindu deities along with the Adi Granth, whereas gurdwaras house only the Adi Granth. Before coming to the United States, Satya did not realize that orthodox Punjabi Sikhs only believed in the ten gurus, excluding the worship of various Hindu deities. In Atlanta, however, no tikana exists, so to maintain this practice from their childhood, Satya and Ram must attend the Punjabi Sikh gurdwara. Satya describes the veneration of Guru Nanak and the reading of the Adi Granth as "really the Sikh religion" even though it is important in her religious life.

The family for the past several years has also participated in the activities of the Sadhu Vaswani Center in Atlanta. Sadhu T. L. Vaswani was a Hindu holy figure from Sindh who settled in Pune, India, following partition. After his death, his nephew Dada J. P. Vaswani succeeded him. When possible,

Satya and Ram attend the *satsangs* (meetings for devotional singing, worship, and study) of the Sadhu Vaswani Center, which occur once or twice a month in the home of a member. At these gatherings everyone sits on white sheets spread on the floor and gives devotion to images of Sadhu Vaswani and Dada Vaswani by singing, presenting flowers and food to the images, and waving an oil lamp before the pictures as an offering of light. The community also watches a video of Dada Vaswani lecturing, either in English or Sindhi. After the satsang, everyone receives blessings by receiving both the food and the flame previously offered to the images.

Ram and Satya also frequently participate in the monthly *seva* (service) of the Sadhu Vaswani Center. Each month the Sadhu Vaswani community meets to visit people in a nursing home, feed the ducks at a park, or provide another type of service to humans or animals. They speak positively about their experiences bringing cheer to the residents of the nursing home, asserting that only a few of the residents do not want them to visit, presumably because of their non-European heritage.

A special religious occasion is the yearly visit of Dada Vaswani to Atlanta. Ram and Satya usually attend the various activities Dada conducts with his followers, as well as the public lecture he presents in English, which also draws local dignitaries. Dada Vaswani also conducts a weekend retreat in New Jersey, including satsangs, lectures, meditation, and other activities to foster the religious spirit of participants. Ram and Satya have attended several times.

Satya describes her participation in the Sadhu Vaswani Center as something new for her. She knew of Sadhu Vaswani in India, but no one in her family particularly followed him. However, since the group in Atlanta started, she has benefited from her participation. She describes the lectures of Dada Vaswani as practical, helping her to become a better person, forgive others, and work with people more easily. Going regularly to the satsangs to hear Dada's lecture also encourages her to continue doing the things Dada has taught her. She contrasts these practical lessons with her attendance at the Sikh gurdwara, where she expresses her devotion to Guru Nanak and continues the practices of her childhood without fully understanding the language.

Beyond these regular religious activities, various families in the Sindhi community sponsor religious functions on significant occasions, such as the birth of a child or a special anniversary. On these occasions, the sponsors invite others in the community to attend the activities, which vary from a *path* (a continuous reading of the Adi Granth in forty-eight hours) to a special *puja* (ritual of worship) for a specific Hindu deity. When Ram and Satya moved to Atlanta in the mid-1970s, most of these events happened in homes. Now, these special Sindhi events are typically held in one of the gurdwaras or the Shri Venkateswara temple, despite the connection of these institutions with other regions of India.

Ram and Satya frequently attend such events, sometimes with more than a hundred other Sindhis. Following the practices of Satya's grandmother, who maintained a copy of the Adi Granth in her home (which entails serving the book every day as one's living guru), Satya and Ram sponsor a path of the Adi Granth every few years. Frequently, they will organize the path in a Punjabi gurdwara in Atlanta, though one year they sponsored it in a Sindhi tikana in Mumbai while visiting India.

Satya's and Ram's lives are also interspersed with various religious holidays and festivals. The Sindhi Sabha of Georgia organizes many of the festivals that are most important for Ram and Satya. Satya and other leaders conduct these festivals entirely beyond the realm of the various temples in Atlanta. In the spring they honor the deity Jhule Lal at Cheti Chand, as described at the beginning of this essay. In the summer they have a picnic and social activities. In the early fall they celebrate Janmasthami, the birthday of Lord Krishna, and in October and November they hold their largest gathering for Diwali, when they worship Lakshmi. While they use community centers for most of their activities, they rent a hotel ballroom for Diwali and have the meal catered instead of cooking the food themselves. All of these religious festivals combine religious practices with food, cultural programs, and socializing. For the first time in several years, the Sindhi Sabha also planned to sponsor a path in the fall of 2001 at the north Atlanta gurdwara.

Ram and Satya also celebrate the birthdays of several religious figures. On Guru Nanak's birthday, they typically go to the gurdwara, where the Sikh community conducts a path and other special practices. The Sadhu Vaswani Center also has special satsangs for the birthdays of Dada Vaswani (August 2) and Sadhu Vaswani (November 25). To commemorate Sadhu Vaswani's birthday, the center encourages people, both within and beyond their group, to sign a pledge not to eat meat on that day. Satya usually signs this pledge, unless November 25 falls on Thanksgiving. Since her family serves meat on Thanksgiving, she does not want to make a commitment to fast from meat if she might decide to eat meat with her family and thus break her pledge.

Throughout their religious activities, Ram and Satya primarily connect with their Sindhi regional heritage and the Sindhi community around Atlanta. In this sense, their broader emphasis is not any particular religious institution, such as a temple or gurdwara. They focus on Sindhi gatherings wherever they occur, within temples and beyond them. When they go to the Venkateswara temple, they usually attend with other Sindhis. The Sadhu Vaswani Center is primarily a Sindhi religious organization, and their attendance at the gurdwara both connects them to the Sindhi tradition of venerating Guru Nanak along with Hindu deities and the special occasions of other Sindhis who similarly connect with Sikh traditions.

While the combination of Hindu practices and a veneration of Guru Nanak challenges the boundaries that frequently separate the religious traditions of Hinduism and Sikhism, Ram and Satya's transgression of such abstract boundaries is not unusual for people of Sindhi heritage, nor for others in India. The experience of re-forming religious practices in diaspora in the South, however, creates additional difficulties for these broader practices. Since the Sindhi community has not built a tikana in Atlanta, the only way for them to participate in communal Sikh traditions is to attend a Punjabi Sikh gurdwara, where the boundaries between Hindu practices and Sikh practices are much clearer than they were in the tikanas in which they worshipped in India.

Being in a different place, such as the South, makes it difficult to continue their religious practices in the same manner as in India. Many Hindus in diaspora, including Satya and Ram, want to give their children an understanding and experience of their heritage and an ethnic social community. Therefore, they commit their time and other resources necessary to build the temples and organize the religious practices. The future of Hindu practices in the South depends partly on the extent that the children and grandchildren of immigrants gain an understanding and appreciation for these re-created Hindu practices. However, as the flow of immigrants from India continues, the generations born in the United States will not be the sole maintainers of Hindu traditions here. They will have to negotiate the differences between their understandings of Hindu traditions from their experiences in the American South with the experiences and ideas of new immigrants from India.

As the experiences of Satya and Ram suggest, the variety of Indian religious activities in the South enables immigrants, particularly those who live in urban areas, an opportunity to create a vibrant religious life, incorporating both practices that they followed in India and some that are new to them. To understand the experiences of Hindus in the region, one must look beyond the temples and other religious institutions to see the plethora of religious activities outside the temples. It is also imperative to recognize the possibility for activity in a variety of temples, small organizations, and other religious sites, even when these activities relate to differing traditions. By looking at the temples but also moving beyond them, the vibrancy and diversity of Hindu practices in the South becomes clearer.

Notes

1. In this, I am revising Raymond Brady Williams's categories of South Indian, North Indian, eclectic, and sectarian that he develops in *Religions of Immigrants From India and Pakistan: New Threads in the American Tapestry* (Cambridge: Cambridge University Press, 1988). This book also addresses further the tension within this immigrant community between pan-Indian and regional loyalties.

2. The first Shri Venkateswara Temple in the United States is in Pittsburgh, Pennsylvania. For a more complete discussion of the process of building that temple and the involvement of the temple in Tirupati, Andhra Pradesh, India, see Fred Clothey, *Rhythm and Intent* (Madras: Blackie and Sons, 1983).

3. The material in this paragraph and the following section comes from a series of interviews and conversations with Ram and Satya in Atlanta in 2000 and 2001. I appreciate their generosity with their time, sharing their stories with me, and also reviewing an earlier draft of this section of the article.

Steven W. Ramey

Kathryn V. Johnson

ISLAM IN THE NEW SOUTH CITY: AN INTRODUCTION TO MUSLIMS IN AMERICA AND CHARLOTTE

ISLAM IS A MONOTHEISTIC RELIGION THAT HAS A WORLDWIDE FOLLOWING of more than one billion people. It teaches belief in one all-powerful God who revealed himself to a series of prophets, culminating with the final messenger, Muhammad, the Seal of the Prophets, to whom the Qur'an was given.[1] The practice of Islam includes five requirements: bearing witness that there is no god but God and Muhammad is his messenger; performance of the five daily prayers; fasting during the month of Ramadan; alms giving; and performing the pilgrimage to Mecca. In addition, all Muslims share six points of doctrine: acknowledgment of the unity of God; acceptance of the series of prophets sent by God, beginning with Adam who was the first prophet and concluding with Muhammad; recognition of the scriptures that God has revealed to humankind, including the Torah, Psalms, Gospel, and Qur'an; belief in angels; acknowledgment of the Day of Judgment; and acceptance of predestination. Muslims have, however, historically been divided as to the manner in which the revelation is to be interpreted and the nature of leadership within the community. Thus, the use of the terms *Sunni* and *Shi'i* (sometimes found as *Sunnite* and *Shi'ite*) to designate the majority and minority positions taken on these issues within the community of faith. More than 85 percent of the world's Muslims are Sunni, the remainder follow various branches of Shi'ism.

Islam also reflects the diversity of cultures and places in which it has taken root. Islam is one, but it has many faces. This has been nowhere more apparent than in the United States in the last three decades. Islam is the fastest-growing non-Christian religious tradition in the United States, with some seven million American followers nationwide. About seven thousand of those followers make their homes in the metropolitan area of Charlotte, North Carolina. This essay presents an overview of the history, denominational differences, and demographics of American Islam and an introduction to the Muslim community in Charlotte.

It would be impossible to understand how Islam is taking shape in Charlotte without understanding the larger context of Islam in the United States. But, perhaps just as well, a closer look at Charlotte's Muslims is a good introduction to how Muslim communities can thrive in America. The presence of Muslims in Charlotte is not difficult to see as one drives around this very automobile-oriented city. One passes strip malls with markets catering to Muslims from Asia and the Middle East. Some Indian restaurants profer signs that read, "We serve *halal* meat."[2] Women wearing the traditional *hijab* (head covering) are visible among the shoppers and workers in Charlotte's businesses. An Islamic school and four mosques are now part of its landscape. Programs from both the Nation of Islam and Muslim American Society are broadcast regularly by Charlotte television and radio stations.

Seeing Charlotte's Muslims means seeing Charlotte in a new light. International business, big-time banking, and miles of strip malls are not the only manifestations of what is "New South" in this old southern city. An increasing religious diversity, of which the growth of Islam is a significant aspect, is also part of its transformation. Indeed, while Charlotte's seven thousand Muslims may be a small minority in this city with a metropolitan population approaching two million, their presence is a significant sign that Islam can thrive in the South, even in the home of Billy and (more significantly) Franklin Graham.[3]

The American Muslim Community By the Numbers

American Muslims today come from a number of racial and ethnic backgrounds.[4] Thirty-six percent were born in the United States. Many are immigrants or the descendants of those who settled in the United States. Sixty percent of those born outside the United States arrived here after 1980. Over one-third (36 percent) arrived between 1980 and 1989, while 24 percent arrived between 1990 and the present. American Muslims come from a variety of ethnic and racial backgrounds. Over 40 percent are African-Americans, 24 percent are of South Asian origin, and 12 percent are of Arab origin.

American Muslims are young. Seventy-four percent are under the age of fifty. Seven in ten adults are married. The average Muslim household is composed of 4.9 persons and is likely to contain well-educated occupants since almost three-fifths of all adult Muslims in the United States have at least an undergraduate degree. They are well represented in the professions and often prosperous, with 50 percent making more than fifty thousand dollars per year. More than 10 percent of employed Muslims work in computer science and engineering; 8 percent work in medicine and health care–related fields.

Most Muslims live in the major urban centers of the nation. Twenty percent of U.S. Muslims live in California, 16 percent in New York state, 8 percent in Illinois, 4 percent in both New Jersey and Indiana, and about 3 percent in Michigan, Virginia, Texas, and Ohio. Some 30 percent of all incarcerated African Americans are converts to Islam who found and accepted their new faith while in prison. Finally, a small number of American Muslims live on military bases; 1 percent of the men and women on active duty in the United States armed forces are Muslim.

More than three thousand mosques, six institutions of higher learning, approximately two hundred day schools, and some five hundred weekend schools serve the American Muslim community. They are generally young institutions. Thirty percent were established in the 1990s, and 32 percent in the 1980s. They range in size from the large, well-funded complexes found in major urban centers like Washington and New York to modest "apartment" mosques that serve the spiritual needs of local families and students. Although four-fifths of all mosques are located in urban areas, suburban mosques have experienced the fastest growth. As American Muslims have joined the exodus from the cities, congregations have sought more convenient suburban locations.

The number of mosques in the United States has grown by 25 percent in the last seven years. This growth in the number of facilities has been accompanied by an increase in participation in attendance at mosque functions. An average of 1,625 individuals are associated in some way with the religious life of each mosque, with an average attendance at Friday prayers of 292 worshipers.

Ninety-three percent of all mosques are attended by members of more than one ethnic group. Most are administered by a board or council elected from the members of the congregation and provide some services such as a school for children (20 percent) or aid to the needy (70 percent). In an average congregation, 33 percent of the members are of South Asian origin (India, Pakistan, Bangladesh, etc.), 30 percent are African American, and 25 percent are from the Arabic-speaking Middle East. Of the remaining members, 3.4 percent are from sub-Saharan Africa, 2.1 percent are from Europe (Bosnia, Kosovo, etc.), 1.6 percent are white Americans, 1.3 percent are Southeast Asian (Malaysian, Indonesian), 1.2 percent are from the Caribbean, 1.1 percent are Turkish, 0.7 percent are Iranian, and 0.6 percent are Latino. On average, 30 percent of those who attend services regularly are converts.

Few Muslim children, only about 3 percent, acquire any formal religious training outside their home. This may be the case because only about 20 percent of mosques have a full-time school. Smaller congregations and families living in areas without an organized community typically must resort to informal instruction by family members. Young Muslims and their parents do, however, continue to uphold the traditions of their faith. While some Muslims admit that they only occasionally pray or attend their mosque (22 percent), two-thirds perform some of the daily prayers and nearly half (47 percent) offer all five required formal prayers. Half of all Muslims likewise report that they had attended either a prayer or the weekly service at their mosque in the proceeding week. Although 79 percent affirm that religion is important in their daily lives, young Muslims aged eighteen to twenty-four (62 percent) and African American Muslims (69 percent) are more likely to be involved in their mosques than American Muslims in general (48 percent).

Muslims are increasingly participating in the traditional political and social institutions of American life. Their ranks are made up of liberals and conservatives and members of all of the major parties. Over a third of American Muslims describe themselves as political moderates, 27 percent as liberals, and 21 percent as conservatives. Forty percent support the Democratic party, 23 percent are Republicans, and 28 percent are independent. They vote in local and national elections. They overwhelmingly supported Bush in the 2000 presidential election, with 34 percent of those interviewed reporting that they had voted for the first time. The majority of African Americans voted for Gore (55 percent), while Arabs (54 percent), South Asians (49 percent), and Pakistanis (56 percent) voted for Bush.

Perhaps the wide variety of political preferences reflects the divisions that typically exist between a strong tradition of support for social welfare programs and conservative social values. Thus, while an overwhelming majority support universal health care and aid to the poor (93 percent) and 77 percent actually volunteer themselves in community organizations that aid the sick, elderly, and homeless, Muslims also support the death penalty (68 percent), a ban on pornography (65 percent), and a ban on gay marriage (71 percent).

And finally, Muslims are concerned about the place of their own faith in twenty-first-century America. Ninety percent believe that Muslims should actively participate in the institutions and political system of this country. Unfortunately, a majority of Muslims (57 percent) believe that the attitude of their fellow Americans has grown more unfavorable since September 11, 2001. Over half report that individuals in their own local community have experienced discrimination. Thus, many congregations have increased contact with their local community by participating in interfaith dialogues, contacting the media and local politicians, and visiting area churches and schools.

Muslims, like other American faith communities, have established a number of national organizations to represent their interests and facilitate cooperation. These organizations have become increasingly important in presenting a genuine, positive image of Islam to the American public. The first national organization to be established was the Muslim Student Association (MSA), which was founded in 1963 to coordinate the activities of student groups. The success of the MSA led to the creation of a number of organizations such as the American Muslim Scientists and Engineers and the Islamic Medical Association to serve groups outside the student population. Although the MSA and other groups operate their own internal committees, their administrative and financial affairs are now under the management of the Islamic Society of North America (ISNA). ISNA groups sponsor national, regional, and profession-specific conferences where members gather. In 1985 ISNA created its own political action committee, ISNA-PAC, to represent the interests of American Muslims in national politics.[5]

The Many Faces of American Islam

Among the seven million people making up the American Muslim community today are African-Americans, recent immigrants and their descendents, mystics, converts, and international students. Each group has made its own distinctive contribution to American Islam and is taking its place in the Charlotte Muslim community.

African American Muslims

The early history of Islam in the Americas remains the subject of much debate among archaeologists and historians. What is known is that perhaps 10 to 20 percent of those captured and transported to the New World to be sold into slavery were Muslims seized from the communities of West Africa. Many of their stories have now been lost. However, one man whose story has survived and whose life is perhaps representative of the period also has an intriguing connection to North Carolina.

Umar ibn Said (or Sayyid) was born around 1770 in the West African state of Futa Toro (modern Senegal). A scholar and trader by profession, he was captured, sent by ship to Charleston, South Carolina, and sold in the slave market in 1807 to James Owen, a planter from eastern North Carolina. Despite the cruel circumstances of his arrival in America, Umar seems to have lost none of his intellectual curiosity. He is said to have requested and carefully studied an Arabic translation of the Bible and perhaps even to have converted to Christianity before his death in 1864. The Arabic Bible sent by Francis Scott Key, author of "The Star Spangled Banner," survives today. It is currently housed at Davidson College, just outside of Charlotte. However, the mystery lingers. Did Umar abandon Islam and adopt the new religion of his master after so many years of separation from his homeland? Or, do the Arabic notes he made in the book's margins confirm that he remained faithful to Islam and had merely indulged in a bit of scholarly inquiry into the religion of his captors? As is the case with pre-Columbian contacts between the Islamic world and the Americas, historians debate the conclusion of the spiritual journey of Umar ibn Said.[6]

Umar's story is a particularly intriguing one because it reveals something of the dilemma confronting African American Muslims as they reexamine their own historical relationship with Islam. Indeed, some would point to Umar as representative of their own ancestors' stories. Like Ibn Said, they were stolen away from African communities and perhaps lulled into forgetfulness of their true spiritual legacy. Now their descendants face the challenge of awakening, returning to their rightful spiritual home, Islam. Thus, when African American Muslims speak of "reverting" to Islam rather than "converting" to the religion, they are alluding to Islam as both the most natural of religions for humankind and the legitimate faith of their ancestors.[7]

The first person to employ symbols and principles that he understood to be drawn from Islam to win converts was not, however, an immigrant. Timothy Drew, a black man born into poverty in North Carolina in 1886, founded the Moorish-American Science Temple in Newark, New Jersey, in 1913. He changed his own name to Noble Drew Ali and taught that for a people to succeed they needed to have "a name and a land." Blacks, he concluded, were actually "Asiatics" and should properly be called Moors. While Christianity was the religion of whites, Islam was the religion of Asiatics. Noble Drew Ali challenged his followers to rise above poverty and oppression and reclaim their true, proud heritage. The Moorish-American movement found adherents in several major cities and in some parts of the East Coast but failed to win a large national membership.[8]

A far more successful movement was led by another southerner. Following Ali's death in 1929, "The Lost-Found Nation of Islam in the Wilderness of North America" was founded in Detroit by an individual of probable Middle Eastern origin who assumed the names of W. D. Fard, Wali Fard, Wallace Fard, and W. D. Muhammad on various occasions. Master Fard, as he is called, soon transferred leadership of the movement to his successor, Elijah Muhammad (born Elijah Poole in Georgia in 1876). Fard designated Elijah Muhammad as the "Messenger of God" who had come to teach the black nation its true nature and mission.[9]

Kathryn V. Johnson

Although known as the Nation of Islam (NOI), many of the teachings directly contradicted the doctrines of mainstream Islam. W. D. Fard was proclaimed to have enjoyed divine status and Elijah Muhammad to be a prophet or divinely appointed messenger, in direct contradiction to the Islamic understanding of the unique nature of God and the designation of Muhammad as the final prophet. The NOI account of creation, which described whites as the flawed creation of an evil scientist named Yacoub and blacks as the chosen people of God, likewise contradicted Islam's insistence that all races are equal. And although mainstream Islam has also acknowledged the virtues of hard work and disciplined living, it has done so without preaching the requirements of racial isolation or the creation of a separate black nation.

Mainstream Islam thus proved to be as uncomfortable with the teachings of the Nation of Islam as did many within the American Christian community. A far greater challenge to the movement, however, was to come from within its own ranks. In 1963 Malcolm X, one of the best-known and most charismatic members of the NOI, was suspended by Elijah Muhammad following his infamous remark about the Kennedy assassination that "the chickens have come have to roost." Soon afterward, Malcolm made the pilgrimage and experienced an extraordinary spiritual transformation. For the first time he encountered the world community of Islam and at last found in Mecca a faith untainted by prejudice and hatred. He returned to the United States prepared to believe that cooperation between races was possible in Islam.[10]

On March 8, 1964, Malcolm X left the NOI and established his own organization, the Muslim Mosque, Inc.; the political wing of the Organization was called the Organization of African American Unity (OAAU). In recognition of his pilgrimage and new identity as a member of the world Muslim community, he changed his name to El-Hajj Malik el-Shabazz and set about preaching a new message of equality and reconciliation through Islam. On February 21, 1965, he was shot while addressing the newly formed OAAU in New York. His killer was never brought to justice.[11]

At the same time that Malcolm X had been making his own journey to Islam and had increasingly begun to doubt the central teachings of the NOI, Elijah Muhammad's own son started to question those same doctrines. Born in 1933 to Elijah Muhammad and his wife Clara, Wallace received a more traditional Islamic education that emphasized the Qur'an, Islamic law, and mastery of the Arabic language. He made his first pilgrimage to Mecca in 1967 and, like Malcolm, concluded that many of the NOI's teachings were incompatible with those of orthodox Islam.

Following his father's death in 1975, Wallace assumed leadership of the movement and quickly began to distance himself from some of the more extreme positions espoused by Elijah Muhammad and his predecessor, W. D. Fard. He abandoned the old racist creation account and the insistence on separatism.

They were replaced by a public commitment to orthodox Islamic doctrines, respect for the Constitution, and support for the institutions of American political life.[12]

By 1985 Wallace Muhammad, now known as Warith Deen, had completed the process of integration into the world faith community. He and his followers defined themselves simply as African American Muslims. The old separatist doctrines that once characterized the organization had come to be regarded as a necessary stage through which a once oppressed people had passed on their way to social and spiritual liberation.[13]

The two predominately African American mosques in Charlotte, the medium-sized and small Ash Shaheed and Ali Shah, joined W. D. Muhammad early in their histories.[14] W. D. Muhammad's presence in Charlotte has been significant. At one time Charlotte served as a base of operation and thus provided opportunities for Muslim presence to be witnessed frequently in local media. He has spoken in the city to large crowds and in 2001 made an important address at the National Convention of Muslim Youth, held in Charlotte the December following the September 11 tragedy.

In contrast to those who saw the need to integrate the Nation of Islam into the world faith community, Minister Louis Farrakhan demanded that believers remain loyal to the old separatist teachings of the organization. How can blacks achieve equality, he argued, when they continue to suffer oppression and live in poverty? Thus Farrakhan chose to rebuild and strengthen the institutions that Warith Deen had abandoned. He continued to preach separatism and racial inequality. Members of the Fruit of Islam, the young men's organization that had been disbanded by W. D. Muhammad, were once again present at public meetings as symbols of the organization's commitment to discipline. Indeed, Farrakhan often pointed to them as the prime example of how the NOI—and not W. D. Muhammad's Muslim American Society—consistently produced accomplished, successful young people in the African American community.[15]

However, Minister Farrakhan, as had Malcolm and, later, Wallace Muhammad, ultimately abandoned the old doctrines. On February 26, 2000, the *Washington Post* reported that Muslim American Society leader Wallace Deen Muhammad and Nation of Islam leader Louis Farrakhan had appeared together for the first time in twenty-five years and announced their reconciliation. Farrakhan announced, "Twenty-five years later, I know your father wanted this. . . . From this day forward, the Imam Muhammad and I, no matter what our little problems are, will work them out for the glory of Allah." He continued, "We bear witness that there is no prophet after Muhammad." With his acknowledgment of Muhammad as the final prophet, he publicly set aside one of the central doctrines of the NOI, that W. D. Fard had in fact been God incarnate and Elijah Muhammad the final prophet sent to humankind.[16]

Just as had been the case with Warith Deen Muhammad's announcement that the NOI would henceforth follow the teachings and practices of the Sunni tradition, some adherents refused. The past few years have witnessed a process in which many of Minister Farrakhan's followers have embraced mainstream Islam. Others, chiefly some younger members of the organization, have rejected his call for reconciliation with the Muslim American Society. They continue to preserve the old separatist teachings. Thus, the future of the NOI cannot be predicted with any certainty. Some observers have noted, however, that time may be the worst enemy of the organization. The NOI is a youth-oriented movement in which members typically drop out of the organization as they approach middle age. Unless the NOI is able to retain middle-aged members or replace them with a new generation of recruits, it is destined to decline. A Charlotte police officer who had some experience working with NOI members in the area echoed this observation. Perhaps age brings a different set of concerns to followers. Whereas the NOI emphasis on discipline, confidence, and success is particularly appealing to younger members, those approaching middle age may well be more concerned with more traditional questions of faith and spiritual development. If this is the case, as they age out of the movement, they may well move to other faith communities.

In his 1983 essay entitled "The American Muslim Mission in the Context of Social History," C. Eric Lincoln offered an analysis of the spiritual issues confronting African American Muslims as they seek to define the future of Islam in the United States. His observations continue to be relevant. Describing the appeal of Elijah Muhammad's message, he wrote, "The essence of his message was that Blacks were separated from the knowledge of Allah and the knowledge of self. They were estranged from the one true God to whom they owed allegiance, and ignorant of their own history and their previous high status in the hierarchy of human valuation. The problem was to restore to the Lost-found Nation the truth that could make them free."[17]

His successor, Warith Deen, believed that the time had finally come when the community built by his father could successfully make the transition from the old separatist doctrines and embrace orthodox Islam. Some within the community comfortably made the transition. The Muslim American Society, as the new organization came to be known, reflected their confident, integrationist perspective. Others saw little reason to reject the original teachings of Elijah Muhammad. As Lincoln noted,

> For the millions of blacks whose lots have not been
> measurably improved by almost three decades of America's

'new' racial policies, the romance of Elijah Muhammad's
Nation of Islam still represents challenge and identity;
and above all, it is a visible expression of the rage and
hostility that still pervades the Black under caste. To them,
it is quite clear that the denied and disinherited are still
Black; the deniers and disinheritors are still white; and
Armageddon remains inevitable. They see no compelling
reason now to deny Elijah, or to reinterpret his teachings.[18]

More than two decades later, the story continues to unfold. It is obvious
that much progress remains to be made before minorities will enjoy true equality in the United States. Thus, the continued appeal of Elijah's message to a
new generation of frustrated young people. But what of W. D. Muhammad's
bold efforts to transform the NOI? Again, Lincoln offered several useful observations. Describing the complex relationship of the Black church and mainstream Christianity he wrote, "Black religion derives, in the first instance, from
that aspect of the Black experience that made it difficult to resolve the apparent incongruity between Christianity and Black slavery. It was not only a repudiation of the concept that slavery was acceptable to God, but has always been
a critical medium through which the Black community has institutionalized
. . . to effect Black liberation."[19]

To the extent that the American Muslim community can avoid becoming
the Islamic counterpart of white Christianity and instead become the vehicle
through which African Americans finally achieve full equality, Warith Deen's
dream will be fulfilled. Its success will depend upon the strength of commitment of immigrant and native-born Muslims to a shared vision of Islam. And
American Muslims believe there is hope for success.

One of the things that Charlotte Muslims point to with great pride is
that, regardless of their shortcomings, congregations are struggling against
the "Sunday morning syndrome." Whereas one of the moments when Christians are most likely to be in an entirely segregated environment is during a
Sunday morning church service, mosques are filled seven days a week with
people from diverse social and economic backgrounds and a rainbow of skin
colors. Integration and cooperation are becoming the norm, rather than the
exception. The proof that Islam is the way to true equality, they point out, can
easily be seen any day of the week. Or, as one young woman commented during a Muslim Women of the Carolinas meeting, "I don't just know these
women, I hang out with them!"

Unity in ethnic and racial diversity appears largely to be up to the younger
generation. If NOI still attracts some young black Muslims, most Muslims in
their twenties and thirties in Charlotte seem well aware that if it is to flour-

Kathryn V. Johnson

ish, American Islam must succeed in bringing together people of diverse cultural and socioeconomic backgrounds. One longtime Muslim resident of Charlotte observed that older individuals, in contrast, are sometimes so distracted by the struggle to survive in a new country or by the struggle to survive the battle against poverty and racism that they are unable to contribute to community building between groups.

Charlotte Muslims increasingly do "hang out" together at local mosques and Islamic schools. And they are able to put modern technology to use to further nurture the growing sense of community. Muslims of all ages now have immediate access to local community news. Muslims broadcast local cable television shows and use listserves such as "Muslims in Charlotte," which serves the entire city, and the University of North Carolina at Charlotte Muslim Student Association listserve, which serves area students and faculty. Something of a cyber-Muslim quarter now exists in the city, a place where local Muslims can log on to catch up on news about upcoming community celebrations, births, and weddings. Money is raised for needy families, and news stories are discussed. Not surprisingly, some Muslims commented that they sometimes knew people online long before they actually encountered them in person at a community function.

Again, young Muslims who are most comfortable with technology and affluent enough to have easy access to computers and online service at home are best able to use the Internet to build community connections. The digital divide—who has access to technology and who does not—is impacting the process of relationship building between congregations. The very fact that invitations to a discussion group or community meeting, for example, are issued by e-mail preselects those who will be in attendance. Young professionals will be there; older Muslims and poorly educated immigrants will likely attend only if invited by phone or in person.

Immigrant Muslims

Approximately 60 percent of American Muslims are immigrants or the offspring of individuals who moved to this country from other parts of the world. The first wave of immigration lasted from 1875 until 1912 and consisted largely of uneducated laborers and peasants who left homes in what are today Syria, Jordan, Lebanon, and Palestine to seek their fortunes in America. Most came without wives or delayed plans to marry because they fully expected to work for a few years and then return home with their savings. Instead, few fortunes were found. Most of the young men remained and sought work as laborers, peddlers, grocers, and shopkeepers. Those who could afford it eventually sent home for wives and fiancées. Young men who could not settled down with local girls. In the Midwest small congregations were established and the first mosques built. In the South immigrants largely lived in isolation. Today their grandchildren and great-grandchildren have largely lost contact with the world and religion of that generation. Although families whose names have now evolved into Hoey, Colley, or Badour are occasionally able to recollect the odd Arabic word or prepare a traditional family recipe, most southern families no longer speak Arabic, and many, both Middle Eastern Christian and Muslim, have been absorbed by the local Protestant Christian denominations after several generations of intermarriage.[20]

A second wave of immigration began following World War I and continued into the early 1920s when quota systems were imposed to restrict access to immigration from particular countries. Most Muslims who succeeded in entering the country were relatives of families already living in the United States. During the 1930s more restrictions were imposed so that only relatives were allowed entrance. The actual number of Muslims did not rise until after World War II.

Only a few of those who came to the United States in the first decades of the twentieth century survive today. However, those who are still able to recollect their youth have genuinely fascinating stories to tell. One elderly woman now living in Charlotte, who has retained a wonderful sense of humor in her advanced years, remembered coming to New York by ship as a timid, seventeen-year-old bride from Lebanon. She arrived speaking no English and was met by her groom, a young man from her village whom she had hardly spoken to before their arranged marriage. For a very long time, she was lonely. There was no one in their small North Carolina town who spoke Arabic. But her life, she said, had turned out well. Her parents had chosen a good Muslim man for her, and the two of them had been blessed with healthy children and a successful little business.

Now, the *nasihah* (good advice) she had for new immigrant women is that they should trust in God and learn English "because it's very hard to talk to just one person for a whole year!" Indeed, young Muslim women accompanying their husbands to Charlotte today seem to have an easier time overcoming isolation. Mosques and Muslim Women of the Carolinas can help enormously. But the advice about learning English is key. A young wife who recently arrived from Saudi Arabia reports that her isolation began to be broken via television. She learned her first bit of conversational English by watching the Home Shopping Network while her husband attended classes at the university. Also, with great humor, she relates that once she became proficient enough to order merchandise by credit card over the phone, her husband decided that she should improve her English by attending classes rather than through television. Now she has a circle of women friends and feels comfortable negotiating life in Charlotte.

A fourth immigration wave lasted from 1947 to 1960. Although the Nationality Act of 1953 set a quota on the annual number of immigrants from each country, the number of Muslims increased. Middle Easterners were joined by Indians, Pakistanis, and Muslims from Eastern Europe. Most chose to settle in urban areas in order to pursue professional careers or advanced degrees. And unlike earlier generations of newcomers, they were able to adjust quickly. Many were well educated and accustomed to a life of modern privilege. Their ranks included Iraqis who fled after the violent 1958 revolution, Egyptians unhappy with Nasser's socialist policies, Syrians at odds with the regime, and educated Palestinians displaced by Israel.

While the older immigrants told of overcoming a sense of isolation and adjusting to a society that was quite different from the world they had left behind, those who moved to the United States following World War II sometimes expressed very different sentiments. Often well-educated and comfortable in the new lives they have built in the United States, they have sometimes been quite willing to walk away from the traditional institutions of organized religion when they feel estranged.

One Charlotte resident tells of a desperate, middle-of-the-night escape to the United States after a violent coup in his country. A well-educated professional who was fluent in English, he married, enjoyed a successful career in industry, and retired quite comfortably. His American-born wife is Christian, and their adult children have all married Christian spouses. And although many immigrants wish to raise their children in the faith, he has never pressured either his wife or his children to convert. Quite the opposite. While retired professionals typically fill the ranks of mosque administrative boards, he has maintained almost no contact with the local Muslim community. He feels "disconnected" from Islam. Religion, or at least public rituals, no longer seem relevant. Instead, he chooses to pray alone. His one remaining point of contact with the mosque is an occasional visit to participate in funeral prayers for old friends.

Others from this generation have chosen to maintain limited contacts with the local Muslim community. In these families the mosque is often seen as a place for children to receive a religious education and for cultural traditions to be passed on to the next generation. One family reflects this perspective. They became dissatisfied with the atmosphere at one of the large mosques in the city, or, more precisely, they felt uncomfortable with the conservative views of some within the congregation. This well-educated Arab immigrant family arrived in the United States in the early 1960s and belonged to the group humorously referred to as "Eid Muslims" by their co-religionists. Like "Easter Christians," Holiday Muslims are so-named because of their relationship to their local mosque. Children are typically dropped off to attend weekend religious education classes so that the teachers can "make them into good Muslims"; adults rarely enter the building. They attend only on special occasions such as Eid.

Although Eid Muslims are generally quite assimilated into mainstream American culture, they may nonetheless see the mosque as fulfilling an important social role in their lives, as the family's story reveals. The incident that finally caused this particular family to stop attending altogether ironically took place at a community-wide celebration. One of the women in the family had joined a group of older women who were singing traditional village songs accompanied by a small drum in the main prayer hall of the mosque during the annual children's party at the end of Ramadan. She was approached, and rather sharply rebuked, by an American convert who told her that a mosque is "no place to dance and sing." She replied to her critic, "Where else should we sing Eid songs?" and promptly rounded up the grandchildren and left. As she finished the story, she added, "And that woman didn't even know enough Arabic to understand the words!"

This story is probably typical of a drama that is played out every day in mosques around the United States. On one level, it reflects the conflict between enthusiastic converts and those who have been born in a faith. On another, it reveals a different understanding of the purpose of an Islamic Center in America. From the convert's perspective, the mosque is a place reserved for respectful worship. However, from the perspective of an immigrant grandmother who is singing the songs of her childhood once again, the mosque is a community gathering place. Perhaps the only place where Eid songs can be enjoyed with friends and grandchildren is the mosque. It also reflects a clash between generations and notions of appropriate speech between young and old. The grandmother returned only when her husband died a few months later and the family came to make funeral arrangements.

The final wave of immigration began in 1967 and continues today. In 1965 President Lyndon Johnson signed the repeal of the immigration law that placed quotas based on national diversity requirements. For the first time in many decades the right to enter the United States was not tied to an individual's national or ethnic identity. Immigration from Asia and the Middle East increased dramatically. Iranians fled their country following the 1979 revolution. Palestinians continued to seek refuge in the United States as conditions in the occupied territories periodically worsened. The growing numbers of political refugees from all parts of the Muslim world have been joined by millions who seek to enjoy the many economic opportunities present in our strong economy. In Charlotte this is reflected in the number of Muslim-owned businesses and Muslim professionals.[21]

Kathryn V. Johnson

Unlike previous generations of immigrants, these recent newcomers are here to stay, and they invest in the institutions of American society. Their vision for the future is often expressed as the desire to build an America that is prosperous, honorable, and accepting of all of its citizens. And because they do have great hope for America, they are often outspoken social activists. They and their children have frequently been the public voice of American Islam during the difficult months since September 11, 2001. All the mosques in Charlotte held community events and made public statements in the media in response to that tragedy. But even prior to it, many members of Charlotte's Muslim community were active in the city as spokespersons for religious understanding and tolerance and as a Muslim presence in community affairs, especially in the school system.

The young generation, those raised in the United States and abroad, often provides an equally critical link between American-born Muslims, converts, and immigrants. Because their parents returned often to their former homeland and insisted that their children learn both languages, these young Muslims are comfortable in both worlds. They are fluent in the languages of the more conservative older members of the congregation and are an indispensable source of inside information on how to survive in America for foreign students. And because they are also absolutely American, this generation understands the concerns of converts and can mentor children with confidence.

One of the most active young Muslim couples in Charlotte could perhaps best be described as a new-generation mixed marriage. He is an immigrant; she is a southern-born convert to Islam. They first met as students at the University of North Carolina at Charlotte, where he was pursuing a degree in engineering and she in education. Today he is well known as a community activist, a frequent contributor to "Muslims in Charlotte Online," and an articulate public spokesman for the Charlotte Muslim community. She is a teacher at the Charlotte Islamic School (currently on leave with a new baby) and secretary of Muslim Women of the Carolinas. Both are active because of a strong personal commitment to Islam and an equally fierce desire to build a Charlotte that will be a "good place" for their baby daughter when she grows up.[22]

Foreign Students

Local colleges and universities in the region enroll thousands of Muslim students who come to pursue undergraduate and graduate degrees. Many of those students have their American experience shaped in large part by their encounters with the local Muslim community and their campus student association. Such is the case at the University of North Carolina at Charlotte, where the Muslim Student Association (MSA) provides a spiritual home on campus for American-born Muslims, converts, students from immigrant families, and international students. It also, perhaps, instills a tradition of activism in those international students who become involved in the organization. During the course of the academic year, MSA members typically participate in the fall International Festival, host Islam Awareness Week in November, and organize a number of community functions for area Muslims as well as holding weekly congregational prayers on campus. During the past years, as students from families who are active in their home communities have joined, the MSA itself has become more visible on campus. Last year, for example, one of the officers of the MSA ran for vice president of the student government, and three others organized a write-in campaign to allow students to take religious holidays off without a grade penalty. And since September 11 many of the members have become articulate community spokespersons for Islam in area schools and churches.[23]

Sunni and Shi'i Communities

As mentioned, the fundamental difference between these two traditions is their divergence of opinion regarding the nature of legitimate leadership within the community and authoritative interpretation of the revelation. Thus denomination, like national origin, shapes the American Muslim community.

Those Muslims who call themselves Sunnis recognize the legitimacy of the men who led the community following the Prophet's death in 632 C.E. The series of caliphs, as they were called, were political and military leaders who possessed no supernatural power or infallible religious authority. Rather, the caliph was a political leader, a chief executive officer whose task was to regulate the affairs of the community according to the requirements of the revelation. By the mid-thirteenth century, however, the reality of history had proven to be quite different from the ideal of the virtuous caliph who ruled over a system guided by Islam.

Often the man who held de facto power was a local warlord or ambitious mercenary. The caliphate consisted of a shadow throne and then finally vanished when the Mongols sacked Baghdad in 1258. In response to the question of whether such a society could continue to be a legitimately Islamic one despite the absence of a proper caliph, scholarly discussions came to acknowledge that it was the presence of Islamic law, Shari'ah, and not the particular individual who ruled, that was the hall mark of a legitimate Islamic society. As a consequence, Sunni discussions of the proper exercise of political power came to de-emphasize the person of the ruler.

Modern Sunni writings on the role of religion in society reflect this legacy. Authors discuss the potential application of numerous political models in Islam.

Kathryn V. Johnson

It is adherence to the Revealed Law, Shari'ah, which makes a society properly Islamic, not a particular head of state or form of government. Further, just as Sunni Islam has chosen to de-emphasize the person of the ruler as an arbiter of the revelation, it has entrusted the ability to properly interpret the revelation to the community itself. Based upon a statement of the Prophet in which he affirmed that the community could not agree upon an error, Sunnis argue that using the tools developed to derive rulings based upon the revelation, the Muslim community can be assured of right guidance. The Prophet himself affirmed the presence of such consensus as a trustworthy test. The Qur'an, Example of the Prophet (Sunnah), and the proper application of the principles of analogy and consensus enable those scholars knowledgeable in Islamic jurisprudence to derive sound interpretations without recourse to the supernatural. Thus, modern Sunni Islam is characterized by its willingness to debate appropriate political models for Islam and its emphasis upon the role of Shari'ah in society. And because the authority to properly interpret the Revealed Law has been vested in the community, it is capable of correctly applying it to the issues confronting modern society. This Sunni heritage is apparent in the characteristics of American Islam.

Approximately 80 percent of American Muslims are Sunni. Like their counterparts around the world, they too debate the role of religion in society and the means of its reform. Those who see the Revealed Law as the hallmark of a truly Islamic society must by necessity discuss its role in a modern community. If God's law provides all that humankind needs to prosper in this world and prepare for the next, then how is it to be applied in a society in which Muslims are a minority community? Some of the most exciting discussions within the American Muslim community focus upon analysis of political models and application of the Shari'ah to such modern concerns as medical ethics and family law.[24]

Sh'ism, in contrast, is a charismatic tradition that emphasizes the concept of the Imamate. Shi'i Muslims believe God sent a series of Imams, individuals descended from the house of the Prophet who were designated as the rightful political leaders of the Muslim community and infallible interpreters of the revelation. The majority of those Muslims who are Sh'i are divided into three groups that differ as to the identity and number of the Imams. They are Zaydis, Isma'ilis, and Ithna Ashiri, or Twelver Shi'is.

Zaydi Shi'is acknowledge five Imams. Today, the largest Zaydi communities are found in Yemen; few Zaydis reside in the United States. Isma'ili Shi'is constitute approximately 10 percent of the American Shi'i population. The Druze follow a tradition that emerged from Isma'ili Shi'ism in the eleventh century. The remainder of American Shi'is are Twelvers.

Isma'ili Shi'is. Isma'ilis believe that the Imamate was inherited through a different line of descent from the Prophet; today their various communities are headed by men descended through the line of the seventh Imam, Isma'il (died 760 C.E.). Mustalis or Boharas form the smaller group in the United States. Their followers are centered in major urban areas such as Chicago, New York, San Francisco, and Detroit. Nizaris are the fastest growing component of the Shi'i population. They constitute some 10 percent of American Shi'is. Nizaris are united by their allegiance to Prince Karim Agha Khan, the spiritual head of the world community. Members of each local congregation select their own lay leaders who represent the interests of the community. Smaller communities, such as Charlotte-Huntersville, are served by religious leaders who travel a regional circuit. Because of doctrinal differences, the Isma'ili community has traditionally chosen to avoid discussions of religious matters with other Muslims. Instead, they emphasize the common elements of faith and practice shared by all Muslims. Most of the Sunnis and Twelver Shi'is interviewed were unaware that there was an Isma'ili community in the area.

Like the Isma'ilis, the Druze community in the United States has chosen to avoid potential conflicts within the Muslim community. The Druze religion or sect of Islam (depending upon one's perspective) began in Fatimid Egypt as an offshoot of Ismai'li Shi'ism in the eleventh century. Because their practice and doctrine differ so profoundly from those of both the Sunni majority and Twelver Shi'ism, the Druze have traditionally concealed their teachings from outsiders and married only within their own community.

Early in the twentieth century, however, poverty and political instability led many Druze to abandon their homes in Syria and Lebanon and immigrate to the United States. A substantial number of them settled in Virginia, Kentucky, and Tennessee. Those early settlers who arrived at the turn of the century typically assimilated into their new communities, many even converting to Protestant Christianity. More recent generations, in contrast, have reclaimed their Druze identity and affirmed their connection to Islam.

Advances in communication technology and convenient international travel have probably facilitated the survival of the southeastern community. Today, families can maintain close connections to other American Druze communities, return home to their old village for summer visits, and incorporate new members through immigration.

The handful of Druze families that live in the Charlotte area have benefited from precisely these factors. Rather than live in isolation, they see themselves as part of a strong southeastern and national Druze community. Their children often return to "spend the summer with relatives and get to know their cousins" in the towns in Lebanon or Syria from which their parents or grandparents originally emigrated. Likewise, parents insist that their children learn Arabic well. And because adults emphasize visits and the acquisition of language skills, young men and women strongly identify with their own community and as Arab-Americans. They move comfortably among members of the local Arabic speaking Muslim and Lebanese Christian communities.

Ithna Ashiri/Twelver Shi'is. The Twelvers, so-called because they recognize twelve individuals as having been Imam, form the largest group of Shi'i Muslims in the United States. They believe that the last Imam, Muhammad al-Muntazar, went into occultation in 878 C.E. and will return at some unknown time in the future. Upon his return, he will create the true, virtuous Islamic society. Twelver Shi'ism thus developed an elaborate explanation of the transference of religious authority within the community. Authority came to be vested in the religious scholars *(ulama)* during the twelfth Imam's absence. Shi'i religious scholars have traditionally exercised guardianship over the faithful in spiritual matters. Modern revolutionary Shi'ism, as expounded by the late Ayatallah Khomeini, claims that both religious guardianship and complete political leadership can be exercised by the ulama until such time as the twelfth Imam returns to assume his role as rightful spiritual and political head of the community. Modern Shi'i discussions often focus upon the proper relationship of religion and politics in this Time of Awaiting the twelfth Imam's return.

Twenty percent of American Muslims are Shi'i. The majority are from Iran, and many came to the United States after the 1979 revolution. Iraqi Shi'is make up the second-largest group. The remainder are from Lebanon, India, and Pakistan. Charlotte's communities reverse the norm. Lebanese Shi'is, chiefly from the towns of the southern Bakaa Valley, outnumber those from Iran. Persian-speaking Shi'is who live in Charlotte tend to develop social and spiritual ties to the much larger and better-established communities of the Research Triangle area. Important religious holidays and national festivals such as Nau-Ruz are celebrated with the Iranian community of Raleigh, Chapel Hill, and Durham. Arabic-speaking Shi'is from Lebanon and the states of the Persian Gulf have yet to establish a permanent Islamic center in Charlotte. Instead, families meet in the homes of various community members for services and fellowship twice a week. On Wednesday evenings, devout Shi'is traditionally meet to ask forgiveness for their sins and pay the *khums,* a 20 percent religious tax on profit. On Fridays they meet again for the weekly communal prayer. Shi'i students from area colleges are invited to attend.

The last year has been a difficult one for Charlotte's Shi'i community because of the publicity surrounding the arrest and June 2002 conviction of Mahmoud and Chawki Hammoud, two local Lebanese businessmen. The brothers were convicted of a number of charges, including the illegal transportation and sale of cigarettes across state lines and contributing part of the profit to Hizballah. North Carolina's low cigarette taxes have made the transportation and sale of tobacco products a rather common crime. The charge that profits were sent to Lebanon to finance Hizballah operations, in contrast, drew national attention to the trial. As a result, some members of the Lebanese Shi'i community admitted their reluctance to attend future gatherings at the homes of families whose political views they do not know, lest they be placed under government observation or be accused of being a part of what Charlotte television stations referred to as "Charlotte's own terror connection." Others expressed mixed feelings. On the one hand, the trial had brought the local Arab community together. For the first time in anyone's memory, Charlotte's Arab community became so incensed by the lurid news coverage that they held a joint news conference and issued a statement signed by the Arab-American Association, all of the local mosques, and representatives of the Lebanese Christian community. The committee also invited the American-Arab Anti-Discrimination Committee to send a representative down from Washington to discuss possible legal action. On the other hand, Charlotte's Lebanese and Shi'i residents were embarrassed. As one prominent member of the community noted, "I'm furious with them whether they're guilty or not! All of us are embarrassed. And our families pay the price whenever Muslims look like criminals."[25]

The Sufi Contribution. While not, properly speaking, a separate division within Islam, Sufism claims both Sunni and Shi'i practioners, and this mystical community merits a special mention in any analysis of the American Islam. Within the Muslim community, a distinction is typically made between those non-Muslims who incorporate elements of practice such as chanting or dancing from the Sufi orders as a form of spiritual experimentation and Muslims who pursue a more intimate relationship with God. The former are dismissed as spiritual tourists who are ignorant of the most basic requirements of Sufism: submission to God and acknowledgment of a tradition of spiritual education that is absolutely dependent upon the truths of Islam. This is the meaning behind the often-repeated description of the mystic's journey. Submission to the Revealed Law (Shari'ah) is the first step that leads to the Path (Tariqah), which concludes with the Absolute Reality (Haqiqah). It is not surprising that many of the mainstream national organizations, such as the Islamic Society of North America (ISNA) and the Islamic Circle of North America (ICNA), refuse New Age–type groups the opportunity to participate. In contrast, those organizations that can demonstrate a clear pedigree linking them to the recognized Sufi orders are more widely recognized as legitimate expressions of Islamic piety.[26]

Perhaps the two authors best known for popularizing Sufism in the United States are Idris Shah and Hazrat Inayat Khan. Both have done much to promote a version of Sufism as a method of spiritual enlightenment that can be pursued without commitment to the religion of Islam. Idris Shah, the author of *The Sufis* and numerous short collections of Sufi tales is the founder of the Society for Sufi Studies. Hazrat Inayat Khan traveled across the United States from 1910 to 1927 initiating disciples and establishing the Sufi Order of the West. Today the organization is active in a number of cities and known for the retreats and therapy sessions it sponsors. Most mainstream Muslim groups do not recognize the Order.

Among organizations with links to the traditional Sufi orders *(turuq)* of Islam are the Bawa Muhaiyaddeen Fellowship of Philadelphia, whose late founder was initiated in the Qadiriyah Order, and several groups affiliated with the Naqshbandiyah. Both are products of the Sunni mystical tradition. Shi'i mystical orders in the United States include the Nimatullahi Order of Sufis established in the 1970s by the well-known Iranian author Dr. Javad Nurbakhsh.[27]

In the Carolinas, individuals affiliated with several orders and those appreciative of the mystical tradition fulfill an important role by providing opportunities for Muslims from diverse backgrounds to come together for fellowship and to explore their rich spiritual legacy. Members are also known for their support of prison outreach programs. At a recent Islamic Studies and Research Association (ISRA) conference held in Columbia, South Carolina, on June 7–9, 2002, approximately five hundred American-born Muslims, immigrants, and guests from abroad joined to celebrate the Mawlid al-Nabi (birthday of the Prophet Muhammad). The three-day program included lectures on Islamic history and doctrine, as well as discussions of how modern Muslims can implement the lessons of their faith in their daily lives. The more sober intellectual discussions were generously supplemented with Qur'an recitations, poetry, and *na'at* (songs) honoring God, the Beloved. Young attendees received Mawlid T-shirts celebrating the Prophet's birthday and presented their own panel discussion on how the Prophet can serve as a perfect model for today's youth.[28]

Today, Sufism continues to be particularly attractive to educated Muslims, whether born into the faith or converts, because of its emphasis on the sincere pursuit of spiritual enlightenment, tolerance of diverse viewpoints within the community, and rich literary tradition. And although many educated Muslims would be hesitant to formally affiliate with one of the orders, even if one were to be active in their local community, it is not uncommon for both men and women to express appreciation for their contributions and enthusiastic devotion to Islam.

Charlotte's Mosques

As we now turn to examine several of the larger Islamic centers found in Charlotte, it will become apparent that many mosques in the Southeast, just as in other parts of the country, are evolving to meet the needs of the growing communities they serve. The Islamic Center of Raleigh, North Carolina, the state capital, provides a particularly informative example related to Charlotte's Muslims and Islamic institutions in America. The Raleigh center conforms to the national profile. Its well-educated, rather affluent congregation is drawn from the Research Triangle area and includes immigrants, American-born Muslims, and recent converts. The center's focus reflects their interests in education, charitable service, and community outreach. It is the largest Islamic center in North Carolina and typical of what some observers have called a "full-service mosque" because it quite literally provides for the needs of members from the cradle to the grave.[29] The Islamic Association of Raleigh (IAR) is often mentioned by members of Charlotte's mosques as a model for the future.

Serving a local population of more than ten thousand Muslims, the IAR typically welcomes seventeen hundred people to Friday congregational prayers—so many, in fact, that the mosque must now offer two Friday services to accommodate all who wish to attend. With an annual budget of more than a million dollars, the association is able to employ a director, Imam Muhammad Baianonie; maintain a full-time preschool and K-8 elementary school, a weekend religious education program, and a Qur'an memorization program; and provide a number of outreach activities.

The IAR has three governing bodies. The Shura Council is composed of the Imam and twenty members elected from the congregation; it establishes the policies of the association. The Executive Committee is composed of eleven members appointed by the Shura Council. Its members manage the daily operations of the mosque and its numerous programs. They are assisted by more than seventy volunteers. The Board of Directors has five members who are also elected by the Shura Council.

Among the most important of the missions of the IAR is to provide children and adults access to a sound Islamic education. To accomplish this goal, the congregation provides a number of programs. Begun in 1992 with an initial enrollment of twelve children, Al-Iman School now has a staff of thirty-five full- and part-time instructors and offers a preschool program and grades K–8. The school has thirteen classrooms, a computer lab, gym, and playground. More than 230 students were enrolled in 2001–2002. The curriculum naturally includes traditional subjects such as Qur'an, Islamic studies, and classical Arabic. Students are also instructed in the standard North Carolina curriculum and are required to take the North Carolina End of Grade (EOG) tests. Students in the third and sixth grades also take the Stanford Achievement Test (SAT). Al-Furqan, the weekend Islamic school holds classes for 330 children from preschool through high school. Al-Bayan, the recently instituted Qur'an school, offers instruction in proper recitation of the Qur'an.

Preschool, elementary, and middle-school students are eligible to join in the center's youth-oriented weekend activities and summer programs. High school students can sign up for a computer class or the popular SAT-preparation course. Adults will find course offerings ranging from the traditional (such as Islamic history and Arabic) to the very practical (basic plumbing, auto repair, and tax preparation).

And finally, in addition to the educational programs and extensive outreach program that includes visits to area schools and frequent participation in interfaith dialogues, the IAR cares for Muslims at death. One of the requirements of a growing religious community that is often overlooked is the preparation of the dead and ensuring the availability of space in a cemetery. This is particularly true of Islam, since traditional practice requires that the deceased be buried within twenty-four hours of death unless exceptional circumstances exist. The IAR thus maintains a cemetery in Zebulon, North Carolina, and assists local families in the preparation and burial of loved ones. Charlotte's Muslims draw on some of the resources of IAR as well and look forward to the time when their own mosques can offer the array of services it offers.

Charlotte's Sunnis are served by three large mosques *(masjids)* and several smaller locations, such as Ali Shah, in the city. The largest and oldest of the congregations began in the early 1980s as a small apartment-mosque in a northeast Charlotte complex. It was leased by local Muslims to provide a place for prayer and small gatherings. Today, the congregation has grown to become the Islamic Center of Charlotte (ICC).

Located at 1700 Progress Lane, the ICC is housed in a former church complex that was purchased and renovated by the congregation. The center currently employs a professional Imam, Shaykh Bassam Obeid, and provides a number of services to the local community, including youth groups, a Sunday Islamic school for children, and a schedule of weekly adult education classes. Most of the administrative work is done by congregation members and the Shura Council. Social activities, such as the Sisters' Islamic Studies Group, Girl and Boy Scouts, and others, are funded and run by volunteers from the congregation.

The Charlotte Islamic School, associated with ICC, provides full-time instruction for children from pre-kindergarten through the fifth grade. The school employs a professional teaching staff and is housed inside the mosque complex. Along with the usual curriculum of math, English, and science, CISI students receive instruction in Arabic, Islam (din), and Qur'an. Enrollment for the 2001–2002 school year consisted of sixty-two students, some of whom were American-born Muslims and others who came from immigrant families from Africa, the Middle East, and Eastern Europe. The school plans to add grades six through eight in the near future, and property has been purchased to construct a new school on Robinson Church Road in northeast Charlotte. The congregation is now in the midst of a drive to raise the estimated $250,000 necessary to build the new school.

Ash-Shaheed Islamic Center is located at 2717 Tuckaseegee Road in West Charlotte in a working-class African American neighborhood. In addition to holding the weekly 1:30–2:30 P.M. congregational prayer service on Fridays, the Center offers classes in religious education for adults and children. Weekly Arabic classes are held on Saturdays, and both men's and women's organizations meet for study and to provide volunteer support for the activities of the center. It raises money for scholarships for its youth, awarded at an annual dinner.

Just as the Islamic Center of Charlotte's efforts to expand the services of the mosque have been limited by the scarcity of funds available to the congregation, such has been the case with Ash-Shaheed's Brick-Buy-Brick fundraiser to collect money to pay for a new mosque and school complex. Since usury *(ribah)* is forbidden in Islam, congregations avoid borrowing money for new buildings or expansion of an existing structure from commercial banks. Instead, they typically undertake construction projects in stages, raising money for each portion of a project before actual construction is begun.

The Islamic Society of Greater Charlotte (ISGC) is located at 7025 Plaza Road in northeast Charlotte. It has recently completed a substantial expansion program to accommodate the needs of its growing congregation that includes both local families and students from the nearby University of North Carolina at Charlotte campus.

In addition to the weekly congregational prayer service at Masjid al-Mustafa, the ISGC also provides social and educational services to area Muslims. A weekly Sunday school offers instruction for children in Islamic doctrine and practice (din), Arabic language, and Qur'an. Children and teens can also join Islamic scouting organizations and participate in center-sponsored social activities and sports. And because many of the center's members are of South Asian and Pakistani descent, the ISGC also includes cricket in the sports offered in its athletic program.

Adult-level classes on Islamic religion, history, and Arabic are also available to the congregation. In addition, the ISGC's staff and members frequently participate in interfaith dialogues and present programs in public schools and area churches.

Conclusions

The Islamic Association of Raleigh Center anticipates the likely direction of growth for Charlotte's three largest mosques. As Charlotte's Muslim population continues to increase, so too will the demands placed upon local mosques to provide for the educational and spiritual needs of all within the community. However, the future of Charlotte's Muslim community will not simply depend upon building projects and funding personnel budgets. Growing service demands do not tell the whole story. Charlotte's story must also include the emergence of a new consensus.

Sunni and Shi'i Muslims in the Carolinas share a number of issues, including counteracting the sometimes disturbing levels of discrimination that have occurred since September 11, 2001, and defining their own relationship to mainstream American culture. However, there are some problems that are unique to each community. The local Shi'i population is numerically smaller and further divided by differences of language and culture. There is no Shi'i Islamic center and only limited participation by Shi'is in the Sunni mosques in the area. Persian-speaking Iranians gravitate toward the much larger Research Triangle community for social and spiritual activities. Arabic speakers gather in the homes of co-religionists and invite area students from Lebanon and the Persian Gulf states to participate in their weekly gatherings. And Ismai'lis, by choice, maintain their own network of social and religious relationships.

Although Sunni Muslims make up the majority in the Carolinas, they too face challenges. Sunnis have a substantial numerical and financial advantage as well as easy access to a strong network of regional and national organizations. Yet because the local community mirrors the national population demographics, it can best be described as a mosaic of people from extraordinarily diverse backgrounds. Immigrant and American-born, African American and Pakistani, rich and poor, illiterate and intellectual, conservative and liberal—North Carolina Muslims are all of these. Muslims in Charlotte recognize the importance of all of them coming together as a minority community, while recognizing that ethnic diversity and other differences (such as location within this sprawling city) will mean the presence of multiple Islamic institutions.

If the greatest challenge confronting Shi'is in the Carolinas is to become more inclusive, that of the Sunni community is to set aside old prejudices of race, class, and doctrine and begin anew to forge a consensus of the faithful. If that victory is won, then Islam can truly become a positive force in the greater life of Charlotte. Muslims in the various Islamic institutions of Charlotte voice this hope with a great sense of responsibility. Without diminishing the reality of discrimination and some negative incidents since September 11, Muslims in Charlotte by and large feel positive about the future of Islam in the South. Many who have lived elsewhere in the United States comment that "it's easier" to live in Charlotte because southerners "respect religion" and "are interested in other people's stories." Yet the burden of responsibility for becoming at home in Charlotte, they realize, rests on the Muslim community, for as one Syrian-trained shaykh is fond of reminding his students: God never changes the condition of a people until they (first) change that which is in themselves (Qur'an 13:11).

Notes

1. "Allah" is simply the Arabic word for God. Jews, Christians, and Muslims who speak Arabic use this same word to refer to the deity. Thus many English-speaking Muslims use "God" rather than "Allah" in translations to emphasize the fact that the deity worshipped is the same supreme being in all three monotheistic traditions. Just as one does not say that a Spanish speaker worships "Dios" or the French believe in "Dieu" because it implies that those who speak Spanish or French worship a different God depending upon the native tongue of the believer, it is rather misleading to claim that Muslims worship a deity named "Allah."

2. *Halal* means "permitted" and refers to meat and other foods that meet Muslim dietary codes. Rules governing the types of meat (no pork, for example) and methods of slaughter compose the majority of Islam's dietary regulations.

3. The Billy Graham Evangelism Association moved its headquarters to Charlotte in 2002. Graham's son and new head of the organization, Franklin, is well known for repeated critical remarks about Islam after September 11, 2001.

4. The number of Muslims living in the United States is said to range from six to eight million people. Statistics cited come from the following Web sites: "Islam in the United States," http://usinfo.state.gov/products/pubs/muslimlife/demograp.htm; Council on American-Islamic Relations (CAIR), "Mosque in America: A National Portrait," released Apr. 26, 2001, http://www.cair-net.org/mosquereport; Sound Vision Foundation, "Muslims in America: Profile 2001," http://www.soundvision.com/info/yearinreview/2001/profile.asp; and "Muslims in the Public Square," http://www.projectmaps.com/. For information on Islamic communities around the United States, see the Pluralism Project Web site at http://www.pluralism.org/affiliates/norman/index.php. The link to profiles of Charlotte's communities, compiled by students at Converse College, can be accessed at the same site.

5. See Islamic Society of North America Web site, http://www.isna.net/.

6. See Ellen Barry, "Owning Omar," *Boston Phoenix,* July 2–9,1998, at http://weeklywire.com/ww/07-06-98/boston_feature_1.html. Also, Thomas Tweed, "Islam in America: From African Slaves to Malcolm X," accessible at the National Humanities Center Web site: http://www.nhc.rtp.nc.us/tserve/twenty/tkeyinfo/islam.htm. The Bible owned by Umar is in the Rare Book Room of Davidson College, Davidson, North Carolina. It is a Saadiah ben Joseph version, edited by J. D. Carlyle, which was published in England in 1811. A number of books and articles are available on early contacts between the Muslim world and the Americas and African American Islam: Allan D. Austin, *African American Muslims in Antebellum America: Transatlantic Stories and Spiritual Struggles* (New York: Routledge, 1997); Ronald A. T. Judy, *Disforming the American Canon: African-Arabic Slave Narratives and the Vernacular* (Minneapolis: Univ. of Minnesota Press, 1993); A. Rashad, *Islam, Nationalism, and Slavery* (New York: Writers Inc. International, 1995); and S. A. Diouf, *Servants of Allah:African Muslims Enslaved in the Americas* (New York: New York Univ. Press, 1998). Articles that can be accessed online include M. A. Ahariof, "The Islamic Community in the United States: Historical Development," accessible at the Islam for Today Web site, http://www.islamfortoday.com/historyusa2.htm; and Youssef Mroueh, "Muslims in the Americas Before Columbus," http://cyberistan.org/islamic/mamerica.html. A number of other online articles can be accessed from Professor Alan Godlas (University of Georgia), "Islam, Islamic Studies, Arabic, Religion: Resources for Studying Islam," http://www.arches.uga.edu/~godlas/.

7. Muslims often speak of "reverting to Islam" rather than "converting" to the faith. This is so because it is believed that the original form of religion of all human beings is submission to God (Islam). Based upon Qur'an 7:171, it is said that our human nature *(fitrah)* naturally recognizes God as Lord. Thus humans are born Muslim and transformed into Jews, Christians, and so on as they grow up under the influence of their parents and community. When an individual converts to Islam, he or she is thus reverting to their original, most natural relationship with God. African Americans, then, are reverting to both the original faith of humankind and that of their Muslim ancestors.

8. Y. Y. Haddad, "A Century of Islam in America," originally published in *Hamdard Islamicus* 21, no. 4 (1997), is now available at http://muslim-canada.org/HamdardCentury.html. See also Jane I. Smith, *Islam in America* (New York: Columbia Univ. Press, 1999), 78–80.

9. Smith, *Islam in America,* 80–85. Also, G. Kepel, *Allah in the West: Islamic Movements in America and Europe* (Palo Alto, CA: Stanford Univ. Press, 1997); Martha F. Lee, The Nation of Islam: An American Millenarian Movement (Syracuse, NY: Syracuse Univ. Press, 1996); and C. Eric Lincoln, *Black Muslims in America* (Boston: Beacon Press, 1973).

10. "Malcolm X: A Research Site" offers an online bibliography from the director of the Africana Studies Program of the University of Toledo: http://www.brothermalcolm.net/. *The Autobiography of Malcolm X* as told to Alex Haley (New York: Random House, 1975).

11. For the aftermath of the assassination, see S. Barboza, *American Jihad: Islam After Malcolm X.* (New York: Image Books, 1995).

12. On the development of Black Islam under Wallace Muhammad, see C. E. Marsh, *From Black Muslims to Muslims: The Transition from Separatism to Islam, 1930–1980* (Lanham, MD: The Scarecrow Press, Rowan and Littlefield Publishing Group, 1984).

13. The official site of the Muslim American Society is available at http://www.masnet.org/magazine.asp.

14. For profiles on Charlotte's mosques, see the Pluralism Project Web site, http://www.pluralism.org/affiliates/norman/index.php.

15. L. H. Mamiya, "Minister Louis Farrakhan and the Final Call: Schism in the Muslim Movement," in *The Muslim Community in North America,* ed. E. H. Waugh, B. Abu Laban, and R. B. Qureishi (Edmonton, Alberta: Alberta Univ. Press, 1983), 234–55; and Mattias Gardell, *In the Name of Elijah Muhammad: Louis Farrakhan and the Nation of Islam* (Durham, NC: Duke Univ. Press, 1996).

16. "Farrakhan and Nation of Islam Move towards Islam," *Washington Post,* Feb. 26, 2000, describes the response of ISNA's Secretary General, Dr. Sayyid Muhammad Syeed, to the event. See also "The Family Grows," *Islamic Horizons Online* (publication of the Islamic Society of North America), Mar./Apr. 2000, accessible online at http://www.isna.net/Horizons/article.asp?section=2&leftbar=1&issueid=6. The Nation of Islam's official Web site is located at http://www.noi.org/.

17. C. Eric Lincoln, "The American Muslim Mission in the Context of American Social History," in *The Muslim Community,* ed. Waugh, Laban, and Qureishi, 222.

18. Lincoln, "American Muslim Mission," 225.

19. Lincoln, "American Muslim Mission," 226.

20. The information on Islam and immigration in this section comes from Smith, *Islam in America,* 50–54. A number of survey histories of Islam in America are available, including Aminah B. McCloud, *African-American Islam* (New York: Routledge, 1995); A. H. Quick, *Deeper Roots: Muslims in the Americas and the Caribbean from Before Columbus to the Present* (London: Ta-Ha Publishers, 1996); R. B. Tucker, *Islam in the African-American Experience* (Bloomington: Indiana Univ. Press, 1997); M. Koszegi and J. G. Melton, eds., *Islam in North America: A Sourcebook* (New York: Garland Press, 1992); Sulayma S. Nyang, *Islam in the United States of America* (Chicago: KAZI Publications, 1999); Yvonne Yazbeck Haddad, ed., *The Muslims of America* (New York: Oxford

Kathryn V. Johnson

Univ. Press, 1991); Yvonne Yazbeck Haddad and Jane Idleman Smith, *Muslim Communities in North America* (Albany: State Univ. of New York Press, 1994); and Amir Nashid Ali Muhammad, *Muslims in America: Seven Centuries of History (1312–1998)* (Beltsville, MD: Amana Publications, 1998). See also Azim A. Nanji, ed., *Muslim Almanac: A Reference Work on the History, Faith, Culture and Peoples of Islam* (Detroit: Gale Research, 1996); and Gisela Webb, "Expressions of Islam in America," in *America's Alternative Religions*, ed. Timothy Miller (Albany: State Univ. of New York Press, 1995).

21. In the Charlotte area, Muslim-owned businesses include auto sales, barbershops, real estate and remodeling companies, restaurants, grocery stores, convenience stores, limousine service, and accounting and consulting firms. Area businesses can be located using Islamic Finder, http://www.islamicfinder.org/.

22. American Radio Works, a PBS program, broadcast a program on North Carolina Muslims in October 2001, featuring an interview with Labeed Alkadi, the Chair of the Islamic Association of Raleigh's Outreach Committee and the couple mentioned here. The interview is available at http://www.Americanradioworks.org/.

23. This is typical of many of the student organizations around the United States. See the Web site of the Muslim Student Association of the United States and Canada, http://www.msa-natl.org/resources. See also Talk Islam's "Library of Islamic Websites," http://www.talk-islam.com/, and the Global Islamic Lobby, http://groups.msn.com/TheGlobalIslamicLobby. The Web site for the Muslim Student Association at the University of North Carolina at Charlotte is accessible at http://www.uncc.edu/msa.

24. Searching the keyword "fiqh" at *Islamic Horizons Online* (http://www.isna.net/Horizons/) results in links to various relevant articles. See also Muslim Family Services Web site, http://www.reliefonline.org/mfs/, and Islamic Medical Association of North America Web site, http://www.imana.org/frmain.htm.

25. Coverage of the trial can be found in the online archives of the *Charlotte Observer* and area television stations at http://www.gocarolinas.com/.

26. Discussions critical of New-Age style Sufism can be found on the Web sites of the Islamic Society of North America, http://www.isna.net/, and the Islamic Circle of North America, http://www.icna.com/.

27. Laleh Bakhtiar, *Sufi Women of America: Angels in the Making* (Chicago: KAZI Publications, 1996), offers a fascinating account of seven women who joined the Naqshbandiyah Order and provides insight into the appeal of Sufism.

28. The Islamic Studies and Research Association (ISRA) is based in South Carolina. Information on members and events can be found at its Web site, http://www.israinternational.com/.

29. The Islamic Association of Raleigh maintains an extensive Web site at http://www.islam1.org/, with the annual report of the administrative board, school information, and a number of Friday sermons.

PART 3

Behind the Red Door: The Episcopal Microcosm in the South

CHAPTER 12

"THE TRADITION CLUB": CULTURE WAR, MEMORY, AND THE REINVENTION OF ANGLICAN IDENTITY IN THE MODERN SOUTH

> "The Tradition Club is the 'must play' new course of the year in Myrtle Beach."
>
> —"Carolina Golf and Family Vacations" Web site

AT THE TIME WHEN THE 1999 WILLIAM PORCHER DUBOSE SYMPOSIUM WAS being planned at Sewanee, I was asked to offer observations on church life in the South from the perspective of someone who studies southern religion but who is neither a resident nor a native of the region. While it is true that my roots are not in the South but in New England, the background of my wife, Cynthia, is in fact quite southern. Members of her mother's family have lived in the South Carolina low country since the eighteenth century, and because of these kinship ties I have spent a good deal of time in Charleston and environs during the past twenty-five years. Over that period, I have also developed a great fascination with the history and culture of the low country, and despite the usual family tensions that arise whenever we go to Charleston (which aunts and uncles are we expected to visit, what do we say if we run into irascible cousin Tillman, et cetera), I am always glad to have a reason to visit the area.

Since I am a priest of the Episcopal Church as well as a historian, social and theological controversies within the Diocese of South Carolina have been a particular focus of my interest in recent years.[1] According to sociologist James Davison Hunter, modern-day Americans are engaged in a "culture war" that has affected most of the major institutions in this country over the past forty years. American society, Hunter believes, is divided basically into two camps with opposing intellectual and moral visions: those who believe in a single, external, objective, and transcendent truth ("the orthodox"), and those of who believe that truth is subjective and is continually being redefined according to the spirit of each new age ("the progressives").[2] The impact of this culture war has been manifested in numerous ways, none more critical than the stark political divisions of the 2000 presidential election—the many, sparsely populated "red" counties of the American heartland that voted for George W. Bush, and the few, densely populated "blue" counties on the nation's geographical periphery that voted for Al Gore. The current cultural divisions have also had a profound effect on church bodies in the United States. Beginning in the midst of the social upheavals of the late 1960s, they have encouraged realignment across traditional institutional boundaries and have been a factor both in the decline of membership in the "mainline" Protestant denominations and in the growth and resurgence of conservative and Pentecostal churches.[3]

The Episcopal Diocese of South Carolina is itself one of the religious battlefields on which the American culture war is now being fought. I was personally made aware of this fact several years ago. Whenever Cynthia and I were in Charleston on a Sunday morning, we used to feel at loose ends about church. Whereas the majority of her family belong to either St. Michael's or St. Philip's, the two oldest and most established Episcopal parishes in the city, the evangelical worship style of those churches is not really congenial to our own, more catholic liturgical tastes. St. Michael's and St. Philip's also tend to use far more contemporary "praise" and renewal music than we like—"frozen chosen traditionalists," they call us. And as liberals from the Northeast, we simply do not enjoy listening to sermons that condemn national political and religious figures whom we support or admire. St. Philip's, in fact, underwent a period of considerable internal discord when the charismatic renewal movement first gained a foothold in the parish in the 1980s. It even drew significant national news coverage in 1986 when its popular but controversial rector resigned abruptly, announcing from the pulpit one Sunday that he had been placed under a witch's curse![4] So we were reluctant to attend those churches in spite of the obvious family ties, but thanks to a friend's recommendation, we found a church where we immediately felt at home and where we now like to go whenever we are in South Carolina: St. Stephen's, a small parish in Charleston's historic Ansonborough neighborhood.

St. Stephen's Church is—like the city in which it resides—a place with a fascinating and varied history. The church was founded in 1822 as part of an effort by wealthy church women to evangelize people who were unable to pay pew rents at other Episcopal parishes in Charleston. As such, it was one of the first "free" Episcopal churches in the United States, and when the original building was opened in 1824, it carried an inscription over the front door pro-

Gardiner H. Shattuck Jr.

claiming itself to be a "house of prayer for all people"—an inscription that remains in place today. St. Stephen's maintained a paternalistic outreach mission among poor whites and a few free blacks in the city throughout the antebellum period, but when membership dropped off precipitously during the period of economic depression after the Civil War, the diocese closed the church's doors. The property was not used again as a parish until 1923, when a congregation of the Colored Methodist Episcopal Church became Episcopalians en masse. From the 1920s through the 1980s, St. Stephen's functioned as an African American mission within a predominantly black neighborhood—one of three black Episcopal churches in the city.[5] During the mid-1960s Henry Grant, the priest in charge, also ran a social outreach center in a nearby area, described (appreciatively) by *The Episcopalian* magazine as "the toughest, meanest slum in South Carolina."[6]

In the 1970s, when the Historic Charleston Foundation targeted Ansonborough for "preservation" by buying, restoring, and selling houses to middle-class owners, racial patterns in the neighborhood began to change dramatically once again.[7] As a result of that shift, only a handful of families remained at St. Stephen's when Father Grant retired in 1987, and at this point the church entered its third incarnation. Alanson Houghton, the former rector of the Church of the Heavenly Rest in New York, was appointed vicar of the mission by C. FitzSimons Allison, then bishop of South Carolina, and Houghton in turn recruited a number of well-to-do whites in the city to work with him in restoring St. Stephen's as a self-consciously interracial, socially progressive parish. The African American families who constituted the church prior to Houghton's assuming leadership held a meeting at which they discussed whether they would accept the new vicar or simply transfer to another black parish. Their apprehension about the proposed changes was understandable, since the St. Stephen's situation was reminiscent of the historical pattern of race relations in the Episcopal Church—a white bishop choosing the white priest whom he wanted to lead a black parish. Despite some opposition to the proposed plan, however, the majority of African Americans decided they would remain at St. Stephen's and work with any new white members who joined them.[8] When parishioners later determined that the vestry would be evenly divided between black and white members and that the church would give away 50 percent of its income to work on behalf of social justice, their commitment to outreach not only was consistent with what black Episcopalians had supported under the leadership of Henry Grant but also recapitulated the aims of the upper-crust Charlestonians who founded the parish in the early nineteenth century.

In recent years, the percentage of African Americans at St. Stephen's has declined a bit, and the racial makeup of the parish is now approximately two to one, white to black. On the other hand, its gay and lesbian population has grown markedly, and despite the disapproval of some older parishioners, St. Stephen's is one of the rare parishes in Charleston where gay and lesbian church members feel openly welcome. Based on the parish profile developed in 1997, St. Stephen's members believe they encourage an inclusive atmosphere that takes seriously issues of race, gender, and sexual orientation. At the annual diocesan convention in 2000, in fact, a St. Stephen's parishioner publicly challenged other South Carolina Episcopalians to celebrate the diversity in their denomination by acknowledging the presence of gay church members like him in their midst.[9] In liturgical matters, on the other hand, St. Stephen's is quite traditional, and it adheres strictly both to the *Book of Common Prayer* (1979) and to the conventional Anglican hymnody contained in the *Hymnal 1982*. Contemporary praise and gospel music is not used in worship, and the renewal movement, which is so influential in neighboring low country parishes, has had little influence on the St. Stephen's membership.[10] The church currently has about a hundred communicants, and as a consequence of both its liberal social outlook and its relatively formal worship style, the parish and its members are regarded (in the words of Jim Bills, the current vicar) as "mavericks" at odds with the rest of the diocese.[11]

If St. Stephen's, Charleston, represents the "progressive" side in the culture war being fought among Episcopalians in South Carolina, the "orthodox" position is defended and advanced most forcefully by All Saints' Church, Pawleys Island—a parish with a history and traditions in some ways different from, and in other ways quite similar to, its urban counterpart. Pawleys Island, which is located a few miles southwest of the city of Myrtle Beach, is part of the fertile coastal region where the richest plantations in the state once were located. Producing nearly one-third of the total rice crop of the United States in the mid-nineteenth century, a wealthy aristocracy, heavily dependent upon the strength and skills of enslaved Africans, flourished there in the decades prior to the Civil War. More Africans came to South Carolina than anywhere else on the North American mainland, and the ratio of blacks to whites (nine to one) on the plantations near Pawleys Island was the highest in the state. The owners of those plantations, committed to maintaining slavery at all costs, also supplied the leadership that took South Carolina out of the Union in 1860 and helped precipitate the outbreak of war a few months later.[12]

Most of the planters in the Pawleys Island area were at least nominally Anglican during the colonial era, and they helped establish All Saints' Church in 1767. Typical of all institutions of the Church of England in rural parts of the South, church life in the parish lay dormant during and for many years after the American Revolution as Anglicans struggled to reorganize and revive their denominational tradition in the changed circumstances of a new nation.[13] However, religious activity was eventually reestablished at All Saints' in the early nineteenth century, and in 1816 the Episcopal bishop of South Carolina consecrated the building in which the congregation worshiped. Although planters in the low country had been reluctant to support efforts to evangelize their slaves before the War for Independence, the next generation of slaveholders eagerly sponsored paternalistic missionary activities on their plantations. Exemplifying this antebellum trend, the vestry of All Saints' called a young English priest named Alexander Glennie to be their rector in 1832, and over thirty years he helped raise the number of active black communicants at his church from a mere handful to more than 525. Glennie's work, however, was seriously disrupted during the Civil War, and when African Americans in the area learned of their emancipation in 1865, most of his black parishioners stopped attending Episcopal services altogether. Disconsolate at this development, he resigned from his position a year later, and the parish lacked stable clerical leadership for more than a decade afterwards. Evangelistic work among African Americans also came to a halt at All Saints' during this period. At the end of the nineteenth century, however, when the Diocese of South Carolina formed a segregated "Archdeaconry for Colored Work," a new parish for black Episcopalians (Holy Cross and Faith Memorial Church) was organized not far from the place where whites worshiped. This also became the site of Camp Baskervill, the diocesan camp that black church members attended in the first half of the twentieth century.[14]

As was the case during the heyday of the rice planters in the nineteenth century, the Pawleys Island area continues to offer a remarkably congenial environment for well-to-do white Americans today. Advertising itself as "the oldest resort" in America, it attracts vacationers and retirees from all over the United States, and both the population and wealth of the area have increased at a phenomenal rate since 1970.[15] Millions of dollars have been poured into the creation of lavish "antebellum" mansions and gated "plantation" communities for the privileged, while lush golf courses and well-appointed country clubs (with imposing but fabricated names like "The Tradition Club" and "The Heritage Club") have sprung up virtually out of nowhere.[16] Despite such dramatic growth in recent years, over 20 percent of the people in Georgetown County (in which Pawleys Island is located) still live in poverty—a figure more than 50 percent higher than the average in the rest of the country.[17] Moreover, throughout the twentieth century the ownership of large portions of the low country was transferred from native South Carolinians to wealthy northerners and foreign investors. As the economic historian Peter Coclanis wryly observes about the ongoing exploitation of the low country, even in today's "rarified, five star atmosphere," the essence of the region's past can still be observed in the fact that "while a few feast, many serve."[18]

All Saints' Church in the year 2001 retains a similarly ironic connection both to this general regional heritage and to the historic roots of its denomination in the low country. Despite its venerable past, the parish today more closely resembles an ecclesiastical version of the nearby "Tradition Club" than an ordinary Episcopal church, offering its membership a thoroughly modern form of the "old-time" Anglican religion.

The extent of the parish's alienation from its denominational traditions is revealed in actions undertaken by its current leadership over the last few years. In January 1999, for instance, Charles H. Murphy III, then rector of the parish, accused liberal Episcopalians of having done a very poor job in managing church affairs, allowing a loss of about a million members between 1963 and 1988.[19] Despite maintaining "the older trappings" of Anglican liturgy and polity, he complained, many Episcopal bishops and priests seemed determined to destroy the true essence of the Christian faith. Murphy asked churchgoers to follow his advice and distinguish carefully between "the packaging and the content" of Christianity. The Episcopal Church would only be able to reverse the downward trend he described when its leaders learned, first, to support wholeheartedly traditional doctrinal and ethical standards and, second, to introduce innovative forms of worship and evangelism designed to encourage non-Episcopalians to join the denomination. Under his direction, Murphy noted, All Saints' had adopted this strategy and reaped substantial rewards. The church dramatically increased in size during the population boom in the Pawleys Island area, and it used some of the new residents' wealth to construct an $8 million parish complex on the sixty-six acres of prime real estate it owns. In contrast to unabashedly heterodox clergy like John Shelby Spong, the retired bishop of Newark (one of various liberals struggling to maintain the institutional fabric of the Episcopal Church in decaying areas of the urban Northeast), Murphy believed that a cadre of truly faithful Episcopal clergy and lay people would have been able not only to resist such decline but also to achieve the same level of success his parish enjoyed during Americans' rush to the Sunbelt in the 1980s and 1990s.[20]

Like the evangelical mega-churches that served as models for Murphy's pastoral leadership, All Saints' Church offers two well-attended services at ten o'clock on Sunday mornings. One of these, billed as "contemporary worship . . . in a casual environment," provides young churchgoers with a Christian message to which they can easily relate: "No pressure, no dress code, regular language, multi media, . . . gourmet coffee," and instead of a priest and an altar, a rock band playing upbeat religious music. The other service, which the parish labels "traditional worship," is designed to appeal to middle-aged and older church members, but it too is quite unconventional by venerable Anglican standards. Most of the texts used in that service are found, not in the denomination's official prayer book and hymnal, but in All Saints' Church's own "Parish Family Worship Book"—a user-friendly collection of photocopied hymns (mainly post-1970s praise and renewal music) and prayers. Church-goers at the "traditional" service exhibit great enthusiasm as they lift their hands heavenward, and the clergy encourage them to view worship as a highly personal and emotional experience. Broadly evangelical rather than narrowly Episcopal, Sunday morning worship at All Saints' dispenses with established Anglican emphases on liturgical and ecclesiastical order in favor of a believer's direct encounter with God through Bible study, singing, and prayer.[21]

Using this concept of new "packaging" for an otherwise conservative faith, Murphy helped transform his two-hundred-year-old church by successfully adapting worship and parish life to meet the spiritual needs of affluent white residents migrating to the Myrtle Beach area. In the late 1990s he continued his innovative approach to church leadership by organizing a nationwide movement of dissident Episcopalians. Similar to the handful of other schismatic groups that have left the Episcopal Church over the years, the organization Murphy helped create was developed as a counterweight to the progressive social and intellectual trends that he thought were threatening traditional moral values in the United States.[22]

This present-day rupture in the Episcopal Church took shape when a select gathering of clergy from dioceses in the Southeast and Southwest met at All Saints' in September 1997. Committed to the reformation of their denomination, those clergy released a statement that accused national leaders of the Episcopal Church of utterly neglecting "the first promise" of their ordination oath: that is, the promise to uphold "the doctrine, discipline and worship of Christ" and "the truth of the gospel" in their ministries. The central issue on which this "First Promise" statement focused was sexuality. The clergy who gathered at Pawleys Island believed that the only divinely mandated form of sexual expression is between a man and a women, united in marriage. They were appalled, therefore, by the apparent willingness of the Executive Council and General Convention of the Episcopal Church to ignore the clear teachings of the Bible by accepting the legitimacy of sexual relations outside of marriage. Homosexuality came under special attack for being a perversion of the natural order created by God. As a consequence of the alleged abandonment of Christian orthodoxy by the liberal wing of their denomination, which had repudiated "the faith once delivered to the saints," signers of the First Promise statement declared that ordinary lines of authority within the Episcopal Church had become "fundamentally impaired." They pledged not only to sever their ties with any bishop whom they viewed as apostate but also to seek "alternative episcopal oversight" from "faithful bishops who uphold our heritage in the gospel."[23]

The principles enunciated in the "First Promise" statement were soon put into action by an international coalition of conservative leaders from several different Anglican churches. At a service at the Anglican cathedral in Singapore in January 2000, Charles Murphy and John H. Rodgers Jr., former dean of Trinity Episcopal School for Ministry in Pennsylvania, were raised to the episcopate by a group of bishops (including FitzSimons Allison of South Carolina) representing provinces of the Anglican Communion in Africa, Asia, South America, and the United States.[24] Although the exact ecclesiastical status of Rodgers and Murphy was uncertain at the time, they were consecrated with the intention of serving as missionary bishops in the United States, founding congregations and encouraging both old and new Episcopalians to uphold traditional biblical values.[25] The crisis created by the Singapore consecrations escalated even further a few months later, when Murphy, Rodgers, and their followers organized a formal religious body, the Anglican Mission in America (AMiA), which was designed to function as a separate ecclesiastical structure for conservatives eager to leave the Episcopal Church.[26]

Since the January 2000 consecrations, the AMiA, now headquartered at All Saints', has expanded and claims to represent nearly forty parishes and over five thousand Episcopalians throughout the United States.[27] Moreover, against the vigorous objections of both George Carey, the archbishop of Canterbury, and Frank Griswold, the presiding bishop of the Episcopal Church, four more men (including two priests who had worked as assistants to Murphy at All Saints') were consecrated AMiA bishops at a service in Denver in June 2001. Acknowledging that he had violated one of the essential tenets of Anglican canon law (namely, the requirement that clergy serve only with the approval of ecclesiastical authorities within the boundaries of established dioceses), Murphy argued that Christians who were faithful to God's word should not be constrained by antiquated notions of geographical jurisdiction. New priests and bishops, dispatched as evangelists from thriving Anglican churches in third world countries, were needed for service in the increasingly secular United States. Murphy himself served under the sponsorship of the Province of the Episcopal Church of Rwanda, and though a white American raised in Alabama, he envisioned his new ministry as an ironic reversal of the evangelistic thrust to enslaved Africans that had taken place at his parish in the nineteenth century: Africa now freely sending missionaries to America to preach biblical truths to unconverted people of European descent.[28]

Such claims to be the authentic voice of worldwide Anglicanism notwithstanding, the AMiA was really constructed on a very narrow theological, liturgical, and ecclesiastical base. As even conservatives otherwise sympathetic to the goals of the organization have been compelled to admit, it is hard to recognize the AMiA as a credible church body when four of its eight bishops serving in the United States are located in a single diocese (South Carolina), and three of the bishops were, until recently, working closely together as priests at the same parish (All Saints', Pawleys Island). AMiA adherents not only represent an infinitesimal percentage of the total membership of the Episcopal Church, but most of them belong to a small cluster of congregations that embrace charismatic renewal, a movement that did not exist in the Episcopal Church prior to the 1960s.[29] In addition, because the founding principles of the organization do not actually require the use of the prayer book—the standard of worship for all Episcopalians—but allow "approaches . . . which are freer and more accessible to those just making their first acquaintance with the Body of Christ at prayer," the liturgical emphasis of the AMiA seems decidedly more evangelical than Anglican.[30] Similar to both the Puritans of the seventeenth century and the Methodists of the eighteenth century—the two most significant breakaway groups in the history of Anglicanism—Murphy and his colleagues have elevated the primacy of scripture and the inner promptings of the Holy Spirit over adherence to traditional Anglican norms of ordered worship and hierarchical authority.

The AMiA leadership at Pawleys Island is also clearly out of step with the role traditionally exercised by Anglicans in the American South. For example, in the late eighteenth century, when Baptist and Methodist opponents of the Anglican establishment stressed the need for individual conversion and inner moral discipline, most Anglicans insisted that they drew spiritual sustenance from the shared, corporate recital of prayers and creeds—an approach to worship that the evangelicals derided as mere "formalism."[31] As Henry May observes in his classic study *The Enlightenment in America,* the Church of England consistently "stood for moderation, comprehensiveness, liberality of doctrine, and stability of custom" in the eighteenth-century South. Evangelicals, on the other hand, condemned those traits as vices, equating Anglican "comprehensiveness [with] looseness; its liberality [with] apostasy; its cheerfulness [with] overweening optimism; its decorum [with] vain ceremony."[32] In his history of southern Anglicanism before the American Revolution, Charles Bolton makes a similar observation. Anglicans, he notes, "scorned both the pettiness of elaborate theology and the uncertainty and ecstasy of experiential religion and advocated 'the religion of common sense'" instead.[33] And as Christine Heyrman writes in *Southern Cross,* her prizewinning book on the origins of evangelicalism in the South, membership in the Church of England in the eighteenth century "did not require testifying to a conversion experience or submitting to an ascetic discipline." Anglicans in those days placed little emphasis on "strict doctrinal conformity," but they "took consolation from carefully crafted sermons emphasizing the reasonableness of Christianity, the benevolence of God, and the moral capacity of humankind."[34]

As the revivals of the Second Great Awakening further strengthened evangelicalism in the early nineteenth century, Baptists and Methodists surged ahead of Episcopalians in numbers. The awakening encouraged ordinary men and women to see their deepest spiritual impulses as divinely inspired, and more and more Americans, southerners especially, accepted the "religion of the heart" that revivalists preached. In contrast to the emotional extremes of the revivals, Episcopalians continued to believe in the value of both their dignified worship services and the claim of antiquity embodied in their polity. Some Christians seeking to escape from the social narrowness of the Baptists and Methodists also responded positively to the Episcopal Church's relatively tolerant attitude toward "vices" such as alcohol, dancing, and the observance of Christmas. Whereas most evangelicals regarded such concerns as impediments to the practice of true Christianity, a few religious people saw them as reasons either to join or to remain a member of the Episcopal Church during the great age of American revivalism.[35]

Evangelicalism in the South has evolved considerably since the nineteenth century, and so has the Episcopal Church in relation to it. While southern evangelicals today have certainly not abandoned their earlier preference for spontaneity and enthusiasm in worship, they have become increasingly more rationalistic in their understanding of the Christian faith. In fact, according to the noted southern historian Samuel Hill, a concern for "rational purity" has now become the driving force in evangelical circles, replacing the heartfelt religiosity that was once the dominant paradigm of church life in the South. Insisting on strict adherence to certain doctrinal and ethical standards, evangelicals have increasingly tended to view anyone who opposes them as an enemy of Christ. Sexuality in particular has become a focus for evangelicals' concern, and "sexual perversion" has even taken the place of drinking as the sin that Christians are expected most strongly to resist. The current situation is especially strange, Hill thinks, because this rationalistic, judgmental approach to Christian orthodoxy used to be a feature of biblical fundamentalism in the North, not of evangelicalism in the South.[36]

Hill's analysis of contemporary southern evangelicalism has special relevance to the intellectual foundations on which the AMiA was created. The constitution of the organization begins with a list of principles that are intended to guide its corporate life. The first of these principles relates to the authority and interpretation of the Bible. Although the exact function of the Bible in Anglicanism has long been debated, the sixteenth-century English theologian Richard Hooker devised a nuanced formula regarding the nature of authority in the church, and it has since become the recognized standard for Episcopalians. Opposing both the biblical idealism of the Puritan movement and the conservative traditionalism of papal Catholicism in his day,

Hooker argued that the church was an organic and evolving institution rather than a static one. Since the scriptures were ambiguous and imprecise in their teaching on certain issues, Hooker thought Christians always needed to bring insights derived from their innate human reason to bear on the resolution of disputes about the Bible's application to contemporary ecclesiastical affairs.[37]

In contrast to Hooker's cautious and pragmatic views on the Bible and its role in the church, the founding principles of the AMiA assert not only the scripture's "supreme authority" for Christians in all matters but also "the clarity of its plain sense . . . understood by ordinary readers." While "the importance of the scholarly interpretation of Scripture" is duly recognized, the tools of modern biblical scholarship are to be used (the AMiA principles say) simply to uncover "the original meaning of the text."[38] This stance toward the Bible is extremely revealing, for rather than affirming the complex intellectual process articulated by Hooker in the sixteenth century, it relies instead on the rationalistic, scientific model endorsed by the first generation of Protestant fundamentalists in the late nineteenth century. Interpreting scriptural texts empirically according to plain-sense reasoning, early fundamentalists thought the Bible was essentially "a store house of facts" intelligible to anyone who chose to read it with an open mind.[39] Thus, despite the AMiA's stated appeal to long-standing traditions in the church, the organization has committed itself, not to historic methods of theological inquiry employed by Anglicans over the centuries but to a form of biblical interpretation developed by one portion of the American Protestant community about a hundred years ago.

As the foregoing discussion suggests, the culture war currently being fought among Episcopalians in South Carolina cannot be reduced to a simple "progressive-orthodox" dichotomy. Using St. Stephen's Church, Charleston, and All Saints' Church, Pawleys Island, as models, it is obvious that "progressives" in the low country can be relatively traditional by accustomed standards among Anglicans in the South, while "orthodox" Episcopalians can be quite innovative and modern. Of course, as anyone who knows the Myrtle Beach area is well aware, "tradition" and "heritage" can mean almost anything today—they are often just names on signposts in front of new housing developments and country clubs. And Charleston's own cultural traditions have themselves been subject to manipulation and invention over the years. For example, as one scholar has recently shown in an article on the beginnings of the preservation movement in Charleston, the city's elite infused the buildings they restored with a concept of history intended to sustain both white privilege and black subordination. Rather than preserving memories about the actual role of slavery in the city's life, they promoted "a socially regressive culture of nostalgia" that fostered amnesia about the past instead.[40]

Present-day discussions about race and the memory of slavery also provide a helpful lens through which the adequacy of the culture war's "orthodox" and "progressive" labels can further be tested. According to Ulrich B. Phillips, the preeminent historian of the South in the early twentieth century, attitudes about race have repeatedly constituted "the cardinal test of a Southerner," and the issue itself must be understood as "the central theme of Southern history."[41] As Phillips himself knew, the South as a region had long been obsessed with the concept of race—white southerners in adherence to the idea of mastery over blacks and black southerners in resistance to the racism and brutality of whites. Although race relations in the South have improved considerably since the era when Phillips was writing, this subject remains a crucial, albeit sometimes unarticulated, concern for all southerners today. It is intriguing, therefore, to compare the ways in which the two congregations examined in this essay deal with an issue that has indelibly marked their respective histories.

Given this historical context, an intentionally interracial church like St. Stephen's, Charleston, seems much closer to traditional southern folkways than All Saints', Pawleys Island, and other socially conservative parishes where attention is focused primarily on sexuality and church doctrine.[42] Simply by paying attention to the public interaction of black people and white people in Charleston—a city once regarded as one of the most racially mixed places in the United States—St. Stephen's marks itself as a very traditional *southern* parish. Although Charleston itself has become increasingly more segregated in recent years, as the gap between rich and poor widens and as the tourist-minded chamber of commerce seeks to expunge reminders of the ugly realities of slavery, the decision of St. Stephen's Church in Ansonborough to reconstitute itself as an interracial parish represents a courageous attempt, at least, to keep the subject of race open for scrutiny and discussion.[43]

It is also noteworthy that this parish serves as the spiritual home of Edward Ball, author of the prizewinning *Slaves in the Family*, who has explored some of the painful history of race relations in Charleston. Ball's book begins with an anecdote about his father, Theodore, an Episcopal priest who grew up in Charleston. There were five things that Ball family members never talked about, Theodore used to say: "Religion, sex, death, money, and the Negroes." A few months before he died, however, Theodore gave his son a history of the Ball family and the plantations they once owned. Edward kept that book, and despite settling in New York after college, he read it periodically and felt drawn to both the land and the era it described. Although he had left the South as a young man, he still believed that "the plantation past was etched in my unconscious," and as a consequence he decided to return to the low country and find out more about his family. Eventually, he moved to Charleston and conducted the research that forms the basis of *Slaves in the Family:* a chronicle of the experiences of both his slaveholding ancestors (about whom some written record already existed) and the "anonymous, taboo" people from Africa who had lived with them and toiled on their plantations.[44] Following his relocation to Charleston, Ball became a member of St. Stephen's Church in the late 1990s. Since St. Stephen's is a place where questions about race and the interweaving of the lives of black and white Charlestonians remain important concerns, one should not be surprised that Edward Ball or anyone else attentive to "the central theme" of southern history would gravitate there.

At All Saints', Pawleys Island, on the other hand, serious discussion about the South's racial history race is notably absent. As the headquarters of the AMiA, the parish does make clear the debt it owes to Christians in Africa, especially to Emmanuel Mbona Kolini, the Rwandan archbishop who consecrated Charles Murphy and who serves as one of the organization's "global sponsors." "Christianity is no longer a white man's religion," an AMiA publication notes, but it "has become a religion of the poor, the marginalized, the powerless" in the developing nations of Africa, Asia, and Latin America.[45] The truth of those observations about "two-thirds world" Christianity notwithstanding, there are very few people of color, especially African Americans, present as worshipers at All Saints' Church on a typical Sunday morning. The parish derives its membership not from any of the largely powerless African Americans who live in surrounding Georgetown County but from the privileged white elite who have moved to the area in the last two decades. Although All Saints' is hardly unique among Episcopal congregations in its lack of an African American membership, there is still an extraordinary discontinuity between the parish's racially oriented evangelism in antebellum times, its stated interest in the faith of downtrodden people in Africa today, and its negligible outreach among the poor in its own community.[46]

St. Stephen's, Charleston, and All Saints', Pawleys Island, are two quite different parishes, but each claims to retain links to the past and to represent the best traditions of the Episcopal Church in South Carolina. Both were very active parishes in the early nineteenth century, and both were inevitably shaped by the realities of race at key moments in southern history. Both were organized by the most privileged members of their society, and both sponsored a paternalistic mission intended to evangelize and aid disadvantaged people during the antebellum period. Both were strongly affected by social and cultural changes within their communities in the twentieth century, and both experienced an institutional revival in the 1980s. But there the similarities between them end, and over the last twenty years their paths have radically diverged. Each fosters an almost opposite version of what its leadership believes are traditional Anglican religious values. Thus, one parish emphasizes ethical purity, biblical literalism, spiritual enthusiasm, and individual conversion; the other stresses concepts such as social inclusiveness, theological latitude, liturgical formality, and pastoral outreach. One has succeeded handsomely as a "winner" in what has been called the American "free market religious economy," while the other, though hardly a "loser," has achieved far more modest material and organizational results.[47] Confident in what it has achieved on its own, one parish has all but repudiated the denomination to which it officially belongs and instead seeks oversight from a foreign bishop thousands of miles away; the other, despite having been ostracized as a "maverick" and outsider within its own diocese, resolutely clings to the Episcopal Church in the United States.

Ironies abound in this depiction of life in two low country parishes today, none more telling than the discontinuity between the vision of "orthodox" Anglicanism espoused by AMiA leaders at All Saints, Pawleys Island, and genuine Anglican traditions in the South. While their parish has unquestionably prospered within the contemporary religious marketplace, its success derives not from any association with the distinctive heritage of the Episcopal Church in the region but from a denial of that denomination's fundamentally generous theological spirit. Despite claiming that they alone have preserved the ancient "faith once delivered to the saints," these modern-day Episcopalians have, in effect, invented an Anglican past that never actually existed.

Notes

A version of this essay was previously published in the *Sewanee Theological Review* 43, no. 4 (2000). The epigraph at the beginning is taken from Carolina Golf and Family Vacations, "The Tradition Club," http://www.thecarolinagolf.com/myrtle-beach/golf-courses/tradition.htm.

1. South Carolina contains two Episcopal dioceses: the Diocese of South Carolina (the southeastern half of the state) and the Diocese of Upper South Carolina (the northwestern half).

2. James Davison Hunter, *Culture Wars: The Struggle to Define America* (New York: Basic Books, 1991), 31–51.

3. Robert Wuthnow, *The Restructuring of American Religion: Society and Faith Since World War II* (Princeton, NJ: Princeton Univ. Press, 1988), 134–64. See also Jeffrey K. Hadden, *The Gathering Storm in the Churches* (Garden City, NY: Doubleday, 1969).

4. Steve Mullins, "Battles Split Churches," *Charleston Post and Courier,* July 3, 1994, http://www.charleston.net/.

5. Albert Sidney Thomas, *A Historical Account of the Protestant Episcopal Church in South Carolina, 1820–1957* (Columbia, SC: R. L. Bryan, 1957), 20–21, 68, 148, 261–65, 660, 748.

6. William McK. Chapman, "But What Does St. John's Mission *Do?*" *The Episcopalian,* Dec. 1967, 8, 10.

7. Robert N. Rosen, *A Short History of Charleston* (San Francisco: Lexikos, 1982), 150.

8. For background on race relations among Episcopalians in Charleston, see Robert F. Durden, "The Establishment of Calvary Protestant Episcopal Church for Negroes in Charleston," *South Carolina Historical Magazine,* no. 65 (1964), 79–81. See also Gardiner H. Shattuck Jr., *Episcopalians and Race: Civil War to Civil Rights* (Lexington: Univ. Press of Kentucky, 2000).

9. Dave Munday, "Bishop is Challenged on Homosexuality Issue," *Charleston Post and Courier,* February 13, 2000, http://www.charleston.net/. See also Eric Frazier, "Homosexuality Is Theological Quicksand for Congregations," *Charleston Post and Courier,* December 7, 1997, http://www.charleston.net/.

10. St. Stephen's Episcopal Church, Charleston, South Carolina, "Parish Profile" (unpublished manuscript in the author's possession, 1997), 4–6, 8, and appendix D.

11. Much of the preceding discussion is based on personal observations as well as on conversations in Charleston with Jim V. Bills, Julia Logan, and the late Frank M. McClain, whose ideas and insights have all added significantly to my understanding of the Episcopal Church in South Carolina.

12. Charles Joyner, *Down by the Riverside: A South Carolina Slave Community* (Urbana: Univ. of Illinois Press, 1984), 1–2, 4–5, 12, 14, 34.

13. David L. Holmes, *A Brief History of the Episcopal Church* (Valley Forge, Pa.: Trinity Press International, 1993), 50–62.

14. Thomas, *Historical Account,* 380–81, 385–87, 453–58; and Joyner, *Down by the Riverside,* 154–57, 229–30.

15. Pawleys Island/Litchfield Business Association, "The Oldest Resort Area in America: Pawleys Island and Litchfield Beaches . . . Map/Guide" [2001], brochure in the author's possession.

16. "The Tradition Club" (Pawleys Island, South Carolina), Web site, http://www.traditiongolfclub.com; Carolina Golf and Family Vacations, "The Tradition Club," http://thecarolinagolf.com/myrtle-beach/golf-courses/tradition.htm; and Carolina Golf and Family Vacations, "The Heritage Club," http://thecarolinagolf.com/myrtle-beach/golf-courses/heritage.htm.

17. Council on Library Resources, "Georgetown Country Library Case Study: The Context" (Nov. 1996), http://www.clir.org/pubs/reports/case/geor01.html.

18. Peter A. Coclanis, *The Shadow of a Dream: Economic Life and Death in the South Carolina Low Country, 1670–1920* (New York: Oxford Univ. Press, 1989), 156.

19. See figures published in *Episcopal Church Annual: 1965* (New York: Morehouse Barlow, 1964), 10–11 and *Episcopal Church Annual: 1990* (Harrisburg, PA.: Morehouse, 1990), 13.

20. Charles Murphy, "We Can Better Perceive What to Hold . . .," *Episcopal Life,* Jan. 1999, http://www.episcopalchurch.org/episcopal-life; and Jan Nunley, "Frustration over Thwarted Mission Propelled AMiA's Murphy out of ECUSA," *Episcopal News Service,* 2001-16S (January 26, 2001), http://ecusa.anglican.org/ens. For a similar critique of the situation in the Episcopal Diocese of Newark, see Rodney Stark and Roger Finke, *Acts of Faith: Explaining the Human Side of Religion* (Berkeley: Univ. of California Press, 2000), 261.

21. The preceding discussion is based on the author's own observations and participation in worship at All Saints' Church. See also photographs and text at the parish Web site, http://www.allsaintspawleys.org/.

22. For an overview of this phenomenon, see Don S. Armentrout, "Episcopal Splinter Groups: Schisms in the Episcopal Church, 1963–1985," *Anglican and Episcopal History* 55 (1986), 295–320. The first major "schism" in the Episcopal Church occurred with the formation of the Reformed Episcopal Church in 1873; see Allen C. Guelzo, *For the Union of Evangelical Christendom: The Irony of the Reformed Episcopalians* (Univ. Park: Pennsylvania State Univ. Press, 1994).

23. Concerned Clergy and Laity of the Episcopal Church, "Online Publications: The First Promise" (Sept. 1997), http://www.episcopalian.org/cclec/paper-promise.htm.

24. The Anglican Communion is a worldwide fellowship of churches that share a common historical and liturgical heritage with the Church of England.

25. Dave Munday, "Pawleys Island Pastor Shakes up Anglican Communion," *Charleston Post and Courier,* Feb. 1, 2000, http://www.charleston.net/.

26. Jan Nunley, "Murphy and Rodgers Launch Traditionalist Anglican Mission in America," *Episcopal News Service,* 2000-117 (Aug. 22, 2000), http://ecusa.anglican.org/ens; Jan Nunley, "First Promise Founding Parish Challenges Diocese for Property," *Episcopal News Service,* 2000-168 (Oct. 23, 2000), http://ecusa.anglican.org/ens; and Nunley, "Frustration over Thwarted Mission."

27. These figures represent about one-half of 1 percent of the total membership of the Episcopal Church, which contained 7,368 parishes and approximately 2.3 million baptized members in 1999. *The Episcopal Church Annual: 2001* (Harrisburg, PA: Morehouse, 2001), 13.

28. Schuyler Totman, "AMiA Consecrates Four More Bishops," *The Living Church,* July 15, 2001, 6–7; Marek P. Zabriskie, "Viewpoint: Breaking Away," *The Living Church,* Nov. 26, 2000, 17; Dave Munday, "Dissident Bishop Cautions Churches to Reform or Perish," *Charleston Post and Courier,* Jan. 19, 2001, http://www.charleston.net; Dave Munday, "Would-Be Reformers Fighting for New Anglicanism," *Charleston Post and Courier,* Jan. 21, 2001, http://www.charleston.net; and Gustav Niebuhr, "Religion Journal: Episcopal Dissidents Look to Expand," *New York Times,* June 16, 2001.

29. "Editorials: Consecrations Harmful to Unity," *The Living Church,* July 15, 2001, 14; Jan Nunley, "Barna Group Reports Drop in Number of Mainline

Evangelicals," *Episcopal News Service*, 2001-178 (July 6, 2001), http://ecusa.anglican.org/ens; and Robert W. Prichard, *A History of the Episcopal Church* (Harrisburg, PA: Morehouse, 1991), 266–67, 277–78.

30. Anglican Mission in America, "Solemn Declaration of Principles" (Nov. 1999), art. II, sec. 1–2; available online at AMiA Web site, http://www.anglicanmissioninamerica.org/meetamia/archives/constitution.html.

31. Cynthia Lynn Lyerly, *Methodism and the Southern Mind, 1770–1810* (New York: Oxford Univ. Press, 1998), 16–17.

32. Henry F. May, *The Enlightenment in America* (New York: Oxford Univ. Press, 1976), 66–68, 75–76.

33. S. Charles Bolton, *Southern Anglicanism: The Church of England in Colonial South Carolina* (Westport, CT: Greenwood Press, 1982), 20.

34. Christine Leigh Heyrman, *Southern Cross: The Beginnings of the Bible Belt* (New York: Knopf, 1997), 11.

35. Samuel S. Hill, *Southern Churches in Crisis Revisited* (Tuscaloosa: Univ. of Alabama Press, 1999), 12–14; Holmes, *Brief History of the Episcopal Church*, 67.

36. Hill, *Southern Churches in Crisis Revisited*, xxxv–lii. See also George M. Marsden, *Fundamentalism and American Culture: The Shaping of Twentieth Century Evangelicalism, 1870–1925* (New York: Oxford Univ. Press, 1980), 15–18.

37. Philip H. E. Thomas, "Doctrine of the Church," in *The Study of Anglicanism*, ed. Stephen Sykes and John Booty (Minneapolis: Fortress, 1988), 224–25.

38. Anglican Mission in America, "Solemn Declaration of Principles," art. I, sec. 1–2.

39. Marsden, *Fundamentalism and American Culture*, 60–62, 110–14 (quotation on 113).

40. Stephanie E. Yuhl, "Rich and Tender Remembering: Elite White Women and an Aesthetic Sense of Place in Charleston, 1920s and 1930s," in *Where These Memories Grow: History, Memory, and Southern Identity*, ed. W. Fitzhugh Brundage (Chapel Hill: Univ. of North Carolina Press, 2000), 230, 240–44 (quotation on 243).

41. Ulrich B. Phillips, "The Central Theme of Southern History," *American Historical Review* 34 (1928–29), 31.

42. According to Fred Hobson, however, there may well be links between racism and homophobia in the modern South, for racial integration and homosexuality both constitute threats to established roles in a social order long held sacred by whites; see Hobson, *But Now I See: The White Southern Racial Conversion Narrative* (Baton Rouge: Louisiana State Univ. Press, 1999), 133.

43. For reflections on the historical interaction of black and white Charlestonians, see Kendra Hamilton, "Goat Cart Sam a.k.a. Porgy, an Icon of a Sanitized South," *Southern Cultures* 5, no. 3 (Fall 1999): 32, 37–39.

44. Edward Ball, *Slaves in the Family* (New York: Farrar, Straus, and Giroux, 1998), 7–21, 356 (quotations on 7, 13).

45. Anglican Mission in America Web site, "The Anglican Mission Story" [2001], http://www.anglicanmissioninamerica.org/.

46. For historical background on the relationship of African Americans to the Episcopal Church, see Harold T. Lewis, *Yet With a Steady Beat: The African American Struggle for Recognition in the Episcopal Church* (Valley Forge, PA: Trinity Press International, 1996).

47. For discussion of the "market economy" model of church growth and decline, see Roger Finke and Rodney Stark, *The Churching of America, 1776–1990: Winners and Losers in Our Religious Economy* (New Brunswick, NJ: Rutgers Univ. Press, 1992), 1–2, 54–59, 71–72.

D. Jonathan Grieser,
Corrie Norman, and
Don S. Armentrout

CHAPTER 13

Quiet Revolutionaries: Stories of Women Priests in the South

IN TWO FASCINATING NOVELS, BEST-SELLING AUTHOR GAIL GODWIN TELLS the story of the Reverend Margaret Bonner. In the first, *Father Melancholy's Daughter,* Margaret deals with the trauma of her mother's departure from home when she was six. Her mother would die the next year in a car accident. She is then raised by her father, a middle-aged Anglo-Catholic priest and rector of a Virginia parish. As the only daughter of a widowed rector, she is both doted on by the people of her father's parish and expected, in the course of time, to grow into the role of "rector's wife": hosting parishioners, serving on the altar guild, and the like. Margaret goes off to college but returns home for Holy Week in her senior year when she first encounters another priest, Adrian Bonner, a former Roman Catholic who has become a close friend of her father. On Good Friday, her father has a fatal stroke. The novel ends with her hoping to develop a relationship with Adrian and sending off for application materials from seminaries. In the second novel, *Evensong,* Adrian and Margaret are married, and Margaret is the rector of a parish in the mountains of Western North Carolina, where the couple had moved earlier so that Adrian could become chaplain at a private high school for troubled youth.[1]

Godwin, then, in some eight hundred pages of text, glides over some of the most emotionally drenching periods of any priest's life, but particularly of female clergy. There is no discussion of the nature of Margaret's call, of any conflict over women's ordination. What might her father have really thought of her decision to enter the priesthood? After all, he continued to use Rite I of the Eucharist after the revision of the *Book of Common Prayer* in 1979. Her husband, too, a former Catholic, even a former monk, accepted her call easily. In the parish, the Reverend Bonner encounters the expected mix of support and diffidence but often attributes the relative ease with which she was accepted by her flock to the fact that her immediate predecessor was convicted of sexual assault on minors.

Godwin's female priest conforms to the model of female priesthood described by Suzanne Radley Hiatt. In her study of women's ordination, Hiatt found a profound contrast in the Anglican communion at large and, in the Episcopal Church, between the characterization of feminist agitators for women's ordination prior to 1976 and those who were ultimately accepted as priests. The first ordinations of women to the priesthood in the Episcopal Church occurred in 1974. They were deemed "irregular" by the church because they took place before changes were made to the constitutions and canons of the Episcopal Church that sanctioned women's ordination. The General Convention of 1976 accepted the ordination of women, paving the way for the first "regular" ordinations in 1977.[2] The status of the "Philadelphia Eleven" and the four other women who were ordained before 1976 remained unclear. In the end they were publicly and ritualistically forced to state their obedience to their bishops, thereby making their ordinations "regular." The women who were ordained in 1977 were lauded for their "patience and devotion to the church."[3] The story of women's struggle for acceptance by the institutional church, however, did not end there. Yet Margaret Bonner's "patience and devotion" seems to have been rewarded with an uneventful ordination process.

Instead of difficulties with institution, bishops, and other clergy who question her call and her ministry, Godwin's female rector struggles with personal and pastoral issues: her relationship with a much older, often distant husband and a miscarriage, religious crackpots on the eve of the millennium, and the rhythms of life in a parish and community. In this respect, Margaret Bonner's fictional experience as a female priest in the South may not be all that different from the experiences of the priests we surveyed. As will become clear in this essay, the women priests in the South have found rewarding and spiritually fulfilling vocations in a variety of ministries. When telling the stories of their priesthood, they tend to focus on the personal and relational aspects of ministry as "real" people to real people.

But real life is more complicated than fiction. Almost all of our respondents have experienced sexism and have named it as such, locating it primarily in the institutional church. Most have pursued a strategy of personal patience and devotion to make their way in the world and in the church. With few obvious role models set before them, they have reached for models of ministry shaped by personal relationships, incarnational spirituality, and southernness. Absent from their stories is a link to the dramatic history of the first women who fought for ordination. Although one of the Philadelphia Eleven, Carter Heyward, was a southerner, and many of the important strategy sessions took place at Virginia Theological Seminary, that early history seems foreign to these southern priests who overwhelmingly agree that the South is "different."[4]

The Statistics

We have established that, in general, ordination of women in the South does not vary significantly from that in other regions of the Episcopal Church. However, closer analysis reveals more startling information. Women were ordained in twenty-six dioceses (out of ninety-three) in the first month that "regular" ordination was possible, January 1977. Of those twenty-six, only three were southern: Virginia, Arkansas, and Alabama. Other dioceses on the "edges" of the South were Rio Grande, West Virginia, and Missouri. By the end of 1977, a total of forty-one dioceses had seen ordinations of women. Of the expanded group, an additional six were southern: East Carolina, Atlanta, Central Gulf Coast, Kentucky, Louisiana, and Southwestern Virginia. On the other hand, of the nine dioceses that finally ordained their first female priests in the 1990s, only two were in the South: Southwest Florida and Georgia. None of the three dioceses that still refuse to ordain women is a southern diocese. We conclude that while southern dioceses may have been initially more reluctant or slower to ordain women than dioceses elsewhere, as a group they did not drag their feet once they had begun.[5]

Another way of looking at the priesthood of women is by attempting to determine how many female priests serve southern dioceses. We draw the following conclusions by examining the data accumulated by Louie Crew. Of the twenty-five dioceses with the most canonically resident female priests, only one southern diocese, Atlanta, appears. Of the twenty-five with the lowest percentage of female clergy (excluding those with none), nine are from Province 4, which comprises much of the Southeastern United States: Southeast Florida, East Tennessee, Alabama, Central Gulf Coast, Southwest Florida, Georgia, Central Florida, Louisiana, and South Carolina. Four more are in former states of the Confederacy (Texas, West Texas, Dallas, and Western Louisiana).[6] These figures support a common perception described by the priests who responded to our survey: the grim sense of isolation from other female clergy.

Statistics alone cannot tell the story any better than novels can. We were interested in getting behind the numbers and fictional accounts to begin to understand the real lives these southern women priests live and how they make sense of them. In our survey we sought to bring out their voices and to allow them space to tell stories about their calls to the priesthood and ordination process, their lives as priests, and their spiritual journeys.[7] We were also interested in their family lives, what they are like as daughters, as mothers, as spouses and life partners. Running as a constant theme throughout the questions we asked, and the stories they told, is a factor that is virtually ignored in Margaret Bonner's story: the South as a context for women's lives and ministries.[8]

Hearing the Call

For many of the women surveyed, the struggle with their role in the church began at an early stage. In describing their call, these priests fall into two large groups, roughly equal in size. Half tend to place their call back into their youth or childhood. One says, "I have never not felt called." She grew up Roman Catholic and followed that call to the convent. She left sadly after a year in vows. Later, after converting with her family to the Episcopal Church, the call to ordination became clear. Other respondents tell of "playing church" as children. One of them recalls taking a vocational test in the eighth grade and being told that she should either become a minister or a cruise director. Another remarks, looking back on her childhood in the days before ordination for women was possible, "I knew I would become a priest if only I were male." Still another reminisces, "My first call came at a very early age—about eight. I just knew this was what I was to be; but I did not know the church would not allow it until many years later."

One priest was recently told by her kindergarten teacher—now in her eighties—that she knew that she would be a priest from a picture she drew in kindergarten. In her case she had not recognized the call herself. When, in her late thirties, she did and confided in her best friend, her friend said, "But you've always wanted to be a priest." She adds, "But I had never even seen a woman priest." For many women, the opening up of ordination to them was a powerful confirmation of a call that had come long before and they often look back with some sadness, saying something like, "I had to wait for the church."

Rarely is the influence of women priests acknowledged in the recognition of call. For a few women who were active in the church in the 1970s, the sudden presence of female clergy was a beacon showing the way to their own ordination. One describes getting to know a woman seminarian in the years just after the Philadelphia ordinations and recognizing that "that was what I was supposed to do." When she told her father, a priest, of this, he replied,

"Well, I was wondering when you would figure that out!" Another describes her experience of "running into brick walls" until the conference on women's ministries that she attended around 1978 paved the way for her ordination.

The other half describe their call as more gradual, often the product of years of searching and in many cases growing out of lay ministry in the church. Somewhat typical is the following story. Confirmed as an adult, this future priest became an active layperson in her parish and was eventually hired as a full-time staff member. A year of seminary in a program for laypeople followed. That year made clear to her that ordination was the next step on her journey. Similar paths are interpreted in different ways. For some, that long period of searching and lay ministry might seem to be an attempt to live out a call to the priesthood in a context where that call was not possible. But many of these women understand their lives differently. It was through such activity, often beginning as enthusiastic volunteers in the parish and developing into paid staff, that they came to recognize their call to ordination.

There are a lot of "in the meantime" stories. While several wish that they had responded to the call to priesthood earlier, most see life prior to priesthood as part of a journey, not a straight path but part of a life that was rich in itself and that also helped to prepare them for ministry. One woman, who spent several years as a church educator, describes her call as "a coal burning for a long time." She felt it first at age twelve; she was ordained at age forty. Another woman experienced a call in childhood "that never left in forty-plus years"; she felt it first at age eight. But she looks back on the "wonderful" jobs she did while "waiting" for the priesthood.

For many women the process was not a smooth journey. One woman describes her call to ministry at age fourteen in a small rural southern church. When her Sunday School teacher told her that she could not be a priest, she left the church, only to return after the birth of her first child. What enabled her return to the church was a vivid experience of the change it had undergone. A friend invited her to a service at which she witnessed a pregnant priest celebrate. Many women tried to live out their call in more traditional roles for laywomen—as volunteer or semiprofessional church workers in education. Some became chaplains and some thought the vocational diaconate would satisfy them.[9]

Another priest writes of a moment in midlife when her call became clear. She had been struggling with what she "wanted to do with her life" for three years. Praying, discerning, she had spent a year in spiritual direction. All she knew was that she needed to make a change. As she was driving to a diocesan meeting one day, reflecting on her situation, she heard a voice ask her a question, the same question her spiritual director had been asking: "If nothing stood in your way—time money, family, ability, etc.—what would you want to do?" Her answer was clear: "I would be a priest; I would go to seminary." But she immediately found herself retracting that response. Then the voice asked, "If you were a man, how would you answer this question?" "Of course," she suddenly realized, "I would have been a priest twenty years ago." In making sense of this experience, the priest now comments, "I needed this bonk on the head to get my attention." What her story reveals is the complex interplay of factors involved in hearing a call. While the institutional church may have been and, in some cases continues to be, reluctant to ordain women, in cases like this one the possibility of ordination is restricted by personal reasons and gender assumptions. Call may come in different ways to different people. But no matter how strong or clear, it seems that for most of the women whose stories we have heard, gender plays a significant role, even when they are reluctant to admit it to themselves.

Wives, Singles, Mothers, Daughters

For most of our respondents, the importance of family and community in clarifying and affirming their call is paramount. One says, "My call came from the people around me, especially my husband and children, who saw in me something that I had not yet given myself permission to see." Another describes hers as "a confusing mix of God and community pushing and pulling me into something that at once was thrilling and terrifying." She goes on to say that she had come to question the whole idea of call in the contemporary world and that she could not imagine herself, "a mild-mannered Southern mom," having anything to say from the pulpit. She wryly adds that at the time she was thinking this, she did not consider the fact that she had sat through many sermons preached by men who "had nothing to say."

For the most part, these priests talk about supportive families. We hear of parents who, if not from the beginning, were proud and supportive by the time of their daughter's ordination. This is true as well for many women who grew up in families outside the Episcopal Church. Several comment that their families might not "really understand" what they are doing, but they voice support and a bemused pride. Many say they have become the "family priest" even for their non-Episcopalian families. Stories of the "moments" they first recognized familial support abound. One priest, who had grown up Roman Catholic, found the most moving part of her ordination to have come when her elderly mother, a devout Catholic, made her a complete set of vestments for the occasion, just as she might have done for a son entering the Roman Catholic priesthood.

Most of the priests who responded to the survey are married, and most of the married ones have remained married to the same man for a number of years. While a few priests tell stories of broken marriages and abandonment during the ordination process (one on her ordination day), most describe their marriages as remarkably strong and without significant career tensions. Still, almost all the married women cite "more time with spouse and family" as the thing they would like to change most about their lives. Two proudly note "the work" their professional husbands have accomplished in coming to terms with "their" careers.

Most of the spouses are Episcopalian, but several continue to practice their own faiths, especially the Roman Catholics. None of the women speak of marital tension because of this, although some worry about children who go with the faith of one or the other parent and fit into neither community. Priests usually comment in these cases on their husbands' "commitment" to their own communities as well as to support of their ministries. The ordination process and seminary were tough going for some couples, and some husbands still have trouble dealing with their wives' professional standing. One doctor still bristles when he is addressed by a parishioner as "Mr. Jones," instead of as "Dr. Smith" (his priest wife kept her maiden name). For the most part, however, husbands are supportive and handle being married to priests well. One woman tells of how funny her husband finds it when people assume he is the priest in the family. Another mentions the response her husband gave to members of a parish search committee who asked about his responsibilities as a priest's spouse. When he said, "I sleep with the rector," the committee's uneasy silence was followed by hearty laughs all around.

While professional couples deal with impossible schedules and career issues, churches seem mostly accepting of these difficulties. However, one priest with a stay-at-home spouse says that this was a problem in her job search: "People did not know what to do with my house husband." Several of the women note that their spouses' associates have more trouble "knowing what to do with me" than parishioners have with the husbands. One, whose husband works in the entertainment industry, has seen her husband's friends overcome their initial shock when told she was a priest. Others try to fulfill the expectations of a southern wife in the professional classes, but social engagements and dinner parties are often preempted by pastoral emergencies.

Four of the women who responded are married to priests. In two cases, the couples serve together. They remark on the "busy-ness" and the occasional tension of living with the men with whom they work. There is also some frustration with the gendered expectations of parishioners about their roles. Still, these women are largely satisfied now that both spouses have positions. The women whose spouses serve in different calls express the difficulties of coordinating work schedules, the rarity of worshipping together, and some problems for children, but they too seem very satisfied, by and large.

Single, widowed, and divorced women tended to underline the isolation and loneliness of being a single woman priest. The loneliness is almost palpable in some stories. Isolated from family and familiar contexts, serving in troubled parishes for meager pay, many women have little support. Some just long for women friends or to be closer to family. Some want more congenial environments, bigger places. Some do not wish to marry or remarry, but others are frustrated by the difficulty of being a "single-and-looking" woman and a priest. One comments, "I've noticed that parishioners like to play matchmaker for single men more than for single women." One woman tells how, when she took a job in a cathedral, she heard from her superior about a previous priest who lost his position there. The message, though indirect, was clear: "There would be no strange cars parked overnight outside my house." Others sense that being single is a handicap when looking for positions. One remarks, "I'm tired of losing calls to the young guys with cute kids."

There are surprises among these stories. A priest in an interracial marriage with a man of another faith emphasizes the support they both have received in the medium-size southern town where they live. A lesbian couple, two priests serving different calls, find support in their small community, although they live a "quiet" life fully aware of the dangers. But another lesbian reports her decision to remain "closeted" and the loneliness she feels as she tries to live out her call. We were contacted by two lesbian clergy who wanted us to know about them but who were afraid to tell their stories, even anonymously, for fear of negative repercussions if their sexual orientation should be discovered in their dioceses.

A woman's priesthood seems to be tougher on children than on husbands, as these women tell it. And women's roles as mother and priest interact in complex, paradoxical ways. One priest tells the story of her call as a conflict with her motherhood: "I was putting my two little girls to bed one night, wondering what to do next with my life. The idea 'I could be a priest' came to mind. Quickly the next thought was, 'Why would I want to do that to my children?'" One woman reports the smoothness of her process, until she decided to delay while her children finished high school. Her Commission on Ministry interpreted this as "lack of commitment." For many women the adolescence of their children coincided with their recognition of call. Seminary moves are particularly difficult at this point, with families handling them in different ways. In one case a woman went on to seminary while her husband stayed behind to allow their daughter to finish junior high school. One mother notes the spiritual difficulty that seminary brought for her daughter, explain-

D. Jonathan Grieser, Corrie E. Norman, and Don S. Armentrout

ing, "She learned while living in seminary housing that priests aren't saints." One priest glibly notes that her children "recovered well" from the seminary and ordination experience, but a single mother reports proudly that her children describe her seminary degree as "theirs."

Many priests talk about profound interrelations between motherhood and priesthood. The poignant stories of officiating at the funerals of children's friends are stories about being mothers and priests to their children and communities. A few women mention how their children came to ask for "priestly advice" from them, quickly reminding them when "mom" entered in and took over from the "priest." An image of the connection between priesthood and motherhood emerges in one priest's story of the evening of her ordination: "We had all gone out to dinner to celebrate. When we got home, my daughter got sick and was vomiting all night. At one point, I was on the floor cleaning up vomit and thinking, 'I may be a priest, but I'm still a mother.'"

Mothers worry most about the effects of their ordination on their daughters. Some stories center on women postponing their seminary training because of their adolescent daughters. Others describe conflicts with daughters that seem to result from the upheaval of being taken off to seminary or of being the daughter of a female priest. While these stories are often told lightly and chalked up to general adolescent embarrassment at anything "abnormal" parents do, there is also real pain here. As the mother of a twelve-year-old put it, "My daughter is proud of me but often asks, 'Mom, can you wear something without a collar?'" One who is chaplain at her daughter's school also says her daughter likes the days when she does not have to wear her collar. Another recalls her fourteen-year-old daughter's reaction to her priesthood: "It's the most embarrassing thing you've ever done to me." Some see it as a sign of moving from the turmoil of adolescence to acceptance when their daughters' friends ask them to participate in their weddings.

The conflict between motherhood and priesthood comes out again when our respondents were asked about children and the church. The numbers of children who leave the church stand out. Mothers speak with audible relief when they can tell of children who remain in and are active in the church. Few push their adult children. When asked how important it is to them that their adult children be involved in the Episcopal church, they say that it is more important that they find a spiritual home where they are comfortable. This is perhaps not surprising in a "generation of seekers," most of whom found their own ways of being religious apart from family affiliation.[10] They are encouraging their children to make their own choices just as they did. But almost to a one, grandmother priests are concerned about their grandchildren. Some dream of baptizing their grandchildren or worry that their grandchildren are not getting spiritual nourishment in religious community. Several are alarmed, however, that their children have chosen or married into conservative churches with which they see themselves at odds and are raising their grandchildren in them.

Only a few of the priests who responded to our survey were ordained before starting their families and are still at relatively early stages in their ministries. They tell mostly positive stories of pregnancies in parish communities waiting for "our baby" and young children growing up in the church, even of the pastoral presence a precocious three-year-old can have when out visiting the homebound with mom. They also recognize the "uncharted territory" they enter with their parishes and children as new mother-priests, and they encounter frustration as well as pleasure in the attention their children and child-rearing receive from parishioners.

The Ordination Process

The ordination process in the Episcopal Church is governed by a strict set of rules, but within those guidelines there is room for considerable variation among the dioceses of the church. Depending on individual circumstances, the process can be quite lengthy, and for many of the women in our study, it brought with it considerable anguish. At the beginning stages, those seeking ordination work closely with the rector of their parish on discerning their call. In the course of these conversations, the rector will generally convene a "parish discernment committee" consisting of parishioners who listen to the individual's story and help her clarify her call. At some point, rector and aspirant will approach the bishop, and then the aspirant follows a battery of medical, psychological, and psychiatric tests. The final decision to accept an individual's candidacy usually rests in conversations among the bishop, the individual, and the diocesan Commission on Ministry, a group consisting of laypersons and priests who examine the candidate's application and meet with her personally. Episcopal Church canons state that, once accepted as a candidate for holy orders, the individual must remain a candidate for at least six months, although generally it is the case that it is only now that a candidate begins three year of seminary training. During seminary, the candidate's fitness for ordination continues to be monitored by her diocese. Upon the individual's graduation, the bishop will usually place the ordinand in a pastoral setting, and she will be ordained a deacon. Again, regulations stipulate that she must remain a deacon for at least six months, at which point the bishop may ordain her to the priesthood. In the Episcopal Church, the bishop is active in placement of clergy only at the very beginning stages of their ministries or to positions on diocesan staffs or to mission churches.

D. Jonathan Grieser, Corrie E. Norman, and Don S. Armentrout

For women, all of these stages are fraught with peril. A tiny number describe the ordination process as having progressed smoothly. One even calls hers "a Cinderella story." But most of our respondents offered horror stories for every step. Stories are similar across generations. A few priests ordained in the 1980s observe that although things are easier now, difficulties persist. To generalize, young, well-educated women seem to have had a slightly easier time of it and still do. But if they have an easier time with the hierarchy in the ordination process and an easier time in seminary (most likely because of their comfort with academia), they cite the resentment and patronizing attitudes they face from male clergy, the institution, and their parishioners once deployed. One young woman wonders how long she will be "the little assistant" whose leadership is easily dismissed. She knows that getting to a rectorate and carrying forth that role will be difficult. Many women say that while they faced opposition from male clergy or parishioners early on, they now feel accepted. Their sense is that this is a personal, rather than an institutional, cross to bear. Moreover, most have little contact with other women clergy, let alone with women priests. And few have enjoyed the benefit of women role models in their experience of priesthood.

Being "smart" may be a jump start in the process, but as a former college professor observes, "Weak males are threatened by smart women whether they are priests or not." On the other hand, the "dumb woman" stereotype still plays against women as well. This shows up especially in stories from seminary and in experiences with Commissions on Ministry and during general ordination exams. Some second-career women who have been outside academia or who do not have advanced degrees perceive that they have had to endure expectations of intellectual incompetence and close scrutiny on examinations. And one wonders whether such scrutiny is as intense for second-career males as it is for middle-aged women. It is a struggle to maintain a sense of competence for many women. One recalls, "I remember one day in beginning Greek class the professor opened the class with a prayer about how our humiliations would help us grow. I began to cry because I felt very humiliated. That was a day when I realized I had submerged [myself] too deeply into this place."

While seminary experiences are often categorized as "challenging," seminaries and supportive seminary faculty come off much better than other church institutions in these stories.[11] One priest comments, "I loved every bit of it. . . . I treat it as a gift from God to be handled with great care and affection." Other respondents describe seminary as a time of great intellectual stimulation and spiritual growth. This is true even for some women who thought themselves ill prepared or were overwhelmed by the challenges. Others are less positive and viewed seminary, like much of the ordination process, as a lengthy hazing. Dominant themes, as women reflect on those years, are trial and sacrifice. As one woman puts it, "As I look back the trial by fire of seminary prepared me. I was headed back to a southern place that expected women to know their place. I finally decided I would no longer live afraid of the place or the consequences of speaking out." For those southern women who attended seminary in the North, the assumptions their classmates and teachers made about them as "southern women" brought additional difficulties. One recalls that another student commented on her southern accent by telling her, "You're much smarter than you sound."

Overwhelmingly, the greatest complaint was about the effects of seminary on family. The logistics of combining seminary with family responsibilities were daunting. A few spouses accompanied their wives to school, abandoning or putting their own careers on hold, or in a very rare instance, receiving a transfer from his employer. Several priests recall the pain of living alone in a dorm room, separated by hundreds of miles from spouse or family; but one remarks on the positive "novelty" of her husband's weekly trips to visit.

Family concerns seem to weigh more heavily on women than on men in Commission on Ministries decisions. One woman recalls being discouraged from pursuing ordination when she was in her thirties with two young children, because it would be "too disruptive" to her family. Her bishop told her to wait "until I was fifty-five" and could take a year in seminary. Soon after that encounter, a male friend of hers in the same diocese who had two young children announced that he was going to seminary. What was seen as an impediment for her was ignored in his case. But that was just the first of the roadblocks placed in front of her. A plan to become a perpetual deacon (i.e., to be ordained and serve out one's ministry as a deacon) was thwarted when the bishop cancelled the program the week before she was going to begin her studies. In the end, she finally went to seminary but was told by her bishop in her senior year that there had never been any plans to place her in a parish. She has been able to serve as a priest under a successor bishop.

The stories of the journey to priesthood are by no means all bad, but the horror stories, some of quite recent vintage, are shocking. Several priests underline the strong support offered by bishops, rectors, and lay people as they made their way through the obstacle course set by the church. One says that although the ordination process "was long, intense, and many found it painful, I did not. . . . [It] afforded me time and space to really get to know myself and to discern the gifts I could offer the church." But almost all of the women recall moments when opposition to their candidacy surfaced.

D. Jonathan Grieser, Corrie E. Norman, and Don S. Armentrout

Priesthood

Many of our respondents are thwarted in their goal of attaining stable, rewarding employment in vibrant religious communities. Obstacles come both from bishops who are reluctant to place female clergy and from parish search committees whose image of a rector is of a young or middle-aged male with a beautiful family. One woman says that every Sunday, as she travels to an interim position in another state and diocese, she passes a mission church that lacks a priest. "It would never occur to the bishop to recommend me for that position," she observes. Many note with frustration the "stained-glass ceiling" women experience. Others perceive that women are "tracked" into "marginally viable and terminally troubled" parishes or missions—set up to fail, in other words.[12] Several mention that salaries in small, struggling parishes are hardly "living." And these same women most often have no other resources on which to rely. Having left careers and not having spouses to provide financial support, they used all their resources to become priests. With retirement approaching, they have little to fall back on but their faith and the support of the laity they serve.

One woman who serves a conservative parish in tandem with her husband says that she occasionally feels like "a glorified Director of Religious Education." This feeling is linked to what her parishioners call her. While parishioners address her husband as "Father," she is called "Honey," although the couple is trying to educate the parish to address them both as "the Reverend." Opposition to her ministry is coupled with a vocal minority's opposition to all change in the church, including the revision of the Book of Common Prayer.

The issue of title comes up repeatedly in these stories, even in congenial parish situations. One priest wishes that "Lady Priest and other unfortunate phrases" were a thing of the past. Some accept "Mother," while others explicitly reject this alternative and prefer to be called by their first names. But this, too, they recognize, is a problem for parishioners who are raising their children "to be polite southerners" by addressing adults with titles. One priest has found an old "southern-ism" acceptable in her context: the children address her as "Miss Anne." These women are well aware that titles are about roles. How one chooses to be (or is) addressed establishes ground rules for how one is going to be perceived in the parish. For those priests who are uncomfortable with the patriarchal connotations of "Father" and are conscious about their relational ministry, how they choose to be addressed sends an important signal about who they will be as priests.

Many identify with pride and satisfaction their successes with female parishioners and staff. One priest finds particular delight in being able to boost the confidence of a female staff person. Another, who had been an administrative assistant earlier in life, has started a retreat program for church staff members in her diocese. A third specifically mentions her joy at seeing a woman in a difficult marriage develop self-esteem and begin to take on leadership in the church.

Being role models for and spending time with young women and girls are often mentioned as important aspects of their role. One priest in a conservative parish saw it as a breakthrough when a young girl presented herself for service as an acolyte—the first in the parish. Another notes with amusement and pride that high school girls often asked to be brought to her office when they feel "sick" at school: "They curl up in a quilt on my couch and talk a lot. They know that they are valued and that I keep confidences. They know that they are safe." Another priest has become known beyond her parish as an effective counselor for troubled teenage girls in her community.

"Feminism" is seldom used to describe these ministries. Only one priest named it when talking about her vocation: "I have always done my ministry from a feminist perspective." With two laywomen in their sixties she began a feminist reflection group in her parish that subsequently has grown into a full-fledged diocesan-wide program and a full-time call for her. Some women identify their mission with a broader mission of liberation, usually mentioning race and class as well as gender. Only one describes her main role as "prophetic." Without calling it "feminism," however, a majority of them describe an important part of their ministry as empowering women of all ages to become more active in the parish, to take on new roles and new ministries, and to explore new forms of spirituality. It is also clear that while isolated from other women priests, the fellowship with and support of the women around them is especially desired and treasured by our respondents.

Many priests cite relationships with elderly parishioners—both men and women—as their most profound experiences in ministry. One young priest says she "identifies more" with the older adults of her parish than with the "affluent yuppies" her own age. The blessing of older laywomen is particularly important. Another respondent says that one of her parishioners, an elderly woman who described her own sister's desire to become a priest in the early twentieth century, was especially supportive of her ministry, seeing in it the realization of a long-deceased sibling's dream. Still another priest tells the story of an elderly black woman's embrace after a service at which she had celebrated the Eucharist and a visiting African bishop had preached. Hugging her, the woman exclaimed, "I am so glad I have lived to see a woman at the altar and a black bishop in the pulpit of my home church!"

Several priests describe how older women signaled the breakthrough in their parishes for their acceptance, which is discussed as a personal and social hurdle. One priest relates how an elderly woman's expression of care was the watershed for her at a critical time in her early ministry in a parish. When the air conditioning broke in the rectory and a vestry meeting seemed to be going nowhere in the discussion of what to do, an elderly vestry woman took her aside and told her to relax, get up, and get a cup of coffee. Her assurance that "we will take care of you" cemented the style of partnership ministry that the priest would develop with her parish.

It is clear that the longing for mature female acceptance and wisdom, even when women come from vastly different circumstances, is very important for the priests who responded to our survey. The maternal nature of these relationships is clear in many stories. Facing death with older women is cited as among the most profound spiritual experiences these priests have. It epitomizes a common idea of ministry in these stories: a shared relationship between "real" people whose presence for each other is spiritually beneficial for both. Many describe the experience of going through death with elderly women as a time of great growth for themselves, when the role of priest as caretaker blends with that of grown daughter caring for mother. As some put it, being a priest is as "natural" as a mother-daughter relationship.

There is a great deal of conflict around female roles, however. Many priests discuss this specifically in terms of southern expectations about women. Several acknowledge an advantage to being southern as "knowing how to be polite" or knowing "how to play the game." Some embrace this. One middle-aged priest confesses that flirting with the men and dressing smartly eases her way as a liberal woman in a wealthy and conservative parish. Others give it a reluctant hug: "I am of a mind that quiet, consistent presence moves us toward acceptance and inclusion." This comes from a priest whose difficulties with ordination and placement she could clearly identify as sexist. Another priest asserts that "patient faithfulness helps folks to see individuals and not issues," even as she acknowledges the profound issues facing women's ministry in the church. So many vacillate between a traditional model of women's quiet patience and individual acceptance (through individual perseverance) and an understanding on another level that the problems are systemic and need to be addressed directly.

The word often used to describe this personal strategy is also more broadly applied to a general attitude about ministry and spirituality: "incarnational." The experience of a flesh-and-blood "real woman" priest, goes the idea, will much more easily overcome fears. Some women describe this as "being regular." One says her call came when she realized the need for "middle-aged mother, regular sort of women to be clergy." Another emphasizes how her parishioners often tell her that she is a "real person" in contrast to the male clergy in the parish. Such strategies and ways of being present may go a long way toward overcoming opposition to women's ordination in parishes. They will also have a significant impact on the overall status and role of women priests and may affect priests as they try to balance the personal and the political.

Even those who wholeheartedly embrace another model of woman and who strongly identify with feminism, have to walk a tightrope between two ways of being. One priest, a native southerner who spent the first half of her career in the Northeast, discusses this. She struggles to find a balance between preaching with a strong voice and not alienating her congregation. She sees herself as a bridge builder and describes this as a very "southern" way of being. Inherent in her southernness are both critical and appreciative relationships to the culture. She has identified resources within southern culture that make change possible. For example, she talks about its multiracial culture offering opportunities for reconciliation.

Along with speaking of their priesthood as "incarnational" and "relational," most women emphasize two aspects of their work that relate in complex ways to gender roles. Overwhelmingly, they cite pastoral care and eucharistic service as key elements of their work and the two that bring them the most satisfaction. Acceptance as pastoral caregivers appears to come rather easily to most of our respondents. Some priests make explicit links between this and gender roles such as "mothering." Pastoral care is done privately, in intimate contexts, one-on-one or with small groups. This may be a more comfortable way to encounter a woman in a new role as pastor. One of our respondents mentions her concern about how little pastoral counseling she had done since moving to a new parish in a small town in the Carolinas. She interprets that as a gauge of how much her parishioners still perceive her as an outsider. Would a male priest interpret a lack of interest in counseling that way?

Healing is another word used frequently for pastoral ministry in these stories. Several women devote much of their time to visiting the ill and infirm. One mission rector remarks, "I've been in more homes of elderly and sick people in the last five years than the former priest (a man) had in fifteen." The emphasis on this kind of ministry relates directly to something else already mentioned: being a "regular person." A priest in a large conservative parish describes the "stealth counseling" she does with parishioners who are uncomfortable about taking their theological issues to her conservative and authoritative male colleagues. It may be a coincidence, but most of the pastoral care stories told by our survey participants are about other women. Indeed, one somewhat embarrassingly admits that she and her male colleague divide pastoral duties along gender lines: she takes the pregnant mothers and breast cancer victims, while he takes those with prostate problems.

Celebrating the Eucharist, or "feeding," also carries female connotations. But few of our respondents make that connection explicitly when they discuss its importance for them. They do link it with pastoral care and many of the stories they chose to tell about their ministries involve giving communion to the sick and dying. But the Eucharist is primarily a public communal event and a direct image of the hierarchy. When consecrating the elements of the Eucharist, the priest is clearly a representative of the institutional church, no matter how ambivalent her own relationship with it is. While one of the aspects of sacramental ministry that women underline is a feeling of "affirmation" they receive as they celebrate, they tend to talk about that affirmation primarily in terms of the "people" and God rather than the institutional church.

Strategizing and balancing roles once in parishes seem easy compared to the struggle to get in the door that many women report. Yet once in the parish, women priests are still likely to encounter considerable opposition and alienation. Most of them are isolated from other Episcopal clergy and especially from other women priests. A few have close relationships with female colleagues—meeting regularly for lunch or, for the very fortunate few, working with other female clergy on a daily basis. One notes the anxiety about "women in numbers getting along" revealed in how often she was asked by parishioners how she felt when her parish was about to get a second female priest.

Women speak of discouraging hurdles on the diocesan level. For every male priest who welcomes and supports them, there seems to be one who is vocally opposed. Perhaps such vocal opposition is passing, some say optimistically, but still the memories linger. One priest witnessed clergy leaving when she celebrated Eucharist at clergy conferences. Another says that fifteen years ago she was often the only woman in diocesan meetings and often sensed unease among her colleagues but that such experiences are no longer the case. But problems do persist. A younger priest recognizes that she remains a "token," given heavy diocesan responsibilities on committees because of her gender. She continues, however, that as a thirty-three-year old, she is much rarer for her youth than for her gender.

Outside the Episcopal Church, there is both acceptance and rejection. One priest serves as president of her community's ministerial association. Another recalls her first attendance at such a meeting with her priest husband. She arrived late, decided to take the chair next to the presider, who turned to her and asked (even though she was wearing a collar), "Can I help you?" Two male Episcopal priests, one of them her husband, quickly jumped in: "Don't worry, she's one of us." Several express the mutual disapproval between them and the dominant evangelical religious culture of the South and, especially, its leaders. Apparent breakthroughs can backfire. One priest's experience of participating in an ecumenical group exemplifies this. They had several ecumenical services throughout the year, and she was asked to preach at one to be held at the First Baptist Church. The senior pastor of First Baptist did not attend the service, and soon after that service he withdrew from the group, taking all of the other Baptist clergy with him.

Spirituality and Formation

When asked to list role models and spiritual influences, several cited spiritual "giants" both within and outside the Christian tradition. Apart from a few mentions of Matthew Fox, these women say very little about anything that might be regarded as other than traditional spirituality. Most often, respondents cite the usual mix of family members, priests, college professors, and spiritual directors. Here again, gender plays an important role. While men, especially fathers, are most often named as "professional" models (even by the few women whose mothers had been professionals), spiritual models are overwhelmingly female relatives: mothers, aunts, and grandmothers.

The "professional" male and the "spiritual" female models may have profound affects on how our respondents come to understand their priesthood. When they discuss what professional models taught them, they mention lessons that have been beneficial in dealing with the institutional church: self-confidence, political savvy, courage. Several are self-professed "daddy's girls" who felt encouraged by fathers from an early age. While that no doubt contributes to their disappointment when they encounter unsupportive males, it also seems to indicate that they are "at home" cultivating male allies and mentors. Several have found "fathers in the church," usually a supportive bishop or rector, essential. The difference between success and failure in the ordination process or in getting on in the church is often told with the heroic intervention of one man as a key factor.

Only a few mention female priests who showed them the way to their own vocations. Two mention "firsts": Peggy Bosmeyer-Campbell, the first woman ordained in the Diocese of Arkansas, and Alice Babin, the first in the Diocese of Chicago. But there is a gaping silence about heroines who paved the way before them. (Some of our respondents were indeed among the earliest "regular" female ordinands.) This extends back into the Christian tradition as a whole. Julian of Norwich is the only female role model named from the broader tradition. One mentions in passing that a great-grandmother had been an independent Baptist preacher and others mention relatives who were nuns. The inspiration and history of women's spirituality and ministry are primarily individual and relational for our respondents.

There are some striking similarities in the ways these women talk about their spirituality. A dominant theme is the importance of prayer and of the monastic tradition. Many of them are affiliated with Benedictine monasteries

D. Jonathan Grieser, Corrie E. Norman, and Don S. Armentrout

or convents. While this provides them with a reservoir from which to draw in their pastoral work, often it also estranges them to some degree from their parishioners. One priest comments, "I am interested in prayer, my congregation is interested in potlucks." Often it is that spirituality that brought them to the Episcopal Church in the first place.

Our survey pool contained a significant number of former Catholics, and they tend to find in the Episcopal church familiar liturgy and spirituality freed from "the guilt" of their childhoods. But they often still identify themselves as "catholic" in the generic sense—catholic spiritually and liturgically. They describe their painful alienation from the Roman Catholic Church and finding a spiritual home in the Anglican tradition. Institutions of the Catholic Church continue to nourish the spiritual lives of many of these priests (former Catholics and not). One remembers with great fondness and appreciation the help and hospitality she received while taking General Ordination Exams. She wrote them at a Jesuit house, and the members of the order fed her, gave her a place to sleep, and helped her through the ordeal. As female priests they occasionally come into contact with Roman Catholic priests, monks, and nuns; and many cite the acceptance they have received. One recalls celebrating a funeral at which a Roman Catholic priest was present. Afterwards, he came up to her to praise her for her pastoral presence. Another recalls sharing an elevator in a hospital with a nun, who told her, "You're doing this for us all."

Another determinant in their spiritual lives is the liturgy. For those who came to the Anglican tradition as adults, it was the liturgy that drew them in; or, as one puts it, "The first time I attended an Episcopal service, I knew I had come home." The liturgy and the sacramental life of the church nourished them as laywomen and as seminarians. It continues to do so as priests. Many mention the profound spiritual experiences they have as they administer the sacraments, even a regular Sunday morning Eucharist. One mentions encountering the sacred when the bell is rung before a service and the acolytes and choir are standing ready to process. There are also those extraordinary times: a service of healing, offering communion to someone about to die. Even as they offer sacramental grace to others, they are aware of receiving it as well, and this experience often serves as a powerful confirmation of their calling.

In addition to the emphasis on traditional spirituality and liturgy, there is an undercurrent of dissatisfaction with the worship and spirituality of the Anglican tradition. Several cite nature as the place they most often encounter God. One goes so far as to say that "profound spiritual experiences seldom happen to me in church." But this is a muted theme, and its relative absence is all the more striking given the spiritual eclecticism that has come to characterize American religion.[13] Instead, our respondents, while often uncomfortable with the institutional church as represented by diocesan structures, tend to find spiritual sustenance in their congregations and in other traditional forms such as monasteries, spiritual direction, and retreats.

One might assume that female priests would be among the most theologically and spiritually liberal of Episcopalians. While our respondents tend to identify a gap between their own theological and spiritual perspective and that of their parishioners and male clergy in their dioceses, these women are by no means radical. And as some of them point out, the gap between the theology (and politics) of clergy and laity is by no means solely determined by gender. One priest notes that it is said in Mississippi that the Episcopal Church is the Republican Party in the pews and the Democratic Party behind the altar. Yet others clearly see themselves siding with the "underdog" in the pew over against the hierarchical males in charge, both theologically and politically.

None of them mentions ongoing discomfort with the language of the liturgy, and there is little discussion of liturgical experimentation. Only one woman highlights gender-inclusive language as a concern. Besides suggesting that our respondents are hardly radical, this also suggests that for our respondents, the church, with all its weaknesses, is still home. And whatever needs to be changed will be changed through the structures of the church, not by battering at the edifice from the outside. Thus, one might be "a seething anarchist inside" but those feelings remain largely unexpressed publicly.

While there has always been a Catholic presence in the South (and in places like Louisiana the dominant religious tradition), Catholicism definitely takes second place to evangelical Protestantism. Many of our respondents grew up in the largest denominations of the South—Baptist and Methodist. But evangelicalism does not leave its mark on the spirituality of most of our respondents. A very few mention the hymns of their childhood as continuing influences on their spiritual lives; there is an occasional mention of a clear and distinct conversion experience, but even those most influenced by evangelicalism or Pentecostalism earlier in their lives seem to have left that behind. Instead, evangelicalism seems for the most part to be something against which these women struggle in their churches, in their ministries, and in their spiritual lives.[14] It may be that their personal struggle for ordination has forced them to look critically at the traditional groupings within Anglicanism and the larger culture, too, and allowed them to appropriate aspects of those various traditions more selectively.

Women Priests and "Southernness"

Our respondents are not all natives of the South, nor are all of them at work in the South today, but the South and what many referred to as "southernness" have affected their ministry and their lives. Slightly over half (54.3 percent) grew up entirely in the South. Of the others, 11.4 percent spent at least some of their childhood in the South, while 17.1 percent grew up in border states or in Washington, D.C. A majority received their seminary education and went through the ordination process in southern dioceses. Most have also spent the greater part of their clerical careers in the South.

Of course, the South is a region with considerable internal diversity. This is expressed clearly by our respondents. One, who has served in parishes in Florida for most of her career, wishes she were able to find a position in the "real" South. Another, in charge of a mission church in the rural South, is convinced that she would have an easier time as a woman priest, and be more fulfilled, if she were in an urban or suburban parish in Atlanta. A third draws a sharp contrast between southern and northern Louisiana. And those who are African American or who are serving primarily African American churches know that the South they experience is very different from the South of white suburbia.

Travel and time away from the South have given many of these women a reflectivity about it. For several, it has reconfirmed their southernness. Negative stories of northern arrogance and being treated as if they were stupid remind some of these women that things are not perfect elsewhere. It also gives them a sense of belonging in their native South that is otherwise compromised by their liberalism, feminism, or other factors that point to their differences with their general surroundings.

Travel and time away also give a critical edge. All of those who have had significant experience away believe that it is more difficult to minister in the South, although they cite one clear advantage: southerners respect and attend church. Others who have not spent time away also believe it more difficult to minister in the South. The most common reasons cited are the expectations of southern womanhood and the sense of a lack of acceptance of women's ordination in the South and in southern churches in general. Even women who do not want to raise negative horror stories, who distance themselves from feminism or gender as issues, acknowledge the complexity southernness raises for women's priesthood.

The pain is apparent in the stories of many native southerners who feel like orphans in their own home. They are caught between their own clear vocation and cultural expectations that call that vocation into question. Some relate the perception that being a *southern* woman and being a priest are especially questionable, as if one abandons one to become the other. One woman describes the painful experience of having her bishop (a northerner serving in the South) question why she would seek ordination in the South after having attended college and seminary in the North. "You're a Yankee now," she repeats with the sting still there.

But that kind of experience only seems to reinforce one's sense of southernness, even if it is uncomfortable. Some women priests revel in being "southern"—usually described as playing the "nice girl" role with the right accent. One priest observes that being a southern woman means knowing when and how to be flirty. Another observes that her "quiet" manner works better in the South than that of the "loud" northern woman. As discussed earlier, their "southernness" is tied to strategic effectiveness. Being southern opens doors in parishes; it helps people overcome suspicions about female priests. Several stated that they were accepted in conservative parishes when northern women would not have been.

Yet many reveal the inauthenticity with which they struggle when they feel they must play the southern lady in order to be the priest. As one puts it, "I am a quiet revolutionary on the outside; but a seething anarchist inside!" One young priest complains that the "passive, compliant model for southern women conflicts" with the leadership role of the priesthood. Others seek ways in which the model of southern womanhood can be adapted to the priesthood. One describes her priesthood in general as "feeding the people." This is directly from the liturgy for ordination, but it is also tied to a traditional female role with which southerners are comfortable.

While one northern-born priest notes that she is often told that she "isn't soft enough," her experience in the church has been better than in the southern professional world, where many of her former male colleagues thought of her as "that northern-Yankee bitch." One northern woman serving in one of the South's historic, tradition-laden cities says that being northern may be to her advantage in her elite, conservative parish: "Parishioners overlook or excuse my 'atypical' behavior as ignorance. But I wonder about southern women priests—if they would get the same slack?" Yet she acknowledges that she has had to learn to play the game by "eating the food, etc." Her bishop approvingly teases her that the parish has "made a southerner of her." She is clearly comfortable playing at trying to be southern while maintaining her difference as a northerner.

Other non-southern women note that demographic changes in the South make this less of an issue when parishes have large numbers of non-southern immigrants. When they acknowledge that difficulties remain, they usually chalk them up to the larger culture, clergy from other denominations, and a

D. Jonathan Grieser, Corrie E. Norman, and Don S. Armentrout

few male Episcopal priests in their dioceses. They tend to excuse parishioners, even when they express their frustration with them. One priest notes that her frustration is tempered by recalling a time when she, as a layperson, resisted the idea of women's ordination herself. The general sense, again, is that with perseverance on the part of women priests, parishioners in the South will come around from the sexism of the general culture to accept them personally, if not always the general idea of, women priests. Indeed, when it comes to sexism, the Church takes more direct criticism than the South. Many, however, underline that is it the church and the South together that present formidable obstacles to women's ordained ministry.

Besides gender roles, several of our respondents identify southernness most closely with the land and with family. Curiously, this identification does not seem to include the church, although family role models—overwhelmingly female—are often cited as spiritual models. Perhaps this reflects their complex relationship to the South. The traditional South offers few resources for a professional way of being for women. But it does offer something very profound: a spirituality that informs their call. This includes gentleness and hospitality, a sensuousness and connection to the land, attention to people's stories and pains, an identification with the underdog, and a questioning (often subtly expressed) of hierarchy and authority.

Primarily, this southern spirituality offers a role model for the "quiet revolutionary": the ordinary woman whose extraordinary faith and example lead the way. Many mention teachers or Sunday school teachers. One woman discussed a family friend, a widow who was a devout Episcopalian and introduced her as a child to the works of C. S. Lewis. Another described the "strong-willed, confident women" who stood out because they were so different from the other women in her family. Now such women in her parish continue to influence her. She identifies a common thread among the female role models. They tend to be women who worked outside the home when that was rare or women who were independent and willing to share their spiritual journeys with younger women. Many priests continue to find such role models as they are deeply moved and strengthened by the faith of older women in their parishes.

One priest's account of childhood influences on her vocation encapsulates the experience of many. She mentions first her anger when she was not permitted to be an acolyte. But then she continues in another vein. She says that "church life was just always a part of my life." She describes accompanying her mother to her stints as a volunteer, waiting after Sunday services while mother and grandmother served on Altar Guild and going with her mother as she chauffeured elderly women to various church functions. Looking back, she comments that "these were very spiritual times as I learned that ministry is just a way of life." Thus, mothers, grandmothers, aunts, and other women who were active laywomen in the church provide models for the spirituality and the ministry of the women we surveyed.

Our investigations, then, have revealed a complex range of stories. As these women have become priests, they have struggled with their own expectations of themselves, with the church, and occasionally with their loved ones. They struggle still. They struggle to find fulfilling and rewarding positions, as well as acceptance from the larger religious community and, occasionally, from their parishes and colleagues. They also struggle to develop modes of ministry in keeping with their personal expectations and goals. They struggle with the expectations set on them from the outside. To be a southern female priest is no easy task. By definition it means being "revolutionary." By necessity or upbringing, it may mean doing so "quietly." Above all, it means creatively adapting traditional roles and expectations to situations that those "ordinary" southern women who so inspired them could only have imagined . . . or, prayed for.

Notes

1. Gail Godwin, *Father Melancholy's Daughter* (London: André Deutsch, 1991); and Godwin, *Evensong* (New York: Ballantine, 1999).

2. The events leading up to and immediately following the Philadelphia ordinations are described by Carter Heyward in *A Priest Forever: One Woman's Controversial Ordination in the Episcopal Church* (New York: Harper & Row, 1976; reprint, Cleveland: Pilgrim Press, 1999).

3. Suzanne Radley Hiatt, "Women's Ordination in the Anglican Communion: Can This Church Be Saved?" in *Religious Institutions and Women's Leadership: New Roles Inside the Mainstream,* ed. Catherine Wessinger (Columbia: Univ. of South Carolina Press, 1996), 211–27 (quotation on 218).

4. Carter Heyward describes her rejection as a candidate for ordination in the Diocese of North Carolina in *A Priest Forever,* 30–31. On the role of Virginia Theological Seminary, see Pamela W. Darling, *New Wine: The Story of Women Transforming Leadership and Power in the Episcopal Church* (Boston: Cowley, 1994), 118.

5. Don Armentrout, "The Ordination of Episcopal Women in the South" *Sewanee Theological Review* 43, no. 4 (2000): 1–10

6. Another interesting question to pursue would be to ascertain what percentage of women ordained in the South have left the region to pursue their vocations and whether that percentage differed significantly from other regions of the country.

7. Because of the lag-time in church record keeping, it was impossible to determine precisely how many canonically resident women priests were in the

South when we conducted the survey in 2001. Relying on church records, we sent five-page surveys, asking for stories about call, ordination, seminary, family life and background, ministry, spirituality, and southern context to some 250 women. We received forty completed surveys, a few partially completed surveys, and several phone calls and e-mails from women who did not have time to complete the survey but who wanted to volunteer information. In addition, we did a number of follow-up interviews with several female priests, some of whom had responded to the initial survey. The authors would like to express their deepest appreciation to the women who participated in the project. We would also like to acknowledge the staff of the School of Theology, University of the South, for administering the survey.

8. In addition to Heyward, who describes her own struggle for women's ordination, the general history of women in the Episcopal Church has received attention. Notable works include Catherine Prelinger, *Episcopal Women: Gender, Spirituality, and Commitment in an American Mainline Denomination* (Oxford: Oxford Univ. Press 1996); and Pamela W. Darling, *New Wine: The Story of Women Transforming Leadership and Power in the Episcopal Church* (Boston: Cowley, 1994). For sociological studies of ordained female clergy, see Paula Nesbitt, *Feminization of the Clergy in America: Occupational and Organizational Perspectives* (Oxford: Oxford Univ. Press, 1997); and Barbara Brown Zikmund, Adair T. Lummis, and Patricia M. Y. Chang, eds., *Clergy Women: An Uphill Calling* (Louisville: Westminster John Knox, 1998).

9. The vocational diaconate refers to those deacons who are ordained as, and remain, deacons for the length of their careers. It is intended for those who are called to specific ministries that do not include celebrating the sacraments and has tended to be an avenue for second-career vocations, especially for women.

10. The quoted phrase comes from Wade Clark Roof, *A Generation of Seekers: The Spiritual Journeys of the Baby Boom Generation* (San Francisco: HarperSanFrancisco, 1993).

11. For a woman's autobiographical account of her first year at an Episcopal Seminary, see Chloe Breyer, *The Close: A Woman's First Year at Seminary* (New York: Basic Books, 2001).

12. On the "stained-glass ceiling" and related issues in the Episcopal and other churches, see Brown Zikmund, Lummis, and Chang, *Clergy Women*, and Nesbitt, *Feminization of the Clergy*.

13. See especially the work of Wade Clark Roof: *A Generation of Seekers*, and *Spiritual Marketplace: Baby Boomers and the Remaking of American Religion* (Princeton, NJ: Princeton Univ. Press, 1999).

14. These competing tendencies have divided the Anglican communion since the nineteenth century, and both Anglo-Catholicism and evangelicalism continue to shape different wings of the Episcopal Church. The two groups do not overlap easily with theological labels such as "liberal" and "conservative"; nor do they clearly denote attitudes toward the ordination of women.

CHAPTER 14

SACRAMENT AND SEGREGATION: EPISCOPALIANS IN THE EVANGELICAL SOUTH

WHEN RELIGION IN THE AMERICAN SOUTH IS THE SUBJECT, ONE DOES NOT think immediately of the Episcopal Church but of dramatic vernacular images of river baptism, communal singing, and populist preaching. The southern religious mood inferred from such experiences is hard, clear, emotional, evangelical, and exaggerated; we tend to personify it in Jerry Falwell, "Daddy" King, Billy Graham, and Jimmy Swaggart—three Baptists and a Pentecostal—who seem to represent those particular markers. When students remember the Lost Cause and southern eloquence expressing the experience of civil war and defeat, however, it is easier to turn from evangelicals to Episcopal priests and the people who founded the University of the South as an almost timeless and imaginary retreat.[1] In addition, if we want religion to bear the regional imprint and at the same time to represent resistance to it through organic connection with the religious of non-Southern jurisdictions and a style of worship distinctly at odds with vernacular informality, we will want to think seriously about Episcopalians. The role of the Episcopal Church in the religious history of American southerners may well provide a key to understanding southern culture in ways we had not thought about before. And, in addition, historic conflicts within the church may also provide an implicit historical criticism of the kinds of religion that have seemed to characterize southerners across class, racial, ethnic, and gendered boundaries.

First, however, it is important to understand context. Students of American religion know several things about the South; they know it has been profoundly affected by evangelical Protestant religion; and they know that slavery, emancipation, and a regional self-consciousness shaped by the politics emanating from those social facts have made the South different from the rest of the United States. For those who insist that there is no such thing as southern culture—only cultures—the anarchy of postmodern orthodoxy has so fractured southern life into the idiosyncratic quaintness of coves, bayous, quarters, landings, lonely churches, dead-end roads, local histories, and family lore as to deny what every southerner (naturalized, adoptive, or native) knows with intuitive certainty (aided by William Faulkner): that "the South" is *different*. Being different from the rest of the United States did not mean that "the South" was *not* conflicted about religion, slavery, race, and authority. Thinking of Dixie as a "whole" did not make it a harmonious, placid, bland, and culturally undifferentiated "place," for it is, as it has always been—while being continuously fabricated by planters, publicists, politicians, pragmatists, and preachers into a "region"—a richly diversified section of the United States. Yet, for about 250 years, that diversity existed in conjunction with slavery, racial politics, and a waxing evangelical hegemony. This latter phenomenon in the waning years of the twentieth century provided a widespread cultural base from which to launch a national resurgence of evangelical Protestantism.[2] To be sure, the range and scope of evangelical dominance differ from place to place; and some scholars may want to think that a subregion such as the southern highlands defies the premise of evangelical pervasiveness clearly enough to distinguish Christianity in Appalachia from that of lower elevations, but their insistence is not enough to convince all scholars that distinctions among evangelicals create significant enough differences to do anything other than amplify the complexity of evangelical dominance.[3]

Evangelical supremacy, as students of Appalachia could argue, is partly the function of varied stories that historians tell about religion in the South: the imperial, ecclesiastical, and evangelical narratives. An imperial narrative of Anglicanism in continental North America avoids engaging the evangelical outcome by beginning with Christian slavery. The men who wrote vestry acts establishing the church in what became the American South also crafted laws establishing slaveholding. Their ministers, insists Jon Butler, could, through "Anglican domination of Christian institutional life" in the southern colonies, sculpt slavery by teaching an ethic of "absolute obedience" (with its draconian disciplinarian implications) on one hand and by urging, on the other, the Christianization of slaves.[4] If the latter goal was supposed to have abated the rigors of the former, ministers, missionaries, and laypeople motivated by this happy thought were corruptly mistaken. If such self-deceit did in fact characterize the founders, stipulating a mythic "Anglican domination" mistakenly implies a self-regulating church capable of exercising influence upon a civil order willing to be disciplined by rules and considerations independent of the interests of elites who ruled colonial life. These elites, however, embraced an

Erastianism that subordinated all spiritual interests to rational self-interest defined by an expanding market and filtered through enlightened rationalism. Modifying the imperial narrative, other stories of southern Episcopal origins emphasize ways in which clerics fought with local elites to achieve some sort of autonomous self-respect by converting Africans, reproving worldliness, preaching an enlightened piety, and disciplining patriarchs in the modulated tones of a latitudinarian sagacity that was ultimately incapable of breathing life into a becalmed church.[5] The presumed lassitude in this ecclesiastical narrative yields to the evangelical mythos that now dominates the others—even the currently correct imperial myth, possibly because it is consistent with the values and assumptions of the most energetic school of American religious history at the present time but also because it explains by an extension into the future how the South became "evangelical."

The evangelical narrative begins with a failed establishment and differs from the ecclesiastical narrative, which was also rooted in failure, by attributing it not to minimal ecclesiastical machinery, overbearing vestries, indifferent governors, and absent bishops but to the deficient piety of both clergy and laity. This assessment included a broad range of people in the late-eighteenth-century South who feared that enlightened reason, natural theology, liturgical formalism, consecrated morality, higher education, and a taste for latitudinarian authors[6] prevented communicants from knowing the true power of religion. This power lay not in affirming the creed, believing the Bible, saying one's prayers, following the Christian year, and attempting to live a responsible and fruitful life but in experiencing a self-conscious, subjective transformation from a state of sin-afflicted guilt and shame to an undeserved condition of renovated innocence. This conversion was interpreted as a "New Birth" so radical and discontinuous from the natural processes of physical birth and progressive maturation as to suggest a gracious gift from God. This phenomenon—from the point of view of the person to whom it happened—initiated a new relationship of trust between the believer and God that was validated by the approval of people who had been similarly affected, the citation of appropriate Bible verses, and a self-conscious inner assurance expressed in a public profession of faith. That this way of understanding authentic piety was associated with New Light Baptists and Presbyterians, the Wesleyan movement, and the dramatic extravagances of George Whitefield the Great Awakener, meant that many Anglican parsons were placed on the defensive at the time, and the evangelical narrative has kept them there ever since.

They were and continue to be personifications of a lapsed, ineffectual, and disgraced clerisy even among Episcopalians. The Right Reverend William Meade of Virginia, for example, could celebrate the episcopacy of his predecessor, Richard Channing Moore, in 1845 by contrasting Moore's proclamation of grace with the homilies of a clergy that, before his consecration, had been more committed to the devilishly "innocent" amusements of dancing, drinking, horse racing, and theatergoing than to a demonstrable piety. Moore, and by implication Meade in the latter's own view, had saved the church by infusing into it a spiritual intensity that rested on the subjective transformation of the New Birth and was expressed in a holy life shriven of aristocratic gaiety, trifling pleasures, and "careless" conversation.[7] If evangelical revival within the church saved it from extinction, according to the approved narrative, evangelical revival beyond the church transformed religious life in what became the South so thoroughly that within two generations after the Revolution, the region had been ploughed, planted, and harvested by evangelicals in all denominations of Protestant Christians.[8]

This success did not mean that the region was more "evangelical" than the rest of the country before 1840, although this would eventually be the case. While foreign immigrants, liberal intellectuals, inventive reformers, and spiritual entrepreneurs were creating American religious pluralism outside the South, religious activists within a region increasingly aware of its differences from the rest of the country and the need to fortify those differences attempted to convince believers that a scrupulous attachment to traditional values confirmed by religious conviction, scriptural authority, popular agreement, and communal solidarity demanded religious conformity. Southerners needed to understand, preachers insisted, that they could justify their institutions more easily by an appeal to the Holy Bible than to the Declaration of Independence. They could make their society function more smoothly if they secured the relationship between superiors and subordinates through the bonds of Christian affection and mutual obligation rather than democratic egalitarianism. They could nurture their youth more dutifully by preparing them for the renovating power of the New Birth than the competitive advantages of a materialistic marketplace. And they could guarantee the safety of their society more responsibly through Christian missions to slaves than by relying on armed patrols. As their young men marched off to defend hearth and home against infidel Yankees and found their courage fortified in regimental revivals, they were transformed into consecrated hosts of the Lord and led by surprisingly devout officers into slaughter and defeat from which they emerged as if from Golgotha. They were encouraged to imagine their sacrifice as sanctified by its similarity to that of Jesus Christ.[9] Thus did two generations of southerners learn in various ways and under a broad range of teachers the importance of religion in fabricating social solidarity and regional identity. That kind of religion embraced, adopted, adapted, or conceded (as befitted the psychology of individual believers) rested on subjective authentication within the minds and experiences of the faithful, as well as on a selective

Donald G. Mathews

memory as to what constituted a biblical foundation. It meant, therefore, that the Protestantism that engulfed the South by 1910 could be called "evangelical."[10] Almost as important to the evangelical mood was the personal assurance that the New Birth provided, as well as commitment to an energetic expansion of the Christian faith and openness to the power of the Holy Spirit expressed in a demonstrable piety that was valued among the pious of different communions and races.[11] The authority of one's spiritual rebirth together with reliance on the Holy Scriptures, however, were and remained the hallmarks of the "evangelical" mood no matter whatever else is added in its various manifestations.

The religious mood of the South was affected, too, by the presence of those whose experiences of authority, sectional conflict, civil war, and Appomattox allowed the imagination to range with vastly different understandings of God's spirit, presence, and omnipotent hand. If Christians came in different colors, conditions, and cultures, the original distance between European and African spiritual birthrights that seemed so dramatic when comparing the elegant English Book of Common Prayer to the expressive celebration of sacred dance was shortened by African transformation of the Christian paradigm. Evangelicals insisted on including Africans in their worship and discipline in ways unimagined and then repudiated by the parsons because Africans seemed to appropriate Christian metaphors and ideas in dangerous ways. The evangelical offer of "liberty" was much different from the politically limited twenty-first-century ideal and was capable of eliciting from enslaved audiences the culturally fabricated earnest of celebration in the spirit that resonated so well with perceptions, ideas, and worship that they had brought with them from the Old World. Emphasis on this subjective authentication of religious experience was not so alien to Africans as it was to Europeans, although the latter nonetheless found the experience evocative enough for themselves to have fueled a religious revolution in the British Isles as well as the English-speaking New World. Although a few Africans were willing to receive salvation within traditional Anglican structures, it was the experience of New Birth that came to them through evangelical missionaries, laity, and preachers that successfully began their Christianization. The resulting voice, which reborn Africans found and articulated within evangelical community, led to authoritative self-expression and action that had to be engaged by whites even if they disagreed.[12] This interaction created a discursive community in which whites were forced to concede authentic African subjectivity.

To be sure, scholars and ideologues will continue to debate whether or not African American Christianity should be called "evangelical" after the people who first brought a widely credible Gospel to Africans. If the adjective obscures the creativity of Africans and implies a repudiation of Africa, it should be discarded, but its importance in emphasizing a shared experience of transcendence resting on the subjectivity of two dissimilar peoples must not be ignored. The act breaching consciousness and culture by the Transcendent Other did not mean that it was interpreted in the same ways, for power, culture, and gender would color interpretation, but acknowledging the breach as authoritative for each people meant that some kind of conversation was possible; it began in the first conversions among the enslaved and continued through the civil rights revolutions of the 1960s. Whether the conversation can continue is for this generation to decide. If it can, African Americans' experience of civil war as victory instead of defeat and emancipation as providential instead of problematic must influence the ways in which "the story" is told. That story is a continuing saga of suffering and redemption from crosses born by Christians under the weight of burdens imposed by those infuriated with constitutionally approved rubrics and infatuated with their own capacity for inflicting pain and humiliation in disfranchisement, impoverishment, and lynching. The story of Christianity in the South would be understood not simply as evangelical triumphalism but white evangelical failure and African American hope.

However the religious historian interprets Southern experiences of religion, race and power, she is obliged in the service of an inclusive story to remember that throughout the making of the South, if religion has continued to express popular, conflicted, and ambiguous views, evangelical discourse has shaped it. If the Bible complemented the New Birth to establish religious authority in Dixie, it was not merely the Bible of white fundamentalists' insistence that each verse has a restricted and condensed meaning, or of those who understand the metaphoric and symbolic power of a richly diverse set of manuscripts gathered by the early church in witness to the power of God, but also of those who still understand the resonance between their own stories and the stories of ancient Hebrews and Christians, whether they are Appalachian whites or Sea Island African Americans.[13]

The question for this essay is, "Where does the Episcopal Church fit into the southern evangelical narrative?" The answer is prefaced by the observation that hitherto the church has been a foil, bad example, or vestigial appendix that (by implication, in an evangelical world) should long ago have disappeared. The church stands not only for itself but also for other non-evangelical religious, such as Quakers, Moravians, Roman Catholics, and Primitive Baptists who with others have resisted evangelical hegemony. For this essay, however, the Episcopal Church is the subject, and the fact that it was itself an arena within which evangelicals did battle with non-evangelicals will help us understand what the experience of the church does have to offer any attempt to understand evangelical hegemony and southern religion. Almost

Donald G. Mathews

any retelling of the story suggests a broad range of religious experiences in the southern colonies; and, in the democratic marketplace in which large numbers denote the good and small numbers the bad, the inability of the church to bring within its discipline and devotion any but a small number of communicants does seem to imply failure—unless the moral of the righteous remnant is invoked. In early America, there were many "remnants": Quakers, Regular Baptists, Moravians (Unitas Fratrem), Lutherans, varied Presbyterians, and happily irreverent "worldlings," all of whom for various reasons and in various ways resisted evangelical importunity and discipline. Episcopalians were similar only to Roman Catholics, Lutherans, and Presbyterians who had also emigrated as members of traditions partially shaped by the fact that somewhere they had been established churches. Anglicans, therefore, whether their heirs are pleased with it or not, are burdened by the imperial narrative; communicants did establish African slavery even if they did not do it by themselves or after having been sobered by the moral implications of having received the Holy Eucharist.

Slavery made the South; abolition remade it. The aftermath of both enslavement and emancipation still afflicts reflective southerners who try to wrestle with the continuing effects of their meaning. Since meaning is so affected by personal as well as collective attempts to fabricate positive images from memories of self and society, it is naturally shaped by knowledge, value, language, and self-interest. By emphasizing only the positive nature of the past, reflection on meaning produces *myth*—that is, those stories that we enjoy hearing. Historical reflection is different; historical meaning is never woven from positive images alone because they obscure more than they reveal. The Eucharist, which is the Christian understanding of God's presence in history, dictates historical meaning because it includes the prayer of confession in which communicants confess in shame and guilt all that they have done and not done, something that is sobering to all those who kneel before that presence in remembering the past. Mythic reflection about the American South falters on the reality of slavery. The imperial narrative concedes very little conscientious historical reflection on the meaning of enslavement among whites, and yet by looking through the Anglican/Episcopal lens at those who made the American South, the historian somehow has to connect that creative process to the church as the self-anointed reflective agency for the culture in which such action occurred. The imperial narrative is correct in telling the story of churchmen's embracing an ethic of absolute obedience so long as the story is about power and white people—which distorts the story. When the enslaved are added to the narrative, the importunate evangelical voice celebrates the many ways in which images, insights, stories, and promises in an "awakening" among cultural Europeans resonated with complementary or evocative affect from within African American culture to allow the enslaved to use evangelical urgency, imagery, and enthusiasm to re-create a presumably undifferentiated, authentic African American culture. The flaws in this narrative are egregious, especially from the viewpoint of those who want us to think about the past not as a steady, heavily cadenced parade into a clearly defined future but as a broad, almost meandering mass move-ment of peoples spreading across a vast landscape with no horizon clearly in view. In this broad movement, there are many adaptations to landscape, exi-gency, institutional options, and religious sensibility, and the observer has an opportunity to notice minor anomalies, principled resistance, and devotion to commitments that may seem to be inconsistent with "major trends," demo-cratic action, and historical generalization. In this broad movement, the Epis-copal Church becomes a site for understanding the complexity of religious life in the South.

A lens steadily held upon the people who made the Episcopal Church in the South will be focused first of all upon Episcopalians of African descent who sustained it while attempting to force it to be, in fact, catholic. In doing so they endured with crucified fortitude humiliation upon humiliation at the hands of whites for almost four hundred years. If the church expected an ethic of absolute obedience in the seventeenth century, it also offered the biblical, educational, and sacramental means for some African Americans to find in the suffering, crucified, and risen Lord the Way to claim from the church what a few whites at least insisted was their right to claim—a place at the Lord's table. This claim was, however, always viewed with reluctance, suspicion, regret, and discomfort even if at first it was thought to be a way to discipline the labor force. White partisans promised that Christianizing slaves would make them less likely to follow African leadership and make them more pli-able by encouraging them to internalize the virtues of hard work, obedience, and self-discipline. By the end of the eighteenth century, African Americans were regularly baptized by Anglican parsons and throughout the antebellum period took communion in chapels scattered across the South; in the Diocese of South Carolina in 1860, a majority of communicants were of African des-cent.[14] In the North a few African Americans also received the Eucharist in a few independent African Episcopal churches where they were under less com-pulsion to do so than were southern slaves. As emancipation proceeded after 1863 and southern African American communicants steadily left the church, a remnant refused to leave. They embraced the Book of Common Prayer, the liturgy, the restrained dignity and presumed universality of the church; they recoiled from the expressiveness, exaggerations, antinomianism, and perceived "superstitions" of independent black churches.[15] As they were not willing to yield to a Christian church defined solely by African American culture, so they were unwilling to concede a Christian church defined solely by Europeans. If, in this awesome commitment to a unified catholic church, they were sometimes joined by a small number of whites, it was always black Episcopalians who carried the cross of racial humiliation and elevated the host of salvation.

Southern Episcopalians benefited from the activism of northern black priests as well as missionary ideology. By 1827, Absalom Jones, Peter Williams Jr., and William Leavington had worked with laity to establish black congregations in Philadelphia, New York, and Baltimore; gradually other Northern cities became sites of black Episcopal activity, too, and it is reported that St. Matthew's, Detroit, was a terminus on the Underground Railroad.[16] These few black priests, through their ordination, activism, and staying power, had established a fragile black presence within a national church that was, by the time of emancipation, eager to extend missions to freed people. The enslaved, churchmen had frequently argued before 1860, clearly should be brought under their care; referring to the obligation was standard rhetorical fare before, during, and after the Civil War. Sometimes it seemed that acknowledging the duty implied its having been met; having done "so much for [the] spiritual care and nurture" of African Americans before the war, southern churchmen believed, they should thereafter renew the mission to enable the freed people "rightly to understand and enjoy the privileges of freedom."[17] Consistent with this public posture, the Protestant Episcopal Church established schools, institutes, a seminary, and eventually colleges for African Americans in the South; it planted mission churches in Florida, Virginia, North Carolina, the District of Columbia, and on into the Southwest. The church attracted to its scattered and small black congregations a well-educated and determined remnant of communicants who were encouraged to believe that they were privileged to "learn for ourselves and our children the noble discipline of freedom," as the prominent black priest Alexander Crummell called it, consistent "with the high teachings of God's church." Such a vision of Christian discipleship, Harold Lewis writes, was a kind of *noblesse oblige noire* that assumed African Americans' discipleship demanded they remain within the church to achieve its egalitarian witness.[18] The obligation was also an eschatological fiction. It was eschatological because it was based on the New Testament principle that ultimately participation in Christ obliterated all invidious distinctions;[19] it was a fiction because the church in the United States was, as Crummell himself confessed in a private letter at the time, a "cold and repulsive stepmother."[20] The challenge for Episcopalians was how to move from the chilling reality of defective relationships into a state of grace within which they could live according to "the high teachings of God's church."

Racial segregation was the issue; as a southern institution established by law as well as custom, it acquired a parochial, perhaps anomalous ambience when outsiders observed it. As insiders lived it, however, its impact on black people was obscured by a restrained public discourse of orderliness, catholicity, and liturgical liminality behind which whites attempted to veil their anxiety lest blacks come to the Lord's table with them. Before emancipation, northern whites had segregated the church; afterwards, when southerners attempted permanently to impose this solution to a biracial presence as official policy, African American resistance from both sections of the country created a continuous creative tension that made almost any solution other than equality problematic.[21] Contrary to the familiar moral rubric that commands humans to talk incessantly about their "true" feelings, ventilate their hostilities, and share all their fears and anxieties—perhaps to confess all their sins—Episcopalians spoke in ambiguous, ambivalent, perplexing, and mystifying ways about race, while deceiving no one. The confusion reflected the inherent contradictions within a church that professed to be universal and heedless of invidious distinctions among the faithful but existed within a culture that was in fact sustained by such distinctions that reflected race and gender. Southern bishops and clergy attempted racially to integrate diocesan conventions as African Americans became communicants, but they met resistance, especially from the laity. Thus frustrated, those same bishops, meeting at Sewanee, Tennessee, in 1883, announced that they would support creating a separate, subordinate African American jurisdiction in each cooperating diocese in the United States. African American Episcopalians, organized as the Conference of Church Workers among the Colored People, persuaded the House of Deputies to reject the "Sewanee canon," but they were unable to dissuade southern dioceses from adopting practices envisioned by the "canon" on their own. Later, the conference unsuccessfully attempted to develop a missionary district plan that would have enabled them to govern themselves in conjunction with fully vested black bishops. To be sure, eventually two black suffragans were consecrated to assist diocesans with "colored work" in the Southwest and North Carolina; they were similar in function to archdeacons previously appointed for the same purpose. But these consecrations were controversial among both blacks and whites: some of the former objected because of the implicit institutionalization of segregation; indignant whites objected because of the implicit institutionalization of racial integration and the possibility that black Episcopal authority might one day actually be exercised over white women. For this very reason—almost a decade after the consecration of black bishops Edward T. Demby and Henry Beard Delaney—as Bishop William A. Guerry of South Carolina was considering the same innovation for his own diocese, he was shot to death in his study by a priest.[22]

The clarity and anger of the murder stand in sharp contrast to the ambiguity and discomfort that usually beclouded southern Episcopalians' experience with segregation. Mystification was characteristic of southern race relations

Donald G. Mathews

among religious white people; it seeped so relentlessly into the nooks and crannies of ecclesiastical life and relations between whites and blacks that it veiled the discourse of both races. Nowhere is this more evident than in "the Newport incident." Paring the narrative down to essentials makes it speciously simple, but it began in the 1932 diocesan Convention of Arkansas. Meeting in Newport, that body elected as bishop the Very Reverend John Williamson, dean of the Cathedral. Subsequently, however, acting favorably on an appeal from the black suffragan, the Right Reverend Edward T. Demby, and two white priests, the House of Bishops nullified the election. Grounds for the appeal had been, in the words of the white priests, the "unworthy, uncatholic, unchristian mind and spirit" that prevailed in the convention and was manifested in the "election of the bishop."[23] The "unchristian mind and spirit" to which the priests objected had been made clear enough to Bishop Demby in a letter from the rector of the host church (St. Paul's, Newport). The Reverend William T. Holt ignored the fact that Demby had already been invited by the white suffragan bishop, Edwin Saphore, to assist in the Eucharist, and observed that there "might be some feeling about the two races taking Holy Communion together" when the convention met.[24] His suggestion that the black clergy commune in St. Paul's basement drew from Demby a cool and ambiguous reply in the tradition of African American forbearance. He wrote that the "Negro churchmen" would do nothing "to make the Convention non-harmonious on our part" but suggested as a remedy that Holt take the matter up with Bishop Saphore who then caved into local usage. Indignant but burdened by the delicate racial politics surrounding the Episcopal election that was to follow, Demby and his clergy resolved to march in procession without forcing their way to the communion table. But then—confronted by an embarrassing black presence—the white rector and bishop suddenly relented in their resolve to exclude African American communicants and beckoned them to come; they refused. The "incident" continued throughout the balloting for bishop, as the priest supported by African American clergy was publicly "stigmatized" as a "nigger lover" who would "raise the Negroes to equality with the whites."[25] Reporting later to the Right Reverend William T. Capers, president of the Province of the Southwest, Demby ignored the racist ambience of electioneering and appealed instead to the integrity of the Eucharist. Speaking for his colleagues and the communicants whom they represented, the bishop confessed that being told to commune separately in the crypt had "meant to my mind nothing less than our Excommunication"; understanding the arrangement to have been approved by the acting bishop of Arkansas meant to Demby that the church's catholicity had been compromised by "Ecclesiastical Authority." The two white priests agreed, and so did a majority of the House of Bishops. The resulting controversy in the Diocese of Arkansas became a festering sore on the Body of Christ.

The "Newport incident" represents such a complexity of images, experiences, and memories that it is almost a perfect representation of Christian life in the segregated South. The anguish and contradictions at Newport, however, were not necessarily and exclusively southern; they were clear in St. Matthew's, Brooklyn, as well. In that parish in 1929 the rector had told West Indian newcomers that they were not welcome; the vestry supported him and he got away with it. Three years later, the vestry of All Souls, Harlem, took their endowment with them when they left the church in defiance of their rector and bishop, who refused to repudiate black communicants. Here were three different congregations and three different outcomes, but characterizing them all was a pervasive nationwide white reluctance to commune with black people. The Newport incident thus could be thought of as a national as well as sectional event but within a distinct local context, too. In Arkansas since the First World War, race relations had been punctuated by frequent and dramatic violence. Even a casual reader of Arkansas newspaper clippings in the Tuskegee files on lynching is nauseated at the wanton cruelty reported in them. A lynching in 1927 had imposed on the Episcopal convention of that year not a sense of whites' moral failure in trying times but what one scholar called a "fanatical enforcement of the color line" that demeaned black Episcopalians in general and the clergy in particular.[26] In response, the native South Carolinian who was rector of Christ Church, Little Rock, William P. Witsell, received permission to plan the convention of 1928 in which the black suffragan would have a prominent role as befitted his office. Thus, in the midst of racial tensions, African American clergy were not entirely without important white connections. They lived in a cultural climate in which they could never be sure of what white clergy would say or do along the color line. They could participate in the election of a white bishop but be forced to endure racist attacks upon them in the process. They could chafe at the double-talk of southern white bishops who could respect them personally enough to invite them into the chancel but not enough to keep them there when local laity objected. They could benefit from certain individuals' abrogation of the humiliating etiquette of race, but they could not be shielded from the racist contempt of alarmists in electing a bishop. Nor could they ever rest secure in white people's overtures to them, as indicated by Demby's being invited to help celebrate the Eucharist and then being expected to disappear.

When Demby declined to act as expected, he was relying on his understanding of the temper and churchmanship of whites among whom he had worked for so many years. He was relying, too, on his own reputation for tact, selflessness, and dignity, carefully fabricated as a black suffragan bishop in an overwhelmingly white church. There he had been under constant surveillance from punctiliously critical whites ever ready to seize on any human lapse into indignation that would betray a conviction that whites had abused him and his people. Such a breach of racial etiquette he had carefully avoided even while insisting in his annual reports how poorly funded African American Episcopal missions and churches actually were. Had he been thoroughly segregated into a "black" denomination, Demby would never have had to endure the indignities of the Newport incident; he would not have been accused of being an Uncle Tom, or attacked for thinking he was as good as white people, or for thinking that he was not; he could have avoided the mortification visited upon him by both white and black. But had that been the case, neither would he have had the opportunity to raise questions so directly relevant to the issue of Christian segregation and the integrity of both the Eucharist and Episcopal consecration. Even though he was an anomaly—a black bishop in a white church—and even though he had very little authority or power as a result of that situation, and even though blacks and whites could agree that the plan under which he was consecrated was terribly flawed (as Demby himself knew on the basis of his own experience), he was nonetheless a bishop, and he had been treated like a "nigger." No one put the matter quite so bluntly, but that was in fact the case. If he had not been willing to carry the cross of racial humiliation as an anomalous bishop and not assumed responsibility for defending the integrity of the Eucharist in the Newport Convention, he would not have been responsible for bringing to Episcopal attention the contradiction between sacrament and segregation at a time when most white Episcopalians would have preferred black Episcopalians to have been neither seen nor heard. This preference shaped the entire controversy. Even though the incident was begun by Demby's objection to the way in which the black clergy had been treated, most parties to the controversy denied that race affected it in any way. Witsell's enemies charged that he had actually encouraged Demby's appeal for the sole purpose of nullifying the election of the man who had defeated him for the episcopacy. Witsell and his allies feared that racial controversy would explode into a wildfire of mindless scapegoating by their opponents, so they insisted that the issue had been the inflammatory and "unchristian" spirit that had cloaked the election. "Race" was too volatile an issue to confront.[27]

The moral confusion of the Newport incident exemplified Episcopal discourse on race before the Second World War. Interested parties found it difficult to speak openly about whites' responsibility for a racially oppressive system; they treated southern segregation as a sociological axiom. Yet when African Americans appealed to that axiom to get the General Convention to grant them black bishops and missionary districts, they failed because of the myth of Christian unity. That belief made the House of Bishops—after the Newport incident—state in effect that the Eucharist and segregation were incompatible, but the bishops could not move beyond the principle to demystify the myth of inexorable segregation. If, in moments of lucidity, black Episcopalians and southern white paternalists agreed that there was something deeply disturbing about race relations in the United States, they could not agree on why this was the case, who was responsible, or how to talk about it.[28] The Second World War changed all that. Instead of working within segregation or waiting for segregation magically to wither away, southerners began to repudiate segregation as an American variant of Nazi ideology. References among Episcopal leaders to "Nazi-like" segregation laws began to come easily, for the images of Nazi death camps had suggested that racism was a prelude to genocide. Southerners of both races began to change, Episcopalians among them. Between 1947 and 1949 the dioceses of Upper South Carolina, Georgia, Arkansas, and Virginia granted equality to black parishes and laity in convention; in 1951 and 1953 African American priests became members of integrated executive committees in Georgia and Mississippi; and in 1954 the Colored Convocation of the Diocese of Southern Virginia was disbanded. Between 1951 and 1953 a hard-fought and bitter battle ended with the racial integration of the School of Theology in the University of the South, and in 1959 activists formed the Episcopal Society for Cultural and Racial Unity (ESCRU).[29] Eventually, Episcopalians were swept along in the swollen currents of the civil rights revolution, participating in marches, sit-ins, kneel-ins, demonstrations, and voter-registration drives. An Episcopal seminarian, Jonathan Daniels, was murdered for his activism. Yet the flood of change that seemed to promise so much for some and too much for so many others became disappointing to still others who, in a complex combination of frustration and hope, raised the standard of black power and presented a bill for reparations to white America.[30] In thirty years African Americans had emerged from the frustrating confusion symbolized in the Newport incident to speak authoritatively in ways whites were not always prepared to heed.

African Americans have continued to speak in many voices as diocesan bishops, suffragans, priests, and active laity. The generation between Bishop Demby's lonely tenure as "Suffragan for Colored Work" in the Diocese of Arkansas and the celebration by the Reverend Pauli Murray of the Holy Eucharist on February 13, 1977, in Chapel of the Cross in Chapel Hill, North Carolina, initiated radical change. On that day, local and national television reporters came to the university town to cover a service of worship in the very chapel where Murray's grandmother had been baptized and consigned to the balcony as a slave. In reading the service and administering the sacrament to an interracial congregation, Murray became the first female priest to do so within the Episcopal communion of that state; she thought of her action as a "symbol of healing."[31] Bishop Demby had died twenty years earlier; it was almost thirty-nine years since the Newport incident. The healing of which Murray wrote was symbolized in her breach of convention as a priest, a woman, a southerner, and an American of both African and European descent. She personified the violence and abolition of slavery, the suffering and victory of faithful people who refused to concede clearly the church to whites and men alone, and she symbolized, too, the unity of the church across speciously defined sectional, ethnic, and gendered lines. This emigrant southerner, educated in North Carolina, New York, and the District of Columbia, returned "home" to a place she had never lived to represent in celebrating the sacrament the full meaning of her enslaved grandmother's baptism. The achievement was not hers alone; Absalom Jones, Alexander Crummell, Edward Demby, and unnamed others had preceded her; they came from both the North and South and used sectional differences to leverage changes otherwise not possible. White southerners, too, like William Witsell and the Right Reverend John Hines, presiding bishop of the Episcopal Church from 1964 to 1974 had played important roles.[32] And so had all the white priests who, with the very worst of intentions as well as the best, had insisted on bringing African Americans under care of the church where they could become, quite apart from paternalists' expectations, a "righteous remnant" that provided an enduring and troubling reminder that the South, the United States, and the church included communicants of more than one race. The South may have held the Episcopal Church hostage to racism and segregation, but it also nurtured those who would eventually free the hostages, for when a white man received the chalice from the Reverend Pauli Murray in the Chapel of the Cross on East Franklin Street, they were both freed from a past that neither could forget.

African American southern Episcopalians may have been evangelized and may have been confirmed in the church as a result of evangelical preaching, but like white communicants they were distinguished from other southern Christian Protestant believers by the fact that they were not "evangelical." This statement will immediately raise eyebrows and hackles, for every religious historian knows that the Virginia Episcopal Church was reborn through the evangelical ministrations of Bishops Richard Channing Moore and William Meade; Meade himself said so.[33] Lieutenants such as Charles Wesley Andrews celebrated an evangelical ethos in their writings and volunteerism,[34] and evangelical women, warmed by Hannah More, the Wesleys, and Hester Ann Rogers, helped to inspire the church through the ministry of parlor prayer meetings and epistolary networks of family and friends.[35] They all agreed that at some moment in the seeker's pilgrimage to salvation, there was a moment in which they knew, as they had never known before, the benefits of Christ's passion as confirmed by the Holy Spirit in a sensible transformation that empowered them to live a Christian life. This experience—in evangelical language—of a "New Birth" was the passage through which one settled into a seriousness of life characterized by denying oneself what many communicants of the church had once thought were "innocent amusements." Evangelical Episcopalians claimed that Bishop Richard Channing Moore had led his parsons to proclaim "grace" rather than to lecture on "morality"—implying the superiority of faith over a theology of works. But in reality the marks of New Birth demanded "morality," too—one that repudiated drinking, dancing, racing, and attending the theater (if one could be found).[36] The experience, sobriety, and self-denial that evangelical Episcopalians shared with believers beyond the church, made them part of evangelical triumphalism in the nineteenth-century South, to be sure. But what made Episcopalians different from other southerners was that their church resisted the prevailing evangelical ethos while it kept one foot within it. Small in numbers though its communicants were, they struggled to create a religious community that could link believers with an ancient past, exemplify the corporateness of Christianity, dignify the holiness of worship, and demonstrate the importance of a learned ministry.

If George Whitefield could dispense with the Book of Common Prayer in Christian worship, his American evangelical descendents could not. Bishop William Meade, who personified southern Episcopal evangelicalism, understood full well that his fellow southerners suspected the Protestant Episcopal Church (as it was called then) of being "Romish" for its liturgy, form, vestments, and prayer book. It was not uncommon for Episcopal communicants to be told that their beliefs were essentially "popish heresies."[37] Such suspicion was unfounded, Meade told a Bible-idolizing public, for the Book of Common Prayer was scriptural, its language was scriptural, its liturgy was scriptural, and its utterances were scriptural so that worshippers in unguarded spontaneity could not blurt out ideas and expressions that were unscriptural and therefore heretical.[38] Throughout the long controversy over what its enemies called Ritualism and what its defenders thought of as purging the church of "subjectivism," there would continue to be Episcopalians—many of them in Virginia—who valued evangelical asceticism and fought against the inroads of liturgical reforms identified with the Roman Catholic Church.[39] They would continue to cherish self-discipline and the intense inner conviction born of divine grace that they shared with other evangelicals, but they nonetheless shared with other non-evangelicals a wariness of the irrational, of undisciplined emotionalism—"impulses and fancies"[40]—and of religious authority based on such "fancies" that could erode the orderliness, elegance, and tradition celebrated in the Book of Common Prayer. In other words, Episcopalians resisted what the more partisan among them considered to be the excesses of a vernacular religion that could transform a clever, semiliterate, eloquent manipulator of emotions into a respected "preacher." If an evangelical braggart could announce at dinner that he never "knew a religious Episcopalian" and Methodists could carp at the "illiberal and unchristian spirit" of the church, one of its communicants could respond by complaining of "ranting and vociferous religionists" who converted their house of worship into a "mountebank show" that dissolved the congregation into "Bedlam let loose."[41] A young layman reading law in Raleigh, North Carolina, William Hooper Haigh did not simply dismiss the democratic drama playing nightly in a local Methodist church with a few well-chosen if impertinent words, for he was fascinated by its power to attract those who seemed to find emotional satisfaction in the noise and histrionics of a three-week revival. Indeed, he himself could not stay away from the admitted eloquence of John Maffitt, one of the most widely celebrated orators of nineteenth-century America, while the Methodist evangelist preached Raleigh into a revival. Haigh wavered between fascination and contempt: Maffitt was a master of the stage; he could move his auditors to tears, groans, expectancy, and ecstasy but then transform them into "poor, blind dupes of a bewildered fantasy."[42] It was genius, young Haigh believed, but it was not religion.

Revivals and camp meetings provided the most dramatic negative images of popular religious culture because Episcopalians believed that these images captured the hedonism, individualism, anarchy, and irrationality of evangelical Protestantism run amuck. Stung by accusations lifted from Wesleyan self-justification that they had the "form" but not the "power of religion,"[43] they struggled throughout the nineteenth century to become a viable alternative to a pervasive southern religious conviction that "power" came out of incessant self-expression, pervasive sentimentalism, uninformed scriptural exegesis, and a populist ministry ignorant of Christian history and unable to inspire true worship for all their conceded eloquence.[44] Stating the position so starkly makes Episcopalians appear to be ill-tempered critics, and some of them could indeed be short with what they considered to be silly, ignorant, and arrogant sectarianism; except in rare cases, however, they tended to avoid theological disputes with other Christians, preferring to make their own case to each other. In a religious ethos that valued a vivid experience of divine grace through which the believer had been "saved" or "got religion," the Episcopal response would have been not necessarily to demean its reality (although the temptation would have been great) but its sufficiency. Conversion, a loving turn to God that evangelicals tied to a once-and-for-all conscious decision, was necessary in the Christian life, they could admit, but it was necessary every day: it was a lifelong process, and it did not await an adult commitment, for it could be an essential part of rearing one's children.[45] Holiness, which some Methodists made into a second experience of grace (after conversion), was, like the emphasis on conversion, also a concept Episcopalians shared with the evangelical ethos. But instead of an achievement of intense piety that separated legitimate from tepid Christians, it was, Episcopal priests could emphasize, a correlative of the Word made flesh. "Ye are Sons of God," they could tell the women as well as men in the pews, and you must exercise your spiritual talents to the utmost in your daily life to perfect your faith; but the decision was the individual's, and its results were judged by God and perhaps the minister but not by one's fellow/sister communicants.[46] The scrutiny of private life among evangelicals, so noticeable before 1850, was transformed into public law during the period after 1885,[47] and in both situations Episcopalians were conflicted, although they tended to be decidedly wary of laying down rules on what they, if not Baptists, considered to be minutiae.[48] Episcopalians' temperament thus shared words and concepts with the evangelical culture in which they were immersed. While encouraging Christian piety and performance, however, they remained suspicious not of sentiment but of sentimentalism, not of emotion but of emotionalism. The corporateness of the church could never be surrendered to insisting on an unscriptural purity—tares and wheat were always intermixed—or to elevating the authority of private vision above that of tradition and scripture, or to elevating proof-texts above reasonable exegesis of biblical texts, or to ordaining presbyters ill-equipped to understand their sacred calling as successors to the apostles.

That corporateness was grounded in tradition, rendered in the Book of Common Prayer and sustained by an authoritative ministry validated not by democratic popularity but by its historical connection with generations who had had the hands of the apostles laid upon them. Evangelicals' emphasis on an immediate, personal religious experience or experiences was anarchic (and to many, idolatrous) because it placed an individual's consciousness (subjectivity) above the presumed objectivity of historical precedence, received Christian wisdom, the liturgical reenactment of Christ's passion, and the ancient language of devotion. The concreteness of the historical and institutional seemed so much more authoritative than ephemeral emotion. Neither intimations of divinity (conversion experience) nor the piety of individual saints or preachers—both of which could be feigned—established legitimacy; only the extension of the Incarnation in the Body of Christ (the church) did so. Episcopal clerics feared that evangelical notions, preaching, self-consciousness, and disorder weakened an understanding of the divine nature of the church and obliterated the sense of awe associated with the Holy Eucharist. The Right Reverend John Stark Ravenscroft, who had himself been a Methodist preacher, thought he understood the subjectivist dangers of the evangelicalism through which he had passed on his way to becoming Episcopal Bishop of North Carolina. He insisted—not entirely in Christian charity—that "the modern doctrine

Donald G. Mathews

of internal consciousness and assumed assurance (that sectarian opiate of deluded souls) [was no] substitute for those external ordinances which designate the covenant of mercy to redeemed man."[49] An "objective" church with specific forms, a definite liturgy, and a historically legitimized clergy who repeatedly led their people through the Christian year and celebrated the Eucharist would not necessarily be embraced by laity for the theological reasons Ravenscroft repeatedly gave his diocese—one of his own presbyters even fled to the Baptists. But the bishop and his fellows were indeed attempting to provide haven for believers who valued tradition, history, order, and the solemnity of a liturgy that reflected not merely the ties of local community but also those of the church universal. The Episcopal Church wherever its priests celebrated the Eucharist was an outpost of what sociologists in the twentieth century would call "cosmopolitanism"—an awareness of the world beyond the local, not only in terms of history but also in terms of reference and identity. It was, as Bishop Edward Demby insisted, a *catholic* church.

Was the church in danger of becoming too Catholic—as in *Roman* Catholic? The question disturbed many communicants in all sections of the country but especially in heavily evangelical Virginia and, because of that state's influence in the region, the South. When the bishop of North Carolina, Levi Silliman Ives, answered the question by submitting to the Roman Catholic Church, it was unclear whether his apostasy indicated a "yes" because the step he took was very small, or a "no" because he had to take it to be satisfied.[50] Such ambiguity throughout American Episcopal history has allowed, perhaps even birthed, a creative theological tension among a long train of parties and divisions that reflected controversy, to be sure, but avoided for the most part the deadly *mentalité* of condensed explicitness and clarity in which the mystery of the divine is surrendered to a specious precision that insists that each word of the Nicene and Apostles creeds and each authoritative text of the Bible must mean certain stipulated things and not others. Because of the mystery associated with the Eucharist, for example, communicants who disagreed on whether or not Christ is "really" present in the sacrament (and why it matters) may receive the elements together at the same time from the same celebrant. The ideal, said Bishop Joseph Blount Cheshire Jr. in a communion sermon early in the last century, was that the sacrament set forth "the crucified Jesus" who invites us to renew our vows of allegiance in "the sight of Calvary" and to take heavenly food. The bishop did not expect to have a debate over what the words of institution meant as long as the communicants submitted to the sacrifice of our Lord in their own lives together with others.[51] If they had to, they could talk about the Real Presence later, and they could disagree, as parties did on baptismal regeneration, predestination, free will, and the atonement, but their discussions should be punctuated by their kneeling once again to receive the elements according to the rubrics and language of the Book of Common Prayer. Cheshire's broad churchmanship was not that of a man necessarily indifferent to theology, although one could make that case. Rather, it was that of a man who thought theological disagreement detracted from vastly superior things—worship and living a Christian life. He shared with Episcopal communicants across the nation a broad theological pluralism.[52]

But what of Bishop Ives and the dangers of (Roman) Catholicism? The question lies within the long lasting discourse about the nature of the historically continuous, visible church that was not simply to be thought a pious body of "agreeable people" but a concrete institution formed by Christ Jesus and of which he was head. There would always be an Episcopal party that insisted more dramatically than others that the church and its sacraments conveyed the Christian faith objectively, that divine grace flowed through them as through nothing else, and that the negatively referenced "nothing else" was to be understood as the subjective experience of grace shaped by an individual's biases and imperfectly effected in a moment of impressionable susceptibility.[53] This did not mean that sacraments and liturgy were "conduits of objective grace," as a Catholic might think, but symbolic means through which the worshipper could be brought to awe, reverence, penitence, faith, and gratitude, and to receive salvation.[54] The church and its sacraments, rather than theatrical performers such as John Maffitt, were the means of grace. Evangelical Episcopalians, of course, would not have accepted the characterization of their position as having anything to do with Maffitt's performances, but they would have shared with the evangelist an insistence on a definite experience of conversion that conceded cosmic significance to *before* and *after*. Non-evangelicals would emphasize process, development, and growing in grace through the ministrations of the church; holiness would not be a subjective sense of trust so much as a commitment to holy living that flowed from personal devotion, reasoned faith, and worship through the liturgy of the church. This view, early in the nineteenth century and under the aegis of the bishop of New York, John Henry Hobart, came to be associated with a High Church party dedicated to nurturing belief in the historicity, visibility, and authority of the church based on studying the ancient fathers as the "rock of epistemological certainty."[55] Authority for the faith lay with the church—not the individual's subjective status; it was the church, not the individual believer, that was the arbiter of what the Bible meant. The phrase *sola scriptura* was meaningless to people who believed that the scriptures never existed alone but always in context, and the proper context was the ancient witness of the church, not the vernacular individualism of the nineteenth century.[56]

Hobart's daughter married an up-and-coming young priest by the name of Levi Silliman Ives, who was consecrated bishop of North Carolina when the austere Ravenscroft died. Having found Hobart's theology as well as his daughter appealing, Ives brought his father-in-law's insistence on the authority of the church with him to North Carolina and attempted to commend it to communicants while rejecting "the enormities of Rome, the gloomy tenets of Calvinism, the lifeless system of Socinianism [Unitarianism], [and] the uncertain vagaries of Methodism, all of which may be distinctly traced to individual opinion and conceit."[57] Against individualism he emphasized Christian tradition in trying to improve the spiritual life of his people and, when he found it exceptionally difficult to attract priests to North Carolina, decided to follow his High Church brother-in-law's example by founding what he hoped would be a combination farm, school, mission, and seminary at what became Valle Crucis in western North Carolina. During this time American Episcopalians were coming under the influence of the English Oxford movement identified with John Keble, Edward Pusey, and John Newman. These men, among others, wrote "tracts" supporting the catholicity of the Church of England through exalting the visible church, emphasizing apostolic succession, and urging acts of devotion that appeared to some to be derivative of "the Roman Church": fasting, frequent communion, and an aesthetically richer liturgy.[58] As the North Carolina laity discovered the "Tractarian" movement, they discovered also that Ives had founded the Order of the Holy Cross at Valle Crucis, which seemed suspiciously like a Roman Catholic monastic order. Participants dressed in monastic garb, possessed a crucifix, read Catholic devotional manuals, and could avail themselves of a father confessor. In fact, in the winter and spring of 1848 and 1849, Ives himself suggested that communicants could voluntarily take advantage of the ancient rite of auricular confession. All of these things were essential to Ives's attempts to bring the church through his priests more directly into the spiritual life of the laity. All of these things could also be perceived as Roman Catholic, and those who did so raised a general protest. After a complex, alarmist, partisan public debate that exemplified the worst characteristics of the American "paranoid style,"[59] Ives was forced to dissolve the order, purge Valle Crucis of its Catholic ambience, and explain himself. He confessed to having considered certain Catholic options without embracing them and to having rejected others after having accepted them; he also denied that he had entertained still other opinions and doctrines of which he stood accused. When the crisis subsided and after one of his closest friends submitted to the Roman Catholic Church, a battered and chastened Ives did so as well.[60]

Ives's story became a cautionary tale in the evangelical South; Episcopal bishops there discouraged "overloading" walls with symbols, decorating the altar, displaying "too many" crosses, and intoning the liturgy.[61] Such caution has since yielded to greater comfort with many of the liturgical practices favored by what Evangelicals feared were "Romanists"; the Chapel of the Cross, where Pauli Murray celebrated the Eucharist to symbolize the liberation of the church from segregation, for example, embraces a rich liturgical life. Yet if the Ives apostasy, like the Newport incident, symbolizes a South frozen in time, both symbols remind Episcopalians that the attitudes revealed within them linger still in a past that cannot die. This essay does not satisfy the need to think about Episcopalians in an evangelical South; simply mentioning the church's engagement with race and evangelicalism is not sufficient. The very fact that the Reverend Pauli Murray was a woman does not mean that women are universally accepted as priests any more than the fact that she was of African and European descent represents the final victory over racism. That she was of southern inheritance and embraced that fact suggests that regional identity is more complex than is indicated in sketching issues of race and evangelicalism; yet surely the discussion about the South and the church must begin with the role of invidious distinctions in crippling the theological and reconciling tasks of the church.

Slavery, the idea of "race," and concepts inferred from "race" are not merely southern matters, but they were peculiarly embedded in the American South where faithful people came to wrestle with them. The attempts to sustain the catholicity of the church in the face of such distinctions were flawed by whites' not accepting as fellow communicants the African Americans among them. Further acceptance still awaits further reconciliation through whites' listening to such historical voices as Alexander Crummell, Edward T. Demby, and Pauli Murray, as well as the voices of their contemporaries. We still await historical analysis of theological insights to be inferred from African American experiences—how they help us understand incarnation, sacrifice, atonement, and reconciliation, for example. The experiences of African Americans in attempting to make the church catholic might also be considered as cautionary in encouraging Episcopalians to be more aware of still other voices desiring to be heard in affirming liturgical language in receiving the elements—voices from those burdened still by invidious perceptions analogous to those Bishop Demby encountered in the Newport Incident. In addition, the experience of Episcopalians making their way in an evangelical South reminds us that Episcopalians are a minority report on regional identity. Sifting through the images of southern religious distinctiveness, one thinks not only of camp meetings, river baptisms, heated revivals, intense conversions, and biblical imagery but also a critique of such markers. Against the democratic celebration of individuals' publicly affirming their salvation within the confines of locality was the quiet confirmation of situating individuals not only within family, community, gender, and race but also within the corporate traditions of the church universal, the orderliness of the Christian year, and the sobriety of silence within the mystery of Eucharist.

Notes

1. Charles Reagan Wilson, *Baptized in Blood: The Religion of the Lost Cause, 1865–1920* (Athens: Univ. of Georgia Press, 1980), esp. 145–52. One of the best recent studies of religion in the American South is Christine Leigh Heyrman, *Southern Cross: The Beginnings of the Bible Belt* (New York: Alfred A. Knopf, 1997). Also important are John B. Boles, "The Discovery of Southern Religious History," in *Interpreting Southern History*, ed. John B. Boles and Evelyn Thomas Nolen (Baton Rouge: Louisiana State Univ. Press, 1987), 510–48. See also John B. Boles, *The Great Revival, 1787–1805: The Origins of the Southern Evangelical Mind* (Lexington: Univ. Press of Kentucky, 1972; Rhys Isaac, *The Transformation of Virginia, 1740–1790* (Chapel Hill: Univ. of North Carolina Press, 1982); Anne C. Loveland, *Southern Evangelicals and the Social Order, 1800–1860* (Baton Rouge: Louisiana State Univ. Press, 1980); Donald G. Mathews, *Religion in the Old South* (Chicago: Univ. of Chicago Press, 1977); Ted Ownby, *Subduing Satan: Religion, Recreation, and Manhood in the Rural South, 1865–1920* (Chapel Hill: Univ. of North Carolina Press, 1990); Daniel W. Stowell, *Rebuilding Zion: The Religious Reconstruction of the South, 1865–1877* (New York: Oxford Univ. Press, 1998); and David Edwin Harrell Jr., *Varieties of Southern Evangelicalism* (Macon, GA: Mercer Univ. Press, 1981). See also Charles H. Lippy, *Bibliography of Religion in the South* (Macon: Mercer Univ. Press, 1985).

2. See, for example, Peter Applebome, *Dixie Rising: How the South is Shaping American Values* (New York: Times Books, 1996).

3. Deborah Vansau McCauley, in *Appalachian Mountain Religion: A History* (Urbana: Univ. of Illinois Press, 1995), believes that the highlands are not southern because the rest of the South is dominated by "denominations" and they are not. The conclusion comes in part from not paying attention to antidenominationalism throughout the United States, much less the South. See also Samuel S. Hill's gentle demurrer in "The Virtue of Hope," in *Christianity in Appalachia: Profiles in Regional Pluralism*, ed. Bill J. Leonard (Knoxville: Univ. of Tennessee Press, 1999), 310.

4. Jon Butler, *Awash in a Sea of Faith: Christianizing the American People* (Cambridge: Harvard Univ. Press, 1990), 135, 135–51.

5. See John Frederick Woolverton, *Colonial Anglicanism in North America* (Detroit: Wayne State Univ. Press, 1984); S. Charles Bolton, *Southern Anglicanism: The Church of England in Colonial South Carolina* (Westport, CT: Greenwood Press, 1982); and Robert Prichard, *A History of the Episcopal Church* (Harrisburg, PA: Morehouse Publishing, 1999), 21–103.

6. After the Glorious Revolution in England, which placed William III and Mary II upon the throne, the monarchs removed the English bishops who refused to swear allegiance to them and replaced them with others who supported the "Revolution." These men also embraced the Cambridge Platonists, followers of

Plotinus, a third-century Neoplatonic philosopher who, as Prichard points out, "characterized faith as a mystery that could never be entirely reduced to logical propositions." As a result, they lived comfortably with the scientific revolution and the mysteries of faith, and generally deplored theological controversies with Calvinists, preferring a Christian faith that allowed for differences of informed opinion on contested points as long as the interpretations could be thought consistent with the Thirty-Nine Articles. Consistency was interpreted broadly, that is in a *latitudinarian* way. See Prichard, *History of the Episcopal Church*, 24.

7. William Meade, *A Brief Review of the Episcopal Church in Virginia from its First Establishment* (Richmond: Southern Literary Messegner, 1845).

8. Boles, *Great Revival;* Heyrman, *Southern Cross;* Isaac, *Transformation of Virginia.* That the evangelical style affected denominations did not mean, as Philip Mulder has pointed out to me, that lions and lambs lay down together in vegetarian harmony.

9. See, for example, Gardiner H. Shattuck Jr., *A Shield and a Hiding Place: The Religious Life of the Civil War Armies* (Macon, GA: Mercer Univ. Press, 1987), 117–19. See also Wilson, *Baptized in Blood*, 161–82.

10. It is common practice among historians of religion in the South to call the hegemonic religious mood of the region "evangelical"; this author has done so in the book *Religion in the Old South*. There I suggested that changes wrought in the religious life of southerners were made possible by similarities among religious innovators who appealed to a popular audience across what would later be called "denominational lines." Rhys Isaac did the same in his brilliant *Transformation of Virginia,* in which he identified changes in the Old Dominion in the eighteenth century with revivalistic Baptists whom he called "evangelicals." Christine Heyrman shared the same assumption in *Southern Cross,* except that she identified evangelical innovation more with Methodists, who were at that time by definition "evangelical." The primary markers of "evangelicalism" can be debated at such length as to make definition a way of defining orthodoxy. Indeed, within the past twenty years, so many books have been written about evangelicals that one now has to write and speak of "varieties" of evangelicalism. (See, for example, Harrell, *Varieties of Southern Evangelicalism;* and Donald Dayton, *The Variety of American Evangelicalism* [Knoxville: Univ. of Tennessee Press, 1991].) Samuel S. Hill Jr., in an essay of about a generation ago, pointed out that one could distinguish between devotional, fundamentalist, evangelistic and ethical (social or public service) kinds of evangelicalism in the South. This variety certainly suggests that evangelicals are not monolithic; but there are at least characteristics that bind them together. See Hill, "The Shapes of Popular Southern Piety," in *Varieties of Southern Evangelicalism,* ed. Harrell, 99–114.

11. See, for example, William Meade, *A Brief Review of the Episcopal Church;* Meade, *Reasons for Loving the Episcopal Church* (New York: Protestant Episcopal Society for the Promotion of Evangelical Knowledge, 1855);

[Meade, ed.], *Sketches of Old Virginia Family Servants with a Preface by Bishop Meade* (Philadelphia: Isaac Ashmead, 1847); Mathews, Introduction, *Religion in the Old South;* Hill, "Popular Southern Piety"; and the other works cited in note 10.

12. See Albert J. Raboteau, *Slave Religion: The 'Invisible Institution' in the Antebellum South* (New York: Oxford Univ. Press, 1978); Sylvia R. Frey and Betty Wood, *Come Shouting to Zion: African American Protestantism in the American South and British Caribbean to 1830* (Chapel Hill: Univ. of North Carolina Press, 1998); and Margaret Creel Washington, *'A Peculiar People': Slave Religion and Community-Culture among the Gullahs* (New York: New York Univ. Press, 1988).

13. See, for example, Loyal Jones, *Faith and Meaning in the Southern Uplands* (Urbana: Univ. of Illinois Press,1999); and Washington, *'A Peculiar People,'* 13–50, 113–210.

14. Harold T. Lewis, *Yet With A Steady Beat: The African American Struggle for Recognition in the Episcopal Church* (Valley Forge, PA: Trinity Press International, 1996), 1–38.

15. The expressiveness of the sacred dance called the "shout" was familiar to many African American worshippers, whether in Pennsylvania or the Sea Islands of South Carolina and Georgia, but some African American worshippers were wary of it. The call and response patterns of evocative preaching in which the congregation encourages the preacher to stay in the right trajectory towards a satisfactory climax are well known. The tendency to emphasize a sense of being overpowered in the Spirit and through that subjective experience to say one had "got religion" placed a greater weight on the psychological satisfactions of religion rather than on ethical and moral implications. Such a tendency has been called "antinomianism" by its enemies, with the implication of little or no self-discipline. See Daniel Alexander Payne, *Recollections of Seventy Years* (Nashville: A.M.E. Sunday School Union, 1888; reprint, New York: Arno Press, 1969), 253–58; Washington, *'A Peculiar People,'* 297–302; William H. Pipes, *Say Amen, Brother: Old-Time Negro Preaching, A Study in American Frustration* (New York: William-Frederick Press, 1951; reprint, Detroit: Wayne State Univ. Press, 1992); Riggins R. Earl Jr., *Dark Symbols, Obscure Signs: God, Self, and Community in the Slave Mind* (Maryknoll, NY: Orbis Books, 1993), 46–69; and William E. Montgomery, *Under Their Own Vine and Fig Tree: The African-American Church in the South, 1865–1900* (Baton Rouge: Louisiana Univ. Press, 1993), 266–92.

16. Lewis, *Yet With A Steady Beat,* 25–34.

17. "Right Reverend Thomas Atkinson in the Journal of the Diocese of N.C. (1868)," quoted in Lewis, *Yet With A Steady Beat,* 49–50.

18. Alexander Crummell, *Africa and America: Addresses and Discourses* (Miami: Mnemoeyne Publishers, 1969), 464, quoted in Lewis, *Yet With A Steady Beat,* 60. Crummell's characterization of this attitude is also on page 60. Emphasis added.

19. Gal. 3:27–29: "For you are all sons of God through faith in Christ Jesus. For as many of you as were baptized into Christ have put on Christ. There is neither Jew nor Greek, there is neither slave nor free, there is neither male nor female; for you are all one in Christ Jesus. And if you are Christ's, then you are Abraham's seed, and heirs according to the promise" (King James Authorized Version).

20. Crummell to [George] Frazier Miller, Sept. 18, 1894, Alexander Crummell papers, Arthur A. Schomburg Collection, New York Public Library, quoted in Wilson Jeremiah Moses, *Alexander Crummell: A Study of Civilization and Discontent* (New York: Oxford Univ. Press, 1989), 284.

21. Lewis, *Yet With A Steady Beat*, 25–38. This is not to say that an eschatological peace has been achieved. The tension continues in anticipation eventually of a Christian solution. See Gardiner H. Shattuck Jr., *Episcopalians and Race: Civil War to Civil Rights* (Lexington: Univ. Press of Kentucky, 2000).

22. Michael J. Beary, *Black Bishop: Edward T. Demby and the Struggle for Racial Equality in the Episcopal Church* (Urbana: Univ. of Illinois Press, 2001), 182, 197. Robert Prichard, *A History of the Episcopal Church* (Harrisburg, PA: Morehouse Publishing. 1999), 215, 226.

23. Beary, *Black Bishop*, 163, 204.

24. Ibid., 201.

25. Ibid., 181, 183, 188–89.

26. Ibid., 140.

27. Ibid., 178–92.

28. Shattuck, *Episcopalians and Race*, 7–55.

29. Ibid., 33–107.

30. Ibid., 187–90.

31. Pauli Murray, *Pauli Murray: The Autobiography of a Black Activist, Feminist, Lawyer, Priest, and Poet* (Knoxville: Univ. of Tennessee Press, 1987), 434–35.

32. Shattuck, *Episcopalians and Race*, 146, 177–79, 188, 193–213.

33. Meade, *Brief Review of the Episcopal Church*; Greenough White, *A Saint of the Southern Church: Memoir of the Right Reverend Nicholas Hamner Cobbs* (New York: James Pott & Co, 1897), 13–31.

34. Mathews, *Religion in the Old South*, 116–18.

35. Richard Rankin, *Ambivalent Churchmen and Evangelical Church Women: The Religion of the Episcopal Elite in North Carolina, 1800–1860* (Columbia: Univ. of South Carolina Press, 1993); Catherine Fullerton DeRosset diary and the entire series of letters in the DeRosset Family Papers, Southern Historical Collection, Univ. of North Carolina at Chapel Hill (hereafter cited as SHC-UNCCH).

36. Meade, *Brief Review of the Episcopal Church*.

Donald G. Mathews

37. William Hooper Haigh diary, Feb. 27, 1844, SHC-UNCCH.

38. William Meade, *Reasons for Loving the Episcopal Church* (New York: Protestant Episcopal Society for the Promotion of Evangelical Knowledge, 1855).

39. See "Ritualism—The Ally of Popery," *Southern Churchman* [periodical supported by the Diocese of Virginia], June 18, 1874. See also report of the Diocesan Council Meeting, *Southern Churchman*, May 28, 1874, 1. There was much debate over the difference between "moderation" [which could condone "moderate" drinking and dancing] and prohibitions. The Council agreed on fourteen points, some of which modern Episcopalians would find very much unlike their worship today. Among the things proscribed were incense, altar candles, bowing, genuflection, communion wafers, and a cross at the head of a procession. These forbidden things were on a list that also included the crucifix, auricular confession, private communion, adoration of the elements, and vestments reflecting the Christian year. The minister was to be thought of as presbyter and not priest. See *Southern Churchman*, June 4, 1874, 1.

40. White, *Saint of the Southern Church,* 70.

41. Haigh diary, Aug. 14 and 18, 1844.

42. Haigh diary, Sept. 11, 1844. See also Aug. 12, 1844.

43. See, for example, White, *Saint of the Southern Church,* 97–98.

44. See, for example, John N. Norton, *The Life of Bishop Bowen of South Carolina* (New York: General Protestant Episcopal Sunday School Union, 1859), 127–31; White, *A Saint of the Southern Church,* 253–56; *Southern Churchman,* December 17, 1874, 1; Thomas Frank Gailor, *Some Memories* (Kingsport, TN: Southern Publishers, 1937): 281; Michael Taylor Malone, "Levi Silliman Ives: Priest, Bishop, Tractarian and Roman Catholic" (Ph.D. diss., Duke Univ., 1970); Walter B. Capers, *The Soldier Bishop Ellison Capers* (New York: The Neale Publishing Co., 1912): 245, 246; and Joseph Blount Cheshire Jr., sermon 112, and Joseph Blount Cheshire, "Memories of my Father," MS vol. 41, 132–33a, both in Joseph Blount Cheshire Jr. Papers, SHC-UNCCH.

45. See, for example, Joseph Blount Cheshire Jr., sermons 165 and 187, Cheshire Papers.

46. See for example, Joseph Blount Cheshire Jr., sermon 100, Cheshire Papers.

47. Ted Ownby, *Subduing Satan: Religion, Recreation and Manhood in the Rural South, 1865–1920* (Chapel Hill: Univ. of North Carolina Press, 1990).

48. See, for example, Joseph Blount Cheshire Jr., sermon 188, Cheshire Papers.

49. John Stark Ravenscroft, *The Works of the Right Reverend John Stark Ravenscroft, D. D.,* vol. 1 (New York: Protestant Episcopal Press, 1830); the quotation is on 151, but see also 249–51, 259–60, and 267–70. See also Joseph Blount Cheshire Jr., sermon 62, Cheshire Papers, SHC-UNCCH.

50. See Malone, "Levi Silliman Ives."

51. Joseph Blount Cheshire Jr., sermon 62, Cheshire Papers.

52. Robert W. Pritchard, *The Nature of Salvation: Theological Consensus in the Episcopal Church, 1801–73* (Urbana: Univ. of Illinois Press, 1997), 171–207.

53. Robert Bruce Mullin, *Episcopal Vision/American Reality: High Church Theology and Social Thought in Evangelical America* (New Haven: Yale Univ. Press, 1986), 20–21.

54. Ibid., 72–80.

55. Ibid., 67, and, generally, 60–96.

56. Ibid., 51–59.

57. Malone, "Levi Silliman Ives," 146.

58. For a recent discussion of the Oxford Movement as a social movement, see John Shelton Reed, *Glorious Battle: The Cultural Politics of Victorian Anglo-Catholicism* (Nashville: Vanderbilt Univ. Press, 1996). See also Mullin, *Episcopal Vision*, 141–77; and Pritchard, *The Nature of Salvation*, 184–98.

59. Richard Hofstadter, *The Paranoid Style in American Politics and Other Essays* (New York: Knopf, 1965). See also David Brion Davis, *The Slave Power Conspiracy and the Paranoid Style* (Baton Rouge: Louisiana State Univ. Press, 1969).

60. Malone, "Levi Silliman Ives," 102–14, 129–75.

61. White, *Saint of the Southern Church*, 123–34.

CONTRIBUTORS

DON S. ARMENTROUT is the Charles T. Quintard Professor of Dogmatic Theology, Professor of Church History and Historical Theology, Associate Dean for Academic Affairs, and Director of the Advanced Degrees Program at the School of Theology at the University of the South. A graduate of Vanderbilt, he is an ordained pastor in the Evangelical Lutheran Church in America. He is the author and editor of numerous works on the Episcopal Church, including *A DuBose Reader: Selections from the Writings of William Porcher Dubose*, *Documents of Witness: A History of the Episcopal Church, 1782–1985*, and *An Episcopal Dictionary of the Church: A User-Friendly Reference for Episcopalians* (with Robert B. Slocum).

SUSAN RIDGELY BALES received her doctorate in religion from the University of North Carolina at Chapel Hill in December 2002. Her dissertation is "Seeing and Being Seen: An Ethnographic Study of Children's Interpretations of First Communion at Two Southern Catholic Churches." She has been a Visiting Assistant Professor in the Religion Department at Wake Forest University and an Andrew W. Mellon Post-Doctoral Fellow in Religion at Carleton College.

HEATHER E. BARCLAY graduated from Converse College in 2003 and is currently a graduate student at Harvard Divinity School and works for the Pluralism Project.

MARK K. BAUMAN is the editor of *Southern Jewish History*, an annual peer-reviewed journal. Recently, he took early retirement as Professor of History at Atlanta Metropolitan College. He is the author of biographies of southern Methodist bishop Warren A. Candler and Rabbi Harry H. Epstein and coeditor of *Quiet Voices: Southern Rabbis and Black Civil Rights*. His current projects include an anthology and bibliographic essay, both on southern Jewish history.

WAYNE FLYNT, Distinguished University Professor at Auburn University, received his Ph.D. from Florida State University, specializing in southern political history. In subsequent years, his research turned to poverty and religion in the South. He has written ten books, two of which have been nominated for the Pulitzer Prize. He has been the recipient of the Lillian Smith Award for nonfiction given by the Southern Regional Council. He is also a community activist, founder of the Alabama Poverty Project, and has spoken around the world on problems of the poor. His most recent works include *Alabama Baptists: Southern Baptists in the Heart of Dixie* and *Taking Christianity to China: Alabama Missionaries in the Middle Kingdom*.

D. JONATHAN GRIESER is Assistant Professor of Religion at Furman University. He has published extensively in early modern religious history and served as Interim Editor of the *Sewanee Theological Review* and on the executive board of the Society for Reformation Research. He is also a candidate for the priesthood in the Episcopal Diocese of Upper South Carolina.

NANCY A. HARDESTY is Professor of Religion at Clemson University, Clemson, South Carolina. She is the author of *Women Called to Witness: Evangelical Feminism in the Nineteenth Century* and *Faith Cure: Divine Healing in the Early Holiness and Pentecostal Movements*, as well as a number of essays on women and religion.

SAMUEL S. HILL has frequently been called the dean of the study of southern religion. Prior to his retirement in 1994, he was Professor of Religion at the University of Florida. He also taught at Stetson University and at the University of North Carolina at Chapel Hill from 1960 until 1972. Among his many seminal works are *Southern Churches in Crisis* and, most recently, *Southern Churches in Crisis Revisited, Religion and the Solid South, The South and the North in American Religion, Varieties of Southern Religious Experience,* and *One Name but Several Faces.* He is the editor of the *Encyclopedia of Religion in the South;* a revised edition of that work, coedited with Charles H. Lippy, is forthcoming in 2005.

KATHRYN V. JOHNSON teaches in the Religious Studies Department at the University of North Carolina at Charlotte. A graduate of Harvard University and a scholar of Islam, she works locally and nationally with law enforcement agencies to increase religious understanding in the aftermath of September 11.

CAROLYN M. JONES is Associate Professor of Religion and in the Institute of African American Studies at the University of Georgia. Her work includes pieces on Toni Morrison, Albert Murray, and Harper Lee. She is a past president of the Southeast Region of the American Academy of Religion.

BILL J. LEONARD is founding Dean and Professor of Church History, Wake Forest University Divinity School, Winston-Salem, North Carolina. From 1992 to 1996 he was Chair of the Department of Religion and Philosophy at Samford University and from 1975 to 1992, he was Professor of Church History at the Southern Baptist Theological Seminary. He holds a Ph.D. from Boston University. Leonard is author or editor of thirteen books, including *God's Last and Only Hope: The Fragmentation of the Southern Baptist Convention, Becoming Christian: Dimensions of Spiritual Formation, The Dictionary of Baptists in America, Christianity in Appalachia: Profiles in Regional Pluralism,* and, most recently, *Baptist Ways: A History.*

CHARLES H. LIPPY is the LeRoy A. Martin Distinguished Professor of Religious Studies at the University of Tennessee at Chattanooga. His most recent book is *Pluralism Comes of Age: American Religious Culture in the Twentieth Century.* Others include *The Evangelicals: A Historical, Thematic and Biographical Guide* (with Robert H. Krapohl), *Christianity Comes to the Americas, 1492–1776* (with Robert Choquette and Stafford Poole), and *Being Religious, American Style.* He has edited *Religion in South Carolina, Bibliography of Religion in the South,* and the forthcoming edition of the *Encyclopedia of Religion in the South* (with Samuel S. Hill). He is currently working on *Do Real Men Pray? Images of the Christian Man and Male Spirituality in White Protestant America.* Dr. Lippy is also an ordained Methodist minister.

DONALD G. MATHEWS is Professor of History and American Studies at the University of North Carolina at Chapel Hill. Dr. Mathews has been largely responsible for shaping scholarship on religion in the South. Among his numerous works are the groundbreaking *Religion in the Old South* and *Slavery and Methodism.* Currently, he is a writing a book on lynching and religion in the American South, and editing (with Beth Schweiger) a book of essays on religion in the American South. Most recently, in the online *Journal of Southern Religion* 3 (http://jsr.as.wvu.edu/), he published "The Southern Rite of Human Sacrifice: Lynching in the New South."

CORRIE E. NORMAN, a graduate of Florida State University and Harvard University, has been Chair of the Department of Religion and Philosophy and Director of the Rome Program at Converse College in Spartanburg, South Carolina. While her field of specialization is early modern Italian religious history, her books and articles include studies of religion in the contemporary American South, women and religion, and higher education as well. Currently she is working on two books: one is a collection of essays on food and religion in early modern Italy; the other is on food, religion, and meaning-making in contemporary American culture. A native of Georgia and an Episcopal laywoman, she organized the Dubose Symposium on Religion in the South that prompted this volume. She is currently President of the Southeast Region of the American Academy of Religion.

STEVEN W. RAMEY completed his doctorate at the University of North Carolina, Chapel Hill, with a dissertation entitled "Defying Borders: Contemporary Sindhi Hindu Constructions of Practices and Identifications." He is Assistant Professor of Religion at the University of North Carolina at Pembroke and continues to research Indian religious activities in India and throughout the global diaspora.

DAVID G. ROEBUCK is the Director of the Hal Bernard Dixon Jr. Pentecostal Research Center and Assistant Professor at Lee University. A minister in the Church of God, he earned a Ph.D. in religion at Vanderbilt University. His dissertation was "Limiting Liberty: The Church of God and Women Ministers, 1886–1996." He is editor of *Church of God History and Heritage,* as well as author of a regular column in the *Church of God Evangel.* He has published articles in *Perspectives in Religious Studies, Pneuma: The Journal of the Society for Pentecostal Studies,* and *CyberJournal for Pentecostal-Charismatic Research.*

GARDINER H. SHATTUCK JR. is the author of *A Shield and Hiding Place: The Religious Life of the Civil War Armies* and *Episcopalians and Race: Civil War to Civil Rights*, and a coauthor of the *Encyclopedia of American Religious History* and *The Episcopalians* (forthcoming). He is an Episcopal priest who has served in parishes in Rhode Island and Massachusetts and has also been Instructor in the History of Christianity at Andover Newton Theological School as well as an occasional lecturer at the Episcopal Divinity School.

THOMAS A. TWEED is Zachary Smith Distinguished Professor of Religious Studies and Associate Dean for Undergraduate Curricula at the University of North Carolina at Chapel Hill. Tweed edited *Retelling U.S. Religious History* and coedited *Asian Religions in America: A Documentary History*, which *Choice* magazine named an "outstanding academic book." He also wrote *The American Encounter with Buddhism, 1844–1912: Victorian Culture and the Limits of Dissent* and *Our Lady of the Exile: Diasporic Religion at a Cuban Catholic Shrine in Miami*, which won the American Academy of Religion's 1998 Award for Excellence.

Religion in the Contemporary South was designed and typeset on a Macintosh computer system using QuarkXPress software. The body text is set in 10.5/13 Adobe Caslon and display type is set in Mason Alternate and Mason Sans Alternate. This book was designed and typeset by Barbara Karwhite and manufactured by Thomson-Shore, Inc.

The Change Policy Papers

The Testing
and Grading
of Students

By Ohmer Milton and John W. Edgerly

54235

From the editors of Change

The Testing and Grading of Students *is one of a series of policy papers to help American faculty become more effective professionals. This volume has been published under a grant from The Ford Foundation.*

About This Special Report

WHEN VIEWED AGAINST THE CURRENT CRESCENDO OF egalitarian sentiments—or at least egalitarian rhetoric—the subject of student testing, let alone its design, leads one to some fascinating formulations about the very essence of an education. But no matter what one's ideological stance, the point remains that the "world outside" metes out rewards and penalties pretty much according to one's competence and talents. This being the current state of affairs, the least one can hope for is a less diffident effort by academics everywhere to evaluate student performance according to the fairest criteria available. There is now abundant evidence—and not only gleaned from student dissatisfaction—that testing and grading are often dispensed with an arbitrariness worthy of a Kublai Khan.

An appropriate design for tests should confirm the essential understanding between faculty and students as to what should be learned and what should not. This achievement is difficult, because it means, as Yale professor A. Barlett Giamatti has put it, "deciding that it is in fact a limited world, that some things are more important than others, that adjustments realistically have to be made. It means deciding that you really know what it is you want to teach and learn."

It is this centrality to the learning process that makes the subject of *Change*'s third policy paper, on testing and evaluation, so timely. The editors of *Change* are particularly grateful to the paper's authors, Ohmer Milton and John Edgerly, for their clearheaded portrayal of what is by any measure a vexing and complex subject. The authors are with the Learning Research Center and the Counseling Center at the University of Tennessee at Knoxville, respectively, and are widely regarded as sensitive authorities on the subject of human assessment. The preparation of their manuscript was facilitated by funds from the American Psychological Foundation, the Ford Foundation, and the University of Tennessee. This *Change* publication has been made possible under a separate Ford Foundation grant, which we acknowledge with thanks.

A number of individuals and organizations have contributed to the final formulation of this policy paper. The authors and editors wish to thank them for their counsel on a difficult and much debated subject. They include John Bevan, College of Charleston; Kenneth Eble, University of Utah; John Gillis, Chapman College; Linda Kahan, Evergreen State College; Lee McDonald, Pomona College; Robert O'Neil, Indiana University at Bloomington; Robert Van Waes, American Association of University Professors (AAUP); Francis J. Wuest, Association of American Colleges (AAC); and Norman Frederiksen and Paul Diederich of the Educational Testing Service. Prior to publication, the AAUP and AAC endorsed this policy paper for its serviceability.

There is, on the editors' side, only one further wish: that this publication will be studied by thousands of faculty with as much care as was put into its preparation. One need not agree with every nuance and every thought expressed here: One need only be open to the possibility for learning much about the neglected subject of student evaluation. Here is as good a starting point as any to bring rational planning into what remain, surprisingly, still rather uncharted waters of academic life.

George W. Bonham
January 1976

The Testing and Grading of Students: Why, Where, and How?

1

The Malignancy of Testing

Throughout American higher education, over 100 million tests are administered each year. Although testing is a subject of increasing contention among students, faculty members remain diffident. But a better understanding of both the purpose and structure of evaluating mechanisms becomes a prerequisite for widespread improvement. Page 11.

2

Setting Learning Goals

Teachers must understand what factors play a part in the measurement of learning. Faculty who pay ample attention to course content are often vague about the process of evaluation. If learning goals and course objectives are properly defined, they will be essential ingredients of success for student and teacher alike. Page 19.

3

Constructing Tests

Faculty widely confuse concepts of measurement and student evaluation. Regardless of the test construction chosen, both concepts must be carefully kept in mind. Multiple-choice and essay tests are most commonly used in college today. A thorough analysis of their structure and purpose clarifies underlying principles of evaluation as a learning tool. Page 27.

4

Grading

A comprehensive evaluation of student performance should provide guidance for academic improvement, but students too often receive scant critical commentary on their progress. Letter grading, the most commonly accepted form of evaluation, is particularly susceptible to the charge of insufficient feedback to the student. A more fundamental grasp of the options for academic measurement is the most direct route to improved grading. Page 43.

5

Lone Efforts Are Not Enough

Growing external pressures are forcing faculty to take a fresh look at student evaluation. The new consumerism, recent legal decisions, and far-reaching social criticism will no longer leave matters of grading and testing to the private academic preserve. The use of external examiners and the establishment of effective campus grievance arrangements are only two of the ways recommended to improve an increasingly nettlesome issue in academic life. Page 49.

6

For Further Reading

For a more comprehensive understanding of testing and evaluation, faculty have access to a number of excellent source documents. Here are some of the best. Page 57.

1

The Malignancy of Testing

Throughout American higher education, over 100 million tests are administered each year. Although testing is a subject of increasing contention among students, faculty members remain diffident. But a better understanding of both the purpose and structure of evaluating mechanisms becomes a prerequisite for widespread improvement.

THERE ARE SLIGHTLY MORE THAN HALF A MILLION faculty members in American colleges and universities. If each teaches an average of two courses and prepares three tests for each course, at least three million exams are given during any quarter or semester. Since these examinations are administered to about 10 million students, about 30 million tests are given every three or four months, or over 100 million every academic year. This is measurement on a grand scale indeed!

Considering that major decisions are made about students' lives—whether they remain in school, enter professional or graduate institutions, secure jobs—partially on the basis of those haloed test statistics, the grade point averages, elaborate care should be required in the entire testing and grading enterprise. Unfortunately, the very terms "testing" and "grading" have come to be used more or less synonymously, with either one referring to the entire process. In this policy paper each term will be used in a restricted and distinctive sense. Here, "testing" means measurement; "grading" means assigning an evaluative symbol—A, B, C, D, F (see Chapter 3).

While there are no documented reports about the degree to which care is exercised, a number of factors indicate that too much academic measurement in the classroom is conducted in a cavalier fashion. On the basis of an inspection of numerous tests over the years, loudly voiced and sometimes embittered laments by many students, and observation of too many untutored graduate teaching assistants assigned the entire chore of testing and grading, we developed a healthy skepticism about the practices in force. To check these initial suspicions, two dozen college and university officials were surveyed. In many instances, a disproportionate share of the complaints they were receiving concerned testing and grading. (The range was from 2 to 80 percent, with the overall average percentage near 30.) Discussions with students and our faculty colleagues revealed additional evaluation problems.

The following cases exemplify many of the responses we received.

Complaints About Test Content

(1) **In an introductory course covering approximately 2,500 years of philosophy, five of the seven questions on the final exam were about Kant.**

Good testing should be based on representative sampling. Five of seven questions focusing on one philosopher within a period of 2,500 years is not adequate sampling.

Considering that major decisions are made about students' lives—whether they remain in school, enter professional or graduate institutions, secure jobs—partially on the basis of those haloed test statistics, the grade point averages, elaborate care should be required in the entire testing and grading enterprise. Unfortunately, the very terms "testing" and "grading" have come to be used more or less synonymously, with either one referring to the entire process.

---

(2) **Five textbooks were assigned in a course designed to promote understanding of the contributions of several individuals to the field being studied. Lectures and class discussions focused almost entirely on one of these people. All questions on the final concerned the one person.**

Instructors need to be much more careful than many seem to be in correlating objectives, assignments, and testing.

(3) **Students in a senior course were assigned 15 journal articles, the shortest of which was 14 pages long. The only examination question over this considerable volume of material asked students to match the articles' authors with the titles. Challenged by a colleague, the instructor argued he could assume that a student who could do this matching understood the material.**

The assumption made by this professor requires a major leap in logic. Moreover, his future students might play the odds and limit their learning to memorizing authors and titles.

Complaints About Grading

(4) Students in a technology course were assigned a project to be completed individually. They were informed that the only grading criterion would be the quality of the product. Several students devoted many hours to the assignment early in the term and finished several weeks before final exams. Other students maintained a leisurely pace and worked throughout the term. All the early finishers received F's, while the leisurely ones received A's and B's. The instructor maintained that many of the F's were awarded because of absences—he had not seen some of these students during the last month of the course. Even when reminded that his announced criterion was quality, not class attendance, he refused to alter the F's.

Many teachers are unduly touchy about class attendance. To be fair and just, measurement should measure what has been asked for and nothing else.

(5) A foreign language class contained students who had lived abroad, graduate students working toward the foreign language exams, and beginners. One error of any kind reduced a quiz or exam grade to a B, two errors to a C, and so on. Many studious and responsible students received D's and F's in this course.

While high standards are important, there should be some demonstrable relationship between reasonable expectations and grading criteria.

(6) After assigning quite high mid-term grades, an instructor declared that students were being coddled. Without any warning, term papers were graded very harshly (after the withdrawal date had passed). The final was graded equally severely. Course grades for the class of over 40 included one A, one C, and a few D's; the rest were F's. Colleagues of the instructor arranged for the students to take another final.

Capriciousness and arbitrariness have no place in evaluation.

(7) A freshman was told by an instructor she would receive a B in his course; her final grade was C. The student was applying for admission to a competitive program for which a few hundredths of a point in her GPA might determine her acceptance. Investigation revealed that the instructor was a teaching assistant who had left school. The department chairman believed this instructor's teaching and testing methods had been questionable and changed the grade. The student was admitted into the competitive program.

Most teaching assistants do not receive formal instruction or guidance about testing and grading. Incidents such as this one may be prevalent.

(8) In a course which had a fairly rigid attendance requirement, a student requested an excused absence for a

mandatory appearance in court and believed the instructor allowed the absence. The student received a final grade of C instead of the B he had expected. The instructor explained the C in different ways: to the student—too many absences (he disallowed the court appearance); to the department chairman—inadequate class participation (records indicated otherwise); to an administrator—poor written work (papers averaged B). The instructor refused to change the grade, but an academic grievance committee directed a change.

If an instructor justifies a grade in so many ways, how can evaluators of the student's transcript interpret the grade?

(9) A freshman who had maintained a C average on all his tests received a final grade of F. The instructor explained that the student had exhibited an improper spirit toward the subject matter and refused to alter the grade.

We have serious doubts about the propriety of grading a student's "spirit" or attitude.

While there are no documented reports about the degree to which care is exercised, a number of factors indicate that too much academic measurement in the classroom is conducted in a cavalier fashion. On the basis of an inspection of numerous tests over the years, loudly voiced and sometimes embittered laments by many students, and observation of too many untutored graduate teaching assistants assigned the entire chore of testing and grading, we developed a healthy skepticism about the practices in force.

---

(10) A student with the highest overall point total in her class (90 percent) received a B rather than an A as her final grade. The instructor explained that his point system was absolute and that while she had a "moral A," he could not give her an A for the course. During the conversation he told her he had given another student a B when that student had only enough points for a C. He rationalized that there was a difference between giving someone a B and giving someone an A but did not explain what the difference was. The student appealed to the grievance committee.

Undergraduates state that they frequently encounter this professorial attitude, although seldom in such a blatant incident. Assigning a grade in such a manner is not responsible evaluation.

(11) A female student was informed by a professor: "Women do not belong in my field." Her grade for the course was significantly lower than the average she had maintained.

The injustice was rectified with the assistance of the department chairman.

Social prejudices must be eliminated in evaluating student achievement, and every effort should be made to minimize personal prejudices.

Complaint About Test Conditions

(12) **A final was administered to 130 students in a crowded classroom where it was easy for students to copy from each others' papers. Although many students thought the situation was unjust, the instructor refused to change the test location, blaming the institution for assigning too many students to the class and for providing the small classroom. An administrator, the department chairman, and the college dean intervened, and the test was given again under satisfactory conditions.**

Inadequate and improper testing conditions are inexcusable.

Most student complaints seem to be about grades or the symbols, not about testing or measurement where the basic problems are. Apparently most students are unaware of the fundamental issues in measurement and evaluation and do not know the questions they should be asking. They are not alone in seeing just the tip of the evaluation iceberg. Thousands of studies have been conducted about grades and grade point averages [GPAs], but the measuring devices from which those symbols are derived are rarely questioned.

Most of the students' complaints seem to be about grades or the symbols, not about testing or measurement where the basic problems are. Apparently most students are unaware of the fundamental issues in measurement and evaluation and do not know the questions they should be asking. They are not alone in seeing just the tip of the evaluation iceberg. Thousands of studies have been conducted about grades and grade point averages (GPAs), but the measuring devices from which those symbols are derived are rarely questioned.

Study Influences

The effects of testing upon learning have been almost totally ignored, yet experimental scientists have been concerned for many years with the effects the act of measurement has upon the object or phenomenon being measured. A good example is a blood-pressure reading. At least two features of the act of measuring blood pressure distort the true reading: the pressure of the inflated cuff and, for some people, the emotional reaction to the procedure. The reading is false to some degree because of either or both of these.

Generations of students have told their faculty that testing influences them. They study according to the type of test they are going to take and in so doing learn different features of the material. A few studies support their assertions. Meyer found, by analyzing notes made and the booklets which contained new material to be learned, that a smaller percentage of students who were to receive an essay test used underlining and a greater percentage of them made summaries than students who were to take objective tests. Thomas and Augstein found that students who were informed that their test on a paper on genetics would be in essay form, but who in fact took objective and essay tests, performed better on both types than did students who studied the same material under the impression that their test would be objective (but received the two types). Felker and Dapra demonstrated that comprehension-type questions were more effective for enhancing problem solving than verbatim-type questions.

Directions

It seems likely that traditional testing and evaluation practices—written tests covering subject matter and grading on curves—will continue on a grand scale, especially in lower-division courses. The remainder of this policy paper is devoted primarily to introducing faculty members to basic principles of measurement and some of the prominent unresolved issues of grading. Improved testing devices and practices will help learning and grading. Numerous volumes have been written about most of the topics that we only mention; carefully selected references are given in Chapter 6. The purpose throughout this volume is to alert faculties to some exceedingly complex problems: The measurement of learning, the assigning of grades, and determining the significance of the process are inordinately complicated procedures.

2

Setting Learning Goals

Teachers must understand what factors play a part in the measurement of learning. Faculty who pay ample attention to course content are often vague about the process of evaluation. If learning goals and course objectives are properly defined, they will be essential ingredients of success for student and teacher alike.

ONE OF THE STUDENT-REACTION-TO-INSTRUCTION FORMS used at the University of Tennessee in Knoxville allows instructors to write in extra items. Just before a term ended, one instructor wrote in, "Rate your progress on the course objectives." We suggested that he might list the objectives himself and ask the students to rate their progress on each one. He replied he wasn't certain what the objectives were, but he would try to determine them after the course was over.

How does one measure at all if one does not know what one wishes to measure? Instructors should not be like St. Augustine when he declared, "For so it is, O Lord my God, I measure it; but what it is I measure, I do not know."

Goals and Objectives

It should go without saying that effective evaluation (testing and grading) is based on well-established goals and objectives, yet frequently it is not. Faculty devote great amounts of attention to the content of their courses (what to include, how to include it, and what to exclude), but too few give as much time or energy to the process of evaluation, even though the goals and objectives of a course and of evaluation are the same.

Goals and objectives are often thought of separately so that their roles in evaluation may be delineated. Goals may be defined as the hoped-for end results or products of a sequence of educational events. Goals may apply to a single course or to a sequential program (e.g., a major). Objectives are the short-range events in a sequence leading to a goal.

Goals can best be measured through the assessment of well-defined objectives. This principle is as true for a professor's course as it is for a college's curriculum. The goal for this volume is "improving testing and grading." One measure might be the number of faculty who seek to apply the principles expounded. The objectives are for faculty to understand the detailed ways of attaining the goal. One measure might be their performances on a carefully constructed written test over the contents.

Goals and objectives should be stated in as empirical a fashion as possible so that they will be susceptible to evaluation. It is true that some educational goals are difficult to state in definitive terms, but difficulty is no excuse for not trying to come to grips with the clarity of goal statements.

True, some curriculum and course goals do seem to defy evaluation. Such goals, often found in college catalogs and course syllabi, usually run as follows: The liberal arts education provides the individual with the ability to comprehend the great outlines of knowledge, the principles upon which it rests, the scale of its parts, its

---

It should go without saying that effective evaluation [testing and grading] is based on well-established goals and objectives. Yet frequently it is not. Faculty devote great amounts of attention to the content of their courses [what to include, how to include it, and what to exclude], but too few give as much time or energy to the process of evaluation, even though the goals and objectives of a course and of evaluation are the same.

---

lights and shadows. A liberally educated person is identified by quality of mind. Educators insist these respectable and cherished goals should not be compromised. As stated, they correspond to the accepted definition of a goal as an abstract statement of a hoped-for result (Mager, 1972). They do not, however, tell how to achieve results. This is where objectives play a crucial role in describing what knowledge, skills, understanding, and behaviors (such as laboratory abilities) the students should possess after completing their experience of the curriculum.

It is in defining objectives that many courses and curricula fall short and thereby complicate evaluation. It is generally assumed that the lauded goals are accomplished through various curricula, but the objectives are stated no more clearly than the goals, and hence the confusion.

Although this presentation of the basic principles of setting goals and objectives is concerned with the level of the individual course and the individual test, what pertains at this level is applicable to an entire curriculum. Courses within a curriculum are assumed to be cumulative. The vast majority of courses have prerequisites that assume that the successful completion of one course's objectives provides passage to the next course. It is assumed that all the courses contribute to the goals of a curriculum or program.

Matching Test Items and Objectives

One of the most frequent violations of good procedure in setting objectives for achievement assessment is a mismatch between the objective and the unit of measurement chosen to assess it. The basic unit of measurement of an objective is the individual test item, and it is imperative that the two be well matched. In courses in measurement, though, even some bright and well-informed graduate students have great difficulty preparing test items that adequately match the stated objectives. Matching is difficult, but not impossible, particularly if objectives have been carefully stated.

As Mager (1973) so aptly states: "The issue of inappropriate test items is a widespread phenomenon. . .and a practice (mal-practice?) most urgently in need of improvement. When we deceive the student by discrepancies between our words and our deeds, both he and we are the losers."

The first task in testing, therefore, is to define objectives clearly. These should be made as concrete as possible. Then matching the unit of measurement (the test item) to the objective becomes somewhat easier and one can choose the appropriate test item format. If, for example, "knowledge of," as opposed to "skill in," an academic area is a course goal, then one would choose a compatible set of objectives and units of measurement (test items) to assess its achievement. These two quite different tasks obviously call for different performances or behaviors.

Students frequently complain that an exam did not cover the content of the course. This often means that there was a mismatch between the test items and the objectives. It is crucial to have a sound understanding of what types of performances are required by the objectives. Only in this way can one construct the appropriate item to measure the achievement of the objective. In this sense, each test item is a criterion-referenced item; that is, each item serves as a means of identifying a student's status with respect to an established standard or of assessing objectives.

We pointed out earlier that some academic fields appear to be more easily accessible to measurement than others. However, one encounters as many errors in tests assessing achievement in mathematics as in literature. In this regard, no academic domain or area seems to be entirely free of error. What appears to be a discrepancy between complex (difficult to get at) and simple (easy to get at) domains could be greatly reduced if the basic principles of setting objectives were followed. In short, one must make the decision whether the objectives will lead to "knowledge of," skills, "concepts about," "understandings of" (all manifested in writing) or overt behaviors (manifested by manipulating laboratory equipment, for example).

There is probably no better way of stating an objective (or initiating thinking about objectives) than to pose the following question at the outset of the course: What do I want my students to be able to do at the end of this course?

This usually generates a long list of rather lofty goals that must be translated into objectives. The key words are *be able to do*: read a map, prepare a brief, test for diabetes, explain how a bill becomes a law, describe the human eye, solve an equation, write an essay.

Domain Dictates Objectives

There is perhaps nothing more frustrating to students than to be told that a course objective is for them to be able to write a grammatically correct theme of 100 words and then have a well-meaning professor discount points for lack of imagination and/or creativity. Errors of this sort are commonplace. Not only is this an error in stating objectives to students, it is also an error in the choice of the appropriate item format or type. Creativity is an extremely difficult

---

One of the most frequent violations of good procedure in setting objectives for achievement assessment is a mismatch between the objective and the unit of measurement chosen to assess it. The basic unit of measurement of an objective is the individual test item, and it is imperative that the two be well matched. In courses in measurement, though, even some bright and well-informed graduate students have great difficulty preparing test items that adequately match the stated objectives. Matching is difficult, but not impossible, particularly if objectives have been carefully stated.

---

area to assess—but not impossible. One first defines it and then chooses or constructs the appropriate items to assess its presence or absence.

The problem of choosing appropriate objectives and subsequent test items for assessing achievement within a given domain or area does point up that the domain determines objectives, to a degree. We are not suggesting that faculty back away from trying to assess those goals that they regard as important just because a goal might seem fuzzy. We are not sympathetic with those who contend that the crucial things within their domain are inaccessible to objective assessment and who often claim that only experience and subjective judgment can serve as bona fide assessment. We repeat: If something is worth being made a goal, it is worth being objectified! This position in no way lessens the admirable qualities of a goal.

A good example is a course in art appreciation. If a goal of the course is to appreciate fine art, one simply has to state what the student should be able to do at the course's conclusion. For example, the student might be expected to be able to choose from a list of paintings five that would be considered as representative of fine art by a panel of experts, fine art, in turn, having been made definable by excluding from it violations of characteristics common to fine art, e.g., good composition, perspective, and so on.

The claim that these types of assessment issues are not accessible or are too open to subjective interpretation is inaccurate. There is little question that today's dime-a-dozen novels will not be tomorrow's literary masterpieces or Pulitzer Prize winners. There is little room for doubt that Dante's *Inferno* is superior. Subjectivity enters when one is asked to indicate whether one likes or dislikes a book. This is a personal rendition of one's own experience, but to be able to discern the characteristics of great literature from a random selection of books is something someone can learn to do and subsequently demonstrate.

To emphasize the importance of defining and specifying performance objectives, Mager (1973) suggests the rather humorous "Hey Dad" technique. Here, one places a course objective within the following context: "Hey Dad, let me show you how I can ____!" If the result of filling in the blank is a seemingly absurd statement, the objective is too broad and needs clarification and simplification. In our example of art appreciation, as a course objective, the following absurdity would be the result: "Hey Dad, let me show you how I can appreciate fine art!" This absurdity can be obviated by specifying the generally agreed-upon component behaviors or performances of art appreciation. The following examples make the initial objective more tolerable:

> Hey Dad, let me show you how I can, when presented with them, accurately identify 10 out of 10 Renaissance paintings, supply their titles and the artists' names, name two additional paintings each has done, when and where each lived, three contributions each has made to the history of art, and two elements of their work that have led them to be judged as outstanding in the history of art.

In this fashion, art appreciation becomes less fuzzy and is more easily assessed.

An Illustration

There are several ways of measuring the extent to which course objectives have been met. As previously mentioned, the domain or area does exercise some influence over the type of test or measurement one uses to assess course objectives. There is, however, a basic reciprocity between the types of test employed and the objectives of a course. For example, it just makes good sense to use performance (i.e., observable behavior) to assess the objectives of performance courses. Most of the physical sciences require laboratory skills, the attainment of which requires the instructor to observe whether the student can do the task in question. Most academic courses are assessed by asking students to perform on a written exam. In other words, instructors are assessing students' ability to do something vis-à-vis their response to a written question. Within this form of testing, we ask them to demonstrate knowledge of or about in a variety of ways: multiple-choice testing, matching, true-false, and essay, to mention just a few of the varieties.

An example demonstrates how a simple objective is amenable to different testing forms. The basic case of "Making a Pot of Coffee" is drawn from Mager (1973). Making a pot of coffee with an electric coffee pot calls for knowing how to do definite things:

(1) Disconnect coffee pot; (2) disassemble coffee pot; (3) clean components and pot; (4) inspect components of pot; (5) fill pot with water; (6) reassemble components of pot; (7) fill basket with coffee; (8) reconnect coffee pot; (9) set dial on coffee pot; (10) note if pot is perking properly.

A student's knowledge can be assessed in a variety of test types. One of the objectives in teaching coffee making might call for a knowledge of (or ability to recognize or state) the correct sequence of action in making a pot of coffee. One multiple-choice question could take the following form:

1. Of the items below, which is the first step in making a pot of coffee:

   (a) fill the basket with coffee
   (b) note if pot is perking properly
   (c) disassemble coffee pot
   (d) *disconnect coffee pot*

An essay question requiring this same knowledge might take the following form: Please describe in no more than 100 words the 10 important steps in making a pot of coffee.

A matching test on coffee making might be prepared as follows:

Take every other step and make a comparison right and left list:

Left		Right	
Step	1 disconnect coffee pot	Step	2 disassemble coffee pot
	3 clean components and pot		4 inspect components
	5 fill pot with water		6 reassemble components
	7 fill basket with coffee		8 reconnect coffee pot
	9 set dial on coffee pot		10 watch to see if pot is perking properly

Then shuffle the right list to derive the following:

Step	1 disconnect coffee pot	Step ___	reassemble components
	3 clean components and pot	___	disassemble coffee pot
	5 fill pot with water	___	watch to see if pot is perking properly
	7 fill basket with coffee	___	inspect components
	9 set dial on coffee pot	___	reconnect coffee pot

The matching test for the students would then be:

The list on the left contains the correct ordering of steps 1,3,5,7, and 9 of the 10 appropriate steps in making a cup of coffee. The list on the right contains steps 2,4,6,8, and 10. However, the steps on the right have been shuffled. Your task is to draw a line from Step 1 on the left to the appropriate Step 2 on the right; a line from Step 3 on the left to the correct Step 4 on the right and so on until you have correctly matched all 10 steps in their correct sequence.

As we shall presently see, test construction is a time-consuming task, principally because the preparation of learning objectives must be done with great care. This is the key to successful testing.

3

Constructing Tests

Faculty widely confuse concepts of measurement and student evaluation. Regardless of the type of test chosen, both concepts must be carefully kept in mind. Multiple-choice and essay tests are most commonly used in college today. A thorough analysis of their structure and purpose clarifies underlying principles of evaluation as a learning tool.

Our INVESTIGATIONS INTO STUDENT ASSESSMENT HAVE led to several conclusions: (1) There is real confusion about the concepts of measurement and evaluation. (2) Many faculty members believe their discipline is so unique that little is to be learned about academic measurement from faculty of other disciplines. (3) Instructors feel there must be no interference in their testing and grading of students—not even by their own disciplinary colleagues.

Tests should promote learning. They should assist the student and the instructor in determining whether learning goals are being achieved. If they do not, then both participants may alter strategies. In this private context, formal measurement is of little importance, because errors in judgment by the instructor can be corrected and honest differences of opinion can be resolved. Central to exchanges between the two is the student receiving detailed criticism of his or her work and constructive suggestions for improving it.

What has happened, however, is that the letter symbols resulting from tests are used almost solely for official record keeping. Many instructors do not view testing as part of the learning process and as a result resent spending class time on it, return exams to students with no correction marks or comments upon them, and never show final exam results to students. Students, in accepting this limited use of tests, strive to gain points rather than to learn.

In this context, it is difficult to understand how the defensive cry of "academic freedom" (meaning "Stay away; I'll test and grade as I please") can be justified. Faculty members are fallible. They can be capricious (Case 6, page 14) in their judgments of student achievement, and poorly constructed tests can support those judgments. In the final analysis, it is the student who pays the price; and the best students are harmed the most. They are the ones who engage in "grade grubbing" because they hope to enter graduate and professional schools, and very tiny fractions of GPA points may decide their fates.

The thesis here is simple: Since the results of measurement of student achievement are currently used more to serve the public than to promote learning (that is, the results are made available to employers and others to be used in the selection process), individual faculty members can no longer pretend infallible judgment about student assessment. While we disagree with this public function, since it will continue it must be improved. This chapter will explain and clarify the concepts of both testing and grading and introduce some of the necessary principles for techniques of measurement.

Concepts: Measure, Evaluate

The word "measure" has at least 40 different meanings (Lorge). In the present context measure is intended to mean all those activities

---

Since the results of measurement of student achievement are currently used more to serve the public than to promote learning [that is, the results are made available to employers and others to be used in the selection process], individual faculty members can no longer pretend infallible judgment about student assessment. While we disagree with this public function, since it will continue it must be improved.

---

which are necessary to quantify learning or achievement: the preparation of single questions or items, the selection of items or questions to make up a test or examination, the conditions under which the test is administered, scoring each individual item, and assigning a score, number, or quantity to the whole. In everyday parlance, all of these activities are referred to as testing.

The goal of objectivity is sought in all measurement. In the hands of several trained people, the same instrument—whether a ruler, a watch, a sextant, a sphygmomanometer, an English test—should yield the same reading. Ebel's (1972) definition applies with equal force to all educational tests: "A measurement is objective if it can be verified by another independent measurement. If it cannot be, that is, if the measurement reported depends more on the person making the measurement than on the person being measured, it is unlikely to be very dependable or very useful...."

The greater the care with which an instrument is constructed, the greater the likelihood that two or more trained people will obtain the same reading (or quantity or score) for the same value or operation. Most people seem to be alert to this principle for physical measurements, but much less attuned to it for educational ones. This general lack of sophistication is illustrated by the prevalence of superficial thinking about so-called objective tests. Multiple-choice and true-false tests are both called objective because two or more scorers will arrive at the same score for an examinee after a key is prepared. But the score or quantity assigned is only one aspect of measurement; if other principles of measurement have been applied carelessly, the test is not objective.

It is a common error to equate quantification, no matter how determined, with objectivity. As Hofstadter has explained: "The American mind seems extremely vulnerable to the belief that any alleged notion which can be expressed in figures is in fact as final and exact as the figures in which it is expressed." Upon reflection, it is clear that, for example, an 85 on a test paper could have been derived arbitrarily, and the instrument on the basis of which it was calculated could have been constructed poorly in the first place.

As we use the term, "evaluation" means arriving at a judgment or decision. The physician, after taking a blood pressure reading, makes a judgment that the blood pressure is normal or abnormal.

The greater the care with which an instrument is constructed, the greater the likelihood that two or more trained people will obtain the same reading [or quantity or score] for the same value or operation. Most people seem to be alert to this principle for physical measurements, but much less attuned to it for educational ones. This general lack of sophistication is illustrated by the prevalence of superficial thinking about so-called objective tests.

The driver, after trying to collect sound information about two automobiles, weighs the evidence and buys car A rather than car B. The instructor examines a student's test performance, reaches a decision about the level of achievement, and expresses it in a letter symbol. Needless to say, such decisions may not be simple in reality. While the goal in measurement is objectivity, one of the chief goals in evaluation is minimizing extraneous factors or variables. In Case 11 (page 15), the sex of the student was an extraneous factor and should have had nothing to do with her final grade (evaluation). Ultimately, evaluation is subjective because human judgment is its essence. The greater the extent to which judgments are based upon carefully constructed and administered measuring devices, the greater the likelihood they will be sound. Factors to be considered in evaluating student achievement (assigning grades) are discussed more fully in Chapter 4.

Test-Question Principles

There is at least one unalterable fact about testing: It is time-consuming. There are no short cuts to constructing a good test. Tests take many forms—multiple-choice, true-false, essay, matching, completion, problems, interpretive, and combinations of these. We have set forth certain principles and recommendations that are applicable to written tests because without question such tests are used almost exclusively in higher education. In this connection the work of Ebel (1966, 1972) has been drawn on heavily, and the reader might also see Adkins and Dressel.

The basic unit in a written test is the individual item or question—improvement in measurement begins at this point. Judging from the literature, less attention has been devoted to item preparation than to any other feature of test construction. For this reason, certain principles of item preparation are emphasized, with many examples.

Instructors who prepare items or questions must possess several abilities:

● *A thorough mastery of the subject matter.* Item writers must be acquainted with facts and principles, attuned to their implications, and aware of popular fallacies and misconceptions. Most graduate teaching assistants do not have such mastery.

● *A rational and well-developed set of aims or objectives for the instruction.* For most courses these will include helping students learn facts and principles, make abstract generalizations, be critical, and apply what has been learned in other settings. The importance of aims and objectives cannot be overstressed.

● *A mastery of written communication.* Those who have written for publication have learned how difficult it is to choose the right words and to arrange them to convey the meaning intended. Students probably give the words in test questions much more critical attention than almost any other prose receives.

● *A knowledge of the special techniques of item writing and how to use them.* Some of these will be discussed further on.

Since the two test forms used most commonly are multiple-choice and essay and since our space is limited, we will discuss the development of only these two in some detail.

Multiple-Choice Questions

Multiple-choice tests have been condemned roundly by many instructors and students (the latter sometimes refer to them as multiple-guess). Much of this criticism is well-founded because many tests are constructed carelessly. Items tend to be ambiguous and to emphasize the trivial. In one study (McGuire), three judges classified test items that covered knowledge in medical subjects and unanimously agreed that over half of the items measured predominantly recall and recognition of isolated information. Fewer than one fourth of the items were thought by any single judge to require even simple elements of interpretation or problem solving.

Properly developed, however, multiple-choice tests can tap many facets of learning. The principles here set forth are merely introductory and may appear deceptively simple, but their application is time-consuming and demanding. Illustrative questions or items* are uncomplicated in the hope they will enable the disciplinary specialist to focus upon the principle.

(1) *Strive for item clarity.* The English language is full of ambiguous words. The printed page cannot convey such clues to meaning as voice inflections and facial expressions. Test items should not be verbal puzzles. A test's purpose is to test or measure knowledge rather than verbal puzzle-solving ability. The major recommendation for attaining clarity in items or questions is: *Every item, before it is used, should be responded to by a colleague and by an advanced student (the latter will detect vagueness, ambiguities, and errors the former might miss).*

(2) *Include in the stem or body all necessary qualifications that are needed for answer selection.* Consider the following multiple-choice question:

> If a ship is wrecked in very deep water, how far will it sink?
> 1. Just under the surface.
> 2. To the bottom.
> 3. Until the pressure is equal to its weight.
> 4. To a depth which depends in part upon the amount of air it contains.

The instructor intended 2 as the correct answer, but several capable students chose 4 because they considered the possibility (which the instructor failed to exclude) that a wrecked ship might not sink completely.

(3) *Generally, omit nonfunctional words. They tend to interfere with comprehension.* Consider:

> While many in the U.S. feared the inflationary effects of a general tax reduction, there was widespread support for a federal community-property tax law under which:
> 1. husbands and wives could split their combined income and file separate returns.
> 2. homesteads would be exempt from local real estate taxes.
> 3. state income taxes might be deducted from federal returns.
> 4. farmland taxes would be lower.

Comprehension of this item may be facilitated by rewording it as follows:

> Community-property tax laws permit:
> 1. husbands and wives to split their combined income and file separate returns.
> 2. homesteads to be exempt from local real estate taxes.
> 3. state income taxes to be deducted on federal returns.
> 4. farmland taxes to be lowered.

Sometimes, though, it is useful to include introductory statements that help to emphasize importance:

> The pollution of streams in the more populous regions of the United States is causing considerable concern. What is the effect, if any, of sewage on the fish life of a stream?

---

*These are from Ebel, Robert L. "Writing the Test Item." In **Educational Measurement**, edited by E. F. Lindquist. Washington, D.C.: American Council on Education, 1966, and are used by permission.

thirty-three

1. It destroys fish by robbing them of oxygen.
2. It poisons fish by the germs it carries.
3. It fosters development of nonedible game fish that destroy edible fish.
4. Sewage itself has no harmful effect on fish life.

(4) *Beware of unessential specificity and/or trivia.* Consider:

What percent of the milk supply in municipalities of over 1,000 was safeguarded by tuberculin testing, abortion testing, and pasteurization?
1. 11.1 percent
2. 20.3 percent
3. 31.5 percent
4. 51.9 percent
5. 83.5 percent

This item, encouraging rote memorizing, is an illustration of the trivia about which so many students complain. Furthermore, such figures are seldom as precise as they appear.

(5) *Be certain the stem is accurate.* Consider:

Why did Germany want war in 1914?
1. She was following an imperialistic policy.
2. She had a long-standing grudge against Serbia.
3. She wanted to try out new weapons.
4. France and Russia hemmed her in.

Who is in any position to say that Germany wanted war? Such inexactitudes may strengthen misinformation on the part of students.

(6) *Adapt the level of difficulty of the item to the group and to the purpose for which the item is intended.* Consider:

If a tree is growing in a climate where rainfall is heavy, are large leaves an advantage or a disadvantage?
1. An advantage, because the area for photosynthesis and transpiration is increased.
2. An advantage, because large leaves protect the tree during heavy rainfall.
3. A disadvantage, because large leaves give too much shade.
4. A disadvantage, because large leaves absorb too much moisture from the air.

The above item illustrates an increased level of difficulty because it requires knowledge of both the answer and an explanation for it.

(7) *Omit clues to the correct response.* Items that contain clues or cues are not measuring what the instructor intended. Including clues is perhaps the most frequent error made in multiple-choice tests. In the following item it is necessary only to know that "exert" is commonly used with "pressure":

What does an enclosed fluid exert on the walls of its container?
1. Energy   3. Pressure
2. Friction   4. Work

In the next item the stem calls for a plural answer, which occurs only in 4.

Among the causes of the Civil War were:
1. Southern jealousy of northern prosperity.
2. Southern anger at interference with the foreign slave trade.

thirty-four

3. Northern opposition to bringing in California as a slave state.
4. Differing views on the tariff and Constitution.

In the next item the correct answer has been stated more precisely and at greater length than the others. Students catch on quickly to such a clue.

Why were the Republicans ready to go to war with England in 1812?
1. They wished to honor our alliance with France.
2. They wanted additional territory for agricultural expansion and felt that such a war might afford a good opportunity to annex Canada.
3. They were opposed to Washington's policy of neutrality.
4. They represented commercial interests which favored war.

In the next item there are common elements in the stem and in the answer:

What led to the formation of the States Rights Party?
1. The level of federal taxation
2. The demand of states for the right to make their own laws
3. The industrialization of the South
4. The corruption of many city governments

Finally, such specific clues as "all," "always," "certainly," and "never" are to be avoided—they are clues to incorrect answers. Moreover, scholars are leery of absolutes and probably should encourage students to be.

(8) *Do not use a negatively stated item stem.* Experience has shown that these tend to confuse students, yet some items contain two and three negatives and seem like intricate verbal puzzles.

Which of these is *not* one of the purposes of Russia in consolidating the Communist party organization throughout Eastern Europe?
1. To balance the influence of the western democracies
2. To bolster her economic position
3. To improve Russian-American relations
4. To improve her political bargaining position

Which of these is *not* true of a virus?
1. It is composed of very large living cells.
2. It can reproduce itself.
3. It can live only in plants and animal cells.
4. It can cause disease.

(9) *Be certain that the correct answer is one on which competent critics agree.* Consider:

What is the chief difference in research work between colleges and industrial firms?
1. Colleges do much research, industrial firms little.
2. Colleges are more concerned with basic research, industrial firms with applications.
3. Colleges lack the well-equipped laboratories which industrial firms maintain.
4. Colleges publish results, while industrial firms keep their findings secret.

Competent authorities could not agree upon the best response to the above. If this type of item is to be used, a qualification should be offered in the stem, such as, "According to ____, the chief difference...."

thirty-five

(10) *Avoid answer alternatives that overlap or include each other*:

> What percent of the total [property] loss due to hail is the loss of growing crops?
> 1. Less than 20 percent
> 2. Less than 30 percent
> 3. More than 50 percent
> 4. More than 95 percent

If 1 is correct, then 2 is also correct; and if 4 is correct, then 3 is correct.

This discussion is not intended to suggest that test questions for college students should be simple or tests easy. For the most part, the examples emphasize item clarity; they do not deal with what should be measured—factual information, concepts, appreciation, and so on. Many authorities believe that multiple-choice items, if constructed with great care, can measure conceptual knowledge, ability to generalize, and so forth. The way to prepare such items is to be clear about one's own objectives of instruction and to enlist the assistance of one's colleagues in judging whether a particular item measures what is intended.

Essay Questions

For a variety of reasons, essay questions or items require less preparation time than multiple-choice ones; on the other hand, the essay type requires much more time to score. We estimate, however, that for classes numbering around 35 students the instructor would invest about equal time for properly prepared multiple-choice tests and for properly scored essay ones. Faculty time, however, is not the sole criterion for deciding between the two types of test. The essay question, permitting freedom of response, can test how students approach a problem, what information they think is important, and what conclusions they reach. Debates continue over other qualities or abilities that essay questions are purported to measure (for a research review, see Yeasmeen and Barker).

Whatever the merits and faults of essay questions, they afford students an opportunity to express themselves in their own words, as Stalnaker, among many others, has emphasized. Essay questions compel students to think about a topic, decide what to say about it and how to say it, and do the writing. These are important abilities in an educated person, and many faculty members are convinced that the development of these abilities has been deterred by the excessive use of objective tests. At the very least, essay questions give students an incentive to write.

Most of the principles for promoting multiple-choice item clarity apply equally to essay questions. The application of several additional principles will increase the chances of attaining scoring consistency (or reliability).

(1) *Limit the scope of the question.* There is simply no way of scoring fairly such broad questions as "Discuss Shakespeare's tragedies" or "Analyze the energy crisis." Moreover, students must guess which replies will please the instructor—they must "psych out the prof."

Restrictions of the scope may vary, of course; limits may be imposed by calling for brevity and conciseness, insisting upon only a few sentences, or even specifying the space to be used. Questions may be structured in other ways—by asking students to compare, contrast, discriminate, note limitations, draw inferences, state conclusions tersely, and so on.

(2) *Avoid items or questions that are based on personal feelings.* Educators are in no position to measure or quantify students' feelings about any issue. Such questions as, What does modern art mean to you?, Do you relate to the writings of e.e. cummings?, and How do you feel about Truman as a President? promote "psyching out the prof." If the answers are honest, there are no standards by which they can be quantified. To many people modern art means nothing; others cannot abide e.e. cummings, and well-informed persons differ about Truman. Where the affective domain is concerned, unfair and improper judgments are more likely to be rendered on official records when students' feelings and opinions do not agree with those of their instructors.

(3) *Be certain that an adequate answer can be given in the time allowed.* It is amazing how often this simple rule is violated, even by those who know from personal experience how difficult it is to organize thoughts and present them coherently. Again, the issue is what is being measured; the quickest student is not necessarily the best one in all respects.

(4) *Use the following procedures for scoring essay items,* bearing in mind that the subject is measurement and the goal of measurement is objectivity:

- Minimize, as far as possible, cues that will identify the owners of the papers; at the very least, remove the names. It is all too easy to allow extraneous knowledge about a student to influence the marking of his or her paper. Such precautions should help to assure minority students that the marking process is free of discrimination.
- Write out an ideal answer ahead of time and ask a colleague to do likewise; combine the two into a standard with which students' replies can be compared.
- Score each item on a point scale without reference to a passing grade (assigning a grade is evaluation, not measurement); that is, determine prior to scoring that item 1 can earn 10 points, for example, item 2 is worth 20 points, and so on. Total all the points and then assign a letter grade.

Test Construction

Most tests are composed of several items or questions that are put together for some specific purpose, measuring students' ability to translate a foreign language, for example. Questions on a given test constitute a sample of all the questions that could be asked. There are no hard and fast rules that will produce a representative sample of questions, but there are guidelines that will increase the chances of a fair distribution:

• *Have the items reflect important objectives you have attempted to promote.* This guideline is difficult to elaborate because goals or objectives will vary from course to course. The trick is to aim for an unbiased sample of questions. In Case 1 (page 13), the test was biased in that the majority of questions were on Kant although the goals of the course were not limited to understanding that gentleman. Perhaps the simplest way to avoid an unduly biased sample of questions on a particular test is to have a colleague criticize it before the test is given.

• *Generally speaking, the greater the number of items in a test, the more representative the sample.* This is one of the arguments in favor of multiple-choice items. In a given period of time, more multiple-choice than essay questions can be answered.

• *Allow ample time for all students to respond to all the questions.* The experience of colleagues about the optimum length of a test for a given time period will be helpful.

Regardless of the care with which tests are constructed, there will be errors just as there are errors in all measurement. In physical measurement, the errors stem from at least two sources, defects in the measuring instrument and perceptual distortions associated with the person taking the reading. For educational measurement there is an additional source—the person being measured. The performance of anyone tends to fluctuate from day to day for a variety of reasons. The goal, then, is to minimize errors in measurement.

Errors in Test Construction

Regardless of the care with which tests are constructed, there will be errors just as there are errors in all measurement. In physical measurement, the errors stem from at least two sources, defects in the measuring instrument and perceptual distortions associated with the person taking the reading. For educational measurement there is an additional source—the person being measured. The performance of anyone tends to fluctuate from day to day for a variety of reasons. The goal, then, is to minimize errors in measurement.

Regarding the instrument or test, clearly written items and a representative sampling of material will decrease errors and increase reliability (i.e., consistency or stability). Also, generally speaking, the longer a test, the greater its reliability. Multiple-choice tests tend to be more reliable than essay ones because more questions can be answered in a specified period of time.

As for reliability of marking, properly prepared multiple-choice tests are the least subject to error. Scoring of essay tests tends toward unreliability or inconsistency. Two or more instructors are likely to arrive at different scores, and the same instructor may arrive at different scores at different times. The reliability of a given test can be determined statistically, and for large introductory courses such determinations are very much in order. Ebel (1972) has estimated the average reliability of college tests to be .45, a coefficient that reflects unreliability, inconsistency, and imprecision. (A perfect coefficient of reliability is 1.00.)

The third source of error, the person being measured, encompasses the day-to-day personal variations we all experience and the conditions under which a test is administered. These can help or hinder performance. For the purpose of averaging out day-to-day variations, conducting several tests during a course will tend to yield more reliable or consistent measures than giving a single one. Although we do not recommend a specific number of tests, it is clear that giving only one test for an entire course is likely to be unreliable. As for physical conditions in a room used for a test, inadequate ventilation, uncomfortable temperatures, poor lighting, or excessive crowding will tend to cause inaccurate measures; in Case 12 (page 16), cheating resulted in inaccurate scores. Poor testing conditions are inexcusable.

Rhodes has summarized the meaning of errors of measurement:

> It is assumed that for each test a student takes, there is a true score he should make that may differ from the score he actually achieves. The true score would be free of the accidental error caused by factors such as the questions selected for the test, how the student feels on the day of the test, the temperature of the testing room, and so on. Theoretically, if a student took an infinite number of equivalent editions of a test, the scores he obtained would vary somewhat but would cluster around an average, or true score. The score a student actually obtains on any given occasion is, then, an approximation of this true score and should be thought of as representing an interval, or obtained-score range, the limits of which are determined by use of the standard error of measurement.

Finally, in this respect, there is a statistical formula for calculating the standard error of measurement that is useful for large classes.

A test can be very reliable, yielding precise and accurate scores, but really not measure anything of importance. Such a test is of course invalid. While there are several concepts of validity (for detailed discussions, see Ebel, 1972), only two need be of direct concern—content validity and predictive validity.

Content validity means that a test measures what it is supposed to measure, for example, critical thinking about economics or problem solving in calculus. Well-formulated objectives for a course are the first prerequisite for attaining content validity of test items. The second requirement is the advice of one's colleagues.

The multiple-choice items in the following table presumably have content validity.

thirty-nine

Multiple-Choice Items Intended to Test
Various Aspects of Achievement*
Understanding of Terminology or Vocabulary

The term "fringe benefits" has been used frequently in recent years in connection with labor contracts. What does the term mean?
1. Incentive payments for above-average output
2. Rights of employees to draw overtime pay at higher rates
3. Rights of employers to share in the profits from inventions of their employees
4. *Such considerations as paid vacations, retirement plans, and health insurance*
What is the technical definition of the term "production"?
1. Any natural process producing food or other raw materials
2. *The creation of economic values*
3. The manufacture of finished products
4. The operation of a profit-making enterprise

Knowledge of Fact and Principle or Generalizations

What principle is utilized in radar?
1. Faint electronic radiations of far-off objects can be detected by supersensitive receivers.
2. *High-frequency radio waves are reflected by distant objects.*
3. All objects emit infrared rays, even in darkness.
4. High-frequency radio waves are not transmitted alike by all substances.
The most frequent source of conflict between the western and eastern parts of the United States during the course of the nineteenth century was:
1. *The issue of currency inflation*
2. The regulation of monopolies
3. Internal improvements
4. Isolationism vs. internationalism
5. Immigration

Ability to Explain or Understanding of Relationships

If a piece of lead suspended from one arm of a beam balance is balanced with a piece of wood suspended from the other arm, why is the balance lost if the system is placed in a vacuum?
1. The mass of the wood exceeds the mass of the lead.
2. The air exerts a greater buoyant force on the lead than on the wood.
3. The attraction of gravity is greater for the lead than for the wood when both are in a vacuum.
4. *The wood displaces more air than the lead.*
Should merchants and middlemen be classified as producers or nonproducers? Why?
1. As nonproducers, because they make their living off producers and consumers
2. As producers, because they are regulators and determiners of price
3. *As producers, because they aid in the distribution of goods and bring producer and consumer together*
4. As producers, because they assist in the circulation of money

Ability to Calculate or Numerical Problems

If the radius of the earth were increased by three feet, its circumference at the equator would be increased by about how much?
1. 9 feet   3. *19 feet*
2. 12 feet   4. 28 feet
What is the standard deviation of this set of five measures—1,2,3,4,5?
1. 1   4. $\sqrt{10}$
2. $\sqrt{2}$ 5. None of these
3. 9

*Adapted from Exhibit 5.2. Robert L. Ebel, **Essentials of Educational Measurement,** © 1972, pp. 111-113. Reprinted with permission of Prentice-Hall, Inc.

Ability to Predict or What is Likely to Happen Under Specified Conditions?

If an electric refrigerator is operated with the door open in a perfectly insulated sealed room, what will happen to the temperature of the room?
1. *It will rise slowly.*
2. It will remain constant.
3. It will drop slowly.
4. It will drop rapidly.

What would happen if the terminals of an ordinary household light bulb were connected to the terminals of an automobile storage battery?
1. The bulb would light to its natural brilliance.
2. *The bulb would not glow, though some current would flow through it.*
3. The bulb would explode.
4. The battery would go dead in a few minutes.

Ability to Recommend Specific Appropriate Action

Which of these practices would probably contribute least to reliable grades from essay examinations?
1. *Weighting the items so that the student receives more credit for answering correctly more difficult items.*
2. Advance preparation by the rater of a correct answer to each question.
3. Correction of one question at a time through all papers.
4. Concealment of student names from the rater.

"None of these" is an appropriate response for a multiple-choice test item in cases where:
1. The number of possible responses is limited to two or three.
2. *The responses provide absolutely correct or incorrect answers.*
3. A large variety of possible responses might be given.
4. Guessing is apt to be a serious problem.

Ability to Make an Evaluative Judgment

Which one of the following sentences is most appropriately worded for inclusion in an impartial report resulting from an investigation of a wage policy in a certain locality?
1. The wages of the working people are fixed by the one businessman who is the only large employer in the locality.
2. Since one employer provides a livelihood for the entire population in the locality, he properly determines the wage policy for the locality.
3. Since one employer controls the labor market in the locality, his policy may not be challenged.
4. *In this locality, where there is only one large employer of labor, the wage policy of this employer is really the wage policy of the locality.*

Which of the following quotations has most of the characteristics of conventional poetry?
1. "I never saw a purple cow;
   I never hope to see one."
2. *"Announced by all the trumpets of the sky
   Arrives the snow and blasts his ramparts high."*
3. "Thou art blind and confined
   While I am free for I can see."
4. "In purple prose his passions he betrayed
   For verse was difficult.
   Here he never strayed."

The predictive validity of college tests is low. That is, scores derived from them do not predict future performance very well. For a better understanding of predictive validity, considerable research is needed to determine what magnitude of difference between scores is significant. Often student X with a score of 91 will receive an A, while student Y with 89 will receive a B. For GPA purposes on most campuses these translate into 4.00 and 3.00, respectively. It is assumed that student X can and will out-perform student Y, but the evidence that this is true is tenuous. How large must the difference be between the two—1, 5, 10, 20 points or more—before the predictive assumption is substantiated?

Why is precision emphasized? Because GPAs are used in an exceptionally precise manner, as when arbitrary cut-off scores are set. A 3.50 may entitle a student to further consideration for admission to a program, while a 3.49 results in categorical rejection. Under these circumstances the least that can be striven for is accuracy in measurement.

4

Grading

A comprehensive evaluation of student performance should provide guidance for academic improvement, but students too often receive scant critical commentary on their progress. Letter grading, the most commonly accepted form of evaluation, is particularly susceptible to the charge of insufficient feedback to the student. A more fundamental grasp of the options for academic measurement is the most direct route to improved grading.

EVALUATIONS SHOULD MEAN PROVIDING A GREAT DEAL OF information to students about their academic performance— strengths, deficiencies and corrective steps to be taken, relative standing, and other pertinent details. Blum has observed in this connection: "It is no secret that students often receive little critical commentary on their papers and examinations. The result is that the prospects for academic improvement are diminished...."

There is this paucity of detailed help for students because evaluation now tends to mean the assigning of letter symbols for record-keeping purposes. The subject of grading is laden with prejudices, dogmas, and unfounded opinions, and for many years it has tended to provoke very unscholarly pronouncements. It is not a new dilemma. In 1890, a Virginia institution had a six-point grading scale—optimus, melior, bonus, malus, pejor, and pessimus. Because the president thought too many mediocre students received the grade of optimus, the scale was changed to a three-point one—distinguished, approved, and disapproved. Soon, however, the president was discontented again, for "some bad scholars were approved, and good scholars were all distinguished" (Cureton).

The purpose in mentioning letter grading is to stimulate scholarly attention to the subject. Such attention is imperative if progress is to be made. Our discussion of the unresolved issues associated with the assigning of grades is followed by some tentative suggestions for improvement.

One reason some of the problems here are not yet being resolved is the fact that several assumptions have not been examined except by a few specialists. Another is the widespread and comfortable belief inside and outside academe that letter grades have considerable predictive validity. In truth, they do not. McClelland has summarized data about the predictive value of grades:

> Researchers have in fact had great difficulty in demonstrating that grades in school are related to any other behavior of importance.... It seems so self-evident to educators that those who do well in their classes must go on to do better in life that they systematically have disregarded evidence to the contrary that has been accumulating for some time.

In a recent survey of studies about grades, Warren found that about half of approximately 200 articles, papers, and reports that appeared between 1965 and 1970 dealt with the form of grades (A,B, C,D,F, P,F, etc.) and with grades as predictive measures. The other half were concerned with a variety of aspects, such as presumed advantages and disadvantages. Warren concluded: "These reports, in spite of their variety, leave large gaps in our knowledge about grades and grading.... These results do not constitute an impressive advance in knowledge about an important, ubiquitous process in higher education...."

**There is this paucity of detailed help for students
because evaluation now tends to mean the assigning
of letter symbols for record-keeping purposes.
The subject of grading is laden with prejudices,
dogmas, and unfounded opinions, and for many years
it has tended to provoke very
unscholarly pronouncements.**

Problems

Single course grades are used to compare students within an institution and across institutions. If measurements are the basis of a comparison, no two of anything, let alone the learning of two people, can be compared unless the same instrument is used for both measurements. Woe be to the cabinetmaker who tries to assemble pieces of rare and exotic wood some of which he has measured with a giveaway yardstick and others with a finely calibrated meter stick. For physical measurements, of course, there are many agreed-upon scales or units—inch, yard, mile, ounce, pound, ton. Each of these can be determined precisely so that two or more measurements in the same units tend to have quite exact meaning. A pound on the West Coast has the same meaning as a pound on the East Coast. Perhaps the basic problem in grading students for purposes of comparison is the absence of any such agreed-upon measurements.

A second problem is inherent in the uncritical acceptance of norm-referenced grading, or what students refer to as "grading on the curve." This may have come into extensive use because of the need to compensate for the lack of a measuring unit. At any rate, norm-referenced grading derives from the mythical "normal curve of distribution" or bell-shaped curve. Its pervasive and often distorted applications have created an illusion of the existence of a standard by which students can be compared equitably, first by the professor who assigns the symbol and then by all others who see it. In fact, the "normal curve" is nothing more than a mathematical ideal or model. Moreover, according to Lindquist, there is an erroneous belief that mental ability test data have been shown to form the bell-shaped curve. The overlooked fallacy is that many standardized tests are constructed deliberately so that the scores will yield such a curve; in some cases foxy statisticians manipulate the scores.

The potency of the false standard is illustrated by this episode (Dressel):

> In one university, the decision was made to section engineering students in calculus on the basis of previous grades. One professor, not knowing this, was assigned a group of students in integral calculus who had received A's in all preceding mathematics courses. Although recognizing that this was an unusually good group...on the first examination, he ended up with the usual distribution of grades from A to F. The reaction of the students forced him to reconsider.... The grades at the end of the term showed 40 percent A's, 50 percent B's, and 10 percent C's. Knowing the caliber of the students, the professor still could not bring himself to report a distribution of grades in which almost every student would be given an A.

This professor thought he had firm reference points for setting cut-off scores for each grade.

It is bad enough when a lone professor grades on the curve for a single class of highly capable students. It is even worse when a gifted student body is judged in this manner. Reed College has established grade guidelines for all faculty to follow (Levine and Weingart). For freshmen the distribution is supposed to be A, 15 percent; B, 35 percent; C, 40 percent; D, 10 percent. For the remaining three categories of students, the recommended distribution is A, 15 percent; B, 45 percent; C, 35 percent; D, 5 percent. Needless to say, such grading can cause talented students to encounter difficulties in being admitted to graduate and professional schools. In the final analysis, grading on the curve means statistical relativism; students are rank-ordered from high to low.

Grade point averages are also used to compare students within an institution and across institutions. Basic errors in testing and grading are compounded by the numerous ways in which GPAs are computed at different institutions. In one survey of these practices (Collins and Nickel) from a sample composed of 650 public and private two- and four-year institutions in the 50 states and the District of Columbia, with 448 schools responding, great variation was found (see table on next page).

The survey revealed that in some schools such grades as Incompletes immediately become F's for calculation purposes, while in others more than an entire term can elapse before such academic capital punishment is applied. As one example of "sudden death," during experimental investigation of instruction at the University of

Texas at Austin (Stice) it was necessary for students to receive Incompletes if they desired. During one term 26 percent did so. None of the investigators knew of the policy that I's became F's for GPA purposes nor did several staff members in the registrar's office. Several good students lost scholarships and others failed to receive invitations to honor societies. More than likely the calculation practices are not specified on very many transcripts.

The assumption that single grades have common reference points has been made about GPAs, too. Who knows what sorts of tests are behind the grades or the standards by which the grades were derived? If anything, GPA statistics as they are presently employed tend to be meaningless—despite what most academicians and others think.

Our numerous deliberations about grading led repeatedly back to several basic facts: (1) Unidimensional symbols report multidimensional phenomena. A given grade can reflect level of knowledge, at-

Practice	Number of Institutions Indicating This Is Present Practice
All grades received in all courses taken at any institution are used in computing the overall grade point average.	159
Only grades in courses which count for the degree are used in computing the GPA.	43
Only grades in courses taken in the institution doing the computing are used in computing the GPA.	246
When a course is repeated, all grades (two or more) are used when computing the GPA.	136
When a course is repeated, only the last grade received is used when computing the GPA.	266

titudes, procrastination, interest or lack of it, and other factors. The lone symbol specifies none of these things. Perhaps each professor assumes that every other interpreter will see in the lone symbol all of the nuances he or she intended. (2) The symbol, by itself, reveals nothing about the quality of the test or tests through which it has been derived.

Suggestions

An emerging model of grading is called criterion-referenced. Its basic feature is the concept of mastery. If anything, criterion-referenced grading requires more complete statements of objectives than does norm-referenced grading. Tests are designed, then, to determine whether a student has or has not attained these objectives. The concept of criterion-referenced grading has been used especially in the Keller Plan (see Ruskin and Hess) and in contract grading. (While this approach appears to be more and more common, there is little about it in the literature.) There are several excellent references for criterion-referenced grading—Popham, Carver, and Angoff.

Criterion-referenced grading is used in the emerging competency-based curricula. For a digest of its important features in this context (as well as answers to questions that are being asked such as, What is competence? and How does the faculty role change in a competence curriculum?), see the report by the Southern Regional Education Board.

This method of grading certainly has its place, especially in professional curricula. When it is used for a given course, a notation should be made on the transcript to facilitate interpretation.

Finally, there is the import for grading of the basic theme of this volume—*improved testing or measurement is the fundamental route*

Our numerous deliberations about grading led repeatedly back to several basic facts: [1] Unidimensional symbols report multidimensional phenomena. A given grade can reflect level of knowledge, attitudes, procrastination, interest or lack of it, and other factors. The lone symbol specifies none of these things. Perhaps each professor assumes that every other interpreter will see in the lone symbol all of the nuances he or she intended. [2] The symbol, by itself, reveals nothing about the quality of the test or tests through which it has been derived.

---

to improved grading. There are no substitutes for clarity about what one is trying to accomplish in instruction and very careful efforts to find out what students have achieved.

Etzioni recently suggested that what is needed is open discussion by departments leading to agreement about grading standards, but this would be insufficient. Once again the tip of the iceberg would be considered while its submerged body would be ignored. A better solution would be open discussions by departments about all facets of testing. A professor can no longer go it alone in certifying students for society.

5

Lone Efforts Are Not Enough

Growing external pressures are forcing faculty to take a fresh look at student evaluation. The new consumerism, recent legal decisions, and far-reaching social criticism will no longer leave matters of grading and testing to the private academic preserve. The use of external examiners and the establishment of effective campus grievance arrangements are only two of the ways recommended to improve an increasingly nettlesome issue in academic life.

IF ASSESSMENT IS NOT IMPROVED FROM INSIDE THE PROFES-
sion, then it most surely will be put under pressure from the outside.
Traditionally faculty members have enjoyed almost complete autonomy in their teaching performance. Until recently the courts had
tended to avoid the academic bastions. But now they are beginning
to intervene, and some observers believe such intervention will soon
accelerate. This has resulted from several trends: an increased
sophistication of students, a new regard for higher education as a
social necessity and an individual right, the expansion of civil rights
protections by public authority, and—perhaps most important—the
new age of majority.

The Courts Intervene

One instance of recent court intervention dealt with a lone grade
(*State Ex Rel. Bartlett v. Pantzer*). A political science student graduated from the University of Chicago in June 1971 with a Bachelor of
Arts degree. During the spring quarter of his senior year he had enrolled in a graduate accounting course to fulfill an admission requirement of the law school of the University of Montana, where he
was seeking admission in September 1971. The law school had informed the student that the requirement would be fulfilled if he received a satisfactory grade.

The student received a D in the course, whereupon he was ad-
vised by the law school that he would not be admitted because the
grade was not a satisfactory one. Testimony in court revealed that

colleges and universities regarded a grade of D as "acceptable," but not "satisfactory." The Supreme Court of Montana was unable to discern the exquisite difference and directed the law school to admit the student.

More court intervention in matters of academic measurement seems likely in the not-too-distant future. The United States Supreme Court made a momentous decision in the *Griggs v. Duke Power Company* case and may have set a precedent for drastically altered interpretations of higher education test scores and grade point averages. The company was found to have discriminated racially by requiring, for an employee to be promoted from laborer to coal handler, either the possession of a high school diploma or the passing of two standardized tests. In rendering its decision, the court ruled: "Nothing in the act (Civil Rights Act, 1964, Title VII) precludes the use of testing or measuring procedures; obviously they are useful. What Congress has forbidden is giving these devices and mechanisms controlling force unless they are demonstrably a reasonable measure of job performance."

Suits have been instituted already in several states charging that bar examinations discriminate unfairly against minority groups.

If assessment is not improved from inside the profession, then it most surely will be put under pressure from the outside. Traditionally faculty members have enjoyed almost complete autonomy in their teaching performance. Until recently the courts had tended to avoid the academic bastions. But now they are beginning to intervene, and some observers believe such intervention will soon accelerate.

The fundamental issue is the predictive validity of such tests for all who take them. It could well be that these assaults upon bar exams are a prelude to assaults on many other licensing examinations, because they, too, are job related. Since higher education in its testing activities is engaged more in credentialing or rank-ordering students than in assessing learning, it is not too difficult to foresee grade point averages being ruled job-related by the courts. (Today a student may be refused admission to a professional school because of a GPA a few hundredths of a point below some arbitrary cut-off score.) Many ramifications of the *Duke Power Company* decision and its innumerable complexities have been examined meticulously and thoughtfully by Huff.

Of more direct portent for the future may be the dissenting opinion of former Justice William O. Douglas in *DeFunis v. Odegaard* (Fields). Justice Douglas was especially critical of scores derived from the Law School Admissions Test and of grade point averages and the fact that they had dominated the selection process. He argued that law schools are not bound to admit students according to mechanical criteria because such criteria often conceal important abilities. Justice Douglas was most persuasive in his plea for more thorough assessment of individual attributes than test scores provide. For example, he maintained that a person who pulls himself from the ghetto via a community college has demonstrated a quality of perseverance and thereby has more promise for the study of law than a rich graduate of Harvard. The poorer applicant should be admitted, said Douglas, because he had shown special potential in contrast to the Harvard graduate who may have taken less advantage of the vastly superior opportunities afforded him.

It is too soon to know the full impact of the so-called Buckley Amendment that gives students access to their test papers and other official records, but scores of students may avail themselves of the access and be so overwhelmed that they will demand careful and honest explanations for selected test scores and grades. This provision of law may give them a basis for court action to enforce their demands. Quite obviously, poor tests and unfair grades are features of instruction that are under the direct control of each individual faculty member. Just how could a student's "improper spirit toward the subject matter" (Case 9, page 15) be documented or substantiated in court?

Unless professors individually and collectively begin to make drastic improvements in testing and grading practices, there will be intrusions on their autonomy from without in several forms. There even appears to be a possibility of compulsory state or nationwide standardized tests of academic achievement. Academic freedom is imperative and must be preserved, but the professoriate cannot avoid its own responsibilities. Grading policies and practices in most undergraduate courses do not bear any relation to inviolable academic freedom.

What does all this mean? Unless professors individually and collectively begin to make drastic improvements in testing and grading practices, there will be intrusions on their autonomy from without in several forms. There even appears to be a possibility of compulsory state or nationwide standardized tests of academic achievement. Academic freedom is imperative and must be preserved, but the professoriate cannot avoid its own responsibilities. Grading policies and practices in most undergraduate courses do not bear any relation to inviolable academic freedom.

How, then, can the process be improved? Classroom tests can be improved by faculty members learning more about measurement and obtaining the assistance of their colleagues. At least three additional reforms must be implemented to improve the test product and demonstrate the professoriate's willingness to put its house in order.

Visiting Examiners

It is a deeply ingrained belief throughout American higher education that instructing and examining are inseparable. The instructor
is supposedly the person best able to judge the work of his or her
student.

There has been at least one historical challenge to this assumption (Coulter). In 1811 the three trustees of the University of Georgia
were named as visitors and urged, along with other distinguished
men of the state, to attend examinations of seniors because: " 'The
test of the pudding is the taste thereof' is a saw honored with age
and truth. Examination times were tasting times and this tasting
should be done by more than the cooks only." By 1825 the examinations for juniors were being attended by any person who desired to
attend.

A modern and refined counterpart to this practice of some 150
years ago is the visiting examiners tradition for the Honors Program
of Swarthmore College (Swarthmore College Faculty, 1941), which
began in the early 1920s, continues to flourish today, and is widely
acclaimed by faculty, students, and alumni.

Around 40 percent of juniors and seniors elect to take honors
work. Normally this means that a student studies six subjects during
the last two years. The work is pursued independently or in small
seminars. At the end of the senior year the student is subjected to a
three-hour written examination in each subject. These exams are
prepared and evaluated by faculty members from other institutions.
In the oral examinations that follow, there is no rigid pattern; they
are conducted in a variety of ways. But the judgment of the visitor
carries the most weight.

A recent evaluation of the program (Swarthmore College, 1967)
describes the rationale and the benefits succinctly:

> Many external examiners...think the system works well, and the exam-
> iners' evaluations of students are generally consistent with the facul-
> ty's. Many graduates of honors have said (in the alumni questionnaire),
> as have many faculty, that the system helps to create an atmosphere of
> faculty-student collaboration.... These are now conventional state-
> ments; but we are inclined to agree with them. The colleagueship and
> the intellectual checks provided by external examiners are widely felt
> to be valuable for both students and the faculty; many of the latter,
> especially, set high store by it....

On all too many campuses faculty and students are two factions
warring over learning. The faculty are so dedicated to the exercise
of their selective function, they cannot see teaching-learning as a
collaborative endeavor, whereas at Swarthmore apparently faculty
members and students work together to meet and impress a sort of
common foe, the visiting examiner. Thus one reason for more extensive use of this type of program is that it serves the cause of learning
for the individual students who participate.

A second reason for having visiting examiners on many campuses
is that their presence should broaden the perspectives of faculties
about the art and techniques of teaching. While the various faculty
organizations help keep the professoriate abreast of disciplinary developments, many pay little direct attention to good teaching. With-

out sufficient stimulation it is very easy to become smug, myopic, and provincial. If, over a substantial period of time, too many students performed poorly, the visiting examiners would be in a position to ask some penetrating questions of the home faculty. Help by colleagues from other institutions is more useful and more palatable than interference from those outside academic life.

Testing Specialists

Another challenge to the notion that teaching and testing are inseparable came during the early 1930s at the University of Chicago with the creation of the Board of Examinations (Bloom). The faculty were

---

Recently, perhaps partly as a result of the joint statement, grievance procedures have been made formal in some institutions and often include a specially appointed committee, which in some cases is given the authority to overrule a faculty member and change a grade. For example, at California State University, Los Angeles, if a grade grievance is not resolved at the departmental level, the student may appeal to the dean of that school who, in turn, refers the matter to a special committee. The dean, after consultation with the committee, may authorize a change of grade. If for any reason a student believes the problem has not been resolved fairly, he or she may submit a signed statement to the standing student grievance committee, which may refer the issue to one of several other committees, any one of which may recommend a grade change to the appropriate dean, whereupon the change is made in the permanent records.

---

concerned primarily with having students assume responsibility for their own learning. Degree requirements were set in terms of comprehensive examinations, and as a result students could make individual decisions about the speed with which they would attain their degrees as well as about their study methods and class attendance.

Since the comprehensive examinations were the sole basis for meeting graduation requirements, they had to be excellent measures of academic achievement. In consultation with faculties, a corps of test specialists constructed the exams, scored them, and assigned grades. The faculty believed that an ideal teacher-student relationship—one which promoted an optimum of learning—was impossible when the teacher also served as judge and jury. The success of the project was revealed, in part, by the high test reliability coefficients that were obtained. These ranged almost without exception between .90 and .95.

Several forces combined during the early 1950s to eliminate this extreme departure from traditional testing and grading practices. In the meantime, several campuses have established offices that serve instructors on a voluntary or request basis. One example is the Evaluation and Examination Service of the University of Iowa (Whitney). The service staff consults with individual faculty members or departments on techniques of test construction and improvement, test and item analysis, and methods of grade assignment. In addition, course examinations are duplicated, scored, and analyzed. The service keeps the faculty and others informed periodically by means of memos and technical bulletins. A current memo is entitled, "Should I Take the Graduate Record (GRE) Again?" Recent bulletins discussed "Improving Essay Questions." There are two professional members of the staff; about 40 percent of a faculty of 700 use the service. Comparable agencies should be available to faculties on all campuses.

In *Change*'s first faculty policy paper on professional development, the authors, in a chapter entitled "Evaluation for What?", suggest the ideal of the separation of teacher from evaluator: "A developmental approach to education calls for a new kind of detachment: for students the detachment of the process of learning from the certification of competence; and for teachers, detachment of efforts to improve teaching from official assessments of performance" (Group for Human Development in Higher Education).

Academic Grievances Committees

Tradition has it that if a student feels a grade is an improper one, he or she may seek redress by consulting the individual faculty member. If satisfaction is not received, the student has had the right to consult with other individuals—department heads, deans, and even the president or chancellor. For the most part the arrangements have been informal and final authority to change or not change the grade has rested with the faculty member.

In 1967 several important organizations* issued a Joint Statement on Rights and Freedoms of Students. The statement included this right: *"Protection Against Improper Academic Evaluation*—Students should have protection through orderly procedures against prejudiced or capricious academic evaluation. At the same time, they are responsible for maintaining standards of academic performance established for each course in which they are enrolled."

Recently, perhaps partly as a result of the joint statement, grievance procedures have been made formal in some institutions and often include a specially appointed committee, which in some cases is given the authority to overrule a faculty member and change a grade. For example, at California State University, Los Angeles, if a grade grievance is not resolved at the departmental level, the student may appeal to the dean of that school who, in turn, refers the

---

*American Association of University Professors, U.S. National Student Association, Association of American Colleges, National Association of Student Personnel Administrators, and National Association of Women Deans and Counselors.

matter to a special committee. The dean, after consultation with the committee, may authorize a change of grade. If for any reason a student believes the problem has not been resolved fairly, he or she may submit a signed statement to the standing student grievance committee, which may refer the issue to one of several other committees, any one of which may recommend a grade change to the appropriate dean, whereupon the change is made in the permanent records.

At Western Michigan University, the arrangements are less complicated. If a student is dissatisfied following informal consultation within the department, he or she may see an administrator, who may decide the grievance is unwarranted or there is sufficient evidence for the case to be considered by a committee on academic fairness, either the graduate or the undergraduate committee. The undergraduate committee consists of three faculty members, three undergraduates, and a nonvoting chairperson. If the committee decides to recommend a change of grade, the faculty member is informed first so that he or she may make the change. If the faculty member prefers not to do so, the committee then makes the change by notifying the dean of records and admissions.

At Pomona College, the procedures are simple and straightforward. If, after the usual informal hearings, the disputants are still disgruntled, the dean appoints a small ad hoc committee of faculty from the department of the instructor or from a related department. "The decision of the hearing committee on the disputed grade shall be final."

There are formal hearing procedures in other institutions, but in these the final judge—whether a committee, a dean, or a chancellor—has no power to change a grade. Appeals for fairness can be addressed to the faculty member, but not a decision that a grade must be changed. After going to elaborate lengths to ensure academic rights for students, Michigan State University (1969) persistently maintains the traditional stance that the instructor is the only person who can assign a grade. In most instances instructors are cooperative, but nothing further can be done if they stubbornly defy the grievance committee, according to an official.

We recommend that formal arrangements be established for reconciling testing and grading grievances and that a final judge other than the instructor have the authority to change a grade. This recommendation is made for these reasons:

(1) Cases such as some of those mentioned in the first chapter reflect almost unbelievable examples of faculty arbitrariness and capriciousness. Students should be able to fight back against such unfairness, and with the balance of power on their side. This presumes our basic system of justice, which is designed to protect the rights of the weak individual who is being persecuted by strong external authorities.

(2) The mere existence of such appeal arrangements should help decrease testing and grading offenses.

(3) Correction by one's peers is both more palatable and more effective than intrusion by outside forces.

6

For Further Reading

For a more comprehensive understanding of testing and evaluation, faculty have access to a number of excellent source documents. Here are some of the best.

References

Adkins, Dorothy Wood. *Test Construction: Development and Interpretation of Achievement Tests.* Columbus: Charles E. Merrill, 1960.

Angoff, William H. "Criterion-Referencing, Norm-Referencing, and the SAT." *College Board Review*, no. 92 (1974), p. 3.

Bloom, Benjamin S. "Changing Conception of Examining at the University of Chicago." In *Evaluation in General Education*, edited by Paul L. Dressel. Dubuque, Iowa: William C. Brown Co., 1954.

Blum, Paul Von. "Needed: A Code of Ethics for Teachers." *Chronicle of Higher Education*, October 21, 1974, p. 20.

California State University. "Student Information." Unpublished. Los Angeles.

Carver, Ronald P. "Two Dimensions of Testing, Psychometric and Edumetric." *American Psychologist* 29 (1974): 512-518.

Collins, Janet E. and Nickel, K. N. "Grading, Recording and Averaging Practices in Higher Education." Mimeographed. Wichita, Kansas: Wichita State University, 1974.

Coulter, E. M. *College Life in the Old South.* 2d ed. Athens: The University of Georgia Press, 1951.

Cureton, Louise W. "The History of Grading Practices." *Measurement in Education*, no. 4 (1971), pp. 1-8.

Defunis v. Odegaard, 416 U.S. 312, 94 S. Ct. 1704 (1974).

Dressel, Paul L. *Evaluation in Higher Education.* Boston: Houghton Mifflin, 1961.

Ebel, Robert L. *Essentials in Educational Measurement.* Englewood Cliffs, N.J.: Prentice-Hall, 1972.

———. "Writing the Test Item." In *Educational Measurement*, edited by E. F. Lindquist. Washington, D.C.: American Council on Education, 1966.

Etzioni, Amitai. "Grade Inflation: Neither Freedom nor Discipline." *Human Behavior*, October 1975, p. 11.

Felker, Daniel B., and Dapra, Richard A. "Effects of Question Type and Question Placement on Problem-Solving Ability from Prose Material." *Journal of Educational Psychology* 67 (1975): 380-384.

Fields, Cheryl M. *Chronicle of Higher Education*, April 29, 1973, p. 1.

Griggs v. Duke Power Company, 401 U.S. 424 (1971).

Group for Human Development in Higher Education. *Faculty Development in a Time of Retrenchment.* New Rochelle, N.Y.: *Change* Magazine, 1974.

Hechinger, Fred M. "An Academic Counter-Revolution." *Saturday Review/World*, no. 131 (1974), pp. 63-68.

Hofstadter, R. *Anti-Intellectualism in American Life.* New York: Vintage Books, 1966.

Huff, Sheila, "Credentialing by Tests or by Degrees: Title VII of the Civil Rights Act and Griggs v. Duke Power Company." *Harvard Educational Review*, no. 2 (1974).

Levine, Arthur and Weingart, John. *Reform of Undergraduate Education.* San Francisco: Jossey-Bass, 1973.

Lindquist, E. F. *A First Course in Statistics: Their Use and Interpretation in Education and Psychology.* Boston: Houghton Mifflin, 1942.

Lorge, Irving. "The Fundamental Nature of Measurement." In *Educational Measurement*, edited by E. F. Lindquist. Washington, D.C.: American Council on Education, 1966.

Mager, Robert F. *Goal Analysis*. Belmont, Ca.: Fearon, 1972.

———. *Measuring Instructional Intent*. Belmont, Ca.: Fearon, 1973.

McClelland, David C. "Testing for Competence Rather Than for 'Intelligence.'" *American Psychologist* 28 (1973): 1-14.

McGuire, Christine H. "An Evaluation Model for Professional Education-Medical Education." *Proceedings of the 1967 Invitational Conference on Testing Problems*. Princeton, N.J.: Educational Testing Service, 1968.

Meyer, G. "An Experimental Study of the Old and New Types of Examination." *Journal of Educational Psychology* 26 (1935): 30-40.

Michigan State University. "Code of Teaching Responsibility." Unpublished. East Lansing: 1969.

Pomona College. "Policy on Disputed Grades." Unpublished. Claremont, Ca.

Popham, W. James, ed. *Criterion-Referenced Measurement: An Introduction*. Englewood Cliffs, N.J.: Educational Technology Publications, 1971.

Rhodes, Douglas W. *The Undergraduate Program for Counseling and Evaluation*. Princeton, N.J.: Educational Testing Service, 1973.

Ruskin, Robert S. and Hess, John H. *The Personalized System of Instruction in Higher Education: An Annotated Review of the Literature*. Washington, D.C.: Center for Personalized Instruction, Georgetown University, 1974.

Southern Regional Education Board. "Learning Your CBC's." *Regional Spotlight*. Atlanta: Southern Regional Education Board, September 1974.

Stalnaker, John M. "The Essay Type of Examination." In *Educational Measurement*, edited by E. F. Lindquist. Washington, D.C.: American Council on Education, 1966.

State Ex Rel. Bartlett v. Pantzer, 489 P. 2d 375 (1971).

Stice. James. "Progress Report on the PSI Project at the University of Texas at Austin." *PSI Newsletter*, no. 3 (1975).

Swarthmore College. "Critique of a College." Swarthmore, Pa.: 1967.

Swarthmore College Faculty. *An Adventure in Education*. New York: Macmillan, 1941.

Thomas, L. and Augstein, S. *An Experimental Approach to Learning From Written Material*. Oxbridge, England: Centre for the Study of Human Learning, Brunel University, 1970.

Warren, J. R. *College Grading Practices: An Overview*. Washington, D.C.: ERIC Clearinghouse on Higher Education, 1971.

Western Michigan University. "Student Academic Rights: Policies and Procedures." Unpublished. Kalamazoo.

Yeasmeen, Nazma and Barker, Donald G. "A Half Century of Research on Essay Testing." *Improving College and University Teaching*, no. 1 (1973).

Suggested Readings

American Psychological Association. *Standards for Educational and Psychological Tests*. Washington, D.C.: American Psychological Association, 1974.
This monograph was developed by a joint committee of members from the American Psychological Association, the American Educational Research Association, and the National Council on Measurement in Education. The contents are directed to both developers and users of standardized tests. "Essential," "very desirable," and "desirable" considerations about tests are proposed.

Anderson, Scarvia, Ball, Samuel, Murphy, Richard T., and Associates. *Encyclopedia of Educational Evaluation*. San Francisco: Jossey-Bass, 1975.
This is one of the first detailed reference works on concepts and techniques for evaluating education and training programs. It is not limited in scope to colleges and universities. The articles—alphabetically arranged from "accountability" to "variance"—are written by specialists. Each article is extensively cross-referenced and is followed by selected sources. The articles cover 11 topics: evaluation models; functions and targets of evaluation; program objectives and standards; social context of evaluation; planning and design; systems technologies; variables; measurement approaches and types; technical measurement considerations; reactive concern; analysis and interpretation.

Bowen, Howard R., ed. *New Directions for Institutional Research: Evaluating Institutions for Accountability*, No. 1. San Francisco: Jossey-Bass, Spring 1974.
As the title implies, this booklet is about program evaluation. The seven papers, prepared especially for this volume by six authorities, deal with the various complexities of assessment and offer suggestions for resolving them.

Bruning, J. L. and Kintz, B. L. *Computational Handbook of Statistics*. Glenview, Ill.: Scott, Foresman and Co., 1968.
This is an excellent "cookbook" of statistical methods, clear and concise in its presentation of the steps necessary to compute the basic measurement statistics mentioned in *The Testing and Grading of Students*.

Buros, Oscar K., ed. *The Seventh Mental Measurements Yearbook*. Highland Park, N.J.: Gryphon Press, 1972.
This work is in two volumes that have a total of slightly more than 2,000 pages. More than 1,100 published tests (achievement, attitude, personality, and others) are listed, along with some 12,000 references. For approximately half of the tests, there are orig-

inal reviews by experts, and there are around 200 reviews excerpted from journals. These volumes are indispensable when selecting a standardized test for either classroom use or research purposes.

Dressel, Paul L. and Associates. *Evaluation in Higher Education.* Boston: Houghton Mifflin, 1961.

This is one of the few books in this field beamed directly to college and university faculty members. Thus the level of discourse is more appropriate than that in many other tomes and examples of test questions tend to be quite practical. Of the 13 chapters, all written by different authorities, 10 deal explicitly with the issues discussed in *The Testing and Grading of Students.* Four of them are especially pertinent: evaluation in the social sciences; evaluation in the natural sciences; evaluation in the humanities; and evaluation of communication skills.

Ebel, Robert L. *Essentials of Educational Measurement.* Englewood Cliffs, N.J.: Prentice-Hall, 1972.

This book, a revised version of the author's 1963 *Measuring Educational Achievement,* is sound, readable, and practical. It is referred to repeatedly throughout the first three chapters of the present work, and many points only touched on here are clearly elaborated therein. The 22 chapters are separated into five categories: Part I—History and Philosophy; Part II—Classroom Test Development; Part III—Getting, Interpreting, and Using Test Scores; Part IV—Test Analysis and Evaluation; Part V—Published Tests and Testing Programs. There is a glossary of the terms and concepts used in educational measurement.

Lindquist, E. F., ed. *Educational Measurement.* Washington, D.C.: American Council on Education, 1951.

This useful book, which went into its sixth printing in 1966, is a comprehensive handbook and textbook on the theory and technique of educational measurement. All 18 articles were especially prepared for the volume by noted authorities. Many of the selections—which are grouped into three categories, The Functions of Measurement in Education, The Construction of Achievement Tests, and Measurement Theory—are of a very practical nature, and all instructors can find good tips here for testing.

Mager, Robert F. *Goal Analysis.* Belmont, Ca.: Fearon, 1972.

Mager's work merits considerable attention. His writing is clear and easily understood; he comfortably translates his theory into application. *Goal Analysis* is a small book (136 pages) that spells out the steps by which instructors can identify goals in their instruction and establish the appropriate steps toward the successful completion of those goals. Assessment and evaluation are both built into the goal-analysis procedure. The book defines procedures that allow instructors to say where they are, where they want to go, how they intend to get there, and how they know when they are there.

Mager, Robert F. *Measuring Instructional Intent.* Belmont, Ca.: Fearon, 1973.

Writing in his unique, informal style, the author describes and illustrates a procedure that will help in selecting or creating test items that will match objectives. Illustrations cover a wide array of performances.

Mager, Robert F. *Preparing Instructional Objectives.* 2d ed. Belmont, Ca.: Fearon, 1975.

While the contents of this book seem deceptively simple, the substance is profound, especially for those who have given almost no thought to objectives. The book is cleverly and wittily written. Beginners in the academic enterprise will benefit greatly; old-timers might.

Mehrens, William A. and Ebel, Robert L., eds. *Principles of Educational and Psychological Measurement: A Book of Selected Readings.* Chicago: Rand McNally, 1967.

This book contains classical articles on measurements, most of them very technical and statistical, which were published over a span of 30 years. The 37 selections are grouped into five categories: measurement theory and scaling; norms; reliability; validity; item analysis and selection.

Pace, C. Robert, ed. *New Directions for Higher Education: Evaluating Learning and Teaching,* No. 4. San Francisco: Jossey-Bass, 1973.

Each chapter was prepared especially for this booklet by authors with widely varying perspectives. The six papers collectively demonstrate how complex problems of evaluation are and the innumerable factors to be considered and are useful as a quick but substantive overview.

Thorndike, Robert L., ed. *Educational Measurement*. 2d ed. Washington, D.C.: American Council on Education, 1971.

The first edition of this book went through seven printings. This second edition, prepared with the assistance of the American Educational Research Association and the American Council on Education, reflects the broadened concern about evaluation that has been developing. The 20 pieces are addressed to four areas: Part One—Test Design, Construction, Administration, and Processing; Part Two—Special Types of Tests; Part Three—Measurement Theory; Part Four—Application of Tests to Educational Problems. Both the specialist and the novice will find this book useful.

Selected Journals
with Special Emphasis on Evaluation

American Educational Research Journal
British Journal of Statistical and Mathematical Psychology
Center for the Study of Evaluation
College Student Journal
Educational and Psychological Measurement
Journal of Educational Measurement
Journal of Research in Science Teaching
Programmed Learning and Educational Technology
Psychometrika
Review of Educational Research

On The Quality Of Teaching

DATE DUE

'88			
GAYLORD			PRINTED IN U.S.A.